## TODAY'S FASCINATING WOMAN—
## MORE IMPORTANT THAN EVER!

"I am more convinced than ever that these teachings are true, and that this knowledge is the most urgently needed knowledge in the world today.

"This claim is not unreasonable. A loving marriage is the foundation of a happy family, and a happy family the foundation of a stable society.

"Most of the problems in this world stem from troubled homes. If we are to have peace in the world, we must begin at home."

# FASCINATING WOMANHOOD®

## Updated Edition

## Helen B. Andelin

**BANTAM BOOKS**

NEW YORK · TORONTO · LONDON · SYDNEY · AUCKLAND

FASCINATING WOMANHOOD

*A Bantam Book / published by arrangement with the author*

*PUBLISHING HISTORY*

*Pacific Press edition published March 1965*
*Bantam edition / March 1975*
*Revised Bantam edition / July 1980*
*Updated Bantam edition / February 1992*

*A WORD OF EXPLANATION BY THE AUTHOR*
*Some of the teachings in this book were inspired by a series of booklets
published in the 1920s, entitled* The Secrets of Fascinating Womanhood.
*The booklets, written to single women, have long been out of print. The
authors are unknown.*

ISBN 0-553-29220-X

*Published simultaneously in the United States and Canada*

**Bantam Books are published by Bantam Books, a division of Ran-
dom House, Inc. Its trademark, consisting of the words "Bantam
Books" and the portrayal of a rooster, is Registered in U.S. Patent
and Trademark Office and in other countries. Marca Registrada.
Bantam Books, 1540 Broadway, New York, New York 10036.**

PRINTED IN THE UNITED STATES OF AMERICA

OPM    18

# Contents

**Part II : THE HUMAN QUALITIES** 245

# WHAT IS HAPPINESS IN MARRIAGE
## FOR A WOMAN?

Is it to have a lovely home? Happy and healthy children? A successful husband? Time for talents? No money problems? Husband and wife having fun together? Is it the feeling of being a successful homemaker? Is it to be admired by her associates?

All of these things are important and some essential, but one need is fundamental. She must feel loved and cherished by her husband. Without his love her life is an empty shell.

Why is it that one woman is happy, honored, and loved, and another—no less attractive, no less essentially admirable, and no less lovable—is neglected, unhappy, and disappointed? *Fascinating Womanhood* explains why, and offers every woman an opportunity to learn the art of winning her man's complete love and adoration.

## FASCINATING WOMANHOOD

A book of inspirational feminine secrets that can save your marriage and enrich your life . . .

# WHAT IS A FASCINATING WOMAN?

Is she the coy coquette who charms men with cute clichés? Is she the stunning sophisticate of the fashion magazines and charm schools? Or, is she the sensuous woman who, in her own clever way, manipulates her man into satisfying her whims and fancies? Is she the intellectual achiever who has made her mark in the world, or the competent, independent woman, well able to make her own way in life? Or, is she the self-sacrificing wife, devoted to making her husband happy at her own expense? No, she is none of these images.

She is a woman of angelic character, dedicated to high standards and values. She is the perfect wife, understanding of her husband's needs and sensitive to his feelings. She is not consumed in remaking him into the man he ought to be, but accepts him for the man he is, overlooking his human frailties and focusing on his better side.

Although she is submissive and giving, she does not allow herself to be trampled on or abused. She is not a doormat, a servant, and a slave. Part of being a true woman, she inherently knows, is to retain her feeling of self-respect, an awareness that she is a person of great worth, deserving of proper treatment. Such a regard for herself helps her maintain a queenly attitude which commands respect.

She is proud to be a woman and does all she can to magnify her femininity, not by an outer showing of softness, but by a total personification of womanliness. This includes an outer femininity of appearance and manner and an inner femininity of attitudes and goals. Because she is a truly feminine woman, she has a charm that knows no age.

She is a free soul, free to choose her life and what it will be. If she marries she chooses life in that direction. Although she devotes most of her time to her family she does not feel trapped in the household. She gives willingly and wholeheartedly, prompted by a tender love and concern for her family. She accepts her work as *a sacred trust of worldwide importance. Her career is a career in the home, her glory the esteem of her husband and the happiness of her children*. Because of this *"her yoke is easy and her burden light."* This makes her free.

Her charms are not cleverness or sophistication, but freshness, wholesomeness, and inner happiness. She is innocent and trustful with the playfulness of a child. On her face is a sort of bloom, a bloom which comes from being loved and adored by her husband. Only a woman so loved can be truly fascinating.

## The Phenomenal Success of Fascinating Womanhood

Since first published in 1965, over two million copies of the book have been sold. Its success, however, is measured not so much by the number of copies sold as by the lives it has changed. The impact it has had on marriages has been *phenomenal*. Those already happy have gained a new kind of happiness, and those in serious trouble have been rescued, restored, and blessed with the same new happiness. Success is evidenced by thousands of testimonials, many of which have been included in this book.

Through *Fascinating Womanhood* there is hope of a new generation of women—happy, feminine, adored, and cherished. This would invoke a new generation of men—masculine and chivalrous.

Why did the author decide to update her already bestselling book? Her explanation is this:

*"I wanted to more clearly explain the concepts and strengthen its message. I wanted* Fascinating Womanhood *to be in its best form for women already dedicated to its teachings and those who will yet read it and accept it as their way of life.*

*"I am more convinced than ever that these teachings are true, and that this knowledge is the most urgently needed knowledge in the world today. This claim is not unreasonable. A loving marriage is the foundation of a happy family, and a happy family the foundation of a stable society. Most of the problems in this world stem from troubled homes. If we are to have peace in the world, we must begin at home."*

## A Special Acknowledgment

*"I wish to express my deepest gratitude to the many women who have so effectively helped to bring this message*

*to women in this country and abroad. I also express my appreciation to the women who have sent in their testimonials, many of which are included in this book. And a special word of appreciation to my husband, Aubrey, for his encouragement, insight, and help, at times given at considerable sacrifice. These sources of dedicated assistance have provided me with tremendous encouragement to carry this message forward, with the hope it will reach women throughout the world.''*

# FASCINATING WOMANHOOD

# Introduction

To be loved and cherished is a woman's heartfelt desire in marriage. This book is written to restore your hope in this desire and to suggest principles to apply in winning a man's genuine love.

Is married life all you had hoped and dreamed it would be? Do you feel cherished, honored, and adored? Or, do you feel neglected, unappreciated, and unloved? If so, are you resigned to this condition, thinking there is nothing better to be had? Or, do you still believe in the dream, continue to search for the guidelines to a happy marriage? Do you find fragments of information here and there, but blind alleys where there seem to be no answers? Do you feel lost in a sea of darkness?

Or, you may be in greater darkness. You may think you are happy, when in reality you are not. Your marriage may seem happy when compared to others, but you fail to see that there is more. You lack the vision to see how happy a marriage can be, and should be. You are satisfied to eat the crumbs that fall from the table, for you have never tasted the banquet. You think the weeds are pretty, for you have never seen beautiful flowers. You may even be content with hell because you have never had a glimpse of heaven.

Or, you may be one of those rare few who has already achieved a happy marriage. But, is it all you dreamed it would be? Do you feel a need for a richer fuller life? If so, are you open-minded, and willing to learn new concepts of how to build a truly happy marriage, one in which you feel not only loved but cherished?

## A Woman's Happiness

What is happiness for a woman? If you are single you may find happiness in service and in your own conquering spirit in reaching goals, solving problems, and personal growth. If you are married, additional things must be considered—happy and healthy children, a successful husband who provides economic security, your personal success in creating a happy home, organizing your life so you have time for talents and other interests. Fundamental, however, is your husband's love. If he doesn't love you, your life will be an empty shell.

## The Answer

The first step to a happy marriage is to understand that all life is governed by law—nature, music, art, and all of the sciences. These laws are immutable. To live in harmony with them produces health, beauty, and the abundant life. To violate them brings ugliness and destruction. Just as unwavering are the *laws of human relationships*. These laws are in operation even though you may not understand them. You may be happy in marriage because you obey them, or you may be unhappy because you violate them without an awareness of the laws in operation.

Through ignorance of *the laws of marriage relationships*, much unnecessary unhappiness exists. We find one woman happy, honored, and loved; and another—no less attractive, no less admirable, no less lovable—neglected, unhappy, and disappointed. Why? This book explains why, for it teaches the laws she must obey if she is to be loved, honored, and adored.

## Fascinating Womanhood

*Fascinating Womanhood* will teach you how to be happy in marriage. There are three essentials in reaching the goal:

1. *Love:* Since the cornerstone of a happy marriage is love, you will learn how to awaken your husband's love. These teachings apply, no matter what your age or situation. Love is not limited to the young or the beautiful, but to those who have qualities that awaken it.

If your husband doesn't love you, you are likely doing something to cool his affections, or have lost something which awakens his love. You may have begun marriage lovingly but romance is fading. Why? Could it be that you have changed? Take a good look. In most cases a man stops loving a woman after marriage because she stops doing things which arouse his feelings. When you regain your charming ways, love can be rekindled.

In winning your husband's love, it isn't necessary for him to know or do anything about it. This isn't to say that he doesn't make mistakes or need to improve, but when you correct your mistakes you bring about *a loving response in him*. Frequently his response is so remarkable that it exceeds your highest expectations.

The art of awakening a man's love is not a difficult accomplishment for women because it is based on our natural instincts. However, in our highly civilized life many of our natural instincts have become rusty due to lack of use. You need only to awaken the traits which belong to you by nature.

2. *Self-Dignity:* Essential to happiness in marriage is self-dignity. Does your husband ever speak to you harshly, criticize you unduly, treat you unfairly, neglect you, impose on you, or in any way mistreat you? The important thing is not what he does but *how you react*. Do you shrink back as if struck by a lash? Do you go into your shell? Do you pay him back with a cutting remark? Or, do you fly off the handle with an ugly temper? If you react in any of these ways you will cause yourself unnecessary grief and lessen your husband's love for you.

No man likes an ugly temper, nor does he want a woman he can walk on, or one who will retreat into her shell and feel sorry for herself. He wants a woman with some spunk—some *hidden fire,* a woman he can't push around. Some men even admire little spitfires, women who are adorably independent and saucy, whom they can't put down with even the most degrading remark.

In *Fascinating Womanhood* the method of handling wounded feelings is called childlike anger, spunk, or sauciness. It will teach you how to handle a man's rough nature without pain, without friction. You can, in a flash, turn a crisis into a humorous situation, so that the man may have the sudden impulse to laugh. Instead of hurting marriage, childlike anger can increase love and tenderness.

3. *Desires:* If you are to be happy in marriage your desires must be considered. I am referring to things you want to have, places you want to go, something you want to do, or something you want done for you. This is not to suggest selfish whims, but worthy desires. Unfortunately, you may have gone without these things for years because you didn't know how to motivate your husband to do these things for you.

As a consequence, his feelings for you have likely diminished. *We love whom we serve.* If your husband never does anything for you beyond the call of duty, he may lose his love for you. In *Fascinating Womanhood* you will learn how to obtain the things you need and deserve without causing a marital stir. Your husband will want to do things for you and will love you more because of it.

Although the teachings focus on building a relationship with your husband, the principles apply in building a relationship with any man—father, brother, son, teacher, student, employer. Take care, however, that you don't use them unrighteously, to win the affections of a married man. You would be guilty of a cruel sin and would destroy another woman's relationship as well as your own. In relationships outside of your marriage, apply them only to eliminate friction and to build harmony and trust.

The teachings are also helpful to the single mother who is rearing a family without a father present in the home. She becomes the feminine image for her children to view, as essential to boys in developing their manliness as to girls in developing their womanliness. She should also teach them about masculinity by providing them with a male image to associate with—her father, a brother, or another male person.

Within these pages you will learn principles to follow if you are to be happy, loved, and cherished. The study centers around *the ideal woman, from a man's point of view,* the kind of woman who awakens a man's deepest feelings of love. Within your reach is the possibility of a happy marriage. You can bring it about independent of any effort on the part of your husband. *So, you hold the keys to your own happiness.*

In accomplishing this you lose none of your dignity, influence, or freedom, but gain them, and it is only then that you can play your vital part in this world. The role of a woman when played correctly is fulfilling, fascinating, and full of intrigue. There never need be a dull moment. The practice of this art of womanhood is an enjoyable one, filled with rich rewards, numerous surprises, and vast happiness. Many years of experience teaching thousands of women has proven this to be true.

# What This Book Can Do for You

*It will teach you:*

1. The Ideal Woman, from a man's point of view.
2. What men find fascinating in women.
3. How to awaken a man's deepest feelings of love and tenderness.
4. How to understand men, their needs, temperament, and characteristics.
5. How to treat a man when he is depressed, in order to build his confidence and respect in himself.
6. How to cause a man to protect you, provide for you, and devote himself to you.
7. How to obtain those things in life which mean so much, things you are justified in having.
8. How to bring out the best in your husband without pushing or persuasion.
9. The feminine role, and the happiness which comes with its fulfillment.
10. The masculine role, and the respect due this divine calling.
11. How to react when a man is thoughtless, unfair, or negligent.
12. How to be attractive, even adorable, when you are angry.
13. How to keep a line of communication open in marriage so that a good feeling always exists.
14. How to gain true happiness in marriage, while placing your husband's happiness as a primary goal.

*Please note: Many success stories appear throughout this book. All are true and came to the author's attention by letter or direct conversation with the party involved. Likewise, all illustrations and examples are taken from true experiences, except those from classical literature.*

# 1

## Celestial Love

Celestial Love is a term used in *Fascinating Womanhood* to represent the highest kind of tender love a man feels for a woman, or a woman feels for a man. It lifts love out of the mediocre and places it on a heavenly plane. It is the flowers rather than the weeds, the banquet rather than the crumbs.

Does your husband feel this kind of love when he tells you he loves you, remembers your birthday, takes you to dinner or is generous and kind? Not necessarily. These attentions are admirable but not proof of real love. He may do or say these things out of a sense of duty, without any feeling of real love.

Celestial love is not dutiful, but spontaneous, warm, and tender. When a man truly loves a woman, he experiences a deep feeling within. At times it can be intense, almost like pain. He may feel enchanted and fascinated, with a tender desire to protect and shelter the woman he loves from harm, danger, and difficulty. Then there is the deeper, more spiritual feeling, almost like worship. Even this cannot adequately describe the *many-splendored thing* called love. The following are vivid examples of man's true love of woman:

### John Alden and Priscilla

An illustration of Celestial Love is expressed in Longfellow's account of John Alden and Priscilla Mullens, in which John speaks tenderly of Priscilla: *"There is no land so sacred, no air so pure and wholesome, as is the air she breathes and the soil that is pressed by her footsteps. Here for her sake will I stay and like an invisible presence, hover around her forever, protecting, supporting her weakness."*

7

## Victor Hugo's Love

A tender, protective feeling of love is found in the words of Victor Hugo, written about Adele Foucher, the woman he loved in real life: *"Do I exist for my own personal happiness? No, my whole existence is devoted to her, even in spite of her. And by what right should I have dared to aspire to her love? What does it matter, so that it does not injure her happiness? My duty is to keep close to her steps, to surround her existence with mine, to serve her as a barrier against all dangers; to offer my head as a stepping-stone, to place myself unceasingly between her and all sorrows, without claiming reward, without expecting recompense . . . Alas! If she only allow me to give my life to anticipating her every desire, all her caprices; if she but permit me to kiss with respect her adored footprints; if she but consent to lean upon me at times amidst the difficulties of life."*

## Woodrow Wilson

Probably one of the finest examples of true and enduring love is found in the love letters of President Woodrow Wilson, written to his wife Ellen. After being married for seventeen years, he writes, *"All that I am, all that has come to me in life, I owe to you. . . . I could not be what I am, if I did not take such serene happiness from my union with you. You are the spring of content; and so long as I have you, and you too are happy, nothing but good and power can come to me. Ah, my incomparable little wife, may God bless and keep you."* And after being married for twenty-eight years, he writes from the White House: *"I adore you! No President but myself ever had exactly the right sort of wife! I am certainly the most fortunate man alive."* And in another letter, *"I can think of nothing while I write but only you. My days are not so full of anxiety and a sense of deep responsibility as they are of you, my absent darling, who yet plays the leading part in my life every minute of the day."* These lines were taken from *The Priceless Gift*, a collection of their love letters. Each is a love letter, warm and intimate.

Some of you may believe your husbands are incapable of such feelings, or at least incapable of expressing them. This is doubtful. The warm, tender letters of President Wilson were a surprise to those who knew his personality, that of an unemotional schoolmaster. Every man has the capability of being tender, romantic, and adoring, if these passions are awakened by the woman he loves.

## Shah Jahan's Love for Mumtaz

In the city of Agra in northern India is the Taj Mahal, an exquisite tomb of white marble, built by Shah Jahan in memory of his wife, Mumtaz. Although it was built in the seventeenth century, it is still one of the most beautiful buildings in the world and the most costly tomb in existence. It stands as a monument of man's true love of woman. In describing the shah's love for Mumtaz, I quote from *Three Wise Men of the East,* by Elizabeth Bisland:

"The young Indian ruler found in this Persian girl the realization of all his high dreams and imaginings. So closely were their lives interlaced, so supremely does she appear to have been his inspiration, that it is necessary to imagine one profile next to the other. And in a poet's words the Shah's feelings are expressed:

> "He preferred in his heart
> The least ringlet that curled
> Down her exquisite neck
> To the throne of the world."

"In the culture of his day, practically no restraint existed either in law or public opinion to control the desires regarding women of a Mogul emperor . . . he was absolutely free to take women where he would and use them as he willed; yet never is there evidence that Shah Jahan gave his wife a rival. He had two other wives, but these were political marriages, not love matches."

The shah also built for his wife a magnificent palace of white marble, probably the most perfect dwelling place in the world at that time. It was exquisite, with light passing through delicate carvings of marble almost like lace, and superb mosaics of birds and flowers in precious stones. Here, indeed, the emperor created a work of art in making a home for his beloved.

And above the rich columns holding up the ceiling in beautiful Persian script in pure gold is the famous inscription, *"If there is heaven on earth, it is this, it is this, it is this."*

Mumtaz died at the birth of their fourteenth child. From an old Persian manuscript is the following account: *"When the emperor learned that she was to die, he wept bitterly because of the great love he bore her, and one would have said that the stars fell in heaven and the rain upon the earth. Such lamentation arose in the palace that one would have said the Day of Judgment had arrived. The emperor, weeping and striking his breast, repeated the words of the poet Saadi, 'God will not rest in the hands of a prodigal nor patience in the heart of a lover more than water in a sieve.' But grief stirred his genius to its supreme accomplishment. He resolved that upon the grave of his beloved should be laid love's perfect crown.*

*"The great buildings of the world have been monuments of the pomp and pride of kings, or temples to gods, or records of rich and haughty cities. But he, in the beauty of white marble, for the first time gave utterance to man's true love of woman. Not physical desire, but the mating of spirit with spirit. No pains were spared to bring to perfection the last dwelling place of his beloved Queen. Twenty thousand laborers toiled upon it for seventeen years."*

And take note of this thought: Mumtaz was of a culture where women were subservient, dependent, and kept their place in the feminine world. It was not a culture where women dominated, demanded, and tried to be equal with men. And yet she gained what every true woman seeks—respect, honor, and the devoted love of her husband. Shah Jahan gave to her the greatest token of love a man has ever given to a woman in the Taj Mahal. We may well ask ourselves, are we worthy of such love and devotion from our husband? Where is our Taj Mahal?

## Is It Selfish?

Don't think it selfish to want to be loved with great tenderness and devotion. Your husband's love for you will be a source of great joy to him, and he will be more of a man because of it. It will provide him with greater incentive to succeed in life, giving him something to work for, to live for and, if necessary, to die for. Awakening your husband's love helps him find greater happiness and fulfillment. When you don't, you rob him of one of his finer joys.

Benefits come to you also. Your husband's love will be the center of your happiness. You can more adequately devote yourself to your family and affairs of your household. Love will improve your health and emotions, will make you blossom and feel queenly.

Love in marriage is the most important element in its success, and a happy marriage the foundation of a successful family. There is no way a man and woman can create a truly successful home without a happy marriage based on a true and abiding love for each other. Love, then, becomes not only the fulfillment of a desire but a responsibility. When the marriage is happy we have happy children who can develop normally and be prepared for the life ahead. The happy home becomes a worthy contribution to the well being of society, bringing peace to the world rather than the discord that arises from lack of love.

## *Your Love for Him*

For a true state of Celestial Love to exist, you should love your husband as much as he loves you. Since we study only the principles which awaken the husband's love for his wife, how is your love for him to deepen? The common answer is, *"He must do something about it by being a better man."* Although it is undeniably true that your husband's initiative to improve himself would increase your love for him, the miracle of *Fascinating Womanhood* is this:

1. *When you apply these teachings, you gain a greater understanding and appreciation for him, learn to see his finer side, and therefore learn to love him more.*

2. *By living the principles of* Fascinating Womanhood, *you become a better woman with a more loving nature. You will have the capacity to love him more.*

3. *As you help him gain confidence and respect in himself and create a happier marriage and family life, he will have more incentive to make something worthwhile of his life. He will become a better man, one you can love more easily, more completely.*

Celestial love is what every woman has longed for since the world began. Even in childhood little girls have tender dreams of romance in which they are the beautiful princess sought after by the handsome prince. Snow White and Cinderella are favorites of little girls. During youth, uppermost in a young girl's mind is finding a man who will love and cherish her. This tender love has long been the theme of great operas, novels, and songs. Romantic love, one of the most moving forces in life, rightfully deserves our study and consideration.

As we conclude this chapter you may ask, "What can I do to inspire Celestial Love in my husband?" To know, we must learn the principles which awaken a man's love. We must study *The Ideal Woman, From A Man's Point of View*, the kind that awakens the emotions of worship, adoration, and love.

# 2

## The Ideal Woman

*From A Man's Point of View*

To understand the masculine viewpoint, learn to view the ideal woman through a man's eyes. His ideas of feminine perfection are different from your own. The things we women admire in each other are rarely attractive to men. On the other hand, the things the average woman ignores or condemns in another woman are sometimes just the characteristics which make her fascinating to men. Women are blind to their own charms, which makes it difficult for them to realize what a man wants.

Haven't you been puzzled at times to know what a certain man sees in a particular woman? To you she doesn't hold any appeal, yet the man may be enchanted. The fascination a man feels for a certain woman seems to be an eternal riddle to the rest of her sex. Even when asked *why*, the man finds himself at a loss to explain the spell cast upon him. And, haven't you also known women who appear to have all of the qualities which ought to please a man, yet they are unappreciated, neglected, and often unloved? So, in our study of the ideal woman, remember that *a man judges with a different set of values*.

Women are inclined to appreciate poise, talent, intellectual gifts, and cleverness of personality, whereas men admire girlishness, tenderness, sweetness of character, vivacity, and the ability to understand men. A marked difference is in regard to appearance. Women are inclined to admire artistic beauty such as the shape of the face, the nose, and artistic clothes. Men, however, have a different interpretation of *what makes a woman beautiful*. They place more stress on the sparkle in her eyes, smiles, freshness, radiance, and her feminine manner.

## The Angelic and the Human

The Ideal Woman from a man's point of view is divided into two parts, the Angelic and the Human. The Angelic side has to do with her *spiritual* qualities. This includes her good character, understanding of men, domestic skills, and a quality of inner happiness. The Human side refers to her appearance, manner, and feminine nature, and includes the charms of femininity, radiance, good health, and childlikeness. The Angelic and the Human combine to make the perfect woman from a man's point of view. They are both essential in winning his genuine love.

These two distinct qualities awaken different feelings in a man. The Angelic awakens a feeling almost like worship and brings him a feeling of peace and happiness. The Human side fascinates and enchants him and awakens a tender feeling, a desire to protect and shelter her from harm and danger. When a woman has both the Angelic and Human qualities, she becomes a man's *ideal woman*, one he can *cherish*.

For illustrations of the Angelic and the Human in women, I will refer to examples from classical literature. Although these women are from fiction, they are as reliable as living examples. This is because skilled authors always draw their characters from people they knew or observed in real life. So these women I will refer to were living examples in the author's lifetime.

Although figures from the past, they apply as well today. Human nature doesn't change. The human family has always been pretty much the same, which is why characters from the Bible have such eternal application. Let us now turn to these examples from classical literature for a view of the Angelic and the Human in women.

### David Copperfield

An illustration of the Angelic and the Human is in the story of *David Copperfield,* by Charles Dickens. Our ideal, however, is not represented by one woman, but by two, Agnes and Dora.

**Agnes**

Agnes represents the Angelic side of our ideal, the side which inspires worship. David Copperfield knew Agnes from childhood and worshiped her from the time he first beheld her. The following is a description of their first meeting:

*"Mr. Wickfield tapped at a door in a corner of the paneled wall, and a girl of about my own age came quickly out and kissed him. On her face, I saw immediately the placid and sweet expression of the lady whose picture had looked at me downstairs. It seemed to my imagination as if the portrait had grown womanly and the original remained a child. Although her face was quite bright and happy, there was a tranquility about it, and about her—a quiet good calm spirit—that I never have forgotten; that I never shall forget.*

*"This was his little housekeeper, his daughter, Agnes, Mr. Wickfield said. When I heard how he said it, and saw how he held her hand, I guessed what the one motive of his life was.*

*"She had a little basket-trifle hanging at her side, with keys in it; and she looked as staid and as discreet a housekeeper as the old house could have. She listened to her father as he told her about me, with a pleasant face; and when he had concluded, proposed to my aunt that we should go upstairs and see my room. We all went up together, she before us. A glorious old room it was, with more oak beams, and diamond panes; and the broad balustrade going all the way up to it.*

*"I cannot call to mind where or when, in my childhood, I had seen a stained glass window in a church. Nor do I recollect its subject. But I know that when I saw her turn round, in the grave light of the old staircase, and wait for us, above, I thought of that window; and I associated something of its tranquil brightness with Agnes Wickfield ever afterwards."*

David and Agnes became the closest of friends. She gave him comfort, understanding, true sympathy, and comradeship. *"As if,"* he writes, *"in love, joy, sorrow, hope, or disappointment, in all emotions, my heart turned naturally there and found its refuge and best friend."*

Agnes always had a sacred and peaceful influence on David. At one time, while under great stress and tension he said, *"Somehow as I wrote to Agnes on a fine evening by my open window, and the remembrance of her clear calm eyes and gentle face came stealing over me, it shed such a peaceful influence upon the hurry and agitation in which I had been living lately that it soothed me into tears.''* But, although he had known Agnes since childhood, although he had worshiped her from the time he first beheld her, and although he sensed all along that she alone could give him sympathy and comradeship, he became madly infatuated, not with Agnes, but with Dora.

## Dora

Dora represents the Human side of our ideal, the side that fascinates, captivates, and inspires an overwhelming tenderness in a man's heart, and a desire to protect and shelter. David describes her in the following words:

*"She was a fairy and a sylph. She was more than human to me. I don't know what she was, anything that no one ever saw and everything that everybody ever wanted. She had the most delightful little voice, the gayest little laugh, the pleasantest and most fascinating little ways that ever led a lost youth into hopeless slavery. She was rather diminutive altogether ... she was too bewildering. To see her lay the flowers against her dimpled chin was to lose all presence of mind and power of language in feeble ecstasy.''*

Her childlike ways, her dear little whims and caprices, her girlish trust in him, her absolute dependency upon others to provide for her, made an irresistible appeal to David's gentlemanly and chivalrous heart. She fascinated him, for he writes, *"I could only sit down before the fire, biting the key of my carpet bag, and think of the captivating, girlish, bright eyed, lovely Dora. What a form she had, what a face she had, what a graceful, variable, enchanting manner.''*

## Married to Dora, David Turned to Agnes

Yet even while such feelings toward Dora were at their highest, he missed the comfort, understanding, appreciation, and sacred influences of Agnes. *"Dora,''* he tells Agnes, *"is rather difficult to, I would not for the world say, to rely upon, because she is the soul of purity and truth, but rather difficult to, I hardly know how to express it. Whenever I have not had you, Agnes, to advise and approve in the beginning, I have seemed to go wild and to get into all sorts of difficulty. When I have come to you, at last, as I have always done, I have come to peace and happiness.''*

## Dora's Homemaking

In marriage Dora also failed as a homemaker: *"I could not have wished for a prettier little wife at the opposite end of the table, but I certainly could have wished when we sat down for a little more room. I did not know how it was, but although there were only two of us, we were at once always cramped for room, and yet had always enough to lose everything in. I suspect it could have been because nothing had a place of its own."* Dora could not manage the household, the finances, or the cooking. David bought her an expensive cookbook but she used it to let her little dog stand on.

## The Void in His Life

While married to Dora he continued to love her. She fascinated and amused him, and he felt tenderly toward her. But it was not a complete love, nor did it bring him genuine happiness, for he said, *"I loved my wife dearly, and I was happy; but the happiness I had vaguely anticipated once was not the happiness I enjoyed, and there was something wanting. An unhappy feeling pervaded my life, as a strain of sorrowful music, faintly heard in the night."* And he said, *"I did feel sometimes, for a little while, that I could have wished my wife had been my counsellor; had more character and purpose to sustain me and improve me by; had been endowed with a power to fill up the void which somewhere seemed to be about me."*

Later on in the story Dora died and David turned to Agnes. When married to Agnes, David enjoyed real peace and happiness. She filled up the void in his life. She was a wonderful homemaker and gave him true understanding. They had children and a wonderful home life. He loved her but here again, there was something lacking. During his marriage to Agnes he had tender recollections of Dora that played upon his emotions. In thinking of her he wrote: *"This appeal of Dora's made such*

*a strong impression on me . . . I look back on the time I write
of; I invoke the innocent figure that I dearly loved to come out
of the mists and shadows of the past and turn its gentle head
toward me once again.''*

On one occasion his little girl came running in to him
with a ring on her finger, very much like the engagement ring
he had given to Dora. The little ring, a band of forget-me-nots
with blue stones, so reminded him of Dora that he said, *"There
was a momentary stirring in my heart, like pain!"*

### The Feeling David Had for Each of Them

The feeling David had for Agnes was one near worship.
She had a sacred influence on him. She brought him peace and
happiness, and without her he seemed to *go wild and get into
difficulty*. Thinking about her *soothed him into tears*. He felt
as though she were a part of him, *as one of the elements of
my natural home*.

The feeling he had for Dora was different. She fascinated
and amused him. *She was a fairy and a sylph; I don't know
what she was—anything that no one ever saw and everything
that everybody ever wanted*. All of her delicate and bright
mannerisms aroused his irresistible longing to shelter and protect her.

I would like to stress that David Copperfield felt two
distinctly different types of love for these two women. He
experienced a type of love for Agnes all along, but it was not
strong enough to bring him to marriage. And even though this
type of love brings men the greatest peace and the truest and
most abiding happiness—it is not the most driving.

The kind of love David felt for Dora was forceful, consuming, and intense. When he thought of her he felt like *biting
the key of his carpetbag*. He was *in fairyland, a captive, and
a slave*. This type of love, however, was not complete, nor
did it bring him real happiness, for he said, *"I loved my wife
dearly and I was happy; but the happiness I vaguely anticipated
once was not the happiness I enjoyed and there was something
wanting. An unhappy feeling pervaded my life, as a strain of
sorrowful music, faintly heard in the night.''*

David Copperfield never had the satisfaction of loving
completely, for his feelings were inspired by two different

women. Neither was the whole of our ideal, so neither could arouse his love in a complete sense.

## Comparing the Two

If Agnes had had Dora's girlishness, her adorable human and childlike manner, and her dependency upon men for their protection and guidance, David would never have made the mistake of marrying another. His worship for Agnes would have turned into genuine love, into the desire to protect and shelter. On the other hand, if Dora had had the sympathetic understanding, the appreciation of his highest ideals, and the depth of character of Agnes, and provided him with an orderly and peaceful home life, David's mad infatuation for her would have developed into everlasting adoration and love. Neither of the two, unfortunately for them, represents the whole of our ideal. Each of them made mistakes, each of them won and lost David, but each of them is well worth emulating in some respects.

## Analyzing Agnes

*What She Had:*

Agnes had four outstanding qualities, all on the Angelic side of our ideal.

1. *She had a pure and lovely character.* David always associated her with a stained glass window in a church, and she had a sacred influence on him. One of the greatest tests of her character came when David married Dora. Even though Agnes loved David herself, she did not become bitter or resentful toward either of them, but continued her unselfish friendship to David and became a friend to Dora as well. She had the courage to keep her love for David a secret and to live a useful life in spite of her disappointment. Further evidence of her character is shown in her devotion to her father and her sacrifices for his sake.

2. *She understood men.* She gave David true understanding. She knew how to rejoice with him in his triumphs and sympathize with him in his difficulties. She brought him comfort, peace, and comradeship.

3. *She had inner happiness.* As a result of her noble character, Agnes had a tranquillity about her and a good, calm, spirit which indicates peace, or happiness within.

4. *She was a capable housekeeper.* From the time she was a child, Agnes was a discreet little housekeeper. She took care of the meals, the house, and her father, with womanly efficiency.

*What Agnes Lacked:*

1. *She was too independent.* She was too able to kill her own snakes, too hesitant to lean on David, didn't appear to need his manly care and protection. She was too unselfish, for David said, *"Agnes, ever my guide and best support. If you had been more mindful of yourself, and less of me, when we grew up together, I think my heedless fancy would never have wandered from you."*

2. *She lacked the girlish, childlike, trusting qualities.*

3. *She lacked the gentle, tender, fascinating little ways that stir a man's heart.*

### Analyzing Dora

*What She Had:*

1. *She had an enchanting manner.*

2. *She was childlike, girlish.* At times David referred to her as his child-bride. She would shake her curls as little girls do. Her attitude was childlike, trusting.

3. *She had tender little ways.* The way she laid the flowers against her dimpled chin, patted the horses, or spanked her little dog fascinated David.

4. *She was radiantly happy.* She had a gay little laugh, a delightful little voice, and the pleasantest little ways.

5. *She was bright-eyed.*

6. *She was dependent.* She was helplessly in need of masculine protection and guidance. She had a girlish trust in David.

*What Dora Lacked:*

1. *She was a poor homemaker.* She could not keep house, cook, manage the household, or manage expenses.

2. *She lacked character.* Dora was good, pure, and kind

but inclined to be self-centered. David said, *"I wished my wife had had more character and purpose to sustain me."* She was too absorbed in her own little problems, cares, and whims, and not conscious enough of a man's needs.

3. *She did not understand men.* This was her greatest lack. She did not have the insight, sympathy, understanding, appreciation, or intellectual interest to be a good companion, for he wrote, *"It would have been better if my wife could have helped me more, and shared my many thoughts in which I had no partner."*

There are many women such as Agnes, women with inspiring characters who make wonderful mothers and homemakers, and are greatly appreciated, but if they lack the adorably human qualities that fascinate men, they fail to win their husbands' true love. On the other hand, there are women such as Dora, women who are adorable and childlike, but if they are too self-centered to notice a man's needs or to be good mothers and homemakers, they win only a part of their husband's love.

There is no reason you cannot be both an Agnes and a Dora, for the Angelic and the Human qualities do not conflict. Both are essential in winning and sustaining a man's love. Happiness in marriage depends on development of both sides of our ideal.

## Deruchette

An example of both the Angelic and the Human is Deruchette, heroine of the novel *Toilers of the Sea*, by Victor Hugo:

*"Her presence lights the home; her approach is like a cheerful warmth; she passes by, and we are content; she stays awhile and we are happy. Is it not a thing of divine, to have a smile which, none know how, has the power to lighten the weight of that enormous chain that all the living in common drag behind them? Deruchette possessed this smile; we may say that this smile was Deruchette herself.*

*"Deruchette had at times an air of bewitching languor, and certain mischief in the eye, which were altogether involuntary. Sweetness and goodness reigned throughout her person; her occupation was only to live her daily life; her*

*accomplishments were the knowledge of a few songs; her intellectual gifts were summed up in simple innocence; she had the graceful repose of the West Indian woman, mingled at times with giddiness and vivacity, with the teasing playfulness of a child, yet with a dash of melancholy. Add to all this an open brow, a neck supple and graceful, chestnut hair, a fair skin, slightly freckled with exposure to the sun, a mouth somewhat large, but well defined, and visited from time to time with a dangerous smile. This was Deruchette.''*

*"There is in this world no function more important than that of being charming—to shed joy around, to cast light upon dark days, to be the golden thread of our destiny and the very spirit of grace and harmony. Is not this to render a service?''*

In another place Hugo compares Deruchette to a little bird that flits from branch to branch as she moves about the house from room to room, coming and going, stopping to comb her hair as a bird plumes its wings, and *"making all kinds of gentle noises, murmurings of unspeakable delight. She is, as it were, a thread of gold interwoven in your somber thoughts. She is fresh and joyous as the lark,''* and *"She who is one day to become a mother is for a long while a child.''*

You may think at this point that Deruchette was a bit insipid. Remember, however, that Victor Hugo was a man, a rugged man who wrote challenging sea stories, speaking more the language of men than women. We can be grateful that he has provided us with a very masculine viewpoint of true femininity.

When the young clergyman in the story proposed to Deruchette, he gave indication of her angelic qualities when he said, *"There is for me but one woman on earth. It is you. I think of you as a prayer—you are a glory in my eyes. To me you are holy innocence. You alone are supreme. You are the living form of a benediction.''*

### Analyzing Deruchette

*Her Angelic Qualities:*
1. *Character:* *"Sweetness and goodness reigned throughout her person.''* She was mindful of the needs of others for she *shed joy around and cast light upon dark days.* Further evidence of her character is her lover's statement that she is

like a prayer, holy innocence, and the living form of a benediction.

2. *Domestic:* She was capable in her domestic duties for *"her occupation was only to live her daily life"* and *"her presence lights the home."* She flitted about the house like a bird, stopping to comb her hair as a bird plumbs its wings.

3. *Inner Happiness:* Similar to Agnes, Deruchette possessed inner happiness, or she could not possibly have had such ability to radiate it to others.

*Her Human Qualities:*

1. *Childlikeness:* Like Dora, Deruchette had childlike ways. *"She who is one day to be a mother, is for a long while a child."* She had *"certain mischief in the eye"* and at times *"giddiness, vivacity, and the teasing playfulness of a child."*

2. *Changefulness:* Deruchette was not at all times the same. Sometimes she was radiantly happy and full of giddiness and vivacity; at other times she had an air of *"bewitching languor."* Although she was sweet and good, at times she had *"certain mischief in the eye."* Sometimes she was full of teasing playfulness, and at other times, *"a dash of melancholy."* Changefulness is also a childlike quality.

3. *Fresh Appearance:* *"She is fresh and joyous as the lark"*.

4. *Gentleness:* Her gentle qualities are described in her voice: *"She makes all kinds of gentle noises, mumurings of unspeakable delight."*

5. *Radiates Happiness:* Her most notable quality was her ability to radiate happiness. This was a part of her character, manner, and actions.

- *She is fresh and joyous as the lark.*
- *She sheds joy around.*
- *She casts light upon dark days.*
- *Her presence lights the home.*
- *Her approach is like a cheerful warmth.*
- *She passes by and we are content.*
- *She stays awhile and we are happy.*
- *She has a smile which has the power to lighten the weight of that enormous chain which all the living in common*

*drag behind them—a dangerous smile which was De-*
*ruchette herself.*

· At times she has *giddiness* and *vivacity*.

6. *Grace:* Not mentioned before, but similar to gentleness and tenderness is *grace*. Deruchette was the *"very spirit of grace and harmony"* and had the *"graceful repose of the West Indian woman."* Her neck was supple and graceful.

## Amelia

Another example of both the Angelic and the Human is Amelia, from the novel *Vanity Fair* by William Thackery. He describes Amelia as *"a kind, fresh, smiling, tender, little domestic goddess, whom men are inclined to worship."* A few pages further he calls her *"poor little tender heart."* In another place he attributes to her *"a kindly, smiling, tender, generous heart of her own."*

He admits that others might not consider her beautiful: *"Indeed, I am afraid that her nose was rather short, than otherwise, and her cheeks a good deal too round for a heroine; but her face blushed with rosy health and her lips with the freshest of smiles, and she had a pair of eyes which sparkled with the brightest and honestest of good humor, except indeed when they filled with tears, and that was a great deal too often; for the silly thing would cry over a dead canary, or over a mouse that the cat haply had seized upon; or over the end of a novel, were it ever so stupid."*

Amelia had *"a sweet, fresh, little voice."* She was subject to *"little cares, fears, tears, timid misgivings."* *"She trembled when anyone was harsh."* Altogether, she was *"too modest, too tender, too trustful, too weak, too much woman,"* for any man to know without feeling called upon to protect and cherish her.

## Analyzing Amelia

*Her Angelic Qualities:*

1. *Character:* She had a generous heart and was kindly. Since men were inclined to worship her, she evidently had a character worthy of that worship.

2. *Domestic Qualities:* Thackery calls her "a little domestic goddess."

### Her Human Qualities:

1. *Fresh health:* She had the freshest of smiles, and her face blushed with rosy health. She had a pair of eyes that sparkled. She had a sweet, fresh little voice.

2. *Childlike Emotions:* She would cry over a dead canary, or a mouse that the cat had caught, or the end of a novel. She was subject to little cares, tears, fears, and timid misgivings. She trembled when anyone was harsh.

3. *Tenderness:* She was *"a tender little domestic goddess."* She was *"too tender, too weak, too much woman."*

4. *Trustfulness:* *"She was too trustful,"* also a childlike quality.

### Is Beauty Necessary?

It is interesting to note that none of the authors of the women just described placed any importance upon natural beauty. Amelia, for example, was chubby and stout with a very imperfect nose. *"Her nose was rather short than otherwise, and her cheeks a good deal too round for a heroine."* Deruchette's complexion was marred by freckles, and her mouth was too large for perfection. So far are the authors from claiming beauty for these young charmers that aside from pointing out the defect mentioned, they make no attempt to describe outward appearances. Agnes and Dora were both beautiful girls, so David's choice was based on other qualities.

The four women we have studied thus far have been examples from classical literature. There are, of course, and always have been examples from history. One, worthy of our review is Mumtaz, lady of the Taj Mahal. Again I quote from *Three Wise Men of the East,* by Elizabeth Bisland:

### Mumtaz

*"Mumtaz was exquisitely lovely. Her glossy black hair hung in two plaits over her shoulders. Her large eyes were perfect in shape and of soft deep black; the delicately arched eyebrows were like a swallow's wings, and long silky lashes*

*added to their beauty. Her velvety skin was fair as a lily.''* In addition to her uncommon external beauty, she had the following qualities:

*"She had a pure, simple, and generous mind. She was amiable in nature, and affable. She had indomitable patience which would not give way even under the most trying circumstances. For example, during one period of their lives before her husband ascended to the throne, there was an attempt made to oust him from his position. Chased by the Imperial Army, he had to move from place to place for shelter. Mumtaz accompanied her husband everywhere, from the forests of Telingana to the plains of Bengal, suffering with a patient cheerful resignation all of the miseries and hardships of a fugitive's camp life. Many of the prince's friends and advisers deserted him in the course of these events, but she clung to him with a most sincere devotion.''*

*"Mumtaz was a wise, prudent, and sagacious lady, and the Emperor had implicit confidence in her in private as well as State affairs. He consulted her on many important affairs of the Empire, and she discharged this function of adviser admirably well. She was charitable and kind. Many suppliants came to her and she never turned a deaf ear to any suitor worthy of her attention. Her intercession saved many a victim from the scaffold and reinstated many who had incurred royal displeasure. Orphans, widows, and other indigent persons won her assistance.''*

*"Mumtaz proved to be an ideal wife. She fascinated the mind of her husband. With all of her beauty, wisdom, and grace, she was the consummate flower of her gifted family. If she used any of these potent charms to bend her husband to her will, it was done with such entire art that the world had no vision of the process. From the story of their lives, however, it is evident that this woman was a strong factor in the life of this man.''*

*"Perhaps her feminine influence was the reason for the extended period of peace during the reign of Shah Jahan. In his long reign of forty years, but three wars took place and these were to suppress attacks or revolts. Public affairs flowed so smoothly that chroniclers find no episodes of blood or violence to record. His extremely successful foreign policy too*

*was a measure of the success of his reign as was his domestic jurisdiction.*

*"In historical records, only by inference do we have the suggestions that Mumtaz helped to shape the life of Shah Jahan, but it must be supposed that she affected his life profoundly. Not that we have any record of his words. One hears nothing of any public action of hers. We get only a most fleeting glimpse of a lovely figure, enshrined like a jewel in a marvelous setting of splendor."*

## Analyzing Mumtaz:

*Her Angelic Qualities:*

1. *Her Character:* She was pure, simple, and generous. She was sweet tempered and kindhearted, affable and courteous. She had indomitable patience, in the most trying circumstances. She was compassionate to the needy, assisting them in their desperate circumstances. She was intelligent and had great wisdom and prudence.

2. *Her domestic qualities:* She had a lofty sense of duty to her husband and proved to be an ideal wife. She bore him fourteen children. (Only eight lived, however, four sons and four daughters.)

*Her Human Qualities:*

1. *She was feminine:* She had a profound influence on her husband's life, but it was done with a subtle feminine art. She played her submissive role admirably.

2. *Radiance:* There was a cheerfulness about her in spite of trying circumstances.

3. *Fascinating:* She fascinated the mind of her husband.

We can find other examples from history of women who had Angelic and Human qualities. Cleopatra's charms changed the course of history. Helen of Troy was so treasured she caused a major war. Ellen Wilson, wife of the President, is worthy of intensive study. Biographies in libraries are sources of examples.

As for living examples of well-known women, intimate descriptions of their charms are scarce. Tradition seems to be

## THE IDEAL WOMAN,
### From a Man's Point of View

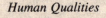

**Angelic Qualities**

**Understands Men**

**Has Inner
Happiness**

**Has a Worthy
Character**

**Is a Domestic
Goddess**

The Angelic qualities
awaken a feeling near
worship. They bring
a man peace and
happiness.

**Human Qualities**

**Is Feminine**

**Radiates
Happiness**

**Has Radiant
Health**

**Is Childlike**

The Human
qualities fascinate,
amuse, enchant,
and arouse a
tender desire to
protect and
shelter.

Together he Cherishes
*Both are essential to his Celestial Love*

that one must die before virtues are revealed. Only recently have the love letters of Woodrow and Ellen Wilson been made public.

What about unknown women? Yes, once in awhile in everyday life we see a shining example of the Angelic and Human. Be alert for such examples. Remember, they will not necessarily be the idol of women, but of men. In their circle of women friends, they are more likely the object of scorn. But, observe such women carefully. There is much to learn from them.

As we conclude our study of the Angelic and the Human, I will combine these appealing qualities into one whole, the total woman. The facing page shows a diagram of the ideal woman, with essential qualities men find appealing. Although she is divided, think of her as one. Together they form the ultimate in feminine charm.

You may wonder how you can know if these teachings are true, if these are indeed the qualities that a man finds fascinating, and if they will for certain awaken his tender feelings of love. Experience with thousands of women has proven these teachings to be true. Results have been unbelievable. Women who have thought they were happy have found a new kind of romantic love. Women who have felt neglected and unloved have seen their marriages blossom into love and tenderness, and women who have all but despaired over their situations have found the same happy results. Time and experience have proved that whenever these principles are applied women have been loved, honored, and adored, marriages flourish, and homes are made happier, as in the following testimonials:

### Earthshaking Results

"I have always been happily married (fourteen years) and have a marvelous husband, so as I read F.W. I was thinking how this could help Jill or Marsha. Then it seemed so easy and like magic that I thought I best put it to work. Well, let me tell you, I could hardly believe the response. I thought perhaps two areas were overstated a bit, so I tried them, and my husband reacted exactly as you said he would. I stand back amazed at the simplicity of F.W., yet the profound truths are nothing short of earthshaking.

"Needless to say, it is hard to be quiet about something that can change marriages into happy, loving units with two partners working together, rather than opposing each other. The very same week I read F.W three women came to me saying they were ready to walk out on their husbands, that they'd 'had it.' Now I had some concrete help to give them. I know you'll believe me when I say that one of the gals three weeks later farmed out her three children and she and her husband went on a week's honeymoon. The second realized she was guilty of self-righteousness and two weeks later there was giggling back in the home. The third gal wouldn't try one thing, and her marriage is still on the rocks."

## Trapped

"I want to thank you for F.W. It has helped me find my husband's real love for me. The one thing I have wanted him to do is to wear his wedding ring. He said he hated it, and he couldn't keep it on because it made him feel trapped. I would find it on tables and dressers, everywhere but on his finger. He knew how badly I wanted him to wear it, but he still refused. So the next time I found it I put it away.

"One day my lovely friend and landlady gave me F.W. and I started to practice it in my life. One evening about two months later we were getting ready for a party when he asked me for his ring. My heart pounded until it hurt while I was getting it and putting it on his finger. He held up his hand and turned it back and forth admiringly. It is a year now and he has not taken it off. Our love seems to grow stronger every day and I, without a doubt, consider you one of my dearest friends and I thank you with all my heart."

## Doctor's Advice

"Every woman should read F.W. I personally wish I had read it years ago. It would have spared my family a lot of pain and heartache. I was on the verge of divorce. I have loved my husband for years, but never knew how to let him know. Last summer we really began to have problems and I was desperate.

I didn't know where to turn, and he refused to discuss anything with me. My doctor suggested I buy F.W., and I'll be thankful forever that I did. My husband told me that he has always loved me but has a deeper feeling for me now than he has ever had.

## Our Marriage Blossomed

"I'm sure you have heard a million success stories but I'll tell you one more anyway. I thank God every day for the knowledge of F.W. My pastoral leader in my church gave it to me and ever since I've begun reading it our marriage has blossomed. I bought the book for each of my eight sisters and even though some aren't married, it helps them learn a lot about men and about understanding them, about the woman's role and their femininity.

"Most of the mistakes I made in the past I was unaware of, but each one drove my husband further from me. Now he treats me even better than when we dated and calls me by many different endearing names and opens doors for me again and calls me twice a day from work. The list goes on and on. I know now that we have what it takes to make a Christian marriage."

## I Was a Different Person

"My husband was drinking heavily, away from home almost every night, hardly speaking to me, and I believe he was seeing other women. He told me I might as well leave because he didn't need me. One night he locked me out of the house and told me to come by in the morning for my clothes. When I did he had my bag packed, met me at the door, and told me he would think about letting me see our six-year-old daughter. Later that day he called me from work and said he wanted me to talk to someone. Then he put some girl on the phone. This kind of thing went on until I became desperate. I was ready to leave him when someone told me about F.W. I thought they were crazy. No book would change my husband, I was sure.

"After some suffering I sat down and read it and when I did I got so excited. I started the very next day and within weeks there was a dramatic change in him and in our marriage. He started staying home, taking me out, buying me things, and his drinking almost completely stopped. But the most important change was that he started talking to me again, sharing things with me. We even went walking in the snow one day with his arm around me. I could go on and on but the thing I would like to mention is this: He told me that I was suddenly a different person, that something had happened to change me. Our little girl is a different person now too. She had become so withdrawn and nervous that I suspected she had an ulcer. Now she is happy and outgoing and her father spends time with her.''

These testimonials are evidence of the success of F.W., but an even more convincing way to find out if these teachings are true is to apply them in your own life. Acquire some of the qualities given in this chapter and see for yourself the loving response in your husband. Study the forthcoming chapters. Apply the assignments and observe your husband's reaction. During this time it is best if you don't inform your husband on the subject. If you apply these principles without his awareness, you will see more clearly his automatic response to *Fascinating Womanhood*. This will be further proof of its truth.

### Assignment

1. In becoming the Ideal Woman, you are not starting from zero. Take a good look at yourself and you'll find things to appreciate. Write down 25 things you like about yourself.

2. Make an Angelic Human chart. Mark with pink pen qualities you have. Mark with blue pen qualities you lack. Take one quality you lack and work on it this week. Notice your husband's favorable reaction.

# Part I
# THE ANGELIC QUALITIES

Understands Men

Inner Happiness

Worthy Character

Domestic Goddess

    The Angelic arouses in man a feeling near worship, and brings him peace and happiness.

    To become *the Ideal Woman from a man's point of view*, first study the Angelic qualities listed above. All of the chapters in Part I are devoted to a study of the Angelic qualities and how to acquire them.

# Introduction to Understanding Men

We begin our study of the Angelic side by learning to understand men. The first thing to learn is that *men are different from women,* so different in nature and temperament that it is almost as though they came from another planet. Men don't think, act, or react as women do, nor do they have the same needs or values. Even needs that are similar differ in value. For example, love is essential to both; admiration is essential to both; but *love is more important to a woman and admiration is more important to a man.* Because we fail to understand these differences, we sometimes provide men with the things we need, rather than the things they need, and are baffled when they fail to respond as we anticipated.

The following chapters cover the masculine needs, temperament, and characteristics. This knowledge should be a basic part of every woman's education. Without a thorough knowledge of the masculine nature, how can we hope to build a good relationship with our husbands and sons? The following relationship rules are based on the nature, needs, and characteristics of men:

*Relationship Rules With Men:*

1. Accept him at face value.
2. Appreciate his better side.
3. Admire his manliness.
4. Make him number one.
5. Let him be the guide, protector, and provider.
6. Let him manage the money.
7. Don't wound his sensitive masculine pride.
8. Be sympathetic, understanding.

# 3

## *Accept Him*

### *At Face Value*

Many years ago, Dr. Norman Vincent Peale delivered a lecture in our community. After the lecture, as was customary with Dr. Peale, he allowed time for questions. A question from a woman went something like this: *"I have tried to make a good home, be a good mother and devoted wife but things have not worked out well. The trouble is that my husband has not put forth equal effort to make our marriage successful."* She then reviewed his faults, some of which were, *"He neglects the children, spends money foolishly, drinks, and is difficult to live with."* Her question to Dr. Peale was, *"After twenty-five years of marriage is there any hope that he will change?"*

Dr. Peale answered firmly and a little impatiently, *"Don't you know that you should accept a man at face value, and not try to change him?"* Dr. Peale's advice is essential to a happy marriage and the foundation of *Fascinating Womanhood*. Therefore, if you want a happy marriage, *accept your husband at face value and don't try to change him.*

### What Does Acceptance Mean

Acceptance means you accept your husband for the man he is today, with no changes. You realize his conduct could be better, and probably should be better, but this is *his* responsibility, not *yours*. You observe his weaknesses, but count them as human frailties. You may not agree with his ideas, but allow him the right to his own viewpoint. You may not fully approve of his interests, dreams, or his lack of dreams, but allow him the freedom to pursue them as he will. In accepting him, you are accepting his right to be himself, for better or for worse.

Acceptance does not mean tolerance, that you *put up with him*. Nor does it mean dishonesty, that you deceive yourself into thinking he is perfect when he is not. Nor is it a matter of resignation. Acceptance is a happy state of mind when you realize that your responsibility is not in making him over but in appreciating him for the man he is.

Acceptance means you recognize him as a human being who, like yourself, is part virtue and part fault. This is an honest look. You realize that his faults exist, but focus on his virtues. You accept the total man with all of his potential goodness and all of his human frailties.

Acceptance is easier to understand if you form a mental picture of a man with a line drawn down the center, dividing him in two equal parts. Visualize one side painted a bright color to represent his virtues; picture the other side painted a dull color to represent his faults. Then, turn the dull side out of view so you see only the bright side. You know the dull side is there but you are not looking at it. You see only the bright side. Acceptance means *to accept him as a human being who is part virtue and part fault, to stop worrying about his faults and look to his better side.*

## What Faults Do Men Have That Women Try to Change?

In discovering how you may be violating this principle, take a careful look at this general review of men's faults:

1. *Personal Habits:* Poor eating habits, bad table manners, neglect of appearance, poor spelling and grammar, bad temper, depressed moods, untidy habits, especially in leaving things around the house, failure to hang up things or put things away in their proper place, lack of courtesy, swearing, smoking, drinking.

2. *How They Spend Their Time:* Spends too much time watching television, in the bathroom, napping on the sofa, away from home with the boys, in sporting events, church responsibility, outside activity, too involved in too many things, always in a hurry, fails to come home on time, or fails to call if he will be late.

3. *Duties:* Neglects home duties such as home repairs,

yard work, painting, fixing, paying bills, neglects church duties, fails to follow through with work, undependable in his job and therefore unsuccessful, lazy and irresponsible about his duties.

4. *Social Behavior:* Brags too much in public, talks too much, talks too little, careless in conversation, crude or loud in conversation. Lacks courtesy and social graces. Doesn't choose friends that wife can accept. Fails to accept wife's friends.

5. *Desires and Dreams:* Has no ambition or zest for living, doesn't have a desire to better himself, underestimates himself, lacks confidence, can't make up his mind what he wants out of life, moves from one dream to another, lets good opportunities go by, no imagination about getting ahead, has dreams that are out of reach or require too much risk.

6. *Manly Qualities:* Isn't masculine enough, indecisive, vacillating, fails to lead the family, too soft on the children, worries too much about past mistakes, too fearful of launching out on something new, flabby muscles, won't exercise.

7. *Money:* Doesn't earn enough money, doesn't manage money well, spends money foolishly, is stingy with money, spends large amounts without consulting wife.

8. *Neglect of Children:* Ignores the children when they come home, doesn't play with them or take them anyplace, doesn't help them with their homework or take part in their care and training, complains about normal noise and contention of little children.

9. *Religion:* Won't attend church, won't listen to religious ideas, isn't interested in religion, takes children on fishing trips or to amusement parks on Sunday instead of to church.

How do you react to your husband's faults? Do you accept him and look to his better side? Or do you set out to change him, as most women do? If you do, why? Perhaps for one of the following reasons:

## Why You Try to Change Him

1. *For Your Own Good:* You may try to change your husband because his faults get on your nerves, create distressing problems, or deprive you of some of the things you want

and deserve. *If he would only change*, you may say, *your life would be better, happier*. Review your husband's faults to see if this is true. If he changed, would your life be more pleasant? Would you eliminate some problems, or have more comforts, money, material goods, prestige, or other benefits to yourself? Your desire for these things can prompt you to try to change him.

2. *For His Own Good:* You care about his comfort and happiness, you want him to be successful and get the best out of life, so you set out to change him for his own good. You may have begun marriage by making a list of his faults, thinking it your duty to improve him. Is it your duty? Are you responsible for making your husband into the man he ought to be?

In answer, if a man is blind to his faults and this blindness causes him to get into difficulty or fail to reach success, you should *wake him up*, as I will explain later in this chapter. But once he realizes his faults, if he chooses to continue don't persist in the matter. Accept him as he is. It is not your duty to push him to success. "But," you may say, "My husband's faults are robbing him of happiness, and therefore I must change him so he can be happy." This seems like a worthy aim, so why not? The following explains why you should *not* try to change him:

## 1. Creates Discord

Even though you set out to remake your husband with the best of intentions, it can create problems with serious consequences. No matter how carefully worded your suggestion, he will likely respond with resistance, resentments, and even anger. If you *pressure* him to change, you can awaken the monster in him and *enrage* his feelings. This can lead to conflict and serious arguments. In turn, you may respond with frustration and even tears, asking yourself, "What did I do wrong? Why did my husband react so violently?" Children, too, suffer when they sense discord between their parents.

Another problem is in regard his feeling of security. A man expects his wife to be the one secure haven where he can relax, be himself, and feel secure. The realization that you are dissatisfied with him threatens his feeling of security, just as you would feel insecure if you felt he didn't love you. This can *unhinge* him, destroying hope and incentive to strive.

With the resentments, angry feelings, conflict, arguments, frustrations, discord, and threat to a man's security, *is trying to change your husband really worth it?* Does what you hope to accomplish in improving him compensate for the discord in your home and the damage to your relationship? Which is more important to your children, to yourself, and your husband? Isn't love and harmony in marriage of greater value?

## 2. Cools His Feelings

Any attempt to change your husband, can dampen his feelings for you. Even only an *implication* that he doesn't measure up to your standards, can cool his attitude. Your *open suggestion* that he needs to improve can lead to his rejection of you. This can be the beginning of a break in communication which can last for hours or even days. He may avoid the situation by spending a great amount of time away from home with his friends, or in other interests or pursuits.

Not only can love be cooled, in some cases it can be destroyed. When a wife doesn't give her husband the freedom to be himself, when she constantly pushes and nettles him to change, it can cause the destruction of a happy marriage. One of the most tragic cases in history is of the Russian novelist, Count Leo Tolstoy and his wife, Sofia:

### Leo and Sofia Tolstoy

Tolstoy is one of the most famous novelists in history. Two of his masterpieces, *War and Peace* and *Anna Karenina,* are considered literary treasures. He was so admired by his people that some of them followed him around day and night and wrote down in shorthand every word he said. Although he was a man of wealth and fame, after studying the teachings of Jesus and other moralists, he gave away his property, worked in the fields chopping wood and pitching hay, made his own shoes, ate out of a wooden bowl, and tried to love his enemies.

He gave away the publishing rights to his books and had the courage to live a life he believed in.

In the beginning of their marriage, Leo and Sofia, kneeling together, prayed to God to continue the ecstasy that was theirs. But as his views of life changed from luxury to peasantry, their marriage changed. She couldn't accept his simple, barren, way of life. She loved luxury and he despised it. She craved fame and the esteem of society, but these things meant nothing to him. She longed for money and riches, but he thought these things a sin. When he resisted her and went his own way, she screamed at him and threw herself into fits of hysteria or threatened to kill herself or jump down the well. This was her way of pressuring him to change.

After forty-eight years, this man who adored his wife when he married her could hardly bear the sight of her. Countess Tolstoy, heartbroken and old and starving for affection, kneeled at her husband's feet and begged him to read the exquisite love passages he had written to her in his diary fifty years previously. As he read of those beautiful happy days that were now gone forever both of them wept. His dying request was that she should not be permitted to come into his presence.

Countess Tolstoy was not all to blame. Her husband could have considered her feelings more and made concessions. He could have met her halfway. But think how noble it would have been for her to have accepted his way of life, let him have the freedom to experiment with his ideas, to test their value. He would have loved her more than in the beginning. She would have lost nothing of any value but gained everything worth having.

### 3. Can Cause Rebellion:

Pressing a man to change can bring out a streak of rebellion in him. This is due to his effort to preserve his freedom to be himself. For example, my son sometimes says, "Mother, don't tell me to do it or I won't want to." This shows how men feel about their precious freedom and how they will sometimes reject the very thing they want rather than be pressed into it. An illustration is in the following experience:

## Escape Out the Bathroom Window

A woman who was devoted to her religion tried to persuade her husband to investigate her church. He resisted. She kept after him night and day, but each effort failed. One evening she secretly arranged for the missionaries of her church to drop by at dinnertime, thinking her husband would feel obligated to invite them to dinner and be friendly. She also arranged for them to bring books, tapes, a film, and other materials from which they could preach to him after the meal.

Everything went as planned. Just as the family was sitting down to the table, the missionaries rang the doorbell. After an enjoyable meal, the wife said, "Wouldn't it be nice if these two gentlemen explained a little about the church." Due to moral pressure and courtesy, the man agreed. As the missionaries were assembling their materials, flannel board, books, and pictures, the husband felt trapped. He excused himself to go to the bathroom, climbed out the bathroom window, and disappeared.

The desperate wife turned to her church for help. Several men came to her rescue and began looking for her husband. After three days of extensive search, he was found. He had no intention of returning home, but due to kindly persuasion and his wife's promise that she would never mention religion again, he returned home. The wife kept her promise, and the man began to relax in peace. The impressive part of the story is the following:

The husband became acquainted with the man who found him and confessed, "*I have wanted to know more about your church, but not from my wife.*" Secretly he learned about his wife's religion, converted, and became a member. One Sunday morning the minister announced the new member of his congregation and asked him to come to the rostrum. When her husband arose, the wife was so surprised and overjoyed she burst into tears.

## Health Foods

Another woman caused a rebellious streak to appear in her husband by doing the following: When they were first married she made many suggestions about trivial matters. She tried to reform his eating habits, encouraged him to take more baths and to take better care of his appearance.

She was radical about health foods. He came from a family that thought nutrition unimportant, so it was irritating to him to be deprived of foods he was used to. This infringement on his freedom provoked him to eat junk foods when away from home. He also began drinking and smoking. Her suggestions were toward health, so his rebellion was against health, almost ruining his once strong body. In a sense it was *give me liberty or give me death*.

An opposite example is a young woman who was also devoted to health foods. She also married a man who was not interested in nutrition. He had been brought up on pies, cakes, jams, candy, and white bread. Soon after they were married she said sweetly to him, *"Honey, I know that you have been used to eating a different way than I, but do you mind if I prepare for myself the foods I want and I'll do the same for you?"* He agreed and she prepared two separate meals for months. After awhile he adopted her good eating habits and was preaching their value to his family. Men are usually wise enough to want what is best for them but don't want to be pushed.

## 4. It Doesn't Work:

You might as well give up trying to improve your husband because it doesn't work. Hints, carefully worded suggestions, or even pressures won't change him. Did Countess Tolstoy succeed in changing her husband? Did the wife who tried to pressure her husband to join her church succeed? Did the wife who insisted her husband eat health foods reform his eating habits? No, men don't change in this way.

Some women *claim* credit for their husband's improvement. They pressured him to change and finally he did. Don't let this deceive you. With very few exceptions, two of which are covered in this chapter, his improvement wasn't due to her persuasion, but a motivation she may not know about. Someone else may have talked to him, as in the case of the man who joined his wife's church. Or, he could have taken a class which opened his eyes, or read something inspiring. It may have been a flash of insight that prompted him to see the folly of his ways. Yes, he changed, but may have changed much sooner without her push.

As you see, efforts to change your husband are unsuccessful. They cause marriage problems, cool feelings, destroy love, cause rebellion, and don't work. _They bring no change or improvement in the man._

## How You Can Help a Man to Change

If you accept a man at face value, is there any hope he will change? He may not, and you need to accept this fact. But in a miraculous way, when you accept him at face value, he is more likely to change. _The only hope that a man will change is for you to not try to change him._ Others may try to teach him and offer suggestions, but the woman he loves must accept him for the man he is, and look to his better side. There are, however, three things you can do to encourage him to change:

1. _Give Him His Freedom:_ Give him the freedom to be himself, to follow his own convictions, set his own objectives, pursue his own interests, or not pursue them, and do the things he wants to do. When given this personal freedom, his mind will function without barriers. He will be receptive to new ideas, even your own, and encouraged to be his better self.

2. _Appreciate His Better Side:_ A steady diet of praise can motivate him to overcome his weaknesses and become a better man. Appreciation can help a man, child, or any individual, grow to a higher potential. More of this in the next chapter.

3. _Live All of_ Fascinating Womanhood: When you apply the teachings of _Fascinating Womanhood,_ in a miraculous way your husband's faults tend to disappear. I have seen this happen again and again. Men have been so obnoxious that neither their wife nor anyone else could stand them, but when the wife lived _Fascinating Womanhood_ the man became pleasant and agreeable. Of course, there is no guarantee, but a wholehearted effort to live these teachings can prompt a man to change for the better.

## The Man's Great Need for Freedom

Free Agency is one of the most fundamental laws of life. Mankind does not develop or experience happiness without it. God was fully aware of this principle when he created man and placed him on the earth. He allowed the forces of evil to be present to tempt him and to try him. And He knew from the beginning that many of the precious souls of men would fall into sin and reap the bitterness which comes from disobedience. But He also knew that without freedom, mankind could not grow and develop. Man has to be given a choice and make that choice himself. *If God could risk man's future happiness in order to extend to him his precious freedom, a woman should allow her husband this same privilege.* Let him do what he wants to do, and be what he wants to be without interference.

A man is particularly in need of *religious* freedom, as all mankind has always been. Wars have been fought over it; men have fought valiantly and died for it; the Pilgrims left Europe because of it; America was founded on this principle. It is still as important to each of us today; it is our God-given right. A man has a right to his personal feelings about religion. When his wife extends this freedom to him, rewards follow. His mind is more open. He is more apt to consider another viewpoint, as in the following example:

A girl was engaged to marry a man of a different religion. Her religion was very important to her, so she hoped he would eventually join her church. She sought counsel from a wise man who said, *"If you marry this man, don't make an issue of your religious differences. If he wants to go to his church, go with him. In return, ask him to attend yours. Hold to your convictions and be an example of what your religion teaches."*

She did marry the man and she followed the wise counsel. She attended his church and in return, he attended hers. After some time he modified his viewpoint and became a member of the same church as his wife.

Men are so touchy about religious freedom that they resist even a gentle hint. For example, on Sunday mornings a young wife sweetly asked her husband, *"Are you planning to attend church this morning?"* This so irritated him that he stayed home just to claim his freedom. He had nothing against his church, but if he attended, he wanted it to be his idea. As soon as she stopped hinting he began to attend more regularly.

When you attempt to drive a man to church, you more often drive him away. If you take credit for your husband's church attendance, supposing it was because you pushed him there, you are suffering a false illusion. Your husband has found another reason for attending than you realize, and would have come into activity sooner with freedom and your shining example.

## Provoking a Man to Righteousness

An early religious teaching states that a woman should *provoke her husband to righteousness. It is her duty*. What does this mean? At the time this religious instruction was given, the dictionary meaning of the word provoke was *to inspire*, or *incite*. It would be assumed then, that a woman should provoke her husband to righteousness by her example, and spiritual influence.

The problem today is that women misinterpret the earlier teaching. Dictionaries of today define the word provoke, *"to nettle or to push,"* which is not what the early teaching meant. This method never works. When a woman pushes her husband to church she usually drives him away.

## Methods Women Use to Change Men

Sometimes women try to change men by force in the form of *demands, ultimatums*, or *threats*. Usually, however, they resort to *pushy suggestions, criticism, disapproval*, or *nagging*. Or, they use subtle methods such as *moral pressure, disapproval, a carefully worded suggestion*, or a *gentle hint*.

Some women try to change a man by *using another man as a shining example*. They may express admiration for their father, brother, another man in the community, or even a famous man from history. If it is done out of admiration only, he may let it pass. But if she calls attention to the other man's superior virtues, hoping her husband will try to be more like the other man, he will resent it.

## Self-righteousness

When you try to improve your husband, you reveal a serious flaw in your character, the fault of *self-righteousness*. You indicate that you consider yourself better than he. You may think you are more righteous, more diligent in living your religion, or more faithful in attending to religious duties. This same attitude of self-righteousness was observed among the Sadducees and the Pharisees in Biblical times. They were proud of their faithfulness to attend church, pay tithes, pray, read the Scriptures, fast, observe the Sabbath, and attend to any number of rituals. The Savior condemned them, not for their faithfulness, but because of their self-righteous attitude about their faithfulness.

When you criticize or condemn your husband you take the position of being a judge. But, are you qualified to judge his worth? Are you a better person than he? When a woman complained to me of her husband's faults, some of them serious, I asked her, *"Do you really think you are a better person than he is?"* She looked at me with indignation, then, after quiet meditation lowered her head and said humbly, "No, I don't think I am a better person than my husband. I know he is a fine man at heart."

## A Feeling of Superiority

Similar to self-righteousness is a feeling of *superiority*. You may consider yourself more intelligent, better educated, more skilled, alert, careful, clever, or successful than he. You may come from a better family background, one with more money and status. With this view of yourself, you may take the initiative to shape him up to your standards. If you want a good marriage, don't count the worth of these things in your favor, or flaunt them before him, making him feel inferior. Instead, learn to appreciate the things which really count, as we will learn in the following chapter.

One thing that makes it difficult to overlook a fault in a man is that *his faults are different from yours*. He may be disorganized and messy, whereas you may be neat and orderly. He may be forgetful and you may be alert. On the other hand, you may be critical whereas he is inclined to be forgiving. You may be tardy and he may be prompt. Because your faults are different, you may focus on his and overlook your own. The next time you are troubled about your husband's faults, say to yourself, "He has this fault but he is better than me in other ways."

### The Key to Acceptance:

The key to acceptance is *humility*—realizing our own human frailties and limitations and therefore *looking to ourselves for change*. The heart of Christian doctrine and other sound religions and philosophies is, *"It is ourselves we must change,"* or *"Cast out the beam from our own eye first, that we may more clearly see the mote in our brother's eye."* Only with this humility of spirit can we build a successful relationship with another person. Remember the Bible account of the man who lifted up his head in pride, saying he was glad he was not sinful as other men. But Jesus approved the humble man who bowed his head, smote his chest, and said, *"Oh, God, be merciful to me, a sinner."*

### Should I Ever Try to Change Him?

First, let it be said that anytime a woman can change or improve a man for the better without causing marriage problems, there is nothing wrong with doing so. But as we have learned, this is difficult to do. Men resist change, and it usually causes serious marriage problems, and in many cases, marriage failures. So, when you attempt to change a man in any way, always tread lightly. Be prepared for his stubborn resistance, problems in your marriage relationship, and even cooled feelings. Make sure your efforts to change him would be worth the loss. However, there *are* situations when *you should try to change him* and when, if you do it right, you may be successful and it may be well worth your effort. They are the following:

1. *When He Is Blind to His Faults:* Sometimes a man's faults bring him serious problems or even failure. When he is blind to these faults he has no insight to understand his problems or correct them. Take for example, the salesman who

fumbles his presentation, or the manager who is too dictatorial, or a doctor who is unfriendly with his patients. If he is blind to these faults he makes the same mistakes over and over again, bringing on the same failure patterns. People he associates with may not be interested enough to say anything, or may feel it is not their business to do so. His wife may be the only one who cares enough, and is in a position to speak out.

In waking up the man who is blind, keep in mind that *you do accept him*. It is the world that does not. In talking to him don't refer to his failures directly. Instead focus on the success that lies just ahead. Assure him that if he would make a few changes, he would be much more successful and people would begin to esteem him for his true worth. Once you have opened his eyes don't persist in the matter. If he continues to make the same mistakes, fully aware of them, allow him this freedom.

Before correcting your husband, be certain that his mistakes are actually causing him problems. A woman asked me if she should correct her husband's poor grammar. In inquiring about him I found that he was extremely successful and had the approval of many friends. I told her it was unnecessary to say anything about it.

In correcting your husband, be feminine; don't appear to know more about his business than he does; don't be motherly; and don't talk man to man. Refer to Chapter 8, How to Give Feminine Advice.

2. *When He Is Abusive to His Children:* Sometimes a man, without fully realizing it, can damage his own children. Habitual harsh words or depreciating remarks can diminish a child's self-esteem in a way to destroy something fine about him and affect his entire life adversely. Or, cruel or unjust punishment, either mental or physical, can endanger the child and his relationship to his parent. Whether mental or physical, it is not fair for a parent to so injure a child. If this is the case, you have a moral obligation to take a stand.

You will have to speak out boldly, and probably frequently, with a patient persistence. If you live all of *Fascinating Womanhood,* and do all you can to build a good relationship with your husband, you need not fear any danger in taking this stand. You are entirely within your rights and he will sense this. If you are patient and persistent, you will be very apt to win, to humble your husband, and change him in regard to his children. And someday he will thank you for it.

I am not referring here to a man who is merely firm in the discipline of his children. This is a masculine tendency which should be respected. Children tend to respect a firm father and love him more because of his firm training. And it is always best for the children to feel their mother's support of the father's authority, and the united front of their parents.

But when a father goes too far, when he depreciates a child with harsh, cruel words, or when his punishment is unjust, or he resorts to belts, buckles, boards or anything which would injure a child in body or spirit, you have a moral obligation to take a stand. And if he will not listen to reason, take the children out of the household and remain away until all danger is past. Don't judge him or condemn him for his actions. Be firm but kind, letting him know that you are doing it for the protection of the children. Your firm but kind attitude, accentuated by your actions, may humble him and bring him to repentance.

3. *When There Are Things You Can't Live With:* There may be things, no matter how hard you try, you just can't live with. These may be small but abrasive things which only irritate you, or something which so grates on your nerves that it makes your life miserable. After you live the whole of *Fascinating Womanhood*, there are ways you can effectively correct a man, such as the following:

a. Tell Him What You Expect of Him: When he does something to irritate you, don't criticize him. Instead, use a positive approach. *Tell him what you expect of him.* First say something like this: "I expect more of a man such as you," or "You can do better than this." These statements suggest you have a high opinion of him he is not measuring up to. In a subtle way this gives him the incentive to live up to your conception of him. After you have thus approached him, spell out what you expect of him.

When Wally Simpson first met Edward, Prince of Wales, his conversation was superficial and boring. Then Wally said something which became history, "I expected more of the future King of England." Her high expectation of him and direct honesty charmed him. It was something special he liked about her.

b. A Feminine Appeal: Or, you can approach him in a feminine way, such as, "Would you consider . . . ," or, "It would help me a lot if you would . . . ," or, "It would mean so much to me if you would . . . ," or, "Would you mind very much . . ."

If you try either of the above methods and they don't work, you can be sure you are not living the whole of *Fascinating Womanhood*. If you are a selfish, nagging, unfeminine woman, or fail to make a comfortable home life for him, he will not likely respond to this method.

## Some Special Problems

There are other occasions when, although you are not trying to change him, you should respond to his faults in a certain way. They are the following:

1. *When He Mistreats You:* When a man is thoughtless, unfair, insulting, harsh, or critical, should you try to change him? Should you try to put a stop to his behavior? No, count these flaws as human frailties, present in most human beings. But, do respond to his mistreatment in the right way: Don't be a doormat. Don't shrink back and act wounded, or retreat behind your shell. Instead, have some self-dignity. Stand up to him and he will love you more because of it. But take care that you do it in the right way. The method of doing this is one of the charms of *Fascinating Womanhood,* taught in Chapter 24.

2. *When He Does Something Wrong:* If a man does something morally wrong, is dishonest, unjust, deceitful, cruel, or in any way sinful, don't overlook it. If you do, you show a weakness in your own character. And don't make the mistake of lowering your standards to his. He expects you to be better than himself and would be disappointed to see you fall from your level to his. He wants you to hold to your ideals and standards, even under trying circumstances, regardless of what he does himself.

When a man does or says something sinful, here is the way to handle it: At first, show reluctance to believe it. Say you thought it impossible for a man such as he to do such a thing. If you are compelled to believe it, indicate that you know it is contrary to his true nature and was only the result of carelessness or thoughtlessness. *You must be immensely disappointed at his temporary lapse but your faith in his better side must be unshaken*.

3. *The Alcoholic Husband:* Alcoholism is difficult to accept due to related problems such as squandering money, ugliness of disposition, dishonesty, unreliableness, other women, and the deterioration of the home. Women almost despair over this problem. They ask, *"How can I accept what he has done to our life?"* The following will make acceptance possible:

First, gain an *understanding sympathy* for the problem. Alcoholism is one of the most difficult of weaknesses to overcome. I know you have been told this before but here is a way to make sympathy real: Once a month fast for three days, going without all food or beverage—nothing but water. Or give up coffee, sweets, or another binding habit. You will soon get the picture, to a slight degree, of what you expect of him.

Next, gain some *humility*. Take a look at your reaction to his problem. Though you've known better, you've probably yelled, nagged, insulted, and abused him for the mess he's made of your life. When he drinks, you've had a bad attitude, lost patience, and exploded. What about your other failings? Are you a good mother? Homemaker? Do you keep the precepts of your religion? Do you live the teachings of *Fascinating Womanhood?* Or do you try, then fail again and again?

If you can admit such weakness in yourself, you will have less reason to condemn your husband for his failings, which are far more difficult to overcome. Yours are relatively easy, his almost impossible. If you will *"cast out the beam from your own eye first,"* you will more clearly see the terrible, enslaving bond of alcoholism.

4. *Other Women:* Two things you have a right to expect in marriage are *fidelity and financial support*. If your husband is involved with another woman, deal with it in the following way: First, ask yourself if you did anything to drive him away. While reading *Fascinating Womanhood*, you will see your mistakes. Take measures to correct them as a means of winning him back. In many cases this has been done quickly and under

difficult circumstances, as evident in case histories at the end of this chapter and throughout this book.

When you have eliminated your mistakes and become a wonderful wife, if he continues immoral practices, it is time to bring him to a showdown. State clearly but firmly that he will have to make a choice, that if he doesn't give her up you will leave him. Be prepared to keep your word. It is morally wrong for a woman to continue to live with a man who is immoral. Also, it can prevent his repentance, for if he has both of you, he doesn't have the incentive he needs to give her up. Don't condemn him. His sin is an addicting weakness, difficult to overcome. After you have left him, try to win him away from the other woman. You have a moral obligation to do so, for as long as he lives in sin he is on the way to destruction. By winning him back, you save not only a marriage but a soul!

5. *Nonsupport:* The second thing you can expect in marriage is *financial support*. This means an income to cover the necessities and a dwelling place. If your husband is disabled, or cannot find work, cheerfully adapt to circumstances until solutions can be worked out. But if he is an able-bodied man physically and mentally, and refuses to look for work or take responsibility for providing the income, there is justification for action.

Since you will not be inclined to let your children suffer hunger or want, you will probably seek employment outside the home, or turn to charity for help. If this is the case, you should ask your husband to leave and not return until he provides an income. If you don't, if you allow him to remain, you will increase the problem. He will be removed from his responsibility, will become accustomed to your income, and you may be stuck with the job for life. Another solution is for you to move out and take your children with you.

6. *Perfect Background:* If you come from an ideal home, where your father was the perfect father, the family the perfect family, you went on outings together, and there were few money worries, it could be a problem. There would be a tendency for you to expect this same life-style from your husband, who may have a different picture of what a life-style should be. You may try to make him fit your mold. Beware of this situation. If you expect too much of him, you may split your

marriage in two and end up with nothing. Accept his background along with everything else. When you do he will be more open to working things out together.

## Acceptance Is Not Easy

When I teach you to accept your husband at face value I'm not asking you to do something easy. Some women have found it so difficult that they have given up trying. Two women talked about this over their back fence one day. They agreed that accepting their husbands' faults was so difficult that it was too much to ask of themselves. They decided to disregard this principle.

Try to understand that any advancement to a better, happier life is difficult. For example, living the Christian religion is not easy. You are taught to love your enemies, do good to those who hate you, and try to become perfect. A devout Christian does not set aside these goals because they are difficult. The ladies talking over the back fence may as well give up being Christians as to give up accepting their husbands at face value.

## Rewards

I can promise you tremendous rewards if you accept your husband at face value. The response in your husband will likely be moving. For years he may have suffered the plaguing thought that you are dissatisfied with him. Your assurance that you accept him as he is will remove doubts from his mind and come as a relief. His appreciation for you and his tender response can be earthshaking, as in some of the following experiences:

## A Brand New Marriage

"When I was twenty-seven I married a thirty-four-year-old bachelor, a rough, tough naval officer and for the next twenty-seven years he remained rough and tough! I leaned over backwards trying to change him into a tender, loving husband. Nothing worked!

"All through his naval career he was spit and polish . . .

and he looked like a million dollars. A few years ago he retired from the navy, and he also retired from the spit and polish. He would go for days without shaving. When we were invited to a dinner party he could care less what he put on—slightly soiled trousers, a wrinkled shirt—and I would be embarrassed to death. If I said, honey, why don't you put on those dark blue slacks, they're clean, the fight would be on. He would bristle, threaten not to go, and I would back down. We'd go and both be miserable. After a few years I changed tactics. I learned to give him *that look with a significant sigh,* but it didn't change a thing.

"Then a miracle happened. I took a course called *Fascinating Womanhood.* I was in a traumatic shock over how wrong I had been in many of my attitudes and responses. During the second lecture the teacher spent two hours talking about the futility of trying to change a man, and the wisdom of accepting him just as he is. And suddenly it hit me: *My husband is an adult, a highly intelligent man, capable of making his own decision . . . a naval officer for years!* When I changed my attitude the miracle happened! I finally realized I had been more concerned about what others would think and say than my husband's happiness.

"On my way home I determined to never again offer suggestions about what he would wear . . . unless he asked, and to not let it bother me. You can't imagine what a load has fallen from my shoulders since I stepped out of my role as my husband's chief advisor. Now my man's happiness and comfort are ten million times more important than what the Jones's say or think. It has changed our going out together from a time of tension and unhappiness to a time of real enjoyment.

"Today he is a tender, loving, husband. But he never changed when I tried to change him. When I stopped trying to change him and started working on me, he changed in response to the change in me.

"Never in twenty-eight years had my husband given me an anniversary present, but on our twenty-ninth we were in Mexico City. He woke me up at dawn and said, ''You know, luv, we've got a brand-new marriage on our hands,'' and he gave me a diamond wedding band. Don't tell me F.W. doesn't work!!''

### A Gem I Must Polish

"Even before I was married I was well on the way to breaking the most important F.W. rule—accept a man as he is and don't try to change him. I remember remarking to a friend, "He really is quite a gem. I just have to polish him up a bit." As soon as we were married I began the polishing process, unaware that what I really was doing was rubbing him the wrong way.

"Instead of producing a beautiful gem, I was creating a massive bulk of cold, hard, rock. My constant barrage of criticism forced him to build a wall around himself, from which he would emerge only after he was drunk, to give me some of my own treatment. Life for me and the children was becoming an unending round of sleepless nights filled with fear, terror, shouting, cursing, nervous tension, heartache, and tears.

"All I could think of was how to get out of this mess, so I got one job after another until I worked my way up to a position where I could support the children and myself. Then I filed for divorce. When the papers were drawn up and ready to be served on my husband, I realized that deep within my heart, this was not the solution I wanted. Somewhere there must be a better way.

"I knew that if I went through with the divorce I would feel for the rest of my life that I had failed as a wife and as a woman. I felt that my three daughters would have a terrible example to follow and that the step I was contemplating would result in not just one divorce, but likely four. "Help me find another way," I prayed.

"God began to speak to my heart about the principle of acceptance. I made up my mind and decreed in my heart that from this time on I would accept my husband as he was, alcoholism and all. No longer would I be offended when he came home drunk. I determined to put my arms around him and try to let him know that I loved him.

"When I did, because I had lived opposite for so many years, he didn't believe me and kept pushing me away. I persisted in my attempts to show him that I cared for him and continued to pray. Later, through F.W. I was to learn that my husband could not accept this change on my part as being genuine until I was willing to humble myself and admit I had been wrong for so many years and ask for his forgiveness.

"In answer to my prayers God next impressed upon my heart that I must submit to my husband in all things. This was an extremely difficult step for me, especially in view of the fact that my husband by now was no longer employed. He was continually either to drunk or too sick to work, and I had become quite independent financially, emotionally, and socially.

"It was the *all things I must submit to* that I balked at, and a great spiritual struggle ensued within me. My chief argument was, But Lord, my husband is not a Christian, so how can I submit to him in all things? His answer was that I should trust Him, that His word may also be brought to husbands through the behavior of the wives. Finally, on the last day of April, I surrendered this stronghold to God and told Him that from that day on I was submitting to my husband in all things. That same evening I met the woman who later introduced me to F.W.

"Within a week of my decision to submit in all things, my husband stopped drinking and sought help through counseling. He has been sober ever since. I was very thankful to have a sober husband but I began to feel a terrible emptiness in our marriage relationship. We were like strangers living under the same roof, not actually knowing one another. My inability to bridge this terrible gap was becoming a source of frustration to me. It was at this point that my new-found friend loaned me F.W. I knew as soon as I read it that it was another answer to prayer.

"One by one, gradually I began applying the principles. 'Honey, I want you to know that I realize I've been wrong all these years in trying to change you. I am sorry and I am asking you to forgive me. In fact, I am glad that you are strong enough to have resisted my efforts to change you. Also, forgive me for not having understood how great a responsibility you have on your shoulders to provide for me and the children. I want you to know how I appreciate your taking care of us. And you know I have always admired your broad shoulders, and those muscles. They're as hard as a rock. And the way you carry yourself. I think you are wonderful.'

"The first two times I tried saying these things to him he said nothing. The third time he didn't say anything either, but he kind of squared his shoulders in a way which to me very eloquently said, 'Well, she's finally discovered me!' Since then he has responded in many heartwarming ways—a bouquet of flowers, a new chair for the living room, invited me to go to an auction sale with him, or invited the neighbors in for an evening. I am grateful for his every response, great or small, which indicates that I have indeed found the key to a happy marriage.

"I feel like a new bride again through F.W. I am just now learning what a good marriage is all about. The only married couples I had known who had a good relationship were either in the generation before mine (and therefore, I reasoned, their circumstances were not relevant to our times), or the husband did not drink heavily.

"Little did I know that the divine order of marriage, as given to Adam and Eve, has not changed, that a man's needs have not changed, and that my marriage could only be successful if I followed the principles God laid down. His laws are eternal and do not change with the times or circumstances."

### The Years That the Locust Had Eaten

"Marriage, for me, at age twenty was an arrangement in which I could begin to change my new husband into the man I wanted him to be and get out of it all that I possibly could. I had been taught that marriage is a fifty-fifty proposition and that I was to do all that I could to be sure that my part of the proposition was secured.

"Seven stormy years later I began to view the shambles I had created, a very unhappy belligerent husband who had retreated into himself and children that also reflected the home situation. I began to ask the Lord what was wrong, and slowly but clearly as I searched the Scriptures I began to see the wonderful role that God had created for the woman in being a helpmeet for her husband and of his place of leadership in the home. Mental assent was given to these truths; yet as to how to put them to practice eluded me. Some improvement was made in our home situation, but my husband remained behind his wall and after a long period of time, I became very discouraged and began to doubt the truths I had previously learned.

"At this point I heard of the *Fascinating Womanhood* course, feeling that this would perhaps give some of the answers I longed and prayed to know. Within six weeks, I sought to put into practice what was being taught and saw my husband begin to shower attentions upon me, so by the end of six weeks our life together was sweeter and richer than it was on our honeymoon.

"Whereas before I was occupied with his faults, now these same faults somehow were the points I could actually admire, finding myself in the freshness of a new love for him. He began to tell me that he loved me for the first time in years. Since then our life together is continuing to improve and grow in love and fellowship. For the first time I feel satisfied and fulfilled as a woman with much thanksgiving for the wonderful gift of womanhood God has given to me and to all women.

"It is written in the book of Joel, *'I will restore to you the years that the locust has eaten . . . and you shall eat in plenty and be satisfied and praise the name of the Lord your God that has dealt wondrously with you.'* (Joel 2:25, 26) I can say with all confidence that this promise is being fulfilled in my life as by the strength of Christ I continue to put into practice the principles in the Scriptures and amplified in *Fascinating Womanhood*."

### His Little Angel

"My husband and I have been married twenty-one years. I had always thought we had a wonderful marriage, that is, for the first half of it. Then things began to happen. We have seven children whom we love very much, but this was not enough to hold our marriage together. A friend and sister had been trying to get me interested in *Fascinating Womanhood*, so in desperation I thought I would try, so I borrowed a book and began to read. To me it was revelation upon revelation.

"My husband at the time was planning to leave me. I told him I thought he should as we had nothing in common anymore. He was two hundred miles away looking for work which would take him further away, so I had to work fast. The night he came home I applied the first assignment, to accept him and tell him so and told him I would like very much a chance to prove to him that I would improve. He said nothing.

"The next night I asked him if he had thought about it and he said 'yes,' but he was convinced it wouldn't work. He was so discouraged, disillusioned, and unhappy that he thought the only thing to do was to go away by himself. I tried to convince him otherwise but nothing would change his mind. Well, with my life at an end, so I thought, I cried the whole night.

"The next morning he asked me if I really meant what I said and I said 'Yes.' He told me that he had always loved me, that he really didn't want to leave, and that his boss had offered him a raise if he would stay. He held me in his arms as if he would never let go. I am remembering our first year of marriage when he kissed my feet and called me 'his little angel,' and I am wondering how I could have been such a fool as to let him down as I have. But I feel very blessed to be given another chance, and by applying *Fascinating Womanhood*, I am praying that I will be able to arouse these feelings again in him."

### Out of the Cellar

"I have a wonderful husband but he has some habits I disapproved of, especially his use of tobacco. I always insisted he go into the cellar to smoke even though I accepted this habit in him when we were married. After learning the principle of acceptance, I realized how awful I had been. When he came home that night I confessed my feelings, asking forgiveness for the terrible way I had treated him, and told him that I accepted him as he is. My husband was so tenderly touched that he cried. Later that evening he told me that he loved me for the first time in two years and he slept with his arm around me all night."

### Rules for Acceptance

1. Get rid of self-righteous attitudes.
2. Accept him as part virtue, part fault.
3. Give him his freedom to be himself.

4. Don't try to improve him.
5. Don't use other men as shining examples.
6. Look to his better side.
7. Express acceptance in words.

## Assignments

1. *List His Faults:* Make a list of your husband's faults which annoy you, things you find difficult to accept. It is best to face this honestly. You need to know what you must accept. Save this list. Later, if your marriage becomes troublesome, refer to the list to see if you are failing to accept something.

2. *As an Icebreaker:* Say something like this: "I am glad you are the kind of man you are. I can see I have not understood you in the past and that I've made many mistakes. But, I am glad you have not allowed me to push you around. You have not been like putty in my hands, but have had the courage of your convictions. Will you forgive me for not understanding you, and let me prove to you that I can be a wonderful wife?"

You may feel insincere in telling him these things, for your critical attitudes may not have disappeared, but do tell him, and look to his better side. When you do, your acceptance will become easier, more natural, more sincere, and will continue to grow.

3. *Love Booklet:* Make or buy a little love booklet to write down loving things your husband says or does as you begin to apply the principles of *Fascinating Womanhood*. Write down any favorable reaction to the above assignment.

*Note: Acceptance is the most fundamental principle taught in Fascinating Womanhood. Your success in living the following teachings depends on your accepting your husband at face value.*

# 4

# *Appreciate Him*

### *Look to His Better Side*

To appreciate a man means to *set a just value on him,* to *esteem him for his full worth,* and *to be grateful for him* and *the things he does for you.* Here are suggestions for developing a keen sense of appreciation:

### *The Third Eye:*

Learn to see him through new eyes. True love has three eyes. One eye is dim, dim to his faults. A second eye sees him as the world does. This is an important perspective. Sometimes you must help him see the way the world sees him, as we learned in the last chapter. A third eye sees him as no one else sees him, appreciates him as no one else appreciates him. Keep this eye sharply focused and you will observe many things to appreciate. Every wonderful wife has a third eye.

### *Develop Values*

Are you inclined to appreciate only superficial things about a man such as his looks, his income, or his status? Is your estimation of an ideal man one with money and success? Is he a high achiever who has earned honors in the community? Do you have a stereotype picture of what he ought to be? Do you expect him to be like other men? To appreciate a man for his true worth, you have to know what true worth implies. You need to develop a sense of values, as here reviewed:

## What to Appreciate

1. *Character:* Look for traits in his character to appreciate such as *honesty, dependability, kindness,* and *love.* When you appreciate these virtues you help him become a better man and strengthen your relationship. For a review of what basic character consists of, refer to Chapter 16, A Worthy Character.

2. *Intelligence:* To appreciate a man's intellectual features, consider his education, knowledge, good judgment, and creative skills of the imagination. Or, he may have a special talent in math, science, sales, or the arts. A man need not be well educated, however, to have intellectual gifts. High intelligence has been found in the rank and file of humanity, and often among the most humble. When a woman is alert enough to perceive it, and believe it, she can magnify the intelligent gifts within him.

3. *What He Does for You:* Notice and appreciate the many little things he does for you, such as when he carries in the groceries, opens your door, remembers your birthday, or gives you a phone call. Appreciate the things he does around the house to help you, such as tending the baby, doing the dishes, or making a trip to the grocery store for a last-minute item you forgot.

Appreciate the fix-it jobs he does around the house to keep things in repair, or the yard work. Appreciate the things he buys for you, furniture, clothes, miscellaneous items, and even your grocery money. And appreciate the time he spends with his children. Yes, these things are his duty, but how nice it is to be appreciated, how much it does for a relationship. Or, perhaps your husband doesn't do any of these things. Then, appreciate the most important thing of all:

Appreciate his occupation in making the living, his many hours of toil and effort away from home, to provide a living for his family. Many women fail in this respect, take this for granted, don't really count his daily grind as *something to appreciate.* It is just part of what is expected of a man, his duty. They could take a lesson from women in the past:

In the early days of America a man was appreciated if he only kept food on the table. This was especially true on the western frontier where life was hard. A man had to build his own shelter, protect his family, and grow his own food. Survival was his foremost concern. Not much more was expected of him. His very existence was appreciated.

Today a man's efforts are less visible and therefore less appreciated. Although he no longer builds his own shelter, he must earn enough money to buy one. Although he no longer grows his own food, he must earn enough money to pay for it. In addition to necessities, he must earn enough for income tax, state tax, property tax, sales tax, and gasoline tax. He not only supports a family but a federal government, local government, school system, highway systems, and various organizations.

When your husband succeeds in earning enough *take-home pay* to provide even the most basic necessities, he is worthy of appreciation. Your *appreciation* may mean more to him than his paycheck. Express your appreciation daily, and do it over and over again. If you grow tired of appreciating him over and over, remember, he must earn it over and over.

One of the most serious faults in anyone is ingratitude. An ungrateful wife is a fundamental cause of serious marriage problems. Be sure your children don't have this failing or they will be offensive. The main way you spoil a child is when you give him more than he can appreciate. This is true of adults also. We are corrupted not so much by the possession of wealth and luxuries, as our inability to appreciate them.

## When You Can't Find Anything to Appreciate

In extreme cases a man deteriorates to the point of not being much of a man, on the surface. You may feel at a loss to find anything to appreciate and would feel insincere praising him for qualities that don't exist. In such a case there are three things you can do:

1. *Have Faith in His Worth:* Have faith that character, intelligence, and kindness are inherent in his makeup as they are in the souls of all men. The German author Goethe wrote, *"If you treat a man as he is, he will stay as he is, but if you treat him as if he were what he ought to be and could be, he will become that bigger and better man."*

When you have an unwavering faith in his better side, you inspire him to live up to your conception of his ability.

You offer him hope that he has not appreciated himself at his true value, that courage, steadfastness, and honor are the underlying traits of his character. You can, in fact, transform a man from an apparently stupid, weak, lazy, cowardly, unrighteous man into a determined, energetic, true, and noble one.

Often a man is at heart a worthy person, and only needs for you to suggest that his life does not do justice to his true character. Once persuaded that he is noble at heart and that you perceive it, he becomes anxious to prove to himself and to you that there is no mistake about the matter. The turning point of his life may come from just such a revelation of his higher capabilities. *Remember, it is not by push or persuasion that you bring out the best in your husband and impel him to a more successful and righteous life, but by an unwavering belief in his better side.*

2. *Go Back Into the Past:* If you can't find anything to appreciate in the present, dwell on past experiences. Tell him what first attracted you to him, experiences in early marriage that aroused your appreciation, difficult circumstances that he faced with courage and persistence. Express appreciation for the diligence he displayed in getting his education or establishing himself in his work. Remember specific instances when he displayed intelligence, character, or ability.

Such a woman remembered the days of the depression, trying years when her husband lost his job and steady employment was difficult to find. She recalled how her husband wore the leather from the soles of his shoes in his effort to provide for his family. Only through his persistence did his family continue to enjoy the comforts of life.

Since that time he slipped in many ways, became difficult to live with, and their marriage deteriorated. But, when she expressed appreciation for his persistence in those early years, he was deeply moved. This was the *bread of life* he needed to make another effort. At that moment a change took place within him; he began to take on a new attitude, a motive for living and striving; his feelings for her revived and their marriage has blossomed once again.

3. *Look for Virtues Beneath His Faults:* Look beneath the surface of most men and you will find things to appreciate, as in the following examples:

## Virtues Beneath His Faults

1. *Obnoxious:* Suppose a man is so obnoxious that his own children run from him. He picks arguments, habitually disagrees with you, and in other ways makes life difficult. It's almost as though he's taking revenge for some mysterious reason you don't understand. Look beneath the surface. He may be a man of high caliber who hasn't been appreciated for his full worth. This can infuriate him. He appreciates himself, but why can't others? When a man of quality, with a good self-image, *is not fully appreciated by his wife,* he can become difficult to live with.

2. *Moody:* Or suppose a man is moody or discouraged for long periods. This was typical of Abraham Lincoln. He sat for hours, brooding or reading the newspaper, according to his law partner. Look beneath the surface of such a man and you will discover he has high aspirations which are not being met. Appreciate not only his high goals, but his frustration for not reaching his goals. If he were a lesser man he wouldn't suffer.

3. *Forgetful, Negligent, or Thoughtless:* Suppose a man is thoughtless or absentminded. Look beneath the surface and you may find a man who is absorbed in things he considers more important. Albert Einstein was well known for his absentmindedness. One rainy day he took his umbrella and walked to his car before he discovered he was in his pajamas. When a man is forgetful or thoughtless, discover the things he considers more important. You will find much to appreciate.

4. *Negligent at Home:* Or, suppose he never gets around to mowing the lawn. The grass is so high you're afraid snakes will nest in it. He doesn't get the house painted, do the repair work, or attend to the little odd jobs around the house. You remind him again and again but his mind is on something else. Look beneath the surface. He may be putting his energies away from home toward being successful. In his arrangement of priorities, he considers the jobs around the house of minor importance and his work away from home of major importance.

The point to remember is this: In looking for things to appreciate, never give up on a man. If you can't appreciate his character, his intelligence, or the things he does for you, have faith in him, appreciate past efforts, and look for virtues beneath his faults.

When you accept a man and appreciate his better side, you lay the foundation for a successful marriage. This is especially true when you *appreciate his daily efforts to make the living*. This means so much to him that when you do, you become beautiful to him in a new way. The following experience, related to me by a man of my acquaintance, is a perfect illustration:

### What Does He See in Her

"There was a woman in our neighborhood that had everyone puzzled. She was not beautiful, was overweight, and always dressed a little dowdy. There wasn't anything about her that was above average, at least not that anyone could see on the surface, yet her husband seemed to adore her. What on earth was it? This had everyone wondering.

"One evening I was in their home about dinnertime. She was busy in the kitchen putting the final touches on the dinner when her husband came home from work. This happened to be payday. He came into the kitchen, kissed her, and handed her his paycheck. She immediately stopped what she was doing, put her arms around him and said, 'I know how hard you have worked for this . . . how many long hours. Thank you for providing us with so many comforts, and making it possible for me to stay home and care for the family.'

"But this was not enough. She went into the living room where the children were all playing on the floor. She made them all stop and stand up. 'Look,' she said as she held up the paycheck. 'See, your father has worked hard to earn this money. Now, Jane, this means you can have a new pair of shoes, and Johnny, you can have your bicycle fixed.' The father stood there beaming. Not only did his wife appreciate him, but taught their children to. In his eyes, she was a beautiful woman.

"I'm not sure she did this every payday, but I know that here was a home where the man was appreciated for his daily efforts. And I know that this ordinary woman was not so ordinary. She knew how to appreciate a man and this is why she was beautiful to him."

### Everything Went Kerplunk

"About two and a half years ago an article entitled 'Expect a Miracle' influenced me to think, 'What would I like for a miracle?' Immediately I thought, 'A miracle in our marriage relationship. If only George would have a deep, deep love for me. And I'd like to be head over heels in love with him.' So I began to pray regularly for this miracle.

"About six months later a friend loaned me *Fascinating Womanhood*. I knew it was a gift from the Lord and my answer, because it showed me what I was doing wrong and how to be the kind of wife God wants me to be. First of all, I learned I was not accepting George as he is. I was not satisfied with what the Lord had given me. I wanted to change George.

"I spent my thinking time looking at his bad side, criticizing him in my heart. Naturally this came through in my attitude. I mulled over his shortcomings and ignored his good side. All the wonderful things about him I just took as a matter of course. I simply did not think to comment about them or even know about them. Undoubtedly this appeared to him as indifference. As soon as I learned about focusing on his good side and expressing my admiration, I began practicing it. He never tires of hearing it. I don't either.

"Immediately our relationship began to improve. As I concentrated on his better side, his faults became insignificant. He began to say the nicest things to me. I am keeping a list of treasures he has said to me, such as 'I love you more and more all the time,' and 'enjoy living with you.' Before, he would say 'I love you,' but that's all, no loving endearments. He had been extremely stingy with money. Now he began buying me anything I asked for. At that time we'd been married sixteen years and I had been cooking with very inadequate pans. He bought me a set of heavy aluminum pans that I wanted. I could go on and on. Also he began to take an interest in the children.

"Occasionally I slip back into my old fault-finding ways. When I do, the atmosphere of our home goes *kerplunk*. The kids crab and fight more. George is his old self. Everything is awful! The funny thing is it's immediate. All I have to do is change my attitude and everything is different. It doesn't take more than five minutes to change either to the good or the bad.

''That's what happened about three months ago. I thought, (undoubtedly Satan helped me) 'Nobody appreciates me. No one cares. All I do is give, give, give. I'm tired of it. I'm not doing it anymore. I'm just going to be myself' (which probably meant my old self). I stopped reading and studying F.W. I did read the Bible and pray, but not as often.

''What I went through! The depths of despair, the unhappiness, the tears upon tears. Everyone was miserable. Finally I decided to go back to the F.W. way. That was a few weeks ago. Last night George said, 'You're so lovable.' (I'd rather not go into what he said when I was going my own way.)

''Last night he said something else that was beautiful. To explain: About two years after we were married, George told me he preferred brown eyes. This broke my heart and crushed my spirit because I knew it was a basic rejection of me. I considered my blue eyes my best feature. Last night he made some nice comments about my blue eyes. I said, 'That's nice but you prefer brown eyes.' He said, 'No, I don't.' I said, 'You told me you do.' He said, 'I changed my mind about two years ago.' This was when I started practicing F.W. You can imagine how deeply happy I felt.''

## I Had Lost All Love for Him

''The first two courses that I've taken in *Fascinating Womanhood* have saved our marriage and been a blessing to our whole family. As I was cleaning out my desk this week, I found some notes that I had written down concerning my life just a year ago. I had reached a real low in expecting any sort of future for our marriage. I had lost all love for my husband and wasn't sure that I had much love for our children. I had even considered suicide during that time.

''I am so grateful to God for leading me out of a pit of despair and into a life that is such a joy and is so solidly stable. The courses in *Fascinating Womanhood,* which I fought against at first, helped to change me from a self-centered, independent, self-righteous mother and wife, into a new person—with a new perspective in all I do.

''As I have really and truly come to accept my husband, I find that my love for him is unbelievable. Before taking the course I was constantly criticizing him. When I asked his forgiveness and let him know how much I love and accept him, he has assumed the responsibility and position of the head of our family for the first time in our marriage of twenty-five years. It is a miracle!

"What a relief it is to me to let him make the final decisions and trust the Lord to lead him. My disposition is one of relaxed confidence. Our children are so much happier and accept their father's authority easily. I don't hear any of the arguing that they used to put me through. Our five children, ranging in age from elementary school through college, are responding with gratitude toward their new mother, as they too are accepted and loved for themselves.

"We are finally having family devotions after dinner each evening! This is something I have been pleading for without success, for years. My husband decided. The children accepted it. We are all growing closer and more understanding of each other. I am so busily enjoying my attempt to fill my role as Angela Human that I no longer have time for nagging, self-pity, or criticizing. Our home finally has an atmosphere of peace, order, comfort, love, joy, and acceptance.

"My husband is so relieved and relaxed as he begins to realize that he can depend on my love. He plans more fun things to do spontaneously. He handles all the family finances now. He's had an electric saw for years that he hasn't used. Suddenly he has begun to build shelves for me—spice shelves, shelves for my sewing accessories, etc. As I admire and appreciate his work he thinks up more and more to do. It is the first sign that I have ever seen of his really enjoying doing something creative.

"I am a schoolteacher, and I have applied many of the teachings of *Fascinating Womanhood* in my work as a teacher. It works miraculously well in the classroom. I have never enjoyed teaching so much. And I have never had a total classroom of children enjoy it so much, regardless of their academic achievement. Actually no child in my class is failing or will be encouraged to repeat the grade—a first in my twenty-five years of teaching in primary grades.

"The most wonderful part of my life is that I really love my husband so much and I know that he loves me deeply in return. This is the greatest joy that anyone can experience! As

we women change within ourselves—following the steps outlined in this course—we do not lose our individuality or identity. We finally find it, with a sigh of relief and unexpected
joy. It is never too late! It really works!''

## *What to Appreciate:*

1. Character
2. Intelligence
3. What He Does for You

## *Assignment*

1. Think of his better side. Make a list of his virtues.
Include his character, his intelligence, and the things he does
for you. During the week express your appreciation for these
things.

2. Make a point of appreciating his earning the living.

3. If he responds favorably, record it in your Love
Booklet.

# 5

## Admire Him

### Admire His Manliness

What does the word *admire* mean? How does it differ from the word *appreciate* in the last chapter? The words are somewhat synonymous but in *Fascinating Womanhood* they are defined in this way: You appreciate a man for his *true worth,* and what he does for you, whereas you admire him for his *manliness*.

Deep in his heart every man longs for admiration of his manliness—his masculine skills, abilities, achievements, ideas, dreams, and manly body. He hungers for it as for bread. Just as you need love, he needs admiration. *In fact, the center of a woman's happiness in marriage is to be loved—but the center of a man's is to be admired.*

Although admiration is all-important to a man, it isn't something he can get for himself. It must be given him by those who respect and love him. He likes receiving it from any and every source, but especially from the woman he loves. The woman who can pass over his human frailties and discover things to genuinely admire, things which others fail to notice or appreciate, is a woman to be treasured. It is such a woman who wins his deepest and most tender affection. *As she gives him admiration, he returns love.*

Sometimes a man will deliberately do or say something in the presence of a woman, hoping to win her admiration, but she fails to notice. She is too busy, too mentally occupied with her own world to notice anything to admire. Her failure in this regard puts him on dangerous ground. When a man's important needs are not met he may be vulnerable to the attentions of another woman who begins to fill these needs. You may be interested to know that designing women have won men away from their wives by nothing more than admiration of their manliness. It is a well-known fact that men turn to other women not so much for sex as for admiration. Many women with loose morals know this, and take advantage of a man's vulnerability in this regard. Unless the wife fills this need, the man can be an easy prey.

## Youth to Old Age

The need for admiration is manifest in the young boy. He doesn't realize this, but it is part of his makeup. When his parents observe his manly qualities and express their admiration, it builds his confidence and helps his growth into manhood, encouraging all the potential within him. Equally important is the kindly feelings it awakens toward his parents, creating a bond of love between them. When he feels close to them he is fortified against youth problems which lie ahead. Because this acute need is not understood by many parents, admiration is sadly lacking. Some young men survive a life of correction without praise, but many don't. There are sad casualties along the way. Some who could have become shining lights fall by the wayside.

Especially is the need for admiration apparent in the young man just beginning his career. His expectations for himself are high. No project is too wild, no dream too fantastic. He is full of plans and proposals, assurance and enthusiasm. He finds flaws in the way the older generation is managing things but waits until he gets his chance to revolutionize things! Meanwhile, life isn't worth living if he can't find someone in whom he can confide. Most of his youthful associates are too occupied with their own aspirations to listen to his. Older people will only laugh at him. Where can he find an uncritical listener and confidante? The cry of his soul is for admiration, and the woman who gives it to him is no less than an angel.

The older man relishes admiration as much as when younger. However, if he has gone without it through the years, time and age have made him less sensitive to the lack of it. The older he becomes, the more inclined he is to believe admiration is not to be had, at least not for him, but the more bitterly he resents this indifference to his manliness.

## What to Admire

What he wants you to admire, more than anything else, are his *manly qualities*. If you admire only those traits which are alike in both men and women, he will be disappointed. For example, if you admire him because he is kind, thoughtful, good-looking, or well groomed, he may appreciate your praise but it will do little to stir his feelings for you. It is his *masculinity* he wants noticed and appreciated, his masculine *body, skills, abilities, achievements,* and *dreams*. When you do, you awaken his tender feelings of affection.

## The Masculine Qualities

1. *His Masculine Body:* These are his *physical features* such as his large build, strong muscles, deep-pitched voice, heavy jaw, beard, mustache, heavy walk, large hands, or anything which distinguishes him as part of the male sex.

Admiring the masculine body includes bodily *strength and endurance,* such as in sports, weight lifting, swimming, managing difficult equipment, sawing logs, taming horses, and even some of the more common things such as mowing the lawn, painting, lifting heavy objects, opening tight jar lids, turning screws, plying a saw, or wielding a hammer. Men's clothes are part of the physical. They are heavier, rougher, and more tailored than women's, and therefore more masculine.

2. *Masculine Skills and Abilities:* This is the skill of the carpenter, the mechanic, the salesman, doctor, lawyer, or other fields of work that men engage in.

3. *Masculine Achievements:* This is the honor of being advanced in his company, taking the championship, winning a debate, an honor for outstanding service, or achieving any difficult objective in the masculine field.

4. *Masculine Goals, Dreams:* I refer here to things a man has not yet achieved, but would like to, in his field of work or outside interests. If he is only casually interested you need not take it too seriously, but if he has a deep desire or dedication toward a worthy goal in a masculine field, it is something worthy of your notice and admiration.

5. *Masculine Traits of Character:* Masculine men tend to be decisive, steadfast, and aggressive. These traits seem to be

uniquely masculine. In contrast, feminine women tend to be vacillating, submissive, and complacent.

Masculine character includes chivalry toward women and children. It includes a sense of honor in masculine duty such as the manly courage to face a situation which, if he were to neglect it, he simply would not feel like a man. Masculine character includes any virtue essential to his manhood.

6. *Masculine Role:* The man who serves as the guide, protector, and provider for his family is performing a very masculine duty. As he leads his family gently but firmly, faithfully goes to work from day to day to provide them a living, he deserves both appreciation and admiration. You appreciate him for what he does and the money he earns from his labors. But you *admire him* for *the masculine skill and ability it required to earn the income.*

Why is admiration of his masculinity so important to him? Because *it makes him feel manly.* This realization of his masculinity is one of the most enjoyable feelings he can experience. When you supply him with the much-needed admiration, you become indispensable to his happiness. He will turn to you again and again for the comfort your companionship gives him, the feeling of manliness he experiences in your presence. Admiring his masculinity is, in fact, one of the keys to winning his love and devotion.

### Discovering Things to Admire:

1. *Think About Him:* Most of your thoughts are probably focused on your own concerns—the children, household chores, personal problems, and things you are involved in. Try thinking about your husband. Think about what kind of a man he is. What problems has he faced? What has he overcome? What has he done with his life thus far? What would he like to do in the future? What are his strong points? Admire these.

2. *Observe Him:* Keep your eyes open and observe what he does and you will find things to admire. Every man has either brains, brawn, or skill—so observe him in these three categories.

3. *Listen to Him Talk:* Your greatest opportunity to admire him will be when he talks, especially when he talks about himself, subjects he is interested in, or his life away from

home. He is most apt to show talent and ability when he talks about his work. And he may display courage or other manly qualities in facing problems or difficulties in his work.

So, encourage him to talk about himself, especially his life away from home. Begin by asking him leading questions about his work. This is not to suggest you be prying or overly inquisitive. But steer the conversation to things he is interested in and then encourage him until he is wound up in his subject. When you see that he is enjoying the conversation, keep it going by your comments and questions. Then learn to listen.

### How to Listen to a Man

Follow this rule and you will be a good listener: *Do not listen only to what he is saying, but to the man who is saying it.* Notice how absorbed he is in the subject, how he has mastered the intricate details, what skill and knowledge he has gained, how he has worked out and developed his own ideas, how loyal and devoted he is to them, what mental and moral power he can wield, what a genuine man he is when you stop to appreciate him.

If he is talking about politics, religion, or world events, don't follow the conversation so closely that you fail to appreciate the man talking. And don't become so wound up in the subject that you form strong opinions which lead to arguments. Follow the conversation, of course, but follow the man too. He may display a special knowledge about the subject, a knowledge which comes from intelligence, experience, or dedicated study. If his attitude shows impatience with how things are, this may indicate that he has ideas on the subject, ideas that need to be expressed and appreciated. As his ideas unfold, look for idealism and devotion to the things he believes in.

If you cannot comprehend all of what he is saying, do not let this lull you to sleep. Look for traits of character which you can admire. In fact, if you only follow his subject and appreciate that, and not the man who is expressing himself, he will be disappointed. You can rest assured that he is not talking only to have his subject appreciated. He wants admiration bestowed upon himself as a man. In fact, you can safely guess that if he *deliberately talks over your head*, he is doing so *only to arouse your admiration*.

You need not be well educated or highly intelligent to follow a clever man's discourse. In his pleasure at having himself admired, he seldom notices that his conversation is not fully understood. Even when he does notice it he relishes it, as in the following words by Maeterlinck:

> *"What care I though she appear not to understand.*
> *Do you think that it is for a sublime word that I*
> *thirst when I feel that a soul is gazing into my soul?"*

If you learn to listen to a man correctly, it doesn't matter if the subject is interesting or dull. You can converse on world affairs, or the details of his business career. You will welcome the most tedious discourse, to seek out things to admire. The following story is an illustration of the right way to listen:

### Alice and Jim

Alice is the perfect listener, with an attentive interest in her husband, Jim. Jim is a man who craves admiration, for out in the world he gets little of it. In the business world he is a terrific success. He is highly intelligent and has ingenious ideas, but who cares or bothers to find out about them? In fact, some have implied that only luck is responsible for his success.

At home it is a different story. When dinner is over and they have a few minutes together, Alice steers the conversation to his work. She prods him from time to time until he is wound up in his subject, and then she listens. Observe her carefully and you will find that she listens only casually to what Jim is saying but nevertheless finds a great deal to admire. What is it? Not his appearance because he is just an average looking man; not his language, for hers is as good as his; and not his ideas for they are quite ordinary.

She sees loyalty, courage, and idealism. Here is a man whose heart rings true to his ideals, to what he believes fair and square. Whether she agrees with him or not doesn't matter. She sits there and admires, not his words, not his ideas, but his manliness. His fervent enthusiasm which might irritate others who do not agree with him, is regarded by her as another expression of the steadfast champion that he is. So long as she can watch the rapt animation of his countenance and the unfolding of his admirable character, she asks nothing else. Even his moods of depression arouse her admiration. Isn't he depressed only because of what he considers the futility of his ideas?

## Natasha

In the novel *War and Peace*, Natasha knew how to listen to a man. When Pierre told her of his experiences in the war, *"He now saw a new significance in all he had been through. Now that he was telling it all to Natasha, he experienced the rare happiness men know when women listen to them—not clever women who, when they listen are either trying to assimilate what they hear for the sake of enriching their minds and, when opportunity offers, repeating it, or to apply what is told them to their own ideas and promptly bring out the clever comments elaborated in their own little mental workshop: but the happiness true women give who are endowed with the capacity to select and absorb all that is best in what a man shows of himself. Natasha, without knowing it, was all attention; she did not miss a word, one inflection in his voice, no twitching of a muscle in his face nor a single gesture. She caught the still unspoken word on the wing and took it straight into her open heart, divining the secret import of all Pierre's spiritual travail."*

## How to Express Admiration

1. *Be Sincere:* Never is sincerity more important than when it relates to a man's most sensitive nature, pride in himself and especially in his masculinity. *This is something not to be trifled with by superficial flattery.* You will have to cultivate sincere admiration before you can express it effectively. If you do not sincerely admire him, even after following the suggestions in this chapter, forgo this part of the subject. Anything you say will easily be detected as insincere and instead of appreciating your praise he may resent it, counting it as a manipulation in trying to gain a benefit for yourself.

2. *Be Specific:* When expressing admiration don't talk in generalities. Don't say, for example, "You are such a manly sort of a man." He may answer with, "How? In what way do you think I'm manly?" If you can't think of a quick answer it could be embarrassing.

Be specific by expressing admiration for particular qualities or incidents when his admirable traits were evident. This is why it is so important to observe him and listen to him, so you will see specific qualities you can admire. If you can pinpoint incidents in which his admirable traits were evident, they will be undeniably true, even to him.

## You Must Accept Him

Although admiration is all important to a man, it will not be appreciated unless it is accompanied by acceptance. If you admire him in some ways but are critical of him in others, it will be like serving him a piece of moldy pie and trying to disguise it by putting whipped cream on top. You will have to accept the total man before your admiration will be well received.

## Rewards

When you sincerely admire your husband it can bring significant rewards to both of you. For the man it fills a most important need. It can also be a tremendous motivation to him, causing him to grow in masculinity and in his success in life, therefore bringing him fulfillment. Rewards to you are equally significant. Your greatest need from him is love. When you give him admiration, he returns love. This is evident in the following true experiences:

## The Look in His Eyes

"Trying to tell my husband that I accepted him and that I admired him for standing up and sticking to his convictions was a very hard thing for me to come out with. First of all, I am not the kind of person to say something like this, and second, I thought I would start to giggle. I tried three or four times to do my little speech, but always ended up turning and walking out of the room. Finally I was going to do it no matter what kind of mess it turned into. So I walked into the room and started, and once I started I realized that what I was saying was really how I felt. This was one of the main reasons I fell in love with my husband. He did stand up for what he believed in and did not let me get away with walking all over him.

"Well, the look in his eyes was just unbelievable. Never can I remember such a look. He had so much pride in his eyes and it was not for himself, it was for me. About a week later he took me out to dinner and made two comments. One hurt, and the other felt great. He said for the first time he felt I really cared; he had never thought I cared what happened to him. Second, that he never loved me more than he did then. What more can a woman ask for? Isn't this what we all really want and makes it all worth it?"

## I Feel Like a Bride Again

"My story is not too spectacular. I have always had a good marriage. I took the course because I felt a need for more self-confidence, but I found I had more problems than I realize. I have always accepted and admired my husband but never told him so, partly because I admired him so much I thought he must know it. It was extremely hard to start saying these things so I started writing notes. When he commented on them I would say 'Well, it's true,' or 'I wanted to be sure you knew how I felt.'

"Then I progressed to saying complimentary things. His response was so great that I realized his need to hear these things. He started telling me the ways I pleased him and this gave me the self-confidence I have always lacked. His tenderness toward me is fantastic. I feel like a bride again. The greatest thing was when he said with tears, 'I have come to realize that you are the sweetest, the most feminine woman in the world, and I love you so deeply I can't tell you how much. You are my whole life.'"

## I Learned to Listen

"For twenty-seven years I never knew what my husband's plans were, what he was thinking or where he was going. The only way I found out these things was if I overheard him talking on the phone or telling someone else. Since F.W. I listen. If I am reading I not only lower my book, I close it and give him my complete attention. I stop, look, and listen! I have been amazed how he has begun to open up and share. He shares things with me that never in my wildest dreams did I think he would.

"Listening to my husband when he talks has done more than anything to bring down the barriers and create love in our marriage. Often he opens up when I just sit quietly with him, saying nothing. I'm just there, available. I'm not in the other room, sewing, or vacuuming. He begins to talk and share his dreams or plans and we both get excited."

## He Holds Them Spellbound

"My husband was a smart man, but a boring conversationalist! When we had dinner guests he would begin to talk, but so low and hesitating, and so long between sentences that people would break in on his story and change the subject. Or, I would pick up on his story, take it away from him, and finish it. This was before I took F.W. After I studied about admiring my husband, when we were at a dinner party and he began to talk, I would fix my starry-eyed gaze on him, refuse to look at anyone else, and thus force everyone at the table to listen to him. Often, probably for a year or more, he would simply talk directly to me . . . as I was so fascinated by everything he was saying. Gradually his confidence in himself as a conversationalist began to grow. Today he is one of the finest conversationalists . . . he can hold a table spellbound. People say to me, 'I could listen to your husband for hours.'

## A New Beginning

"My husband and I had been married thirteen years, most of them unhappy. We had been separated three times and I had decided to leave him for the last time. I had given up on him. About this time a friend told me about *Fascinating Womanhood* and tried to encourage me to take the class. I told her that nothing could be done for that stubborn husband of mine and I might as well give up, but she begged me to read it. By then we had actually separated.

"I don't know if you know how a woman feels when she is going through a separation, but it is worse than miserable. A numbness went through me. I may as well have been dead. I prayed as I have never prayed before that God would help me through each minute, each hour, and that I would depend entirely upon Him to lead me through this as I didn't know where to turn.

"I prayed that my husband would want to see me and talk to me. He did. At first it was accusation and bitterness, then quiet talking and understanding. I decided to take him back, but I was afraid; how was I to know that it was going to work. I asked him if he cared if I took a course called *Fascinating Womanhood*. He asked me what it was about. I told him all I knew was that it was supposed to make a marriage happier and a better wife of me. He told me to go ahead and he was enthusiastic about it.

"At the first class the teacher told us to compliment our husband on *his manliness, muscles, etc*. I didn't think I could bring myself to say something like that. Finally, just before the next class, I knew I had to do something because the teacher would ask us about it, so I waited until we were in bed and the lights were out. I thought I would faint. Finally I told him what beautiful muscles he had. This is when our new marriage began. "I was told not to expect material rewards, but a happy marriage. I received both. Some of the things my husband has bought me without my asking are: a beautiful nightie, typewriter, trip to Hawaii, kitchen stove, table and chairs, couch and chair recovered, bedroom carpeting, perfume, flowers, and others I can't remember."

### His Honey-Eyed Girl

"It was final exam week at the university just prior to my husband's graduation. It had taken him seven years to complete college as he had to stop and work full time every so often to support our growing family. He held jobs while attending school also and held positions in church, as well as carrying out home responsibilities.

"He had many moments of feeling sad and discouraged.

He couldn't see his accomplishments. All he could see was the time it had taken him to get through college. I hadn't helped much. The only time I praised him was when he had problems and then I didn't do it right. I had a very self-righteous attitude. I was handling the finances and trying to push him into greater activity in the church and nagging him to do things for me such as open my car door. I thought I was helping him by pointing out his mistakes.

"Then my sister-in-law enthusiastically told me about *Fascinating Womanhood* and I started reading it. I was thrilled because it told us exactly how to do it and what to say instead of just lots of do's and don'ts. I read it over and over, and when my husband came home I was all worked up about it, yet so nervous I was trembling. I told him I was glad he is the kind of man he is and that I could see I had not understood him in the past, admitting I had made mistakes and that I was glad he hadn't been like putty in my hands, but had the courage of his convictions. I asked for forgiveness and told him I wanted to prove to him I liked him the way he is.

"It was just like turning on a radio. His expression changed and his whole being seemed to be affected. He started radiating happiness instead of misery. The next day I applied admiration and told him I was proud of him for his courage in completing his education and not giving up as others would have done with the same hardships. I told him I appreciated how he worked to provide the necessities of life for us. I also explained to him that I realized I had been holding him back by trying to lead and that I really loved him just the way he is and that I would stop trying to change him.

"This seemed to turn the volume up more than it had been the day before. He treated me like a queen. He even started opening the car door for me. He started leading our family with kindness, love, and strength that I had never seen in him before. He called family councils regularly, and I felt like we truly had a Celestial marriage. What's even better, the other day he took me to our dream home site and told me what wonderful plans he has for me and our adorable family (five children). He is in summer school now and thought he would be home only twice, but he has made it home every weekend. He sang 'Honey-Eyed Girl' to me and told me I was the loveliest wife in the world."

### I Have Never Been Happier!

"I am so excited about telling my story that I hardly know where to begin. My husband and I have been married nearly fifteen years. Eleven of those years were spent struggling with the disease of alcoholism. Anyone who has ever had to deal with this baffling problem with a friend or relative knows the agony of watching those you love destroy themselves. But looking back I can see that my husband's problem with alcohol was a very convenient scapegoat for my own shortcomings. I could always blame his drinking for my attitudes. Well, naturally he rebelled, and no matter how remorseful he felt about his drinking habit, he would not give it up. At this time I was so far from being a *fascinating woman* that it is a miracle I am writing my story today.

"He did finally stop drinking, however, on his own initiative and by the grace of God. Even so, we were in complete agreement about getting a divorce. I really can't say what I expected our life to be, but it was very disappointing to find we still argued and had serious communication problems. He didn't come up to my expectations at all. In fact, he seemed to think more of his friends than of me. We had suffered so much because of him. You can tell my attitude had not changed since he stopped drinking. Instead of criticizing and cursing his drinking, I attacked his character. I didn't realize what an ugly person I had become.

"After about two years of floundering I slowly started drifting away from him. I was very disillusioned with life and I even got to the point where I thought I loved someone else. Thank God this didn't lead to a total disaster. My husband sensed my deep unhappiness but was helpless in this situation.

"During this whole time I had in my possession a copy of *Fascinating Womanhood*. It had been loaned to me by a friend who sensed my trouble, and for some unknown reason I had not opened it. I am one of those people who cannot leave any book unread. I think God must have known I wasn't ready for *Fascinating Womanhood*. It lay on my bedside table for weeks.

"I came to my senses and faced reality about leaving my husband for another man. We were to go on a vacation in

August, and I decided if there was no hope for a change in our marriage I'd ask for a divorce when we got back. In October we agreed to a separation in January. We were glad we were doing something about ending this bad marriage.

"Well, in exactly three days I picked up *Fascinating Womanhood* and couldn't put it down. This will sound unbelievable, but my whole life changed. I've had to struggle to apply the principles of *Fascinating Womanhood,* but it works. Everything seemed to fit for me. All my misconceptions about men and marriage were pointed out to me. I didn't feel I had to give up anything to gain everything.

"Needless to say, for the next few weeks I did a lot of soul-searching. It was a beautiful thing to see my husband respond to F.W. In January there was no talk of separation. In fact, we took a weekend trip with friends. It is a thrill to remember. The comparison between this trip and the one before F. W. is hard to believe. I was so ignored and miserable before I almost cried. This time I used admiration and praise in small cases and with real sincerity. My rewards came immediately. He showed such concern about a slight cold I had at breakfast the next morning that I was completely surprised! After walking with me to the café, he sat with the other husbands, but I could feel him watching me. As we walked along after breakfast, he said, 'I think I'm falling in love with you again.' I'll never forget that sunlit morning.

"It is so hard to believe that it has been only a year since I discovered *Fascinating Womanhood.* I sing its praises to everyone I meet and so does my husband, even though he has never read it. He says, 'I don't know what it is but I love it!' I have never been happier!!"

## Rules for Admiration

1. Accept him at face value.
2. Think about him.
3. Observe him.
4. Listen to him talk.
5. Express admiration in words.
6. Be sincere.
7. Be specific.

*Assignment*

1. Write down ten masculine things you admire about him.

2. During the evening ask him to write down ten things he likes about you and you'll do the same for him. Read your lists to each other, taking time to explain why you admire these traits. No fair just handing each other the list. Observe his reaction. Record favorable results in your Love Booklet.

3. During the coming week observe him. If you see any masculine qualities express your admiration. Record results.

4. Listen to him Talk: Follow rules as explained.

*The center of a woman's happiness in marriage is to be loved, but the center of a man's is to be admired.*

# 6

## *Make Him Number One*

A man wants a woman who will place him at the top of her priority list, not second but first. He wants to be the king-pin around which all other activities of her life revolve. He doesn't want to be the background music to her other interests and dreams. This desire is not necessarily a conscious one, but an *inner need* which surfaces violently when not adequately met, when his wife places other things first, such as the children, homemaking, or a career. Being placed in this inferior position can cause a man to form bitter resentments toward his wife and even his children.

A man does not expect his wife to neglect important duty in his behalf. He is aware of the demands of her life and wants her to give each responsibility the attention it requires. He does not want his children to suffer neglect. And he knows she is entitled to other interests and diversions. But, he doesn't want to be *less important*. And he doesn't want to be regarded as a convenience, a paycheck, an escort, a social asset, a ticket to security, or even just a sex partner. He would like to feel that she married him for him, and not as a means of filling her needs or reaching her objectives.

There is a tendency for women to fail in this respect, to place other things ahead of their husbands. This tendency began in early childhood, clearly evident in our world of dreams. When we were little girls, if we were typical, we dreamed of a little vine-covered cottage with tie-back curtains, flowers in the windows, pots and pans in the cupboards, and children playing on the floor. It was a perfect little home scene except— *there was no husband present.* (This was some time before we dreamed of a handsome prince sweeping us off our feet.)

An early edition of Childcraft Books describes this little girls' dream, minus a husband:

### The Shiny Little House

I wish, how I wish, that I had a little house,
With a mat for the cat and a hole for the mouse,
And a clock going "tock" in the corner of the room
And a kettle, and a cupboard, and a big birch broom.

To school in the morning the children off would run,
And I'd give them a kiss and a penny and a bun.
But directly they had gone from this little house of mine,
I'd clap my hands and snatch a cloth and shine, shine,
   shine.

I'd shine all the knives, all the windows and the floors,
All the grates, all the plates, all the handles on the doors,
Every fork, every spoon, every lid and every tin,
Till Everything was shining like a new bright pin.

At night by the fire, when the children were in bed,
I'd sit and I'd knit, with a cap upon my head,
And the kettles, and the saucepans they would shine,
   shine, shine,
In this tweeny little, cozy little, house of mine!

Nancy M. Hayes

As you can see, no mention is made of a husband. Her focus is on children and homemaking joys. Little girls also dream of the splendor of the wedding, the dress of satin and lace, the wedding cake, candles, ribbons, and bells, everything except the groom. He doesn't come into the picture at this point. Later on, as the little girl reaches puberty, the handsome Prince Charming comes into the scene.

The tragedy is when, after she wins her husband, she reverts to the earlier dream. She now has her little cottage, children, and the domestic comforts and joys she looked forward to. Her husband has been only a means to this end. As she devotes herself to the affairs of the household, her husband drops into the background. As life progresses, duties of family life increase, as do other demands and pressures. She may also include other interests, to make life more meaningful. If time permits, she may even turn to a career. All of these things tend to push the man further into the background. Now, let's take a close look at the things women tend to place ahead of their husbands:

## 1. The Children

You probably feel a sacred responsibility for your children, an obligation to nurture them in body and spirit, and provide them with every opportunity to grow to their highest potential. This noble feeling of motherly devotion, when moved by a strong feeling of mother love, can cause you to so focus on the care and training of your children that you automatically place them in priority.

### Clara

An example of this is a woman I knew years ago, whom I shall call Clara. Clara was the perfect mother, all kindness, patience, and love. She usually wore a kindly smile and talked with a gentle voice when speaking to her children. But she was firm, too. She had studied books on the subject of training children so was not without the strength needed to be a good mother.

Clara was a model of unselfish devotion. I remember her sitting by her children, helping them practice the piano or helping them with their homework. She kept extensive scrapbooks for each child and gave them the most lavish birthday parties in the neighborhood and everything which delights little children. Her children were the center of her life. I have never seen a finer example of mother love and sacrifice, or a more devoted sense of duty. I admired Clara and for a long while wanted to be like her, until I realized what problems her devotion had caused.

Her husband was the unhappy second fiddle to all of this, merely an appendage to the family scene. He was the father and provider but not the king. I think Clara really loved her husband and treated him well enough, but he obviously took second place to his children. He bitterly resented this excessive devotion to his children and the inferior position it placed him in.

In earlier years he was a gentle man, but this situation brought out an ugliness to his personality, a surprise to those who had known him before. Not only did he resent his wife, but he also resented his children, and found it difficult to be a good father. He would leave home for days, to get away from it all, but would be hard to live with when he returned.

This inferior position can cause a man to resist the birth of more children. He may only subconsciously realize it, but more children means more motherly demands and will intensify his problem of feeling neglected. Or, if a new baby does arrive, he may resent the child, or ignore it. He may struggle with a feeling of guilt for this lack of love for his baby, without realizing it is caused by his own feeling of neglect.

Making your husband number one does not diminish your sacred duty to your children, nor does it indicate less love for them. You can serve both husband and children without conflict. Your husband does not want you to neglect his children. He is, no doubt, as interested in their care and training as you are, but would like the assurance that your love and devotion to them does not exceed your dedication to him.

Children miss nothing when their father comes first, but rather feel *more* secure and happy. This is because when you make your husband number one, you build a happier relationship with him. Your happy marriage will be the foundation of a happy home in which the entire family benefits. If you find it hard to understand how to make your husband number one in priority, without neglecting your children, keep this rule in mind:

> *Don't put the comforts and whims of your children ahead of your husband's basic needs.*

## Ways We Put Children First

1. *A Place of Residence:* Suppose your husband finds it necessary to move his business to a new community. The new location will bring more money, opportunity, and other ad-

vantages. If you feel your children will be put to a disadvantage, you may stubbornly refuse to move. Is this wise?

If your husband has overlooked *serious* disadvantages to his children, so that the move would be an injustice to them, you should make an appeal to him to seriously reconsider their welfare. But, if you are only trying to avoid the children's unpleasant adjustment to the new community or some other discomfort, you are pampering them. You are putting their comfort ahead of his important needs. Let your children have a little adversity. It will be good for them. And help your husband *reduce* his adversity. This will be good for him.

When your husband's reason for a move is based on a whim or selfishness, this is another matter. Make an appeal to him to consider the children's welfare. In this case he will not feel in a secondary position, since you have not disregarded his important needs in preference to the children, but only his selfish whims.

When buying a house, don't consider your children's comforts and whims ahead of your husband's needs and requests. Don't press to buy a house beyond his means, feeling it best for the children, or ignore a feature in a house that pleases him, while yielding to whims of your children. He may have always wanted a view, a deck, a pool, or a private study. Although he may forgo these preferences to honor his wife's choice, he's not inclined to place his children's wishes ahead of his own.

2. *Time and Attention:* Does your husband have to compete with his children for your time and attention? Are you so busy attending to them that you haven't a moment to spare? Or if you do give him a few minutes, are you in a hurry to get back to the children? There are times when family demands can't be put aside, but it's often a case of excessive devotion.

Is your husband a salesman or in a profession which takes him away from home a great deal of time? Some women feel fortunate to have their husband gone so much. This gives them time to devote themselves to their children without a husband to worry about. When he returns home he'll somehow sense this unwelcome attitude, that beyond his paycheck he's not wanted. If his wife seems unaware of his need for time and attention, which is now more acute than ever, he will definitely not feel number one in her life.

3. *Money and Things:* Do you pamper your children by giving in to every little thing they want? An entire chapter could be written on how overindulgent mothers harm their children, but the point here is not harm to children, but to fathers. If you buy things he can't afford, you place an added strain on his life. You are placing your children's whims ahead of your husband's health and financial welfare, their *wants* ahead of his *needs*.

4. *Interest and Thought:* Are you more interested in your children than your husband? Are your children uppermost in your mind and thoughts? Are your interests focused on them? Do you spend much time thinking of your husband and his problems, how you may comfort or encourage him? Do you have an ear open for his small requests, what he likes for dinner, how he would like to spend the evening, or what is important to him? In these and many more ways you help him feel number one in your life.

## 2. Homemaking

A man appreciates a clean, orderly home, made comfortable and homey by the touch of a woman's hand. He would consider it a miserable disadvantage if his wife were to fail in this important duty. However, he doesn't want her homemaking to become more important than he is. The house is made to serve the family, not the family to serve the house. He wants his wife's efforts to be mostly for his sake and the children's, not to satisfy her pride or impress others.

If you are an excellent homemaker, don't place your goals of perfection above the needs of your family. Make certain your motives are to comfort them, rather than to please yourself or impress others. An example of such selfish motives is found in an early movie, *Craig's Wife:*

Craig's wife scrutinized the servants to see that they overlooked nothing in the polished perfection of the house. She wouldn't let her husband sit on his bed because it would wrinkle the beautiful bedspread. She didn't like fresh flowers in the house because the petals dropped off and cluttered the tables. Her husband realized that she adored the house more than him, so he left. As the trucking company came for his things and moved a large trunk down the hall, it scraped the highly polished floor, leaving a deep scratch. Craig's wife sat on the floor and wept, not because her husband was leaving her, but because of the scratch in her beautiful floor. And such is the way some women worship a house more than their husband.

Although good homemaking is an admirable virtue, *it can be overdone*. Create a *home*, not a *showplace*. A man appreciates efforts for his sake, but doesn't want homemaking to take priority over him, or things he considers more important. The castle is not *more important than the king that dwells therein*.

### 3. Appearance

All human beings should have enough self-respect to keep themselves well groomed and well dressed as a matter of principle. Even if far removed from civilization, we should maintain a proper appearance, for our own feeling of self-esteem. But, when a woman spends too much time and attention on her appearance, there is reason to question her motive.

If your efforts are to please your husband, he may well appreciate it. But if you spend endless hours shopping, sewing, and grooming, and in so doing *neglect* your husband, it will give him the impression that it is others you are trying to impress. He will feel second place to the public you dress for.

### 4. Parents

Do you have an attachment for your parents that exceeds the one you have for your husband? Are you overjoyed at the prospects of returning home to them? Do you seek excuses to be with them and spend excessive time with them? The love between parent and child is a very fine thing, but after marriage cut the apron strings and transfer your major attachment to your husband. If you don't he may feel second place to your parents and resent them for it.

### 5. Money and Success

Sometimes a man's money and success become more important to the wife than the man himself. Here is an example:

A woman was married to a man of modest income. He was satisfied but his wife wanted more money and prestige. She suggested he return to school and become a surgeon. After considerable pressure she talked him into it and he laid plans in that direction. After two grueling years he quit. He didn't have the interest or motivation to meet the challenge. She was obviously disappointed.

The wife's attitude was injurious to their marriage. She made money and success more important than her husband, his personal desires, and feelings. If he had wanted to become a surgeon it would have been a different matter. He would have appreciated her support. What he resented was her making money and success number one. What a mistake women make when they put other things ahead of the most important thing in the world, their marriage.

Another woman had an opposite situation. Her husband wanted to get ahead by expanding his business, making it necessary for them to sell their home and move to an apartment. Not only did she object, she put her foot down and refused to move. Regardless of how much he wanted to pursue his plans for success, she felt security more important. Was it? There was a possibility the business plans would fail and the whole thing prove a mistake. Although a woman has a right to express herself and have her viewpoint considered, it's a mistake to stand in his way. Regardless of how important security is to a woman, it is not more important than the man, his work, and his worthy goals.

Remember: *It's better to let a man have his way and fail, than to stand in his way and make him feel thwarted.*

We can see from these two illustrations that when you make a man number one you must also make his work, plans, and goals number one.

## 6. Careers, Talents, and Activities

One of the greatest threats to your husband's position of priority would be if you were to earnestly pursue a career. The dedication and drive required for success would push him into the background. If you finally reach a pinnacle of success, you would overshadow him and make him feel relatively unimportant.

This is a serious problem with highly successful women. The greater their success, the less important the man becomes, at least in his opinion. He is automatically placed in a secondary position. This is a challenging problem but not without a solution. If you are a successful career woman, keep your priorities straight and let your husband know by words and actions that he is in the number one position. Always be willing to sacrifice something in your career for his sake, if necessary. But, even if you are not pursuing a career, if you just work outside your home, the demands on your time and energy to hold your job can cause your husband to feel less important. Take special care to assure him that your job is not more important than his welfare and happiness.

Another threat to your husband's position may occur if you pursue other interests such as the development of talents. He may extend you this freedom and may even encourage you, for your own personal development. If you work at your talent, it can be a very fine thing. However, if you pursue your talent with such dedication and enthusiasm that it overshadows your husband, he may feel second fiddle and resent it. Sometimes a man senses this may happen, so for this reason, when you wish to pursue a talent he says "no." However, if you are careful to keep him in the number one position and let him know it, you can usually win his cooperation in devoting a reasonable amount of time to outside activities.

## When a Man Comes Home

A special time to prove to a man that he is number one in your life is when he comes home from work. Make it a pleasant time for him. Have all of the housework out of the way and things as quiet as possible. Be sure the washing machine, dryer, or vacuum cleaner is not running. If you have been sewing, put it all away, out of sight. Be attractively groomed and greet him with a smile. Don't let the children rush to him with their problems. See that they wait until later, after he has gained his composure. Such a greeting will make an amazing difference in his life, in reducing strain and bringing peace and rest. Your thoughtful consideration for his welfare, will give him the impression that he is number one in your life.

## Should He Make You Number One?

It is not always possible or even right for a man to make his wife number one in his life. This is due to the nature of his life. His number one responsibility is to provide the living. His work and life away from home may be so demanding that it must take priority over all else if he is to succeed. This often means he must neglect his family. In reality, he *is* putting you first. He is working for you and your children. Try to interpret his dedication to his work in this way.

In addition to making the living, men have always shouldered the responsibility of making the world a better place. They have largely been the builders of society, have solved world problems, and developed new ideas for the benefit of all. This challenging role of public servant is not easy and also demands the man's attention away from his family.

If you examine the lives of these noble public servants, you usually find a wife who was willing to make the man and his work number one and be content to take a second place. President and Mrs. Dwight D. Eisenhower are a good example of this. Mrs. Eisenhower recalls that during the first two weeks of their fifty-three-year marriage, her husband drew her aside one evening and said, ''Mamie, I have to tell you something . . . My country comes first and you second.'' Mamie accepted this, and that is the way they lived. So, when you make a man number one, you also make his work and outside responsibility number one.

When you fail to make your husband number one, when you put your children, homemaking, career, or other interests first, your husband will feel a deficiency. This is often the very reason a man is driven to another woman. As I have said before, men are seldom driven to a mistress because of sex passions. It is usually her ability to fill an emotional need, to make him feel appreciated and important. The following experience is an illustration of how sex failed to keep a man home, and his emotional needs drove him to other women:

## It Wasn't Sex That Drove Him to Other Women

"Our sex life was good, the only good part of our marriage it seemed. I told my husband so and complimented him on being such a wonderful lover but the trouble was, that was the only thing I complimented him for or admired him for. I found nothing to praise in him; I certainly didn't accept him, and he was never treated as number one. In other words, I counted him as good for nothing except as a sex partner.

"Because of this, he turned to other women who made him feel number one and admired his manly attributes; he turned to women who would listen to his stories and give him the time and attention every man needs. Of course, I hated him for having other women. I couldn't understand why he wasn't satisfied with the sex I gave him.

"But after *Fascinating Womanhood,* I could see that it wasn't sex he needed from these other women but acceptance, admiration, and being number one. By withholding these things from him, I had driven him to unfaithfulness. But I have no fear now that he will ever have another escapade, because I know what kind of a woman a man wants."

## My Husband Was a Second-Class Citizen

"Our three children were born bright, healthy, and beautiful. I was awed by them and apologetic about the world into which we had brought them. I mistakenly thought I could make up for the inevitable hardships they would face by devoting myself to them.

"For five years I put them ahead of everything and everyone. I spared no expense buying baby pictures, toys, clothes, etc. I felt no one could care for my children as well as I could and got baby-sitters only when they were asleep. I felt personally responsible for their happiness and was miserable carrying this burden on my shoulders. My husband, naturally, was a second-class citizen in our home. He had to compete for my time and attention. I even made him be quiet when the children wanted to talk at the same time he did.

"Then my husband had a serious accident, and for a time we thought he might die. As I sat in the intensive care unit waiting room, I was filled with such guilt that I was physically sick. I thought of my husband's status in our family unit. I thought of how much he had wanted a swimming pool and of how much I had made him do without so we could buy a larger house someday. When I thought I was losing him forever, I realized how much he meant to me. I realized that our children would leave home someday and that my husband was my life partner. Our friends and families had lives of their own. I was the one who had the most to lose. I prayed and prayed for another chance.

"God did give us another chance. We put in that swimming pool as soon as he got home from the hospital. My husband thrives on being number one in our home. The children have responded and are becoming less selfish and self-centered. I have given them the responsibility for finding their own happiness and this has let me be more free. Because they no longer feel 'the sun rises and sets' on them, I feel they will be better prepared to face maturity.

"Had we not had this great warning and fear, I feel that by now my husband and I would not be living together. I would be living through my children, resentful, tied down, and envying my husband's freedom. I now feel we are both free, free to love each other and our children."

### Women Tend to Put First:

1. Children
2. Homemaking
3. Appearance
4. Parents
5. Money and Success
6. Careers, Talents, Activities

### Assignment

Tell your husband that he is the most important person in your life and then prove by your actions that this is true.

*If you treat him like a king, he'll treat you
like a queen.*

*Don't put the comforts and whims of your
children, ahead of your husband's basic needs.*

# 7

## *Masculine and Feminine Roles*

| *Man's Role:* | *Woman's Role:* |
|---|---|
| *Guide* | *Wife* |
| *Protector* | *Mother* |
| *Provider* | *Homemaker* |

The masculine and feminine roles, clearly defined above, are not merely a result of custom or tradition, but are of divine origin. It was God who placed the man at the head of the family when he told Eve, *"Thy desire shall be unto thy husband, and he shall rule over thee."* The man was also designed to be the protector, since he was given stronger muscles, greater physical endurance, and manly courage. In addition, God commanded him to earn the living when he said, *"In the sweat of thy face shall thou eat bread, till thou return to the ground."* This instruction was given to the man, not to the woman. (Genesis 3:16,19)

The woman was given a different assignment, that of *helpmeet, mother, homemaker*. In Hebrew the word *helpmeet* means *as before him*. This dispels the notion she was an afterthought. It was clearly understood that she was created to be his equal. In *Fascinating Womanhood* we apply the word *helpmeet* to mean the role of the *wife* as she offers understanding, encouragement, support, and sometimes help. Since she is biologically created to bear children, her role as a *mother* is unquestioned. Her *homemaking* role is assumed: She must nurture her young and run the household, to free her husband to function as the provider. (Genesis 2:18)

The masculine and feminine roles are *different in function* but *equal in importance*. In Henry A. Bowman's book *Mar-*

*riage for Moderns* he compares the partnership of marriage to a lock and a key which join together to form a functioning unit. *"Together they can accomplish something that neither acting alone can accomplish. Nor can it be accomplished by two locks or two keys. Each is distinct, yet neither is complete in and of itself. Their roles are neither identical nor interchangeable. Neither is superior to the other, since both are necessary. They are equally important. Each must be judged in terms of its own function. They are complementary."*

### Division of Labor

As you can see, the design for the human family is based on a *division of labor*. You may be interested to know that modern research has proven this ancient plan to be the best means of people working together. In the 1970s several large industries in America joined forces in a research project to discover the best system for people to work together in groups, especially to get along with each other, without contention.

Part of their study took place in hippie communes which had begun earlier, in the sixties. These idealistic groups were not based on a division of labor, but on *equality*. Men and women shared equally in all daily chores. Women worked side by side with men in the fields or building shelters. The men shared household chores and care of the children.

The interesting discovery was this: They found that equality didn't fit masculine and feminine differences. Women were better at some jobs and men at others. Women's hands, more delicately formed, were better for mending and sewing on buttons. Men were more capable of hauling and shoveling. The most significant discovery, however, was that when they shared work *equally*, they didn't get along with each other. There was contention, frequent hostility, and even hatred. Such dissension caused whole communes to fall apart. The conclusion of the research was this: The best way to work in groups is by a *division of labor*. What a perfect plan God designed for the family.

The greatest success in marriage occurs when husband and wife devotedly live their respective roles. On the other hand, the greatest problems occur when either of them fails to perform his or her duties, or when one steps over the boundaries and forcefully takes over the partners role, or shows an anxious concern for performance or lack of performance.

To succeed in your role, accept your womanly duties with a *keen sense of responsibility*. Let it be *your* concern, *your* worry. You can of course employ servants, or assign your children to help. But you are the one who must see that it's done.

To further succeed, *learn the feminine arts and skills*. Learn to cook, clean, and manage a household. Learn the womanly art of thrift and how to rear children. Forget about yourself and devote yourself to the welfare and happiness of your family.

### Three Masculine Needs:

To further succeed, help your husband succeed in his role by understanding three masculine needs:

1. *A man needs to function in his masculine role as the guide, protector, and provider.*
2. *He needs to feel needed in this role.*
3. *He needs to excel women in this role.*

1. *Function in His Masculine Role:* First, he needs to function, as *the head of the family,* and to have his family honor and support him in this position. Second, he needs to succeed in *earning the living,* in meeting his family's essential needs, and to do so independently, without the help of others. And third, he needs to serve as the protector, sheltering his family from harm, danger, or difficulty.

2. *Feel Needed in His Masculine Role:* He needs to feel that his family *really needs him* as their guide, protector, and provider. When a woman becomes capable of providing for herself, able to make her own way in the world, independent of her husband, she loses her need for him. This is a great loss to him. So deep is his need to feel needed as a man, and to serve as a man, that when he is no longer needed he may question his reason for living. This can affect his tender feelings for his wife, since his romantic feelings partly arise from her need to be protected, sheltered, and cared for.

3. *Excel Women in Masculine Role:* A man is not usually

aware of his need to excel women until a situation arises which threatens him, such as when a woman outsmarts him in his own field, advances to a higher position, brings home a bigger paycheck, or excels him in anything which requires masculine strength, skill, competence, or ability.

## Failures in Society

Unfortunately, we see these principles violated in modern life. Women have invaded the man's world. We have a generation of working mothers, competing with men for greater achievement, the more honored positions, or a bigger paycheck.

At home it is almost as bad. The woman takes control and tries to run things her way. Disappearing is the trusting wife who looked to her husband for strong guidance, a solid arm to lean on. The masculine arm may be there, but she is not leaning on it. She does many of the masculine chores herself. The independence of women is making masculine care and protection unnecessary, and this is a loss to both of them.

As the man is deprived of his masculine function he feels less needed and therefore less masculine. As the woman assumes masculine burdens she takes on male characteristics, to fit the job. This means a loss of femininity, a loss of gentleness. The male responsibility adds strain to her life, more tension and worry. This results in a loss of serenity, a quality very valuable if she is to succeed in the home. And when she spends her time and energy doing the man's work, she neglects important functions in her own role. This results in losses to the entire family.

## To Succeed

To succeed, keep well in mind his masculine role as the guide, protector, and provider. Remember, if he is to be happy, he must *function, feel needed, and excel you* in this masculine role. Let him lead the family, do the masculine jobs around the house, and provide the living. Only in rare emergencies should you step over into his role and do the masculine work.

As he functions in his masculine role, don't expect perfection. Don't scrutinize his performance to see if he is doing things right. If he neglects his masculine duties and it causes you severe problems, don't complain. Instead say to him, "I have a problem." State clearly your problem and the trouble it has caused. Then ask, "How do you think I should handle it?" This honors him as the leader, puts the problem on his shoulders, and helps him feel needed. If he continues to fail in his duty, be patient. Change comes slowly.

To further succeed offer him appreciation. A man's role is not an easy one, as I will soon explain. His greatest reward is your appreciation for his daily efforts. Be lavish in your appreciation. It may mean more than his paycheck. And last, be faithful to perform your domestic duties. This more sharply defines your roles and helps him succeed in his.

### Blurring of Roles

When a man's and woman's roles are not distinctly divided it is called a *blurring of roles*. In this case the woman does part of the man's work and he does part of hers. When this arrangement is temporary, it is not a problem, but if it becomes a life-style it can be injurious to the family.

If children are to develop their sexual nature, they need a strong masculine and feminine image to pattern from. The mother demonstrates this feminine image when she functions in her feminine role. As she moves about the house in feminine clothes, tending to her domestic work, tenderly caring for her children and nursing her baby, she provides this image. If she also indicates contentment and happiness in her role, she gives her children a positive picture of femininity.

When the father functions in his masculine role as a strong leader, protector, and provider, and when his children are given the opportunity to see him in action once in awhile, and see that he willingly assumes his masculine responsibility and enjoys his work, he provides them with a favorable masculine image. With this distinct masculine and feminine image in the home, boys grow up to be masculine men and girls feminine women.

When this is not so, when there is a blurring of roles it can lead to problems. Much homosexuality is traced to homes which have a blurring of roles. The girls and boys from these homes have not had a sexual image to pattern from. This has denied them normal sexual development.

When we think of all of the things children need to learn as they are growing up, and what we need to teach them if they are to become normal, successful, happy human beings, nothing is more important than a boy becoming a masculine man and a girl becoming a feminine woman.

## Is It Fair?

Frequently women who are *up to their necks* in domestic work, tied down to the sixteen-hour-a-day routine of caring for children, challenge this concept of roles. They claim this arrangement is unfair because women must work harder and longer hours than men. Therefore, they claim, men don't have a right to come home and relax while the wife keeps on working. The men, they say, should help more with housework and especially with the care of the children.

This does seem fair, on the surface. But there is another viewpoint: A woman's role, difficult as it is, lasts only about twenty years. Even if she has a large family, twenty years sees her through most of it. Then her life takes a turn. She has freedom and usually plenty of time. But the man's responsibility to provide the living lasts a lifetime. Even if he is fortunate enough to retire, he is never completely free from the feeling of responsibility to provide an income. Yes, when you see it this way, the division of work for the man and woman is fair.

I suggest you keep in mind the twenty-year span. Do your work willingly and don't expect too much of your husband. Instead of complaining because he doesn't help you more, keep your marriage intact and cultivate romantic feelings. If you do, there are golden years ahead for you, as in the following experiences.

## A Large Miracle by Simple Means

''My husband and I were seriously thinking of separation when I started to read F.W. We could not even be in the house together without a fight. We were both miserable. There were children to consider, both our folks, his business, and our years of building a home together, but we were both to the point of not being able to endure life together anymore.

"Then I began practicing what I read in F.W. When a battle would begin I would run to our bedroom where I kept the book hidden, and read some advice on that particular situation, then I would come out and be calm and reasonable. Within a few days a noticeable change had taken place in our household. My husband began to look at me in astonishment, then curiosity, then with awe, then with affection. When he saw my changed attitude, he began to change too.

"It is one of those times when a large miracle is brought about in simple ways, and in a short time. We were both so grateful for peace and harmony at last. We are still at peace around here and it's been about fourteen months since I first read the book. There are still some things we don't approve of in each other, but we have learned tolerance and patience.

"This has been the greatest year of growth for the entire family that we have known in eleven years of marriage. My husband has not only become a better husband, but an incredibly better father. Our home at last has a strong foundation on which to build the kind of life we always dreamed of. This is why I continue to tell everyone about F.W. and give the book as gifts to my loved ones and friends, hoping they will find the same kind of treasure in the book I did."

## I Decided Never to Marry

"I grew up in an unhappy marriage. Mom and Dad were always fighting. Many nights I cried myself to sleep, hoping and praying that they would stop fighting and love each other. As a result of Mom and Dad's unhappy marriage I decided that I would never marry. I knew I didn't have the knowledge necessary for a successful happy marriage, and I didn't want another child to live in the battlegrounds as I had.

"One day about two years ago I changed my mind about marriage and about men's and women's roles in life. After years of doing everything I could to discourage boyfriends, I began encouraging them. I stopped competing with men and became more feminine. I even changed my college major to one more suitable for a girl. I was happier than I had ever been. I was in love with life.

"What brought about this change? A wonderfully perceptive roommate saw what was wrong with my attitude about life and gave me her copy of *Fascinating Womanhood* to read. I still have to work hard and there are things that I forget, but the last year has been the happiest year of my life.

"I have been married about a year to the world's most perfect husband. I wonder how I ever thought that I couldn't make a marriage work. Thank you with all my heart. F.W. has given me my most prized possession—a happy contented husband.

"As for Mom and Dad, your book is helping them have a happier marriage, too. Mom has read F.W. and she is working hard to get her marriage working right. Last night Daddy bought her a new stove that she had mentioned she'd like to have. The change in this marriage makes me thrill. May God bless you and may *Fascinating Womanhood* come into the hands of every woman in the world."

### A Stagnant Marriage Blossoms

"We looked like the model couple on the outside, but there was so much emptiness it hurt. We were not really unhappy, but neither were we truly happy. I had come to abandon my original idea of romantic love in marriage. However, I still prayed occasionally for ways to improve our stagnant marriage.

"Shortly thereafter a friend introduced me to F.W. and loaned me her book. I bought and read the book and since have spread my enthusiasm to others. My marriage is now so perfect that it is hard to find a chance to practice childlikeness, there are so few moments of friction! I now enjoy a tender love from my husband which he had never shown before.

"A friend who was on the verge of divorce borrowed my book. Her husband had given her thirty days' grace before he would leave. He told her to sell their house and said he did not love her anymore, after thirteen years of marriage. She was guilty of many serious mistakes. But she recognized them and was willing to work hard to save her marriage. Several months have passed now and, although their problems are not over, they have come a long way from their bed of troubles. I know of many other instances here in town where the advice in F.W has been put to good use. How thankful we all are!''

## Assignment

Read to your husband the scriptures which define the masculine and feminine roles in the family. (Genesis 3: 16, 19) Discuss with him the following: The masculine and feminine roles are different in *function* but equal in *importance*. They are *complimentary* (lock and key). They are a *division of labor*.

# 8

## *The Leader*

*A man needs to function, feel needed, and excel
women in his role as the guide, or leader.*

The father is the head, president, or spokesman of the
family. He was appointed by God to this position, as clearly
stated in the Holy Scriptures. The first commandment given
to mankind was given to the woman, *"Thy desire shall be unto
thy husband and he shall rule over thee."* Evidently our Creator
felt it so vitally important that the woman understand this, that
He directed the instruction to her.

The Apostle Paul compared man's leadership of his wife
to Christ's leadership of the church. *"For the husband is the
head of the wife, even as Christ is the head of the church.
Therefore, as the church is subject unto Christ, so let the wives
be to their own husbands in everything."* He also instructed
women to *reverence* their husbands and to *submit themselves
to their husbands.* The Apostle Peter said, *"Ye wives, be in
subjection to your own husbands."* (Genesis 3:16, Eph.5:23–
24,33, Col.3:18, I Pet.3:1)

There is also a *logical* reason why the man should lead:
Any organization, to have a smooth-running system, must have
a leader—a president, captain, supervisor, director, or chief.
This is a matter of law and order. The family, a small group
of people, must be organized to avoid chaos. It doesn't matter
how large or small the family; even though it be just man and
wife, there must be a leader to maintain order.

But why should the man lead? Why not the woman? Using
logic again, a man is by nature and temperament a born leader,
who tends to be decisive and have the courage of his convictions. A woman, on the other hand, tends to vacillate. An even
more sound reason for the man to lead is that he earns the

living. If he must work diligently to provide the living, he needs jurisdiction over his life to do so. Women and children can more easily adapt. The final say rightfully belongs to the breadwinner.

There is a great effort now to do away with the patriarchy and replace it with equality, in which the husband and wife make decisions by mutual agreement. Although this idea may sound good on the surface, it is impractical and unworkable. Some decisions can be reached by mutual agreement but many others cannot. A man and wife may never agree on some issues. When a decision must be made, someone must take the lead.

Mutual agreements may take time, hours of deliberation. There isn't always time. Some decisions in daily living must be made quickly. For example, "Should Jane take her umbrella and walk to school in the rain, or should her father take her?" When the father makes the decision, matters are settled at once. And whether Jane gets her feet wet or not is not as important as order in the household. But, keeping the man at the head of the family isn't mainly a question of logic. It is a matter of following God's instruction, which like all other commands is for a wise purpose.

### Rights of the Guide or Leader

1. *To Determine Family Rules:* When a family is organized, rules for living must be established such as rules of conduct, care of the house, table manners, expenditure of money, social behavior, and use of the family car. Family members may help shape these rules. A prudent father may hold a family council, to get their ideas. He may delegate considerable authority to his wife to establish rules of the household, since she more closely supervises this area. But, since he is the head of the house, he has the right to the final say.

*A family is not a democracy, where everyone casts his vote. The family is a theocracy, where the father's word is law.* In the home the presiding authority is always vested in the father, and in all home affairs and family matters, no other authority is paramount. This arrangement is not arbitrary or unfair. It's a matter of law and order in the Kingdom of God.

You may tend to claim jurisdiction over your children,

since you have given them life and are in charge of their daily care. You may feel the right to determine discipline, instruction, religious affiliation, and other important things. If you clash with your husband on these matters, you may feel an inalienable right to the final say. This is not so. Although you have the sacred responsibility of motherhood, you are not their leader. *Your husband is the shepherd of his flock and in full command.*

2. *To Make Decisions:* The father also has the right to make *final decisions* on matters which relate to his personal life, his work, and his family. In an ordinary family many decisions must be made daily. Some of these are minor, such as whether to take the dog on a picnic or leave him home. But even though such a decision is small, it must be made, and often quickly. When the husband and wife don't agree, someone must decide. The final say belongs to the father.

Major decisions must also be made. The man may be faced with decisions about his work, such as whether to enlarge his business, make investments, change occupations, or move to a new community. These plans may mean a cutback in expenses or other adjustments. If a man is wise, he will first talk things over with his wife, to get her ideas and win her cooperation.

It is interesting to note that in the account of Jacob in the Bible, after he had worked for his father-in-law for many years, the Lord said to him, *"Return to the land of thy fathers and I will be with thee."* But, although he had this instruction from God, he first called Rachel and Leah into the field and talked with them to win their support. After he had explained his situation Rachel and Leah answered, *"Whatsoever God hath said unto thee, do."* He now had their support. This is what he needed to go in peace. (Genesis 31) You may want to read this passage to your husband. It may encourage him to seek your viewpoint and support more often.

Sometimes a man may seek his wife's support but is reluctant to explain his reasons. He may think she lacks the business knowledge to understand. Or, he may be unable to justify his plans or explain his reasons. He may be guided solely by inspiration. If this is the case, don't probe too deeply. His strong feelings are likely a better guide than his reasons.

In marriage, the man and woman are not like a team of

horses which pull together equally. They are like a bow and cord, as Longfellow described in his poem, "Hiawatha":

> *As unto the bow the cord is,*
> *So unto man is woman;*
> *Tho' she bends him, she obeys him;*
> *Tho' she draws him, yet she follows;*
> *Useless each without the other.*

### Role of the Wife in Leadership

Although your husband is the undisputed head of the family, you have an important part to play in his leadership. Yours is a submissive role, a supporting role, and sometimes an active role in which you express yourself clearly and even strongly. Your support is essential to him, and your ideas sometimes invaluable, if given in the right way. Much rests on his shoulders. He has a family to lead and decisions to make, some of them highly important. He alone will be responsible for these decisions, regardless of the outcome. Your understanding, support, and even your ideas may be all important to him.

Mumatz, lady of the Taj Mahal, played an important part in her husband's leadership, even in governing his country. Daughter of the prime minister, she was well educated, highly intelligent, and had a worthy character. The shah consulted her in many of his decisions, even technical matters of government. There was no doubt about her subtle influence in his life, but she did it with such art that her husband felt not the slightest threat to his position as the supreme ruler of India. And the world at large had no knowledge of her contribution. This womanly art is taught in this chapter. The first step is to *eliminate mistakes*. Review the following list to see if it applies to you:

### Do You Make These Mistakes?

1. *Lead:* Do you hold the reins in the family and run things your way? Do you make the important plans and decisions and expect your husband to go along with them? Do you consult him about family matters but always end up doing things your way? Why do you do this? Perhaps you don't know

any better, or you don't trust your husband's judgment, or think you can do a better job.

Or, when you try to lead, do you meet with resistance? Is there a power struggle? Do you find it difficult to surrender to your husband's authority? Do you feel the end justifies the means, that it's better to have things turn out well than to honor his leadership?

2. *Pressure:* Do you pressure him to do things your way, sometimes resorting to nagging or needling? If he resists does this lead to frequent clashes or arguments? Or, does he give in against his better judgment, just to keep peace? If you have done this you have probably found it pays to pressure, that this is how you get what you want. Your children copy this method.

3. *Scrutinize:* Do you scrutinize your husband's plans and decisions because you're afraid he'll make a mistake? Are you overly concerned about his judgment, watchful of him, quick to approve or disapprove? Are you overly inquisitive about his business? Do you ask probing questions with a fearful tone in your voice? This shows lack of trust, gives him the impression that you think he is incapable of leading. A woman should *build* a man's confidence, not *destroy* it.

4. *Advise:* A common mistake is to give a man too many suggestions, too much advice, to tell him what to do, and how to do it. Or, when he brings up a matter he is considering, instead of waiting to hear his point of view, to hasten to give him advice. Or, to spend a lot of time thinking of what he ought to do, and then outline a course for him to follow. This also shows lack of trust and gives him the impression that you know all the answers, that you don't really need him, and can get along as well or better without him.

5. *Disobey:* Do you obey your husband when you agree with him but when you don't, do it your own way? Or when you really feel strongly about something he does not approve of, do you do it anyway? It's easy to obey a man when you agree with him. The test comes when you don't agree. How to handle such a situation is taught later on in the chapter.

### How to Be the Perfect Follower

1. *Honor His Position:* Honor his position as the head of the family and teach your children to do so. Have faith in the

principle that God placed him at the head and commanded you to obey him, as stated in the Bible. If this doesn't seem fair, remember that God's ways are better than our ways.

2. *Let Go:* Let go of the reigns in the family. Turn the control over to your husband. Let him lead and you follow. You'll be surprised how well he can get along without you. This will build your confidence in him and his confidence in himself. After you let go he should delegate control of certain affairs of the household to you. Work this out together.

3. *Have a Girlish Trust in Him:* Don't be overly concerned about the outcome of things. Let him worry about it. Have a girlish trust in him. This is not the same trust you have in God, for He doesn't make mistakes. Men do. Allow for his mistakes and trust his motives and his overall judgment. In this way you help him to grow, for nothing makes a man feel so responsible as when someone places a childlike trust in him.

Sometimes your husband's decisions may defy logic. His plans may not make sense to you, nor his judgment appear the least bit sound. Perhaps it isn't, but there's a possibility it is. He may be led by inspiration. The ways of God don't always follow logic. Don't expect every inspired decision your husband makes will be pleasant, or turn out the way you think it should. God may lead him into problems for a wise, unknown purpose. We must all be tried in the refiner's fire, and God has mysterious ways of bringing this about. When your husband is led by inspiration, if you follow him devotedly you can look back and see the hand of Almighty God in your life and be grateful for how things turned out.

There may be frightening times when you would like to trust your husband, would like to feel he is guided by inspiration, but you cannot. You detect vanity, pride, and selfishness at the bottom of his decisions and see he is headed for disaster. If he won't listen to you, how can you avert it? The answer is this: If you can't trust your husband, you can always trust in God. He has placed him at the head and commanded you to obey him. You have a right to ask for His help. *If you obey the counsel of your husband and ask your Heavenly Father to guide him, things will turn out right in a surprising way.*

4. *Be Adaptable:* Don't be rigid and set in your ways. Adjust to life's circumstances. Follow your husband where he

wants to go and adapt to the conditions he provides for you. Every woman who is an ideal wife and makes a man happy has this quality. Rare in women, it is treasured by men. To be adaptable you have to be unselfish, care more about him than yourself, and put your marriage in priority, above all else. But, *when you cast your bread upon the waters, it comes back buttered*. To make it easier, follow these rules:

To be adaptable, don't have *inflexible preconceived ideas* about what you want out of life, such as where you want to live, kind of house, life-style, economic level, or plans for the children. It's all right to have preconceived ideas as long as they are not inflexible. Rigid ideas may clash with your husband's plans, plans he must carry out to succeed in his masculine role.

In my youth I had some preconceived ideas. I wanted, when I got married, to live in a white, two-story house on an acre of ground, with tall, rustling trees in the backyard, and a cellar filled with barrels of apples. This was to be on the outskirts of a city of about twenty thousand. There was snow in the winter and green fields in the summer. I found through the years that this dream got in my way, made me less adaptable than I should have been. When I discarded it I was happier and a better wife.

To be adaptable *make your dreams portable* so you can carry them with you. Plan to be happy anywhere—on a mountaintop or a burning desert, in poverty's vale or abounding in wealth. If you focus on making a success of your home life, it's easy to make your dreams portable.

5. *Be Obedient:* Obey your husband's counsel and instructions and it will work for your good. The *quality* of obedience counts. If you obey, but at the same time drag your feet and complain, it won't get you far. But if you obey willingly, with a spirit of sweet submission, God will bless you and your household and bring a spirit of harmony into your home. Your husband will appreciate you and be softened by your yielding spirit.

The wife who refuses to obey her husband's counsels or instructions brings serious disharmony into her marriage. Even more serious, she is doing something morally wrong. Since God placed the man at the head, the wife's rebellion is a sin.

Therefore, when she allows her will to arise against his, she will lose the Spirit of God. The subject of obedience will be covered more fully later on in the chapter.

6. *Present a United Front to the Children:* Even when you and your husband don't agree, present a united front to the children. Never take sides with your children against their father, hoping to win their favor. This can infuriate your husband and cause him to deny them favors. He will be reluctant to yield to his children when you are pleading their case. But, when you present a united front he will be much more yielding, as the following experience clearly demonstrates:

## Dotty

Dotty wanted to attend a particular college but her father said no. Her mother was on Dotty's side. The two of them plotted and prevailed but couldn't change her father's mind. Dotty came to me for advice. I explained the principle above and told her to tell her mother to get on her father's side. Then I told her to tell her father something like this: *"I respect your position as my leader and will do whatever you wish, but I would like very much to attend B.Y.U."* She followed my instructions to the letter. The mother stopped needling her husband and stood by him in whatever he decided to do. Dotty said what I told her to, and what was the result? As soon as he felt their support he said, *"Of course you can go."* It was as simple as that.

7. *Support His Plans and Decisions:* Sometimes your husband needs not only your submission, but your support. He may face a decision he doesn't want to take full responsibility for. He may want you to stand with him. In this case you will have to take a look at his plans to see if you can support them. If you can, give him the encouragement and support he needs. If you can't, assert yourself, as explained in the next point. He may be grateful to you for expressing your point of view. If he insists on having things his way, you can still support him, even when you don't agree. You can support, not his plans, but his authority or his right to decide. You can say something like this: *"I don't agree with your decision but if you feel right about it, follow your convictions and I'll support you."* More on this later in the chapter.

8. *Assert Yourself:* In being the perfect follower, the points I have listed thus far are all submissive qualities—honor his position, let go, trust, be adjustable, obedient, and supportive, even when you don't agree. There are times, however, when you should speak out. When you have a keen feeling about an important issue, *assert yourself.* Your perspective may be a valuable one, your voice an important one. Whether he invites your opinion or not, express yourself honestly and if necessary, strongly. You don't have the final say, but you do have a say. In asserting yourself follow these rules:

First, think things through in your own mind. Be sure of yourself. If it's something you want to request or suggest, ask yourself, is it selfish, an imposition, or unfair? Or, if you oppose your husband's plans, are you just negative, filled with unnecessary fears, or again, selfish? If you put a lot of thought to it you may discard the idea yourself. Or, perhaps you will be more convinced than ever. Many women skip this part and expect their husband to do the thinking. He may not be in the frame of mind to think it through. If so it will be easier for him to stall, or just say no. If you are convinced you are justified in expressing yourself, go to the next step.

Next, pray about it. Through prayer you will see more clearly. You will either be strengthened in your convictions, or made aware of the flaws. If you see the errors in your thinking, abandon the idea and don't think about it anymore. If you are uncertain, continue to pray about it and ponder the idea in your mind. If you receive a positive answer to your prayer, proceed to the next step.

Go to your husband in confidence. Don't shrink. Be self-assured. Speak plainly and if necessarily, a little strongly. Tell him you have thought about it and prayed about it. Now you would like him to think about it and pray about it. After that, trust in God. In asserting yourself, follow suggestions on How to Give Feminine Advice, as now explained:

### The Feminine Counselor

A man needs a woman at his side, not only to support him but to counsel him. Shah Jahan turned to Mumtaz for advice and David Copperfield relied on Agnes. Married to Dora he had no one to turn to. *"I did feel sometimes,"* he said *"that*

*I could have wished my wife had been my counselor; had been endowed with a power to fill up the void which somewhere seemed to be about me."* All wonderful wives are their husbands' counselors, mentors, and best friends.

As a woman, you have special gifts in counseling, gifts of *insight* and *intuition*, unique with your sex. You have a perspective of your husband's life that no one else has. You are closer to him than anyone, yet not so close to his problems as he is. He is too close. His vision may be distorted. Your viewpoint is better. You are near the center of his life, yet stand back a step or two. Your vision is broader, your perspective clearer. You care about him more than anyone else, are willing to sacrifice more. Although you may have less knowledge than others, your advice may be more reliable.

Here are requirements for being a good counselor: First, drop the habit of giving *daily advice* or *suggestions*. This can weary him. He may turn his ears off and not listen. Save your advice for when he asks for it, or when it is very important. If you give advice rarely he will be more open to it.

Next, eliminate negative thinking. Overcome your doubts, fears, and anxieties, or your advice could do him harm. Good counselors are positive thinkers. They are cautious but not negative. If you are inclined to be negative, read a good book on the subject such as *The Power of Positive Thinking* by Dr. Peale, or *Psycho-Cybernetics* by Dr. Maltz.

Then, a good counselor must have something worthy to give. Develop your character, gain wisdom, and deepen your philosophy of life. Broaden your knowledge of the world and what's going on around you. Become an unselfish, giving person who is interested in someone besides yourself. If you become a wonderful person your husband will put his trust in you and seek your advice. But if you are shallow and self-centered you will have nothing to offer him. This was Dora's problem. She lacked too much in herself to be a good counselor. When giving advice, here are guidelines to follow:

## How to Give Feminine Advice

1. *Ask Leading Questions:* A subtle way to give advice is to ask a leading question such as, *"Have you ever thought of doing it this way?"* or *"Have you considered the possibility*

*of . . . ?''* The key word is *you*. The man may reply, *"Yes, I have thought of the idea"* or *"No, but I'll consider it."* In either case, he will claim the idea as his own and discuss it freely, without feeling threatened.

2. *Listen:* After the leading question, listen. Prod him from time to time to keep things going, then listen. All through your conversation listen more than talk. Every good counselor knows the importance of listening carefully before giving advice. It is better to reserve advice for the end of the conversation. Sometimes a clever woman will not give advice at all. She will lead the man into coming up with the answers himself.

3. *Express Insight:* When expressing your viewpoint say, *"I feel," "I sense,"* or *"I perceive,"* as it indicates insight. He will not argue with a feeling or perception. Avoid the words, *"I think,"* or *"I know."* He can put up a good argument to what you *think* or *know*.

4. *Don't Appear to Know More Than He Does.* Don't appear to be overly wise, have all the answers, or surpass your husband in intelligence. Don't appear as an authority in his field, or hope he notices how smart you are. Don't ask too many whys or probing questions. If he has made mistakes, and *you knew all along what he should do and wondered why he didn't know better,* he'll resent you for your smug attitude.

5. *Don't Be Motherly:* Your motherly nature and charitable attitude may make you seem motherly. Don't regard him as a little boy you must look out for, shield from the hard world, take responsibility for, and worry about as you would a child.

6. *Don't Talk Man to Man:* Don't hash things over as men do, putting yourself on an equal plane with him. Don't say for example, *"Let's come to some conclusions,"* or *"Why don't we go over it again,"* or *"I think I've spotted the trouble area."* Keep him in the dominant position to help him feel needed and adequate as the leader.

7. *Don't Act Braver Than He:* If you are giving advice to a man on a matter in which he is filled with fear, don't make the mistake of acting braver than he is. Suppose he wants to create a new business, change jobs, ask for a raise, or try out a new idea. He is nervous and fearful about the outcome and there's a possibility the whole thing will fall apart.

If you courageously say, *"Why are you hesitating,"* or

*"You have nothing to be afraid of,"* you show more manly courage than he does. Instead say, *"It sounds like a good idea, but it seems so challenging! Are you sure you want to do it?"* Such meekness tends to awaken manly courage and prompts him to say, *"It isn't so tough. I think I can handle it."* Whenever a man detects fearfulness in a woman, it naturally awakens masculine courage.

8. *Don't Have Unyielding Opinions:* When giving advice, don't have unyielding opinions. Such opinions awaken opposition, lead to argument, obligate him to take your advice, and make you appear unfeminine.

9. *Don't Insist He Do Things Your Way:* Let him drink from your fountain of advice as much or as little as he likes, with no pressure. Use a *take it or leave it* approach. It is better to let him make a mistake, than pressure him into doing it your way, and harm your relationship.

## Obedience

Now let us turn our attention more fully to one of the most important requirements of a man's successful leadership—your obedience. The first law of Heaven is *obedience*, and it should be the first law of every home. It is the foundation of an orderly home, a successful family, and the successful lives of the children. The wife is the key. When she sets an example of obedience to her husband, the children follow. It has not only immediate benefits, but far-reaching effects on their entire lives.

On the other hand, when the wife refuses to obey her husband, she sets a pattern of rebellion for her children to follow. They learn from her that they don't have to obey an instruction if they don't want to. There is some way to get around it. When such children are turned out into the world they have difficulty obeying the law, or a higher authority, such as leadership on campus or in their work. The problems of rebellious youth can often be traced to homes where the mother disobeyed the father or showed lack of respect for his authority.

English satirist C. Northcote Parkinson passed judgment on the campus revolution in America in the 1970's, and blamed the whole thing on women. He told a Los Angeles audience that the trouble in American colleges is based on disrespect for authority learned in the home. *"The general movement, I think, begins with the female revolution,"* he said. *"Women demanded the vote and equality and ceased to submit to the control of their husbands. In the process they began to lose control of their own children."* Mr. Parkinson said that in his own Victorian childhood, *"Pop's word was law, and Mother's most deadly threat was, 'I shall have to inform your father.' Nowadays, the mother can't appeal to the children in that way because they have denied paternal authority themselves."*

On the other hand, women who are strictly obedient to their husbands, showing honor and respect for their authority, set an example of obedience for their children to pattern from. Several years ago I was visiting my daughter in a distant state when our son came from a neighboring university to visit. They visited for some time while I listened in. One point in the conversation caught my attention acutely.

Paul said to Kristine, *"When we were growing up I would never have thought of disobeying Dad, would you, Kristine?"* She said emphatically, *"No, I would never, ever have thought of disobeying Dad!"* I broke into the conversation by asking, *"Why would you never have thought of disobeying your father?"* Their quick response was, *"You were the key, Mom, because you always obeyed Dad, even when it was very difficult."*

Immediately there flashed in my mind an experience that had taken place a few years earlier. For months we had planned a trip to the Florida Keys. The children were marking off dates on the calendar in eager anticipation of this exciting trip to a distant state. When the time arrived we bought a new traveling van and had the time of our lives traveling along the way.

When we arrived in southern Florida we bought fried chicken and sat under a banyan tree while our daughters played their guitars. My husband left for a few minutes to call our son, who was in Sweden serving time as a missionary. He had had some trouble with his health and we were concerned about him. When my husband returned he had a strange look on his face. *"We're going to have to go back to California. He's not well and they're sending him home."*

At this point I didn't take it too seriously because I am an optimist. I tried to talk my husband into having our son sent to us in Florida. It would be good for him. It's just what he needs. I thought I had him convinced so we all got in the van and traveled toward the keys. In the middle of the night I woke up to find we were traveling north, heading back to California.

For miles and miles, in the presence of the children, I did everything I could to appeal to him. I just knew my way was best. I felt returning was unnecessary and would be a tremendous disappointment to the children. It just wasn't fair. I remember distinctly how tempted I was to *put my foot down*. But I didn't. I knew my limitations and surrendered. The children observed all of this and remembered. They knew how hard it was for me.

Now I could see it all clearly. I thought the disappointment would do them harm, would leave a scar on their lives. But think of the greater harm I would have done to set a pattern of rebellion. I brought this experience up to Paul and Kristine and ask them if they had been disappointed. *"No,"* they both said, *"We always remembered it as a time we all made a sacrifice for the welfare of one of us."* Our son recovered and all is well, but I consider it a close call. I could have made a serious mistake.

## Problems in the Patriarchy

1. *When the Wife Fears Failure:* Women the world over have a hard time supporting their husbands' plans or decisions, because they are afraid of failure. Women need to take a look at success and failure. No man ever succeeded to any extent without running the risk of failure. He can't climb to the top of a mountain, so to speak, without taking risks. In fact, failure seems to be the history of success. Take for example, Abraham Lincoln's record of success:

When he was a young man he ran for the legislature in Illinois and was defeated. He next entered business and failed and spent seventeen years of his life paying off the debts of a worthless partner. Entering politics he ran for Congress and was defeated. Then he tried an appointment in the U.S. land office and failed. He became a candidate for the U.S. Senate and was again defeated. In 1856 he became a candidate for the Vice Presidency and was again defeated. In 1858 he lost the election to Douglas. Yet he eventually achieved the highest success attainable in public life. Much of his success is attributed to his wife Mary Todd, who maintained, *"He'll be a great man someday."*

The wife is an important key to a man's success. When she supports his decisions, for better or for worse, he can survive his mistakes and keep going forward. If not, she can be the means of keeping him in obscurity. Men who could have contributed great things to life have fallen into obscurity because they failed to have the support of their wife on the *risky* road to success.

2. *When the Wife Rebels:* The fear of a mistake or failure may invoke the wife's rebellion. A Christian writer, Orson Pratt, writes on this subject:

*"The wife should never follow her judgment in preference to that of her husband, for if her husband desires to do right, but errs in judgment, the Lord will bless her in endeavoring to carry out his counsels; for God has placed him at the head and though he may err in judgment, yet God will not justify the wife in disregarding his instructions and counsels; for greater is the sin of rebellion than the errors which arise from want of judgment; therefore she would be condemned for suffering her will to arise against his . . . be obedient and God will cause all things to work for good, and He will correct the errors of the husband in due time . . . a wife will lose the spirit of God in refusing to obey the counsel of her husband."*

3. *When He Flounders:* Does your husband sometimes vacillate, unable to bring himself to a firm decision? If he is overly cautious by nature, accept this tendency and learn to live with it. He may, however, be moved by fear, a fear that you should understand. A common fear is that his decision will put his family to disadvantage. For example, the man may desire to return to school to further his education, but fears it will threaten the security of his family. In this case, you can encourage his decision by assuring him that you are willing to make the necessary sacrifice.

Or, your husband may fear that a decision will lead to the loss of money or prestige. He may wish to proceed with plans but lacks courage to do so. If you detect his fears are groundless, build his confidence to help him make the decision.

4. *When He Won't Lead:* You may want very much for

your husband to take the lead. You want a strong arm to lean on, but he backs away from his position as the leader. In this case you may become frustrated and take over the leadership of the family out of necessity. How can you encourage him to lead?

First, read him Scriptures which appoint him as the leader. Reason with him that someone must lead. He is more qualified than you, and you don't want to lead. Let him know that you need him to take over this responsibility. Then, offer your loyal support. After this, devote yourself to your domestic duties, making a success there. By so doing, you clearly define the division of responsibility between you and your husband.

5. *When He Leads His Children Astray:* If your husband is leading his family into corruption, if he encourages your children to cheat, lie, steal, be immoral, or follow other evil practices, you have a moral obligation to take them out of the household, away from the evil influences. If you are without children, you have the same obligation to remove yourself.

However, if he is just weak, and due to weakness has only slipped so that he doesn't maintain the same high standards as you, or if he is negligent in his religious devotions or in other ways a weaker individual than you, be patient with him and keep your marriage intact.

## Rewards

A home where the father presides is a house of order. There's less argument and contention, more harmony. Taking the lead helps him grow in masculinity. Out of necessity he acquires the traits of firmness, decisiveness, self-confidence and a sense of responsibility. When the wife is removed from leadership duties, she has less worry and concern, can devote herself to her domestic duties and succeed in her career in the home.

Children who grow up in a home where father's word is law have a natural respect for authority, at school, church, and all areas of society. In a world where men lead we would have less crime and violence, less divorce, and less homosexuality. There would be happier marriages, happier homes, and therefore happier people. If the patriarchy could be lived widely, it would be a world of law and order. Rewards of living this principle along with living all of the teachings of F.W. are clearly indicated in the following true experiences.

## My Life Will Never Be the Same

"The past few weeks have meant so much to me as I have learned what my true role as a wife, mother, and child of God is, all based on scripture. As the Chinese students peacefully revolt against communism, so also has my spirit revolted against what my culture has told me were my rights and role. Praise God! I'm now free.

"My first marriage ended in divorce. I have been married the second time for thirteen years. I have strongly supported the E.R.A. and N.O.W. and have fought for thirteen years to be equal with my husband. I made demands, nagged, and worst of all, humiliated my precious husband to get my way. I couldn't understand why he didn't treat me with gentleness. In the end, my quest for equality was met with frustration for both of us, neither of us winning control of our home life and both of us with great needs not met.

"I had a chance to begin a new Bible study on Thursday mornings the same week the F.W. class began. After praying, God gently urged me to attend the F.W. class. My life will never be the same. The results:

1) My husband has always given me silly, humorous cards for our anniversary. I've always yearned for sentimental ones and had told him so but never received one until . . . I opened and read the most beautiful, mushy card! We both wept as I read it.

2) My husband works for the government and is on call twenty-four hours a day and rarely gets home before seven-thirty P.M. I have begged, screamed, and thrown tantrums, but not gotten him home early until . . . two hours early on our anniversary, and he has since come home several times early, has even come home for lunch when in the area, things he has never done before!

3) We have never tithed, as he opposed it and we are over our heads in debt. We'll tithe when we're back on our feet. Right? Wrong! When we received our income tax refund I suggested we tithe it since we have been so blessed materially and in health, but he refused. I had prayed prior and told God

I knew how he would respond but requested strength to hold my tongue (no small miracle) and let God deal with him. When he refused I simply said, 'Ok, it's your decision and I'll support you.'

"Several weeks later the woman who runs the soup kitchen in our community came to speak to our church. It was quite moving. Then a friend shared with us how our church had been trying to tithe and the blessings that had been received as a result. When we got home from church he announced we would tithe our tax refund—half to the soup kitchen, half to our church for missions. Knock me over with a feather!! Since then God has promised me we will be financially stable in six months, and God keeps His promises!

"Our marriage is now as God intended it to be all along. He opened my spirit to hear His word and sent the most precious woman, my *Fascinating Womanhood* teacher, to deliver that word. I have finally been released from my burdens and self-imposed responsibilities and am actually finding warmth and security and comfort in being submissive. After the first few weeks of class my husband would comment *every* day. 'What's going on?' or 'Why are you being so nice?' or 'What did you buy today?' Finally in exasperation of the *new me* he threw up his hands and said, 'Go buy it! Whatever you want, go buy it.' We both laughed! Praise, Jesus.''

### What Heaven on Earth Is All About

"This letter is long but every word comes from a full and grateful heart. Next to my Bible, *Fascinating Womanhood* is the most valuable book I have ever read. And like my Bible, it has changed my life and continues to guarantee peace and harmony in my home as long as I practice the principles taught.

"I have been married eighteen years. Seventeen of them were very stormy ones. My husband and I loved each other very much, but our marriage was often in a turmoil. We were either really happy together or miserable—frequently arguing about every little thing and ending up saying cruel and hurtful things to each other. Our love life was either feast or famine and becoming more famine all the time.

"We were both very strong-willed. I think there was an unconscious power struggle to see who could get the upper hand, the last word, and ultimately win the argument. I am a survivor by nature and a fighter for what I believe is right. So naturally I was right in there pitching for my ideas and principles, and my expectations and needs. Well, this foolish woman may have won many battles with her tongue, but she nearly lost the war and the thing most precious to her—peace and harmony in her home as well as the love and respect of her husband and children.

"Marriage left me so depressed and disillusioned with life. Where was the heaven on earth I had heard about? Why were some marriages smooth and others rough? I was so discouraged and tired of it all. After considering divorce for the umpteenth time, because I was unfairly yoked to an impossible man, I found *Fascinating Womanhood* in the family section of a religious bookstore.

"Deep down I still wanted to save our marriage. I picked up the book. It looked like just what I needed. I brought it home and began to devour it. I was so impressed by its godly principles made practical and easy for me to follow. Not only did it tell me *what* to do, but *how* to do it and how to put my feelings into the right words. Plus, it was not a gimmicky book that said, 'just be more sexy in bed and that will solve all of your problems.'

"Well, reading *Fascinating Womanhood* was a real eye-opener for me!! I thought that I had been doing the right things all the time when really I had been doing exactly the opposite. For instance, I didn't praise my husband because I thought it would make him too conceited. I thought it was my job as his loving wife to keep him humble. I couldn't accept him for what he was because I felt he could always do better.

"I tried everything from overt criticism and nagging to icy silence to try to get him to change. Of course, he only got worse and we only fought more. I was trying so hard to change him, focusing on his faults, that I couldn't even begin to see that he had a better side. Then, of course, to let him be the leader without *my* help and guidance would be unthinkable. What if he made a terrible mistake?

"After reading F.W. I soon realized how terribly wrong I had been and how much I needed to pray and work toward changing *myself*. I am a slow learner in matters of the heart, but right away, little by little I began putting these principles into action. I can look back over the last year and actually see changes in my attitudes and behavior. I have found that it takes a great deal of humility to be truly fascinating, and for me that has not been easy. With my quick temper I still have problems expressing childlike anger properly but am still working on it.

"The results of practicing these principles have been well worth all the effort. I thank God and thank you for writing this book. It has opened my eyes to see the truth about myself and my marriage relationship. Acting on the principles of F.W. has saved my marriage and home. After eighteen years I finally know what heaven on earth is all about and I never want to lose it again."

"When I told my husband that I accepted and appreciated him for the way he is, and I started praising his masculine traits, he opened up like a beautiful rose. When I told him how much I appreciated the way he cares and provides for his family by going to work every day, when it is the last thing he wants to do, he lit up like the sun. When I told him that I understood why he had to be firm in saying no to me, and that I respected him for not being easily pushed around by me, he breathed a sigh of relief as if a ton of weight had been lifted from his shoulders. His look to me said, 'At last she is on my side.'

"We women don't realize how our behavior affects our husbands. We truly have the power to make them or break them and oh, how much better it is to make them the best they can be by understanding them and loving them, and making ourselves the best we can be.

"My husband has simply amazed me with so many thoughtful and generous responses to my changed behavior. He said, "I love what is happening here. You are much more beautiful and precious to me now than you were eighteen years ago. I could never marry anyone else." This came from a man who had been, just a short time before, so angry and frustrated with me that he was ready to leave home any day for good.

"I did not really expect material rewards. With two teen-agers, a home, and one salary, money is spent wisely. How-ever, my husband began to show me his gratitude in gifts as well as words. He started to take me out to eat again, frequently ordered out on nights I was too tired to cook, came home with a Mozart CD because he knew I loved Mozart. He bought an expensive lounge chair for me so I would be more comfortable sewing and watching TV. On top of that, he cleaned and fixed the fireplace so we could enjoy sitting and snuggling by the warm fire. Snuggling has been something foreign to us for a long time.

"One evening when we were sitting by the fire he proudly showed me new photographs he had taken. I told him he would exceed even Ansel Adams, the great photographer. He laughed a deep laugh and looked at me with the most adoring look I had seen in a long time. He told me I was the most beautiful woman in the world and he loved me very much.

"He is much more tender and gentle now. Even when he occasionally gets angry with me it's different. He is kinder and not as harsh. He is so thoughtful and generous too. I know now he was *always* like that, but I had to learn to love and understand him in order to find out. I have seen the differences in children of strong families whose fathers are in the lead, as opposed to those who are not. Thank you for *Fascinating Womanhood*. May the Lord bless this ministry a hundredfold."

### How to Let Him Lead and You Follow:

1. Honor his position.
2. Let go.
3. Have a girlish trust in him.
4. Be adaptable.
   Don't have inflexible preconceived ideas.
   Make your dreams portable.
5. Be obedient.
6. Present a united front.
7. Support his plans and decisions.
8. Assert yourself.

### How to Give Feminine Advice

1. Ask leading questions.
2. Listen.
3. Express insight—I feel, sense, perceive.
4. Don't appear to know more than he does.
5. Don't be motherly.
6. Don't talk man to man.

7. Don't act braver than he is.
8. Don't have unyielding opinions.
9. Don't insist he do things your way.

**Remember:** *It's better to let a man have his way and fail, than to stand in his way and make him feel thwarted.*

## Assignment

1. *If You Have Been in Control:* If you have been running things your way, let go. Tell your husband that you know he is the God-appointed leader of his family, that you're sorry you've not understood this in the past, and that from now on you'll do everything to honor his position.

2. *If He Doesn't Lead:* Read him the scriptures at the beginning of this chapter. If he agrees, read him The Rights of the Guide. Then say something like this: "I want you to be the leader. If you take this responsibility I will support your plans and decisions, even though I might not always agree. I want you to do the masculine things so I can become more feminine."

3. *If He Has Been Domineering:* Read to him about Jacob in Genesis 31. The Lord instructed Jacob to return to the land of his fathers but he first called Leah and Rachel into the field, to discuss it with them and win their support.

# 9

## The Protector

*A man needs to function, feel needed,
and excel women as a protector.*

When we consider the natural man, we can see that he was created to be the protector for his wife and children. Men are larger, have stronger muscles, and greater physical endurance than women. Women are more fragile, weaker, created for the more delicate tasks, like a fine precision machine which runs smoothly and efficiently, *when used for the purpose intended.*

### What Women Need Protection From

In all periods of time, women have needed protection from *dangers, strenuous work, and difficulties:*

1. *Dangers:* In the early history of our country, the very conditions under which people were forced to live made manly protection necessary. There were dangers everywhere. Savage Indians, wild beasts, and snakes created situations which called for masculine courage, strength, and ability, to protect women and children from danger.

Today dangers are different, but just as real. Women are in danger of abduction and rape, sometimes followed by brutality and murder. Lesser dangers are vicious dogs, snakes, a high precipice, a deep canyon, or other dangers of nature.

There are also *unreal dangers.* Amusing as it is, women are afraid of such things as strange noises, spiders, mice, and even dark shadows. Whether the danger is real or not doesn't matter. If she *thinks* it is real she needs masculine protection.

2. *Strenuous Work:* Women also need protection from heavy work, *work beyond their capacity*—hard labor in the

fields, hauling, lifting, spading, or anything requiring masculine strength, skill, or endurance. Protection is also needed in the household—lifting heavy objects, moving furniture, painting, carpentry, and other heavy or rough work. This is man's work. Women should expect them to do it. Such work is injurious to women and lessens femininity.

Women also need protection from *work that is not appropriate* for the feminine sex, such as driving a truck, construction work, road work, or anything greasy or masculine. Some types of office work are inappropriate, such as executive jobs, management positions, police work, or top political posts.

3. *Difficulties:* In day-to-day living, difficulties may arise that require masculine assistance. Examples are financial entanglements, belligerent creditors, or dealings with people who are harsh, offensive, imposing, or who make unreasonable demands. You become the *maiden in distress,* dependent upon masculine chivalry. Women tend to be more emotional and less objective than men in dealing with such problems. Men are more composed, more able to cope.

Men inherently have a sense of chivalry, an *inborn feeling of masculine duty* to protect women. This was evident in John Alden's feelings for Priscilla when he said, *"Here for her sake will I stay and like an invisible presence hover around her forever, protecting, supporting her weakness."* Victor Hugo made known his sense of chivalry when he said, *"My duty is to keep close to her steps, to surround her existence with mine, to serve her as a barrier against all dangers; to offer my head as a steppingstone, to place myself unceasingly between her and all sorrows . . . if she but consent to lean upon me at times amidst the difficulties of life."*

## Do Men Protect Women Today?

Is this kind of chivalry dead? Is the tender care and protection of John Alden and Victor Hugo offered today? Do we see men hovering around their women, protecting their weakness, defending them or serving them as a barrier against all dangers? It sounds like something from a romantic novel, and yet it was common in the past.

Today chivalry seems to be disappearing. We see women walking down dark streets alone, taking long-distance automobile trips, and even hitchhiking. We see them doing the rough work, lifting heavy objects, repairing automobiles, changing tires, driving heavy equipment, fixing the roof, doing the carpentry, and many other masculine tasks.

In the working world, women are doing the men's jobs. They are hauling lumber, driving trucks, and climbing scaffolds. We see women police, steel workers, pilots, and even engineers. Women also battle the world of difficulties—face angry creditors, fight financial battles, and learn to cope with people who take unfair advantage of them.

## Why Is Chivalry Dead?

If men have an inborn sense of chivalry, why don't they offer it? The answer is very simple: Men don't offer their chivalry because women have become capable. They no longer appear to need men. Men only feel a sense of duty to protect women who need their masculine care and protection, or at least appear to need it. When a woman can do a job as well as a man, why should he offer his masculine assistance? He would feel humiliated to offer his assistance when not needed.

If chivalry is dead, women have killed it. They have killed it by becoming capable, efficient, and independent, able to kill their own snakes. They prove by their strength and ability that they don't need masculine care and protection, that they are well able to take care of themselves. They commonly display their capacity to solve their own problems and fight their own battles.

To awaken chivalry we must return to femininity. We must stop doing the masculine things and become the gentle, tender, dependent women we were designed to be, women who need masculine care and protection. When we do, men will delight in offering their chivalry. Femininity is fully explained in the chapters on that subject. When you become feminine, many painful problems disappear and you awaken your husband's tender love, as in the following experience:

## He Wasn't Needed at Home

"We were constantly being moved every two or three years, and with each move my husband had a new job to manage and did not want the family to interfere with his time. A constant remark was 'When I get this under control I'll be able to spend time with the children, or help with the house, or take time to relax.'

"I was a very capable person so I managed the children, did household repairs, took care of the house, and was active in the community. In the meantime, my husband spent more and more time at work. He also drank more because of the pressure he was under (or so we both said). I criticized his devotion to his work, his drinking, his overeating, and finally decided to leave as we had stopped speaking. He usually was drunk when he arrived home so conversation was useless.

"The children had left and I finally decided to leave, for watching him destroy himself was destroying me. Then I picked up *Fascinating Womanhood*. What a shock to find all the things I had been doing wrong. I'd been so capable and independent that he wasn't needed at home. People in the community admired me, for I was so kind and helpful, but my husband didn't, for at home I was critical.

"It was very difficult for me to change, but I kept trying and he started coming home a bit earlier and didn't drink until he was home. Eight months later he stopped drinking for a year. We have been so happy. He comes home in the evening so glad to see me, calls me each noon to see how everything is. He is even buying Christmas gifts this year and is so proud of it.

"He is drinking again and overeating too, but they don't bother me now for I know they are his problems. He had started overdrinking and being secretive, because I used to nag so. One day I told him, 'I don't care if you drink as long as you control it.' He was so surprised at my saying, 'I don't care' that he is much better. I've passed this book to over thirty people in Mexico (mostly North Americans) and about twenty people here in Minnesota. We've had many discussions and it has helped so many of them."

## The Change Is Overwhelming!

"During the past few weeks I have been taking the *Fascinating Womanhood* class. The results in my own home are remarkable. My husband and I are both Christians and very active in our church, but even so, our marriage seemed rapidly heading for the divorce courts. I knew I needed help so I secretly started seeing a psychiatrist, had many counseling sessions with our pastor, and finally a marriage counselor, and still continued having deep, prolonged depressions, lasting for days.

"I happened to see a lady in the beauty shop with a F.W. book. She told me about the classes so I enrolled. I have learned more from these classes than all the professional counseling sessions put together! The change in our home is almost overwhelming! My husband can't seem to do enough for me. For the first time in twelve years of marriage he has taken over the bill paying, has started doing the yard and gardening, and wants to do some home improvements.

"I seemed to always get stuck driving our pickup truck (which I hated to drive). He has now put it up for sale and is buying a small car for me to drive! He has become more devoted to our church, and instead of complaining of my activity he tells me he is proud of me! He is a real estate broker and his business has increased to the point our accountant says it is going to be a profitable year! His formula: A successful church life and a successful home have to equal a successful business. I am so thankful for F.W."

## Assignment

1. Tell him something like this: "I'm glad I have a strong man to protect me. It would be difficult to go through this life without you."

2. When you need him to lift something heavy say, "This is too heavy for me. Will you please lift it for me?" Or, "Will you please lend me your masculine strength?" Or, "Man of muscles, will you please give me a helping hand?"

# 10

## *The Provider*

*A man needs to function, feel needed,*
*and excel women as a provider.*

Since the beginning of time, the man has been recognized as the provider. The first commandment given him was, *"In the sweat of thy face shalt thou eat bread, till thou return unto the ground."* This command was given, not to the woman, but *to the man*. The woman was instructed to *bring forth children*. From this time forth their duties have been thus divided.

This arrangement has been honored by tradition, custom, and even courts of the law. In the event of divorce men are still legally bound to pay alimony; thus they continue to earn the bread so the mother can nurture the children. This plan is important to live, however, not because of custom or law but because it is God's command.

Another reason the man should provide: Inborn in a man is a *keen sense of responsibility to* provide the living and to *function effectively* in this role. Being successful in this area of his life is as important to his feeling of worth, as a woman's in succeeding as a mother and homemaker.

As the man fulfills his masculine duty as the provider, it presents a tender, romantic scene, as in the following nursery rhyme:

> *By, baby bunting,*
> *Daddy's gone a hunting,*
> *To get a little rabbit skin,*
> *To wrap his baby bunting in.*

Picture, if you can, a mother at home nurturing her little ones, making a comfortable home for her family; the father goes out into the world, struggling against the elements and oppositions of life to bring home the necessities and comforts for his loved ones. This romantic scene, instead of being taken for granted, should be viewed as the heart and core of life which, when lived properly, brings soul satisfaction that cannot be measured. There is nothing to equal it and nothing more important.

A man also has an inborn *need to feel needed* as a provider, to feel that his wife depends on him for financial support and can't get by without him. In addition, he has an inborn need to *excel women* as a provider. A man's feeling of worth can be undermined when he sees women in the work force doing a better job than he, advancing to a higher position, or earning more pay. How much worse when his own wife excels him.

## What a Man Should Provide

An excellent description of *what a man should provide* is from my husband's book, *Man of Steel and Velvet*:

*"Simply stated, the man should provide the necessities. This means food, clothing, and a shelter, plus a few comforts and conveniences . . . Through all generations of time it has been recognized that when a man marries, his wife and children are entitled to his financial support. Failure to meet this obligation has been just cause for divorce, and even after the marriage separation, a man is still under financial obligation. Financial support, and along with this, fidelity have always been the two main entitlements for a woman in marriage. But whether these laws remain in force or not, the moral and sacred obligation is just as binding, the need just as great.*

*"It's important that a man provide a shelter separate from anyone else. This is important for the sake of privacy and giving the wife the opportunity of making a home in her own way. Perhaps this is why a special instruction was given by God in the very beginning: "Therefore shall a man leave his father and mother and cleave unto his wife" (Gen.2:24) Under stress of circumstances there may be occasions when a man must move his wife and children into another household. Although there may be justification temporarily, it's contrary to the divine plan and unfair to the wife if this situation extends beyond a brief emergency.*

"Although a man has a sacred and binding obligation to provide the necessities, he is under no such obligation to provide the luxuries. Women and children are not entitled to ease and luxury, to style and elegance. His duty is not to provide a costly home, expensive furniture and decor. Concerning the education of his children, he has an obligation to provide a basic education, but such a binding obligation doesn't extend to a higher education, music lessons, the arts and cultures. He may wish to provide these, and it may bring him much pleasure to do so, but it's not mandatory.

"In providing a high standard of living, some men make near economic slaves of themselves, with great disadvantage to themselves and their families. Too often a man is so consumed with meeting ever-increasing demands, not only by his family, but by himself, that he does not preserve himself for things of greater value. He has little time to give to his wife and children, time to teach them the values of life, how to live, standards to follow, and time to build strong family ties.

"A man is also entitled to time for himself, for recreation, study, and meditation. He has a further need to be of service outside his own circle, a commitment to society. Church service is an important part of this, as is civic responsibility. Men have talents which need to be shared, ability which could be developed to make the world a better place. It is not right for a man to spend his entire time and energy to provide luxuries for his own family circle."

### His Pressing Responsibility to Provide

A woman needs to understand with an *all-comprehending sympathy* what a man faces in earning the living. An excellent description is found in Dr. Marie Robinson's book, *The Power of Sexual Surrender*, from which I quote:

"For the majority of men, when they come of age and marry, take on an enormous burden which they may not lay down with any conscience this side of the grave. Quietly, and without histrionics, they put aside, in the name of love, most of their vaunted freedom and contract to take upon their shoulders full social and economic responsibility for their wives and children.

"As a woman, consider for a moment how you would feel

*if your child should be deprived of the good things of life;
proper housing, clothing, education. Consider how you would
feel if he should go hungry. Perhaps such ideas have occurred
to you and have given you a bad turn momentarily. But they
are passing thoughts: a woman does not give them much cre-
dence; they are not her direct responsibility; certainly she does
not worry about them for long.*

*"But such thoughts, conscious or unconscious, are her
husband's daily fare. He knows, and he takes the carking
thought to work with him each morning (and every morning)
and to bed with him at night, that upon the success or failure
of his efforts rests the happiness, health, indeed the very lives
of his wife and children. In the ultimate he senses he alone
must take full responsibility for them.*

*"I do not think it is possible to exaggerate how seriously
men take this responsibility; how much they worry about it.
Women, unless they are very close to their men, rarely know
how heavily the burden weighs sometimes, for men talk about
it very little. They do not want their loved ones to worry.*

*"Men have been shouldering the entire responsibility for
their family group since earliest times. I often think, however,
when I see the stresses and strains of today's marketplace, that
civilized man has much harder going, psychologically speaking, than his primitive forefathers.*

*"In the first place, the competition creates a terrible strain
on the individual male. This competition is not only for pre-
ferment and advancement, it is often for his very job itself.
Every man knows that if he falters, lets up his ceaseless drive,
he can and will be easily replaced.*

*"No level of employment is really free of this endless
pressure. The executive must meet and exceed his last year's
quota or the quota of his competitors. Those under him must
see that he does it, and he scrutinizes their performance most
severely, and therefore constantly.*

*"Professional men—doctors, lawyers, professors—are
under no less pressure for the most part. If the lawyer is self-
employed he must constantly seek new clients; if he works for
an organization he must exert himself endlessly to avoid being
superseded by ambitious peers or by pushing young particles
just out of law school and fired with the raw energy of youth.
A score of unhappy contingencies can ruin or seriously threaten*

*a doctor's practice, not the least of which is a possible break-
down in his ability to practice. A teacher must work long hours
on publishable projects outside of his arduous teaching assignments if he is to advance or even hold his ground.*

*"There is no field of endeavor that a man may enter where
he can count on complete economic safety; competition, the
need for unremitting year-in, year-out performance is his life's
lot. Over all this he knows, too, stands a separate specter upon
which he can exert only the remotest control. It is the job-
lessness which may be caused by the cyclical depression and
recessions that characterize our economy."*

## Do Women Who Work Feel the Same Pressure Men Do?

Women who work do not feel the *same kind* of pressure
men do. This is because they have a different orientation to
the world of work. Whereas a man feels he cannot turn aside
from his work with a clear conscience, a woman doesn't feel
this same sense of duty. She can resign her job at any time
and for any reason, *without a feeling of guilt*. Economic problems may result but she won't have a lower opinion of herself
or feel disgraced in the eyes of the public.

On the other hand, if an able-bodied man were to stop
working it would injure his feeling of worth and his image to
the public. He and everyone else would consider him a failure
if he were to neglect this important duty. A woman feels pressure, but of a different kind—a *time pressure* which comes
from living a double role. A man feels a *binding moral
pressure*.

## How You Can Help

These thoughts cannot help but awaken your concern for
your husband, and motivate you to want to do something to
help, to relieve his strain and make his life easier. You may
even feel impelled to seek employment outside the home, or
assist him in his work. Noble as these thoughts are, they are
not the best solutions. Instead, do the following:

1. *Reduce Expenses:* Do everything you can to reduce
expenses, so you are living well within your husband's income,
and hopefully with some to spare for savings. When you do,

you will greatly relieve his anxieties over money. Suggestions on doing this are given in the next chapter, Family Finances.

2. *Reduce Demands on His Time:* If your husband works long hours or gives himself devotedly to his work, when he comes home he needs time to relax and recover. You may have to forgo places you want to go, or things you planned for him to do, and adjust your life to his.

3. *Live Your Feminine Role:* Instead of helping your husband provide the income, provide a wonderful home life. *Let him make the living, and you make life worth living.* Keep the home intact so it is running smoothly, with all daily needs met. Be feminine, cheerful, and do all you can to bring a peaceful spirit in the home. Such an atmosphere will relieve his anxieties and help him succeed as a provider.

4. *Live All of* Fascinating Womanhood. When your marriage is free of problems and you have a loving relationship, he can better withstand the stresses and strains of his work. If not, if there is trouble in the marriage, it can greatly add to his burdens. If you do all of these things you will do far more than if you join the work force with him.

## His Drive for Status

Parallel to his pressing responsibility to provide the living is his *drive for status*. This again we need to understand, with an *all comprehending sympathy*.

The driving desire for status is noticeable in all male members of the animal kingdom. Robert Ardrey, in his book *African Genesis*, states that in the animal world the instinct for status, for the acquisition and defense of territory are more compelling for the male than is the sex instinct. *"The pecking order in the barnyard, the formation in which a flock of wild geese fly, the hierarchy in a colony of baboons, and the ranking within a herd of elephants is a more driving force for the male than is the sex function."*

This drive for position is evident in the human male, as he pushes for a higher rank in his work. Don't think his sole motivation is money. Although money is usually the main incentive, the desire for position is also a factor. This is evident in the man who doesn't need more money but drives on for a higher level of achievement.

The desire for status is noticeable even if a man is only trying to win a game, or toss a basketball better than other men. Or this desire may impel him to higher heights—the championship cup, the gold medal of achievement, or president of his company. This is a strongly masculine characteristic, lacking in the truly feminine woman. It is not the nature of women to seek superiority over one another. The man, on the other hand, desires to shine out brightly, to seek an honored place in the world of men.

To some extent, the desire for status is a negative trait. It would be better if men were moved to action by a feeling of love or a desire to serve humanity. But men are human and this trait is not without some merit. The drive for status, if not mixed with greed and a lust for power, can impel men to strive earnestly for worthy goals, or bring them out of obscurity where they can more adequately influence and serve mankind.

## Status with His Wife

When a man has achieved an honored position, it may be heartwarming to receive the acclaim of the world, but greater is his satisfaction in receiving the acclaim of his wife. Although he would like to be a hero to his friends and colleagues, he would rather be a hero to the woman he loves. This is all-important to him so that if he does not receive her praise, he can be painfully disappointed.

And yet, how many heroes have been honored everywhere but home? A man may work for years for an educational degree. He may receive the honor and acclaim of friends, but his wife may not give him the time of day. If she does, it may be *"It's about time."* Or, if her husband has received an award for meritorious service, she may imply another man could have done as well. Or, imagine how painful if she esteems another man a hero, such as her brother, her father, or a man in the community. Although modest comments about other men are proper, don't be overly enthusiastic about another man's accomplishments.

There are women who actually have a great appreciation for their husband's achievements but deliberately withhold praise for *his own good*. They are afraid that too much praise will make him arrogant or unprepared for a possible defeat.

Thus, they feel it their duty to *keep his feet on the ground* by being lukewarm about his achievements.

## Excellence in His Work:

A man may dedicate himself to his work for a different reason than status. It may be for *excellence* in his work. He is motivated by a feeling of satisfaction and self-worth, which only excellent work can bring. This is the joy of the artist, the carpenter, or the musician who finds rewards in his inner feeling of achievement, in creating something of beauty or value. Such men may work with great dedication, giving their *all* to their work. This can cause considerable distress to the wife and children. An example is the following letter of complaint I received:

*"We live in a peculiar area where most of the men work for the government in highly skilled jobs, most of them experimental. The mental challenge is extremely keen, the competition great, and the personal satisfaction tremendous. But the children don't have a father and the wives a husband. The short time my husband is home we are happy, but the job has his heart and soul."*

My comment is this: Men who lose themselves in their work have to neglect wives and children to some extent. They are the men, however, that make the most notable contributions to society. Our world couldn't exist as it does now if it weren't for such men. Men who have been fortunate enough to have wives who have understood and given them loyal support have been blessed and been able to reach their goals much easier. If you are married to such a man, count yourself fortunate.

> **Remember:** *It's better to have ten percent of a hundred percent man, than a hundred percent of a ten percent man.*

If your husband has a worthy and impelling goal in mind, give him the freedom to *reach for the stars*. When he is in pursuit of his goals his life may not be easy. He may have to work long hours and give himself wholeheartedly to his work. He may have *mountains to climb, rivers to cross, and battles to win.* Be supportive and you will be a key factor in his success, such as in the following experience:

### And Touch a Star

"I sat in *Fascinating Womanhood* class and listened while another wife told how in the past she had always pointed out her husband's flaws to prevent his ego from being inflated. Until *Fascinating Womanhood,* she said, she clearly saw it as her duty. Somewhere, deep inside of me, an alarm went off. Why were those words so familiar? Suddenly I knew. They were echoes of words I had probably never said out loud, but I had surely thought a thousand times and worse, believed them to be true. 'I saw it clearly as my duty . . . .'

"My husband, Bob, is a successful and well-known writer of songs and scripts for movies. He is like most creative men, a dreamer of dreams, his eyes on the stars. He expects each new project to be a great and wonderful success. Now I, on the other hand, am a realist. Nothing is perfect . . . everything cannot be great . . . there are degrees to success, I would point out. There is always another picture which gets better reviews, other songs getting more play, other writers getting more recognition. Clearly it was my duty to point this out and more.

"Please understand, I never meant to be unkind. Indeed, wasn't it kindness to show Bob reality? If the balloon doesn't go too high, would it then, not have so far to fall? Was I not his anchor? Surely I was helping my love to see the pitfalls on the ground by forcing his eyes off the stars. Until now, I believed that . . . but now that alarm was ringing in my head. I knew now what a terrible thing I had been doing to the man I loved and who loved me. An anchor? An anchor is a dead weight which keeps the boat from moving. I would not be that again. There are plenty of people to help keep Bob's feet on the ground—critics who are paid to judge his creative talents to others, producers who know if his product is good or bad, and of course, the audience, who ultimately applaud or not. There is no excuse for him to be criticized by me, the one person from whom he needs approval and admiration.

"Later that week we went to a screening of his new picture. He watched my reactions throughout the movie. Even before it ended I told him how really good it was—how proud

I was of him. He glowed with pride. Later, when we returned home our children asked, 'How did it go?' He looked over their heads and into my eyes and said, 'It must have been a masterpiece, your mother loved it.' Let others criticize—my husband still dreams his perfect dreams. The only difference is that he has a wife who now understands that a creative man cannot touch the stars unless he reaches out for them, without concerning himself too much with the pitfalls on the ground.''

Another thing to avoid is *outdoing* your husband for position or acclaim. Never try to achieve in a field in which he is trying to win acclaim, or seek an honor which would overshadow his success. If you are the one who has won recognition, it degrades his position of status. This problem is apparent with many famous women, especially movie and stage actresses. If they marry men who can outdo them there's no problem, but if the man simply cannot meet the competition of his wife's acclaim, it can defeat his drive for status. How can he impress her or anyone else with his meager efforts, if she has already won the honors of earth?

In summary, a man has a sacred duty to provide the living. He has an inborn need to *function* in this role, to *feel needed,* and to *excel women* in doing so. Everything is more ideal when the man is the sole provider. Work to this end, and put such a goal in high priority. However, many women of today work outside the home to help provide the income. This subject is covered in Chapter 21, The Working Wife.

### Why a Man Strives Diligently in His Work:

1. To provide an adequate living.
2. For status.
3. For excellence in his work.

### Assignment

If your husband is an adequate provider, tell him something like this: *"I appreciate how hard you work to provide the living. It's a great responsibility. How do you manage it so well?"* In this way you help him feel adequate as a provider.

# 11

## Family Finances

The man, in his duties as the leader and the provider, and the woman, in her duties as the wife and homemaker, share the responsibility of family finances. The proper division of concern is this:

| Husband's Role | Wife's Role |
|---|---|
| *Provide the Money* | *Be Thrifty* |
| *Manage the Money* | *Cooperate With His Plans* |
| *Concern, Worry* | *Provide Peaceful Home Life* |

As made clear in the Holy Scriptures, the man has the responsibility to provide the living. Since he is also the leader, it falls to him to manage the money and worry about it. Therefore, it is not the wife's responsibility to earn the living, manage the money, or worry about it. She should be given a household budget but should not be responsible for the overall management of the income.

As the wife, you have an important part to play in the success of family finances. You should be given a budget for household expenses. Manage this money well by developing *the womanly art of thrift*. You can measure your standard of living, not so much by your income as by how well you manage the money. Do your part by being thrifty and making your portion cover the needs. If your husband's income is low, you can be the key figure in the financial success of the family, being in a position to make or break him. Families with low incomes sometimes live in more comfort than those with more, due to the skill of money management.

If your husband is to succeed financially, he may have to

set new goals from time to time. This may mean a change of plans. Your cooperation, your willingness to sacrifice when necessary and adapt to new circumstances may be vital to his financial success. In such situations, if you do not approve of the change you have a right to express yourself. Take care, however, that your objections are not based on selfishness such as a fear of inconvenience, personal sacrifice, or minor disadvantages to your children.

Also provide a peaceful home atmosphere. When things are right at home your husband can think more clearly, and will be renewed in body and spirit, prepared to go back into the world to make another effort. When his home life is on an even keel he's more apt to succeed in his work.

### The Wife's Budget

A simple solution to common money problems is the wife's household budget, which covers food, clothing, household goods, personal items, or anything in regular demand. It should not include occasional things such as furniture, appliances, major household repairs, or remodeling. The budget should be advanced weekly or monthly. It should be a fair allowance, based on the husband's income, but hopefully generous enough to have some left over. This you should be allowed to keep, to save or to spend as you please, with no questions asked. This provides personal freedom and incentive to be thrifty.

Your husband should manage the rest of the money, paying the monthly bills such as gas, electricity, telephone, water, house payments, insurance, yard care, car expense, income taxes, and other expenses. As for furniture, household equipment, and other items not in the regular budget, work this out together, conscious of living within your income. If he manages his money well and accumulates an excess, although you are entitled to discuss its use, he should have the major jurisdiction and final say. This will provide him with incentive to be diligent in his work and increase his income.

When he contemplates spending a considerable amount of money from his savings for investments, he should consult you, but it's bad policy to make this a binding obligation. Disputes over money matters are a source of painful problems in marriage. Whatever you gain by having more control is lost in a dampened relationship. Try to understand that a man works hard for his money, and it's wise to allow him freedom over his excess, as long as you are not deprived of what you need.

## In Times of Financial Distress:

In periods of financial difficulty, when there never seems to be enough money to cover expenses, instead of getting a job as most women are inclined to do, consider the following:

1. *Reduce Expenses:* Review monthly expenses with your husband, such as house payments, utilities, car expense, insurance, music lessons, food, clothing, and anything else which you must pay for on a regular basis. Cut expense wherever possible. You may think this can't be done, but with a little thought it probably can. Selling one car may be possible, and could turn your situation around. Difficult as this may seem, it is not so difficult as the oppression of worry.

2. *Trim the Luxuries:* Next, trim the comforts and luxuries more drastically, so you are living well within your husband's income, with something to spare for savings. You may find it hard to forgo luxuries in a world that entices your desire in every conceivable way. Clever advertisements tempt us to buy the latest models in household equipment, furnishings, and even a bigger and better house. This desire is enhanced by an awareness that *other families have them.* Although these material things bring convenience, comfort, and pleasure, they don't compare to the peace which comes from living within your income. Many small luxuries, too, increase expenses. Make a list of them and see how many you can forgo.

## Problems in Family Finances

1. *Confusion of Roles:* The problem in our society is that some men and women have their financial roles confused. A man may think his only duty is to provide the living. He brings home his paycheck, hands it over to his wife, and expects her to manage the money. She pays the bills and worries about where the next dollar is coming from.

If, through her initiative, she is able to save part of the income, what happens? Her husband, as the leader in full command, reaches into the savings and spends the money for luxuries or investments. It would be different if he managed the money and worried about it. He would then have more right to use the excess money according to his best judgment, but not otherwise. The role of money management and control of the purse strings belong inseparably together. If the wife manages the money and worries about it, she should have the power of decision in investing it, or spending it.

There is further confusion of roles with women working to help provide the living. Because they are so busy working and worrying about finances, they neglect home duties. Their homes are in such a state of confusion that when the man comes home he doesn't have the peace he needs to revive himself. No wonder he has difficulty solving his money problems or making greater strides in his work.

Because women spend so much time away from home working, they learn extravagant habits of spending to save time. Food, clothes, and household goods are bought to save time rather than money. Fast disappearing is the womanly art of thrift, which is such a feeling of security to a family. What is the solution to these common problems we see in our society? The answer is to recognize financial roles and live accordingly.

2. *Stress for the Wife:* Serious problems can occur when the wife manages the money. For example, a man brought his paycheck home each week and handed it to his wife. She managed it well until several more children came along. It became increasingly difficult for her to cover expenses, causing her considerable stress and worry. In the meantime, her husband was quite carefree about money matters. She tried to explain their problems but he was not used to thinking about them.

The man was offered a higher-paying position in another state. When the husband and wife considered the proposition, the wife wanted him to accept the position to solve financial problems, but the husband saw no reason to do so. He preferred to stay in his comfortable environment. Because he was not managing the money he did not feel the financial pinch. This was not fair. *When a man forfeits his position as money manager, he should also forfeit his power of decision over money.*

Women were not designed to worry about money. They become depressed, lose sparkle and charm, and sometimes even become mentally and physically ill. They worry more intensely about money than men because, not being the bread-winner, they are helpless to increase the income. Of course they can go to work, but in so doing increase problems. Men worry about money, too, but they have more temperament for it and can do more about it. If they don't have enough money they can work a little harder to increase their income.

Some women take over financial management by choice or even by demand. This is usually because they don't trust their husbands to do a good enough job, or think they can do better. But even if the wife assumes this role by choice, there are losses to her. Being an efficient money manager can burden her with responsibility which can interfere with her domestic role. And if she becomes capable as a financier, it can mean a loss of womanliness.

3. *When a Man Makes a Mess of Things:* How would you handle this problem? Suppose you have been handling the money all along, then suddenly decide to give the job to your husband, trusting him to handle things. He willingly accepts and you peacefully turn your back on this part of your life. What if he makes a mess of things, gets behind in the house payments, doesn't pay the bills, overdraws the bank account, and a few other things? You are a nervous wreck. You don't want the job back, but what can you do? If you have this situation, try the following:

Let go more completely and turn your back on things. Don't be on the anxious seat, checking the books to see if he added right, or is neglecting anything. If he makes a mess of things let him suffer the consequences, no matter what they are. This is the only way he will learn.

Remember, if you have been handling the money, he has been denied experience and will have to learn by doing. Also, if you let go completely, the psychology is right. He will begin to feel responsible, to know that if anyone is to worry about the money, it will have to be him. And he will notice your relief, that you are happier. Let him know you are. As he sees you brighter he will try harder to make a go of things, to keep you happy.

## Children and Family Finances

Children should be protected from financial worry. They do not have the maturity to cope with money problems and therefore the problems seem exaggerated in their little minds. They should, however, be given a realistic picture of the income so they will not expect too much. And they should be taught how to earn money, save it, and spend it. The following are suggestions for reaching these objectives:

1. *Allowances:* Questions often arise in a family about allowances. Should a child be given an allowance or should he be taught to earn his money? A reliable rule to follow is this: When a child is small he should be given an allowance so he can learn the value of money. However, when you give a child an allowance, don't expect him to do jobs around the house as a compensation. He should be taught to do his jobs as his part of the family work. Otherwise he will get the idea that he must be paid for everything he does.

2. *Work:* When a child is old enough, he should be given a regular job with pay, and the allowance can be discontinued. The work can be part of the family routine, but it should be in addition to his regular jobs. It would be better if the job could be outside the family routine, such as a paper route or baby-sitting for another family, or producing something needed in the world.

3. *Managing the Money:* Even more important is for the child to learn to manage his money. Here is a good formula: Teach him at an early age to give one tenth to the Lord. This should go directly to your church. Out of what is left, instruct him to put half *or more* into his bank account. This is his solid saving for the future. This money will work for him, even when he is asleep. Out of the remaining half, encourage him to save half of this for something he wants. He could keep this in a special place such as a jar. If he saves for something he really wants, it will help him learn the purpose of working and the value of money. The rest of the money can be put in his purse for immediate needs and wants. With this amount he can be generous with himself and others.

## Rewards

Interesting things happen when a woman turns finances over to her husband, as in the following true experiences:

### He Exploded

"The turning point in my marriage came dramatically when I learned through *Fascinating Womanhood* of the separate responsibilities of husband and wife. During the six years we have been married my husband has handed all but a small amount of his salary to me to spend and pay bills as I wanted. After the third *Fascinating Womanhood* class I drove home with my mind made up that I didn't want control of the money. I approached my husband by saying that I could no longer carry the burden of handling the finances, he could do it much better, all the worry was getting me down, and I was not doing a very good job.

"Well, he just exploded, saying, 'So, you don't want to worry! Tough, you are going to, because I don't want it. If you haven't done a good job, it's your fault and you're going to learn to do a good job, and you're going to continue.' He walked around saying he had never had a say in the money or what I did. I assured him I would change and I would consult him before I did anything. He just laughed as though he didn't believe me. I was crying, but his attitude didn't change. He was so angry he threw all the books and bills on his footstool.

"I then got my *Fascinating Womanhood* book and asked him to please read the pages I opened for him, the ones *Fascinating Womanhood* said to have our husbands read. After reading the first pages about the man's role, where he is to be the guide, protector, and provider, his voice softened and he asked me about the book. I had not told him about the book before. I then had him read about family finances and the man's and woman's responsibilities there. He was quiet for a little while, then a very small smile came across his face and he said to please bring all the bills, bankbooks, and checkbooks. He worked from ten-thirty until midnight.

"The next week he gave me fifteen dollars, saying he had that much extra and to buy some things I had been wanting. My husband has complete control of the money now, and I am very happy. I used to spend several hours a week placing the money here and there. My husband spends only a few minutes every two weeks and has everything under control. I now ask my husband for what I need. I know he will give it to me if my desires are not selfish and if he can afford it.''

## My Mathematical Jungle

''After we lost two homes, one new car, and went through bankruptcy, I was almost a nervous wreck, trying to make the money go around. My checkbook was a mathematical jungle and statements never balanced. My husband was after me because we were always overdrawn at the bank. He wrote checks for what he wanted, and then I had to worry about bills. Then came *Fascinating Womanhood*. I soon found out that I shouldn't worry about these things, so I really made an effort to stop worrying. Now, I don't open the bills when they arrive.

''We recently had some friends come to visit us on their vacation. We hadn't seen them for about three years. She had only been in the house a short time when she said, 'What has happened to you?' I said, 'Nothing, just that I have gained weight.' 'No, not that,' she said, 'you aren't nervous any more. You used to shake all the time.'

''So I told her about *Fascinating Womanhood* and what it had done for me. She said she often wishes she didn't have to take care of the finances, so that night she told her husband about *Fascinating Womanhood* and the way to handle finances and asked him to take over the responsibility. Much to her surprise and delight, he said as soon as they got home he would try. It is so good to be free of the worry of the bills, and we are doing better financially than we have ever done before. Thank God for *Fascinating Womanhood*.''

## It Was a Risky Feeling

''In the past I have tried to handle the finances in the family, since my husband has been very irresponsible about money. You just can't imagine how foolish he has been, spending his money on motorcycles and other luxuries, always negligent about paying bills, and never able to hang on to any money. After studying *Fascinating Womanhood*, I became convinced that I should hand over the finances to him, regardless. It was a risky feeling, but he was willing to do it. To my surprise and even amazement, he has become a changed man. He is responsible and thrifty with his money and has developed leadership qualities. He now manages our money better than I used to.''

## Assignment

If you have been managing the finances and want to be relieved of this worry, read the principles in this chapter to your husband and discuss it with him. If he agrees, you're off to a good start. If not, say something like this: ''I can't handle this any longer. It's a burden to me. It wouldn't be nearly as difficult for you. You are a man. Please relieve me of this responsibility. Will you take it over completely?'' If he still refuses, don't make an issue of it at this time. Wait until you have applied all of the principles of *Fascinating Womanhood*.

# 12

## *Masculine Pride*

### *Don't Wound His Sensitive Masculine Pride*

What is a man proud of? He is proud of his *masculine qualities* we reviewed earlier. He has an inborn pride in his strong muscular body, his manly skills, abilities, and achievements. If any of these masculine traits are weak or missing, his pride will prompt him to obscure this lack from the world as much as he can. He is also proud of his capability as the guide, protector, and provider, and sensitive when not functioning fully in this manly calling, or when his efforts are not appreciated. Status in the world is important to him, impelling him to high achievements. Again, he is sensitive when his status is not recognized or appreciated, or when he fails to achieve the status he seeks.

The most important thing to learn on this topic is that *masculine pride is very sensitive*. A man cannot stand to have his masculinity *belittled, ridiculed, or treated with indifference*. Such an attack on his manhood is one of the most painful experiences he can suffer. Lacking insight into this subject causes untold misunderstandings between men and women. How many times have you made a casual remark to a man, only to have him snap back with a harsh reply or appear distant? Unaware of your mistake you may have wondered, "Now what did I say wrong?" Understanding these mistakes and how to avoid them should be a part of every woman's education.

### *How to Avoid Wounding His Pride*

*Never belittle, ridicule, or be indifferent to any part of his masculinity. Never suggest that he doesn't measure up in his manhood—in his masculine body, skills, ability, or achieve-*

*ments. In his efforts to care for his family, never imply that he could do better, or that someone else is doing better. Never indicate that his manly care and protection are not needed, that you could make it without him. Never ignore a demonstration of his masculinity. And take care that you never excel him in anything masculine.* Apply these rules to the following:

1. *His Masculine Body:* You can wound a man's pride if you ridicule or show indifference to any part of his masculine body, such as his beard, hair on his chest, muscular strength, endurance, or sex function. Never say, for example, *"I don't like beards,"* or *"Why did God make hair on men's chests?"* If he stands before you with his chest bare and his muscles flexed, hoping to win your admiration, don't act *indifferent.* And never imply that you dislike the male sex organs or their function.

Even more serious, a man cannot stand to have anyone notice a *lack* of masculine features such as if he is short, frail, or beardless. Never suggest he build up his muscles, or compare him to someone stronger or taller. If he is lacking in his sex function, avoid making an issue of it. Try to discover the cause and work for a solution, being careful not to injure his pride.

A man can be painfully humiliated to have *a woman excel him* in anything requiring masculine strength or skill, such as to lift a heavier weight, run faster or longer, or excel him in a sport which is considered masculine, especially one in which he takes pride. To excel a man in anything masculine is to *belittle him.* It makes him feel less of a man.

2. *Masculine Skills and Abilities:* Don't belittle, show indifference, or excel him in anything which requires masculine ability. This applies not only to skills in his work, but to other things such as carpentry, mechanics, fishing, hunting, masculine sports, math, or anything in which he has masculine pride. For example, if your car is stalled and he is trying to fix it, don't suggest he call a repairman. This would suggest that you think he is incapable of doing it himself. And if, through necessity, you must perform some masculine skill yourself, don't outshine him.

3. *Masculine Achievements:* A common way to hurt a man's pride is by *indifference* toward his achievements. For example, do you ever make the following mistakes?

- When he is talking about his latest accomplishment, yawn, glance out the window, continue reading the paper, or change the subject.
- If he recalls past triumphs, act bored and say to yourself, "How many times have I heard this before?"
- If he receives an honor for an achievement, act calm. Withhold praise so he won't get a big head.
- If he rushes home to tell you about the day's achievements, be too busy to listen.

4. *Masculine Goals, Dreams:* He is even more sensitive about achievements for the future. With goals already reached he knows he has something to be proud of. With those yet to come he's not so sure. Take care, therefore, not to wound his pride: Don't take a dim view of his dreams, throw cold water on them, dampen his enthusiasm, or doubt his ability to achieve them.

5. *Masculine Traits of Character:* A previous chapter referred to character traits which seem to be distinctly masculine—decisiveness, steadfastness, and aggressiveness, whereas women tend to be vacillating, submissive, and complacent. Do not, therefore, indicate that he is lacking in the masculine traits, or in any way inclined to be vacillating or submissive.

6. *His Masculine Role:* A masculine man is conscientious about his role as the guide, protector, and provider. Never indicate that he is not measuring up in this manly function, or that someone else is doing better. Never give him the impression that you could do better, or could get by just as well without him. Since his main function in life is to make the living, it is here his pride is most at stake. Let us, therefore, give careful attention to this part of the subject:

### Pride in His Role as the Provider:

Anything to do with his work—his masculine skills, ability, money, success, or achievements, will involve his manly pride. He has a special pride in seeing that his family is well cared for, that they do not suffer neglect, or lack the comforts and advantages of life. If he is to feel like a man, he must measure up in his masculine duties as their provider. The following are common ways women injure men's pride as breadwinners:

1. *The Working Wife:* If you work outside the home you lessen your husband's esteem as the sole provider. If you must work, be careful to not further diminish his pride in any of the following ways:

- Remind him that he couldn't make it without you.
- Complain about how hard you work, or how much you sacrifice because you work.
- Explain to everyone that you work because you have to, that the family could not get by without the extra income.
- Tell everyone how much your parents do for you and how you could not get by without their help.
- Excel him in your work: Do a better job. Advance to a higher position. Bring home more pay.

2. *The Stay-at-Home Wife:* Even if you never work outside the home, beware of mistakes which injure his pride in making the living. For example, never say, *"We can't afford it,"* or *"I wish we had a little more security."* Don't offer suggestions about how he can increase his income or admire someone who earns more money. And don't remind him how you scrimp and save to make his paycheck do, as in the following dialogue:

## Tom and Mary: (The Wrong Way)

Tom: (As he looks over his bills) *"It takes a lot of money to support a family."* (Hoping for praise)

Mary: *"Well, it's not my fault! I scrimp and save, sew all the children's clothes myself, make our bread, and never buy a thing for myself. Other women go to the beauty salon to have their hair done and buy a lot of expensive clothes, but I go without these things."* (Hoping to win appreciation)

Tom: *"Do you really go without?"* (Hoping she will reassure him that she doesn't)

Mary: *"I'm only trying to help. I would rather go without the things I need than see you worry."* (Hoping again for appreciation)

Tom: (Something inside of him happens, a mixture of resentment toward his wife for making him feel like a failure and a miserable feeling of being one.) He says with irritation, *"Guess I'm not much of a provider in your eyes, am I?"* (Mary looks up in bewilderment at his irritation and lack of appreciation for her self-sacrifice)

This is a perfect illustration of the lack of understanding between the sexes. The only reason Tom complained about the high cost of living was to win Mary's appreciation. She took it as criticism, that he thought her a spendthrift. Her defense as the scrimping wife was to let him know she was really trying to help. This was a blow to his pride. The following is an illustration of what she should have said:

### Tom and Mary: (The Right Way)

Tom: *"It takes a lot of money to support a family."*

Mary: *"Doesn't it, though. How have you managed so well? It must be a tremendous responsibility to provide for a family."*

Tom: (His self-esteem has doubled.) *"Oh, I don't mind it, but it does have its trying problems. But, I feel capable of the job! Yes, quite capable!"*

Mary: *"It's wonderful to feel secure and know that you will always provide for us!"* In the first illustration Mary made her husband feel like a failure, in the second, like a hero!

### Common Mistakes Women Make

The following true experiences demonstrate how women blindly wound masculine pride:

1. *Investment:* A man presented an idea to his wife for a business investment which would require considerable money. Although there were risks involved, returns were to be high. He thought the proposition over carefully, and acting on his best judgment, decided to go ahead. He then turned to his wife for approval. After hearing the plan she said, *"Well, if you want to lose all your money, go ahead!"* This belittling remark crushed his pride and made him angry.

This is a *touchy situation*. There's a ten-to-one chance the man could be *fleeced*. He very likely *could* lose all his money. When the wife feels it a hazard, she should speak out honestly, but in a feminine way, a way to not injure masculine pride. She could say, *"It sounds like a good idea and I can see why you are excited about it but for some reason, deep inside, I just don't feel right about it."* A man can't argue with *feelings*. To express yourself in a feminine way refer again to Chapter 8.

2. *Sports Equipment:* A man had an interesting and new idea for sports equipment. He was enthusiastic! When he explained the device to his wife, she said blandly, *"Let's consider the pros and cons."* This cold-water method dampened his enthusiasm and diminished his dream. Some other *cold-water* expressions are *"Let's be practical,"* or *"Let's be sensible."* It is not necessary to support an idea you lack confidence in, but remember, if you diminish masculine enthusiasm, you diminish masculine pride.

3. *Sunday School Teacher:* A woman wrote the following experience: *"My husband taught a Sunday School class and he did it very well. One day I suggested he ask our son to give part of the lesson in the form of visual aids. With an aggravated tone in his voice he said, 'What's the matter? Don't you like the way I do it?' 'Well, you could do better,' I said. He became violently angry, said that I had never appreciated him, that I had depreciated him in the eyes of his children and he had about had enough. He rushed out of the house, slammed the door, and was gone for several hours."* In this situation, when a man must rely on his son to give an adequate lesson, it would be painfully humiliating.

4. *Dinner Time:* A woman was stirring gravy on the stove. When her husband arrived he came into the kitchen and began talking to her, telling her of an incident that happened at work. With enthusiasm he told how his boss, who rarely gives compliments, had commended him for his performance on his job. The wife responded with, *"Well, isn't that wonderful! Jimmy, go out and turn off the water,"* then gave full attention to other details of the meal. Once again he tried to win her attention, but she said, *"Go tell the girls to wash for dinner."*

Remember, ladies, although cooking is a womanly virtue, the way to a man's heart is *not* "*through his stomach.*" Even more important is your interest and appreciation for him as a man. Although having meals on time deserves a high priority, there are times his soul is more hungry than his body.

5. *Business Failure:* A man was despondent over problems in his business. With loving affection his wife tried to cheer him. As he unfolded his problem she could see clearly that he was faced with possible failure. Eager to play the part of the perfect wife she courageously said, *"Honey, don't worry. If you fail in your business it won't matter. I will be content if you merely run a small grocery store."* The man snapped back harshly, *"Sometimes you say just the wrong things."*

What did she say wrong? She projected him as a failure, at least a failure in his eyes. His dream was not to run a small grocery store. He had high hopes for himself, but according to her he would have to settle for something less. Although a man must know that his wife will accept failure and cheerfully adapt to humble circumstances, he would like her to regard their situation as temporary, with *unshakable confidence in his ultimate success.*

What should she have said? She could have said, *"These are discouraging days for you, but they are part of being a success, as is evident in the lives of all successful men."* But she should not say, *"You will not fail."* This is unrealistic, is expecting too much of a man and again, the wrong thing to say.

Some women instinctively know the *right* thing to say when a man faces failure. For example, a man was faced with possible failure in a professional college. At a time when he was painfully discouraged and plagued with the probability of failing the semester exams his wife said, *"George, if you fail you will probably be a bigger and better man than if you pass."* This came as such a relief to the pressure he had been under that in spite of great odds, he passed.

Another case was a man who had been fired as manager of his company. At a moment of discouragement his wife said to him, *"Henry, this may be the door to opportunity, a stepping-stone to success."* He was so relieved he cried. And it was the door to opportunity, for he became more successful ten times over than when manager of the small company. The main point is this: The first lady projected her husband as small in the face of failure. The second and third ladies projected their husbands as bigger and better.

6. *Drama Teacher:* A drama teacher in production of a play asked his wife to be in charge of making the costumes. She worked long hours sewing, hoping her husband would be proud of her. Instead she noticed his growing antagonism. One evening he said, *"You're not interested in me. You're only interested in the costumes."* Surprised and hurt she couldn't understand his reaction.

Her failure was her all-consuming interest in the costumes rather than the play. She missed the opportunity to observe his talents as director, organizer, and teacher. Burying herself in the costumes, she felt the success of the play rested heavily on her shoulders, that he couldn't make it without her. He felt hurt by her indifference to his talent and success. And such is the sad misunderstanding between men and women.

## Who Wounds Him?

1. *His Background:* Undermining of pride may have begun in his earlier years. As a young man, the first sign of a beard may have brought ridicule from his brothers and sisters. Even his mother may have viewed it with disdain. His ideas and achievements were often passed over lightly. Most severe was likely his school environment where young people, anxious to elevate themselves, cut down their fellow students. Teachers, too, sometimes make belittling remarks.

2. *The Working World:* In the working world a man's pride is often brutally cut down. In some companies ability is questioned, backbiting common. Sadistic employers deliberately undermine employees. In the struggle for position men discredit one another. Often a creditor or customer offers cutting remarks. Workers are derided by their superiors. In professional schools a common policy is to cut down students' pride and undermine their confidence, to weed out the weak ones. The same policy is found in military training programs.

3. *His Wife:* As we have already learned, the wife is often the one to wound masculine pride by belittling remarks or indifference. Since she is present on a daily basis, she has a more profound effect on him than anyone, to build or destroy.

Now, let us turn our attention to the harmful effects of wounded pride:

## 1. Humiliation

The most immediate effect of injured pride is the *pain of humiliation,* which is felt in a variety of sharp, biting, or deflating ways. You have touched upon the most sensitive part of his nature. It is one of the most uncomfortable feelings a man can experience so that the woman who causes it becomes repugnant to him. No wonder he reacts by being cold or explosive. In addition to humiliation, the following problems may occur:

## 2. Reserve

By reserve we don't mean bashfulness or timidity. The latter applies to few men, whereas reserve is an attribute of all. When a man's pride is wounded over and over again, he tends to build a wall of reserve, to protect himself from the pain of further humiliation. This wall is called *his reserve*.

When a man's reserve is present, it presents a problem: On the one hand he has a continuing need for admiration. Receiving admiration builds his pride, makes him feel manly. Therefore he longs to confide his feelings, to reveal his noble deeds and secret dreams with the hope of receiving admiration. On the other hand he is reluctant to do so. Why? Because he fears the possibility of ridicule or indifference. This would diminish his feeling of masculine pride.

Nothing is so frightening to a man as the horror of making a fool of himself. He therefore subdues the impulse to seek admiration. Nothing but the absolute certainty that his ideas will be met with appreciation rather than contempt or indifference will induce him to throw off his armor of reserve and reveal to others the things that mean the most to him. And even when he does, the slightest hint of misunderstanding or disrespect will shatter the illusion and drive him behind his wall of reserve again.

To understand the nature of this reserve, take for example a young girl who has won a young man's confidence so that he is unfolding his secret hopes and dreams. As he begins to reveal the finer traits of his character, she has a wonderful opportunity to acknowledge his manly qualities. At this point, let her but indicate by a yawn or a glance out the window that she is not the least bit interested, and he will wince as if struck by a lash. It may be the first time in his life he has ventured to express such feelings. If the girl acts indifferent at such a crisis and fails to recognize its significance to him, she has, so far as he is concerned, a heart of stone. In the future, no matter where or when he meets her, he will not risk a similar rebuff. He will be behind his protective wall of reserve.

Such is the case with every man. His longing for admiration, great as it is, is not sufficient to make him throw off his habitual cloak of reserve except in rare instances. And even then he will quickly resume it unless he can bask in the full glow of an all-comprehending sympathy. The one characteristic seems diametrically opposed to the other. Together they constitute a problem difficult enough to tax any woman's wits.

Occasionally a man will clam up and not talk at all. This is called *going into his shell*. He climbs inside himself, locks the door, and pulls down the blinds, making it impossible to get next to him. This tendency for a man to go into his shell is common. The higher the caliber of the man, the more he tends to draw into himself when his pride is hurt.

In the ideal marriage there should be no wall of reserve. A man should feel comfortable expressing himself without fear of humiliation, confident that his conversation will be met with sincere respect. If you detect this reserve in your husband, take measures to eliminate it. If you don't, he may be tempted to seek the company of another woman who can fill this important need in his life.

### How to Break Down the Wall of Reserve:

When a man is behind his wall of reserve, you can't pull him out by saying "Why are you so quiet?" or "Why don't you ever tell me anything?" Break down his wall by doing the following:

1. *Accept Him:* This again is the first step. When you overlook his faults and look to his better side, he will be more trusting of you, can more easily confide his innermost feelings.

2. *Don't Belittle Him:* Make sure you do not make mistakes which only strengthen his wall of reserve, the very mistakes which created it. You will have to completely eliminate any belittling remarks or forms of indifference, or his reserve will be a permanent problem.

3. *Admire Him:* Your generous and sincere admiration will do more than any other measure to win his confidence and break down his wall of reserve.

4. *Don't Be Critical of Others:* If you are a faultfinder, with an eye open to the faults of others, he will be afraid to expose his innermost thoughts to your criticism and contempt. You must not tell him of your poor opinion of this person or that, or reveal the faults of envy, jealousy, or contempt. You must not make light of anyone. Even when you cannot approve of what someone says or does, show appreciation for his motives or basic character. The more ability you manifest as a critic, the less inclined he will be to expose himself to your criticism. He must be assured that his confidences will be met with an admiring interpretation and not a faultfinding one.

5. *Appreciate the Good in Others:* If you appreciate the good in others, he will be assured that you will see the finer side in him too. When he confides his innermost feelings, he will not fear your ridicule and contempt. Search for the good in everyone you meet and express your appreciation for them. In this way you develop a charitable character that encourages him to lay down his reserve.

6. *Hold Confidences Sacred:* Never repeat to others things which have been told to you in confidence. If you disclose the secrets of others, he will take it for granted that you will disclose his also, and thus subject him to the same ridicule or indifference he hopes to avoid. Unless he thinks he is confiding his innermost hopes and ambitions to one who will not betray them to others, he will not confide them to you no matter how sure he is of your personal admiration of him. Even though he knows you admire him, how does he know *others* will? He cannot risk contempt from anyone.

When his reserve seems to be disappearing and he begins to disclose things about himself to admire, do not imagine that his reserve has disappeared altogether. Further eliminate it by continuing to follow the six steps suggested. During this time make certain that everything he confides to you is met with understanding. Otherwise his first confidence will never be followed by another.

If your first response is always appreciative, he will add another confidence and another until at last, if your reaction is never disappointing, he will lay bare before you every motive, ideal, and hope, that stirs within him. Admiration is too important to him to deny himself, once he has had the full enjoyment of it.

Remember, however, that his reserve is always in the background, ready to appear at the first sign of criticism or indifference, even when the criticism is only apparent in your attitude toward other people. You can therefore understand how difficult it is for a woman with a weak, faultfinding character to keep the reserve in the background long enough for the man to express himself.

### 3. The Numbing Effect

When a man's pride has been injured over a long period of time, he learns to protect himself from the hurt by hardening himself against it. He learns not to care. His senses become dull or numb.

In Dr. Edrita Fried's book, *The Ego in Love and Sexuality,* she speaks of this numbing effect. Dr. Fried says the danger is this: When we become numb to pain, we become numb to pleasure as well. *"We pay dearly for the self-induced numbness, for while it relieves pain, it also reduces our ability to experience pleasant emotions and respond to pleasant stimulation. Unresponsiveness, like an indiscriminate scythe, mows down the flowers with the weeds."*

The man who becomes numb to the pain of humiliation separates himself from pleasure as well. He no longer feels the hurt, but neither does he see the beauty of a summer day, delight in the laughter of little children, or respond to his wife's affection. His sexual feelings may diminish and he can even become impotent.

### 4. Dishonesty

A man with a sensitive pride is sometimes tempted to be dishonest. For example, when he faces failure, his fear of humiliation can prompt him to conceal the truth, make false statements, or put the blame on someone else. Since his pride is most sensitive with his wife, she may have the most distorted picture of all. This leads to problems, as in the following example:

A man facing a business failure was afraid to tell his wife the truth. Because he withheld important facts, she mistakenly believed her husband innocent and demanded restitution from others involved, placing her husband in an embarrassing position. Why did he deceive her? Because of masculine pride. He was afraid of what she would think of him. Although all human beings try to avoid a disclosure of their failures, when masculine pride is at stake the problem is painfully acute.

If a man is unable to obscure the truth, he may rationalize his mistakes by justifying himself, blaming circumstances, others, or even his wife. A man sometimes puts up quite a tough argument in an effort to preserve his pride. But the more he tries to conceal the truth, the more confusing it can become, for what he says may be in contradiction to what appears to be the true facts.

You can help a man avoid dishonesty by understanding his pride in the face of failure. Keep in mind that what you think of him is uppermost in his mind. Assure him that you will always uphold him, even in the most trying circumstances. With your complete trust in his manliness, he will be less afraid to expose the hard truth to you.

## 5. *When a Man Belittles Himself*

In this case a man deliberately puts himself down by emphasizing his weaknesses, mistakes, or failures. Why does he do this? Because his pride is weak or injured, and he needs someone to bolster it. The only means he has to obtain the admiration he needs is to belittle himself. He hopes that when he puts himself down, someone will disagree, and build him up. To respond, offer a kind word of encouragement, but it's best to not lavish him with praise. This may encourage his tendency to belittle himself. Instead seek other opportunities to appreciate and admire him, and thus strengthen his masculine ego.

## Your Responsibility for His Masculine Pride

1. *Don't Wound Him:* Take care that you don't wound his masculine pride, that you are never the guilty one. If he returns from the battleground of life and is further subjected to contempt or indifference, it will undermine his confidence and alter his feelings for you.

2. *Heal His Wounds:* Heal the wounds inflicted by others. Become his good angel, the one who builds him up when others have torn him down. When you do, you become indispensable to his happiness and contribute greatly to his overall success in life. No one can take your place in ministering the healing balm that keeps men going.

If you fail on both counts, if you add injury to injury and utterly fail to build his self-esteem in his hour of need, you can destroy him and his feelings for you. A woman is in a precarious position; she can *build or destroy a man* according to how she deals with his masculine ego.

When you see the sensitivity of a man's nature, you know how careful you must be in conversation. You cannot permit yourself to have an *unbridled tongue* and say anything you please. You cannot pour out your heart to him as you would to a mentor. You must withhold feelings and confessions which would wound his sensitive pride. However, when you learn to converse in a way to build rather than destroy, you can carry on intimate conversations with a man and feel a closeness that will be *bone of his bone and flesh of his flesh.* You will bridge the distance as in the following true experience:

### He Resigned His Ship

"My husband was away on a four-month oceanographic research expedition off the coast of Peru for the U.S. government when I took the F.W. class. These expeditions have been his life. For the past five years the trips have been longer than the usual six weeks, but always they are professionally exciting and all our men friends envy the color and glamour of his life.

"As for me, I was beginning to think I had all the disadvantages and none of the advantages of a divorce. Growing resentment colored all facets of my life. The task of keeping the house and four children fed and clothed grew harder, and I was beginning to find my children increasingly irritating. As the resentments grew I found his times at home less and less a pleasure. I could feel a frightening hatred beginning to build up within me toward my husband. I have never hated anyone before in my life.

"Though we weathered many serious storms, our marriage seemed to be drifting toward the shoals, and we both seemed helpless and powerless to do anything to rescue it. We even talked about it. Did other people have this problem? Of one thing I was certain. I simply did not understand men!

"The first shock of the F.W. class jolted me out of my former pattern of thinking. I had the courage, for the first time in my life, to look inward, not out there for someone to blame. In the honest probing I found something (unknown to me before) that stood out like a neon light! Many of the things which are in F.W are actually things my husband tried to tell me, but I didn't listen. Also, the times in our marriage we had enjoyed long stretches of happiness and satisfaction were the times I was unconsciously going along with its teachings.

"Over and over again I can see a long series of mistakes. Now I marvel that this proud brilliant man did not leave me long ago. I wept at the humiliations I had inflicted on him. How many other women, through lack of understanding, continue to wound the men they have professed to love?

"I started to write him letters, applying the principles of F. W. as best I could, and undoing my mistakes. I also talked with him by phone, and due to my changed attitude I immediately noticed a warm response in my husband. He even called me 'darling' a few phone calls later.

"One of his letters included a brochure on his present expedition. It is so exciting and represents the peak of his career. Even though I have wanted for twenty-three years to have him resign his ship and spend his life with me and the children, it came to me crystal clear that I really haven't the right to ask him to give up work in which he finds so much genuine joy. I told him this in my next letter.

"To my surprise, his next letter ran down his job. He said he was disappointed in much that I had taken for granted as exciting. The unbelievable part is that he is resigning his position and coming home to us! He is buying a farm in Washington where we can all be together permanently. His letters now say, 'Hurry June.' That's the month he gets back home."

## The Great Wall of China

"I was feeling very depressed and discouraged with life. There seemed no purpose or reward, and I seemed to myself a very unimportant thing. I would try to pull myself out of this by saying, you are the mother of two children, so therefore you do have at least an obligation to raise them to be good citizens. The things I had always enjoyed held no joy anymore. I would sit and knit or sew and strive for that ounce of pleasure I was sure it would bring. But nothing, I was empty.

"I can look back now and see where my trouble started, but at the time I was lost. My husband and I had been married ten years before we had any children. Our marriage was average; really no troubles or problems were insurmountable. I worked most of those years and was content. Then two children later and in the midst of building our dream house I started becoming ill. I experienced a dreadful, 'anxious' feeling that I was to be tortured with for eighteen months. It was an endless round of doctors whom I tried to convince that something was wrong with me. They could find nothing.

"Finally in desperation, convinced that my sanity was leaving, I went for psychiatric treatment for three months. I learned that I was emotionally mixed-up. In the course of the sessions the doctor managed to convince me that I was married to an immature, selfish tyrant (which is not the case at all). He convinced me that I was right and my husband wrong.

"Well, I thought I had problems before, but now I set about to change my husband. I managed to do it, all right. I changed him from a loving, tender, and very understanding man to a violent, uncommunicative, withdrawn tyrant who did things so out of his character that even he could not account for them. Bit by bit, nag by nag, accusation by accusation, I built the biggest and most insurmountable wall of reserve in my marriage anyone ever saw. It made the Great Wall of China look like a child's toy.

"Once the wall was up, I tried to tear down my husband, instead of the wall. In return I received threats of desertion, violent outbursts, and saw a happy man retreat into such deep depressions that I feared at times he might take his own life. Of course, I was all right. I even told him it was a phase he was going through and I wished he would hurry up.

"I used to ask him why he didn't appreciate me. I was everything a wife should be. Ha! Oh, yes, I kept the house clean, the children clean, and I couldn't help it if I was moody and depressed and didn't ever feel good. Anyone who tried as hard at marriage as I did and sacrificed so much just trying to win my husband's approval had a right to feel like me.

"One day when I was reciting my usual tale of woe and misery to a friend, she gave me *Fascinating Womanhood* and said, "Please read this and pay careful attention to Inner Happiness and Worthy Character." I read it and it seemed too deep for me. I thought, I will never be able to be like that. I will try, but I just don't think I can.

"And I can say here and now that I never would have been able to without the help of my *Fascinating Womanhood* teacher. She was a magnificent inspiration. I began to live *Fascinating Womanhood,* and the walls of reserve soon came down. *Fascinating Womanhood* has saved my marriage and made my husband happy once again. I am now enjoying the flowers and trying very hard to remember *Fascinating Womanhood* every day."

### He Became a Changed Man

"My husband and I have been married six years and we have two children. When I became pregnant with my last child, my husband became very cold and indifferent. He said he didn't love me and said I was like a mother to him. He began having an affair with another woman. After the baby was born I filed for divorce, and we got a settlement and separated. But my husband didn't want a divorce.

"We went to a marriage counselor for help, and he told us what was wrong but didn't tell us how to make things right. After being separated for three months, we went back together on a six-month trial. We were both miserable separated. We were from very religious homes and attended and were very active in our own church when this happened.

"During this trial period our marriage was doing fairly

well, but was shaky and wasn't what I wanted. I didn't feel the tenderness I wanted and needed so desperately. I didn't feel loved like I wanted to be. I felt like our marriage was very insecure, but I didn't know what to do about it. I felt helpless and worried constantly that my husband would find another woman to have an affair with.

"At this time I heard about *Fascinating Womanhood*. The first time I practiced it, I saw my husband's face light up and felt a tenderness, though small, toward me. We had had very little communication, but when I started admiring him and giving him the sympathetic understanding that you describe, he became a changed man. His shell has disappeared, and he tells me all his problems and treats me with a lovely tender feeling. It is a marvelous experience, one I have always dreamed of but never had. The more I admire him the more love I feel from him.

"I now have a wonderful peace within. I have no fear of him leaving me for another woman because I am giving him the admiration and love he needs and wants, and in turn I receive the love I so desperately need."

### Sensitive Masculine Pride:

1. Masculine Body
2. Masculine Skills and Abilities
3. Masculine Achievements
4. Masculine Goals and Dreams
5. Masculine Traits of Character
6. Masculine Role

### Assignment

1. Don't belittle him or show indifference to his manliness.
2. If he has a wall of reserve, take steps to break it down.

# 13

## Sympathetic Understanding

To be a sympathetic, understanding wife, you need to comprehend what a man faces in his total life. If you have taken the message of *Fascinating Womanhood* to heart, you already have a broad view. You have gained insight into his masculine needs and feelings. You have learned of his pressing burden to earn the living, his drive for status, and his sensitive masculine pride. This perspective helps you understand his anxieties, concerns, and pressures. It should have made you patient, forgiving, and more adaptable to circumstance. It should have given you understanding in the broad sense. Let's see if you have dropped any of the old tendencies and become a more sympathetic, understanding wife.

### The Unsympathetic Wife

If you have lacked sympathetic understanding you have probably shown it in a number of ways. You have probably complained when your husband was late for dinner, retreated to his den to be by himself, neglected the children, didn't get around to doing the yard work or repair jobs, was tight with his money or worked long hours away from home. You failed to count his many hours of labor away from home as doing something for the family. This has always been a mystery to me. If a man doesn't play with his children when he comes home it doesn't mean he is neglecting them, since he has spent his entire day working for their support.

### The Sympathetic Wife

Let me portray the sympathetic wife who understands her husband's world of work: When he is cross or irritable, she

173

tries to understand the pressures of his work. Her sympathy makes her forgive his bad behavior. If he is late for dinner, she measures her own inconvenience against what may have been required of him and counts her problem as insignificant. Her husband, instead of coming home to more problems, enters a haven of rest and comfort.

When he comes home each day, he is always greeted with a warm smile, and never problems. She does not let the children rush in and climb on him, or make complaints. After they greet their father, she leads him into the bedroom where she can make him comfortable. She arranges his pillows, takes off his shoes and encourages him to relax. She allows him this time of peace before exposing him to the rest of the family. He works to protect and shelter her, and this is her way of protecting him.

If he doesn't get around to repairing the fence or painting the kitchen, she tries to understand that although these jobs seem important to her, they may seem insignificant to him in comparison with the responsibility of his work. And she also understands that when he comes home, he often must regain something of himself for the next day's work. The household repair jobs seem secondary to his rejuvenation of body and spirit. Her sympathetic attitude makes her patient with his neglect of home duties.

If he doesn't take her out to dinner or other social events, she understands this neglect, also. She, of course has been home all day and needs the diversion. But he has a need which supersedes hers, the need to recuperate from his strenuous life. Taking her out would only add to his burdens, or so he feels. In weighing out both of their needs, she forgoes her own in preference to his greater need to unwind.

She may have a desire for a few additional home furnishings which would make their home life more enjoyable. But she asks for only those things they can well afford. Much as these things mean to her, her husband's health and happiness mean more.

She has a sympathy for his desire to get ahead and plan for the future, a future which means added expenses and less capacity to earn a living. She cooperates fully with his efforts to save money. She is not jolted when her husband wants to invest money to make more money. If she doesn't agree with his plans to invest, she expresses herself honestly but her opposition is softened by her sympathy for his motives.

A challenging problem is when the husband spends a great amount of time away from home striving for success. He may neglect his wife and children, so that much of the training and care of the family is left to the wife. The wife and even the children may interpret this as a lack of interest in their welfare and even a lack of love. The home and family life, which is the very center of their existence, seems secondary to the father's success. But the sympathetic wife doesn't look at it this way. She understands that her husband's motives are not due to lack of interest but *because of his love and concern for them*. He is conscious of their needs now and in the future, and wants to provide opportunities for their future welfare.

The woman with this attitude doesn't feel neglected, nor does she feel her children are neglected. Children tend to adopt the attitude of their mother. If she doesn't feel her children are neglected, they won't feel neglected. With such a family atmosphere the husband is greatly aided toward success. He has the comfort and assurance he needs to function at full capacity. And if he is always met with understanding, you can count on it he will be home as often as possible. This is the way to bring a man home to your side, *not by the force of an unwholesome obligation*.

Sometimes a man spends time away from home for a different reason. Instead of working for the welfare of the family, his time is spent in pleasures, sporting events, or with his men friends. In this case the man's neglect seems without justification. But the sympathetic wife will not condemn him. She looks to herself for the answers, asks herself if she may have driven him away by an unsympathetic attitude of the past. If she resolves to give him the sympathy he needs, he will probably lose his other interests and realize that his greatest pleasure is his family. Here again, she doesn't bring him home by force, but by building a home life he will seek of his own free will.

We have been referring to his need for sympathy in general, for his burdens in making the living, his drive for status, and his sensitive pride. The following are specific times he needs true sympathy:

## 1. When He Lets Down at Home

The burden of his work and his drive for status explains why men so often let down at home, why they become cross, impatient, difficult to live with, or fail to fix the roof or mow the lawn. These jobs may seem unimportant compared to the demands of his work. He may ignore his children and neglect his wife. Women have said, *"My husband doesn't treat his family as well as he does total strangers."* The truth is that he is often tired of being his best for total strangers and would like to relax and be his worst for his family, hoping they will overlook it. In Florida Scott Maxwell's book *Women and Sometimes Men,* she explains this tendency for a man to let down at home:

*"One of the poignant paradoxes in the life of a woman is that when a man comes to her, he so often comes to recover his simple humanity, and to rest from being at his best. So a woman frequently has to forego his better side, taking it on trust as a matter of hearsay, and she accepts his lesser side as her usual experience of him. . . . While she wishes to admire him she may lack the knowledge, and perhaps the intelligence, to understand the side by which he wins acclaim. She sees him collapse into his home, accepts his need of collapse, indeed receives him with every antenna alert, yet she may forego his superiority with regret. She longs to see his greatness, but has to meet the claim of his smallness."*

## 2. When He Is Discouraged

The tendency to be discouraged is common among men. Whether rich or poor, learned or unlearned, few men escape this unpleasant experience. In fact, the more learned, talented, and aggressive men tend to have the most intense suffering. Abraham Lincoln had periods of depression in which he merely sat and brooded or read the newspapers. At one time he wrote, *"I am now the most miserable man alive."* Most men of great responsibility have periods of discouragement. But all men have times when they are depressed, times when they need sympathetic understanding.

Realizing the nature of men in today's world, we can see

why they become discouraged. It's a world with many demands and little security. Men worry about money, their work, children, and the future. In striving for advancement, a man may have lost rather than won the position he had been seeking. Or, perhaps too much is expected of him. There are demands he can't meet, problems he can't solve, or just a bad day.

A woman has the power to break this spell of gloom and turn his attitude around. But she must know *what to do,* and especially *what not to do.* If she succeeds, she can be of service to him in a most important way. Remember, one of the functions of a woman is to *shed joy around, and cast light upon dark days . . . is not this to render a service?*

## How to Give True Sympathy

1. *Suffer With Him:* Without asking too many questions, try to understand what he is going through. Share his feelings. Suffer with him. *It is not necessary to understand the cause of his problems,* but try to understand his pain and express sympathy for that pain. Say something like this: "You poor dear, oh, you poor, poor dear. You are discouraged now but remember, this is a dark hour that will pass." Inspire hope in his heart that there is a brighter day ahead.

2. *Build Him:* No matter what the situation, have an unshakable faith in his better side. Express appreciation for his true worth and admiration for his masculinity. Let him know that you still believe in him and his ability.

3. *Don't Minimize His Problems:* Don't say, for example, *"There isn't anything to worry about,"* or *"Your problems are just in your imagination,"* or *"Life isn't as tough as you think."* And don't advise him to *count his blessings,* by saying such things as *"Think of all you have to be thankful for."* These statements show a lack of sympathy, make him feel ashamed for letting life get him down, and that if he were a stronger man he wouldn't be discouraged. Pointing out blessings has merit on some occasions, but *it is not sympathy.* The realization that he has blessings makes his discouragement worse. It seems more inexcusable.

4. *Don't Offer to Help Solve His Problems:* In the early stages of his problems don't give suggestions or offer your

help. This may be appreciated later. What he wants now is your sympathy, your appreciation for his efforts, and your willingness to overlook his errors in judgment.

5. *Don't Let His Gloom Rub Off on You:* Try not to become discouraged along with him. Maintain a cheerful attitude, especially optimism. But don't be too lighthearted as this shows lack of sympathy for suffering. He wants you to feel *with him*.

Don't expect an immediate change in spirits. Allow time for him to recover. Even if he says nothing, be assured that your sympathy has been helpful and appreciated. In the meantime, whenever he seems discouraged continue to show sympathy.

It is interesting to note that when a woman is discouraged her needs are different. Although she wants sympathy, she wants something more from a man. She looks to him for help and guidance in times of trouble. He is her guide and protector, and therefore her advisor and helper. A man is different. *It is not her advice he hungers for, no matter how much he may need it, but her sympathy, comfort, and a restoration of his confidence in himself*. And such is another difference between men and women.

### 3. When He Faces Failure

A particular time a man needs sympathetic understanding is *when he faces failure*. This can be a time of agony for a man, not so much for the failure itself as the humiliation. His status is at stake as never before, with the world and especially with his wife. His protective feeling for his family, to provide for them adequately, is ever in his mind. If he must lower his standard of living he faces the painful realization that he must subject them to humiliation and discomfort. The wife who can meet her husband's failure with understanding sympathy, and has the fineness of character to adapt to humble circumstances, meets a need in his life that nothing can equal.

A man may never fully appreciate his wife until she is put to the test of his failure. His defeat is her golden opportunity to show her true worth. When a woman meets such a crisis with *sympathetic understanding,* and *the strength of a noble character,* her husband can come to idolize her and love her as never before. An illustration of a woman who met such a crisis with *angelic perfection* is found in Washington Irving's essay, *The Wife*, which I quote in full:

## The Wife

My intimate friend Leslie had married a beautiful and accomplished girl, who had been brought up in the midst of fashionable life. She had, it is true, no fortune; but that of my friend was ample, and he delighted in the anticipation of indulging her in every elegant pursuit and administering to those delicate tastes and fancies that spread a kind of witchery about the sex. "Her life," said he, "shall be like a fairy tale."

The very difference in their characters produced a harmonious combination—he was of a romantic and somewhat serious cast; she was all life and gladness. I have often noticed the mute rapture with which he would gaze upon her in company, of which her sprightly powers made her his delight; and how, in the midst of applause, her eye would still turn to him as if there alone she sought favor and acceptance.

When leaning on his arm, her slender form contrasted finely with his tall, manly person. The fond, confiding air with which she looked up to him seemed to call forth a flush of triumphant pride and cherishing tenderness as if he doted on his lovely burden for its very helplessness. Never did a couple set forward on the flowery path of early and well-suited marriage with a fairer prospect of felicity.

It was the misfortune of my friend, however, to have embarked his property in large speculations; and he had not been married many months, when, by a succession of sudden disasters, it was swept from him, and he found himself reduced almost to penury. For a time he kept his situation to himself and went about with a haggard countenance and a breaking heart. His life was but a protracted agony; and what rendered it more insupportable was the necessity of keeping up a smile in the presence of his wife; for he could not bring himself to overwhelm her with the news.

She saw, however, with the quick eyes of affection, that all was not well with him. She marked his altered looks and stifled sighs and was not to be deceived by his sickly and vapid attempts at cheerfulness. She tasked all her sprightly powers and tender blandishments to win him back to happiness; but she only drove the arrow deeper into his soul. The more he saw cause to love her, the more torturing was the thought that he was soon to make her wretched.

A little while, thought he, and the smile will vanish from that cheek—the song will die away from those lips—the luster of those eyes will be quenched with sorrow; and the happy heart which now beats lightly in that bosom will be weighed down like mine, with the cares and miseries of the world. At length he came to me, one day, and related his whole situation, in a tone of the deepest despair.

When I had heard him through I inquired, "Does your wife know all this?"

At the question he burst into an agony of tears. "For God's sake!" cried he, "if you have any pity on me, don't mention my wife; it is the thought of her that drives me almost to madness."

"And why not?" said I, "She must know it sooner or later; you can not keep it long from her, and the intelligence may break upon her in a more startling manner than if imparted by yourself; for the accents of those we love soften the harshest tidings. Besides, you are depriving yourself of the comforts of her sympathy; and not merely that, but also endangering the only bond that can keep hearts together—unreserved community of thought and feeling. She will soon perceive that something is secretly preying upon your mind; and true love will not brook reserve; it feels undervalued and outraged when even the sorrows of those it loves are concealed from it."

"Oh, but my friend! to think what a blow I am to give to all her future prospects—how I am to strike her very soul to the earth, by telling her that her husband is a beggar! that she is to forgo all the elegances of life—all the pleasures of society—to shrink with me into indigence and obscurity! to tell her that I have dragged her down from the sphere in which she might have continued to move in constant brightness, the light of every eye, the admiration of every heart! How can she bear poverty? She has been brought up in all the refinements of opulence. How can she bear neglect? She has been the idol of society. Oh! it will break her heart—it will break her heart!"

After additional patience, I finally persuaded Leslie to go home and unburden his sad heart to his wife. The next morning

I was eager to know the results. In inquiring, I found that Leslie had made the disclosure.

"And how did she bear it?"

"Like an angel! It seemed rather to be a relief to her mind, for she threw her arms round my neck, and asked if this was all that had lately made me unhappy. But, poor girl!" added he, "she can not realize the change we must undergo. She has no idea of poverty but in the abstract; she has only read of it in poetry, where it is allied to love. She feels yet no privation; she suffers no loss of accustomed conveniences nor elegances. When we come practically to experience its sordid cares, its paltry wants, its petty humiliations, then will be the real trial."

Some days afterward he called upon me in the evening. He had disposed of his dwelling house, and taken a small cottage in the country, a few miles from town. He had been busied all day in sending out furniture. The new establishment required few articles, and those of the simplest kind.

He was going out to the cottage where his wife had been all day superintending its arrangement. My feelings had become strongly interested in the progress of the family story, and as it was evening, I offered to accompany him. He was wearied with the fatigues of the day, and as he walked out, fell into a fit of gloomy musing.

"Poor Mary!" at length broke, with a heavy sigh from his lips.

"And what of her?" asked I; "has anything happened to her?"

"What!" said he, darting an impatient glance; "is it nothing to be reduced to this paltry situation, to be caged in a miserable cottage, to be obliged to toil almost in the menial concerns of her wretched habitation?"

"Has she, then, repined at the change?"

"Repined! She has been nothing but sweetness and good humor. Indeed, she seems in better spirits than I have ever known her; she has been to me all love and tenderness and comfort!"

"Admirable girl!" exclaimed I. "You call yourself poor, my friend, you never were so rich, you never knew the boundless treasures of excellence you possess in that woman "

"Oh! but, my friend, if this, our first meeting at the cottage were over, I think I could then be comfortable. But this is her first day of real experience; she has been introduced into a humble dwelling; she has been employed all day in arranging the miserable equipment; she has for the first time, known fatigues of domestic employment; she has, for the first time, looked around her on a home destitute of everything elegant, almost everything convenient; and now may be sitting down exhausted and spiritless, brooding over a prospect of future poverty."

There was a degree of probability in this picture that I could not gainsay; so we walked on in silence. After turning from the main road up a narrow lane, so thickly shaded with forest trees as to give it a complete air of seclusion, we came in sight of the cottage. It was humble enough in its appearance for the most pastoral poet; and yet it had a pleasing rural look. A wild vine had overrun one end with a profusion of foliage; a few trees threw their branches gracefully over it; and I observed several pots of flowers tastefully disposed about the door, and on the grass-plot in front.

A small wicket gate opened upon a footpath that wound through some shrubbery to the door. Just as we approached, we heard the sound of music. Leslie grabbed my arm. We paused and listened. It was Mary's voice, singing in a style of the most touching simplicity, a little air of which her husband was peculiarly fond. I felt Leslie's hand tremble on my arm. He stepped forward, to hear more distinctly. His step made a noise on the gravel walk.

A bright, beautiful face glanced out of the window and vanished, a light footstep was heard, and Mary came tripping forth to meet us. She was in a pretty rural dress of white; a few wildflowers were twisted in her fine hair; a fresh bloom was on her cheek, her whole countenance beamed with smiles. I had never seen her look so lovely.

"My dear Leslie," cried she, "I am so glad you are come! I have been watching and watching for you; and running down the lane, and looking for you. I've set out a table under a beautiful tree behind the cottage; and I've been gathering some of the most delicious strawberries, for I know you are fond of them, and we have such excellent cream, and everything is so sweet and still here! Oh!" said she putting her arm within his, and looking up brightly in his face—"Oh, we shall be so happy."

Poor Leslie was overcome. He caught her to his bosom, he folded his arms around her, he kissed her again and again, he could not speak, but the tears gushed into his eyes; and he has often assured me that, though the world has since gone prosperously with him, and his life has, indeed, been a happy one, yet never has he experienced a moment of more exquisite felicity.

In making application to this story, remember, you may be required to adapt to something less romantic than a cottage in the woods. It may be a cold house in a crowded city, or a barren home in a dry desert. But, adapting to these dreary situations cheerfully will deepen his appreciation and love for you.

## Sympathetic Understanding:

*In the broad sense, sympathetic understanding for:*

1. His needs and feelings.
2. His pressing burden in earning the living.
3. His drive for status.
4. His drive for excellence

*Specific times he needs sympathetic understanding:*

5. When he lets down at home.
6. When he is discouraged.
7. When he faces failure.

## Assignment

1. To show sympathetic understanding for his role in providing the living, say something like this: "I am beginning to understand the heavy responsibility you have, to provide for me and the children. I want to cooperate in every way I can to make life easier for you." He may want to discuss ways you can do this.

2. If he is discouraged, follow the suggestions given on how to give true sympathy.

# 14

## *Pandora's Box*

And now, I would like to describe a surprising problem which may occur as you begin to practice the principles of *Fascinating Womanhood:* When a marriage has had real problems, and the wife makes a devoted effort to improve it by applying the principles of *Fascinating Womanhood,* it can cause a peculiar reaction in her husband which I call Pandora's Box.

In a Pandora's Box reaction, instead of the man responding with love and tenderness, he becomes angry and pours out hostile feelings toward his wife. Why does he do this? Up to now he has been afraid to express his anger. In the face of his marriage problems he has felt he must suppress his anger to hold his marriage together. This is not to say that he acted wisely, but only to say that he did so out of what he felt was a necessity. A high-principled man who loves his children will make every effort to hold his marriage securely together.

When his wife applies *Fascinating Womanhood* over a period of time, he begins to feel secure in his marriage. He no longer feels he must hold his troubled feelings within and loses his fear that speaking out will cause marriage problems. Then one day, at last, he dares to open Pandora's Box and release the resentful feelings he has kept hidden there.

If you should face this situation, allow him to empty Pandora's Box. You should, in fact, encourage him to speak freely and completely. And you should not make the mistake of defending yourself, justifying yourself, or fighting back. You will have to sit there quietly, taking it all and even agreeing with him by saying, "I know, I know, you are right." But, when the last resentful feeling has been expressed and Pandora's Box is empty, he will have a feeling of relief, and a love and tenderness for you not known before. And if he has had a reserve, it will probably come tumbling down along with the Pandora's Box reaction, as in the following experiences:

## Wham! A Pandora's Box Reaction

"After I learned and applied *Fascinating Womanhood*, my husband seemed happier, but that lasted only about three to four months, when tension began to build a little (not bad). Then one evening, wham! A Pandora's Box reaction. It seems as if all the pent-up feelings he had came out, and at the same time the walls of reserve came tumbling down. Pretty dramatic, and pretty wonderful. Now he tells me he has never been so happy in all his life, and I feel the same way. Even friends comment on it and ask if I am really as happy as I look.

"I really feel the spirit of *Fascinating Womanhood* and the deep happiness it can bring when one lives it. Tonight my husband spent three hours just talking to me, telling me more about himself, his past, and dreams than I have learned in ten years of marriage. He also said that he came closer than I had realized to leaving me during that time and would have if it hadn't been for the children."

## He Opened the Lid of Pandora's Box

"I had been extremely happy all day, but when my husband came home he cast a shadow of gloom and was grumpy. I was determined to not let his gloom rub off on me. I made him comfortable and invited him to talk over the day. He just wanted to relax so I continued to prepare dinner.

"When I went to call him to dinner, his head was bowed and wet tears on his cheeks. Tenderly, I softly said, 'Dear, share it with me.' All of a sudden he burst into deep sobs, and he opened the lid of Pandora's Box. He had lost all faith in womanhood through the tragic experience of a previous marriage. Out stormed all of his resentments, hatred toward women, and fears of the future. He had opened his shell. Since that evening, our love has had the freedom to grow, even to the height of him telling me with a big hug that I am everything a man could want in a wife."

## The Darkest Time of My Life

"My husband and I have been married almost twenty-two years. I always thought we had a good marriage. We had been through the usual ups and downs but I was confident we would get old together. During this time I took charge of the money and paid the price for it. I was constantly plagued with depression, worry, moodiness, and everything that goes with them, including phobias. I also worked as a teacher and did everything around the house. My husband would come home from work, eat, and watch T.V. for the rest of the night. He also worked in the yard and at our ranch.

"I began to gripe and nag that I had too many responsibilities and needed him to help. The only time he helped was when I nagged, and then he helped very reluctantly. We started criticizing each other rather severely. After going to The Psychological Service Center to help me with my phobias, I became more assertive and demanding. I felt marriage was a fifty-fifty proposition and I wanted my husband to help me more. Very often the word divorce would creep into the conversation, although I felt sure we were just threatening and nothing else.

"After attending a dance with some friends I felt alone and unloved for some reason. My husband was attentive but cool and I felt my first pang of fear. I felt for the first time in my life that he didn't love me as much anymore. The next few months I felt depressed and worried and the only thing I wanted to do after work was fix supper, eat, and go to sleep. I also had spells of crying and feeling sorry for myself. Sometimes I would go to our bedroom crying, hoping that my husband would come and comfort me, which he did by patting my head and talking to me. This was not what I wanted. I wanted closeness and it wasn't there.

"I had another crying spell during the night. He tried to comfort me. I told him that we were growing apart and I didn't like the feeling. The next day he said, 'You rejected me and now I'm not sure I love you.' I was scared out of my wits. I'm Catholic and had been on the Billings Ovulation Method of birth control which calls for a lot of abstaining. He never did like this method.

"Soon after I made an appointment with the doctor to

have 'Band-Aid' surgery. Even though I was Catholic, I was not going to lose my husband because he wasn't getting enough sex. The usual had been twice a month. My husband tried to discourage me from having this operation, saying that I shouldn't go against my convictions. He said that it was too late anyway, that he felt impotent and had no desire for me.

"I went ahead with the operation, hoping against hope that one day he would love me again. On the dreadful day after the surgery, I had a visit in the hospital from a strange woman. I was woozy from the ether and she started talking to me. I had no idea who she was or what she was doing there. Finally she said she had been my husband's mistress for the past nine years! My world came tumbling down around me and I got hysterical. Not my good, Catholic, wonderful husband. Not him. That was the darkest time of my life. In all my life I would least suspect my husband of having an affair.

"A priest came to speak to me and told me to forgive my husband. Then my husband came in. He was really shaken and said, 'It's not what you think it is, honey.' He told me that because I had rejected him he had found her. My disbelief was incredible for I had not one inkling that my husband was having an affair. Since that fateful day he has not seen her. I am finding it very difficult to forgive this dreadful sin, even though I said I would forgive him and I didn't want him to leave. He didn't want to leave either.

"We started going to a marriage counselor and he helped some but I didn't find real hope until I found *Fascinating Womanhood*. I had gone to the library to find a book on how to get my husband interested in me again. I just know that God had a hand in leading me to it.

"I started reading *Fascinating Womanhood* and I cried and cried at all the mistakes I had made. I started applying the assignments and began to see a little response in my husband. Oh, I could have kicked myself for all the years I didn't admire him and wounded his pride so deeply. I began to admire him often. I would write him notes in his lunches, admiring him, and telling him that I loved him. He reacted very guardedly but accepted my compliments. I tried desperately not to feel sorry for myself and not to think of the other woman but it was most difficult. When I felt depressed I reread a chapter from F.W. and felt better.

"I was impatient, however, about progress. Oh, I wanted him to throw his arms around me and tell me that he loves me deeply so badly that I ached inside. He did hug me and kiss me lightly on the lips. We had sex but the closeness was still not there. I listened intently to his conversations and praised him and admired him without sounding too gushy. He talked to me openly about his job and let me know what had been going on.

"One night Pandora's Box opened for the first time. During our engagement his hopes and dreams of our marriage were fantastically high, only to be shattered and not at all what he had expected. He told me about the time I had smeared his face with a dirty diaper just because he wouldn't help me change the baby. He said he could have killed me, and would never forgive me for that.

"He said I had refused to let a cousin live with us for awhile because I wanted my privacy. This cousin was the son of an uncle he had truly loved as a father. This uncle had helped him immensely when he was growing up, gave him money, advice, and let him live with them during our engagement so my husband could save the money he was earning for our wedding. I had refused to let the cousin come live with us and he had to tell his uncle that he was sorry.

"Then he went to bed. He put his arm around me several times during the night. When he got up he put his hands on my face, kissed me, and told me he loved me. All this happened the first time Pandora's Box opened. Pandora's Box kept opening once or twice a week for three months. He had stored up anger for twenty-one years and he was finally releasing it. Every time Pandora's Box opened I sat quietly and looked at him and listened. I followed your advice completely and just said I was sorry. I could not believe all the pent-up anger he had been storing.

"I cried every day for three years. My only consolation was reading F.W. and another book called *God Calling,* and listening to spiritual music. I also started reading other Christian books, and the Bible, and praying in the morning and at night.

"During these three years the other woman hounded and harassed me incessantly. She would call at all hours and use obscene language. She would call me at school. Once she even came to school to ask my principal something. She would pass by my house and wave and make faces. Sometimes I would get so distressed I would go into a room and scream into a pillow and pound the pillow. My children were still at home and I didn't want them to see me agitated.

"My sexual need for my husband made a complete turnaround. Once I found out that he didn't love me, my need for him increased and his for me diminished. In our case the sexual relationship was *very* important. When we had sex it made my husband feel like a virile, strong man and when I rejected him (which was very often) he felt desperately alone and unloved.

"It has been eight years since the hospital incident. I can truly say that it was the turning point in my life. If that woman had not gone to see me at the hospital my husband and I might have been divorced by now. But God was truly with us. He took that black day in our lives and turned our lives back to Him.

"My husband and I are happy and content. He feels loved, admired, and like a man again. I feel loved too! I don't nag him anymore. It was a long and difficult struggle but the rewards were worth it. My husband can talk to me about his innermost feelings. We discuss problems. Every once in a while we fly off the handle, but once we cool off we tell each other the *real* problem and don't try to get the other person to guess why we got angry.

"My husband's confidence in himself went up a hundred percent. He got promoted twice and received an award for outstanding work. Now he's a supervisor and the men who work for him respect and admire him. At home he has taken over the discipline of the children, pays the bills, and does all the heavy work. He will not allow me to help him lift heavy things because he says that's a man's job. His relationship with our children is great. He openly tells them he loves them and they love him back. We are a loving family now.

"Every time I'm around women and they talk about their marital problems I tell them of things I learned in F.W. Many of the younger women do not agree, however. They feel marriage should be a fifty-fifty relationship. I ache for them because

I know what will happen eventually. I still buy F.W. books and give them to people I know need help. Thank you *Fascinating Womanhood*. As you can see, it changed my life. I can never go back to my old ways.''

# Summary of Understanding Men

As we come to the end of the section on Understanding Men, it appears that we must do a lot of giving. We are expected to overlook his faults, appreciate his better side, and make him number one. We must yield to his authority and allow for errors in his judgment. The wonderful wife has an all-comprehending sympathy for his duty to provide the living, and cooperates by living well within his income. In addition we must take great pains to not wound his masculine pride. If it seems you are expected to do a lot of giving without much thought of reward, remember, *when you cast your bread upon the waters, it comes back buttered*.

As you apply these principles, it will awaken your husband's love and tenderness. As one wife put it, *"Our marriage blossomed like a plant that had been placed in the sun after a long, dark winter."* As a man feels accepted, free, respected as a man, and understood, love is awakened. But, remember, you are not to expect material rewards, such as new clothes, a new dishwasher, flowers, or frilly nightwear. These things may come as fringe benefits, as they often do, but the promise of *Fascinating Womanhood* is not material rewards, but a stronger relationship and a tender, romantic love. Evidence of such rewards has been given by testimonials at the end of the chapters. Here are several more:

### I Thought He Was Unlike Any Other Man

"F.W. has been the salvation of my marriage. The book sat on my bookshelf, even through all the moves we made, for about ten years. I don't even know how I acquired it. But, one day last fall my brother was at my house. He pulled it out and read a chapter while I was busy doing something else.

When I came back into the room he said, 'Man, oh man, this book is good. This author is right about this and that.'

"I started reading it, figuring it wouldn't fit my husband because most books are just not the right advice for his character. I thought he was so unique, unlike any other man. I got so excited while reading it and putting the principles into practice.

"Eight months later our marriage has undergone many wonderful changes. Now I am the wife I have always wanted to be, and he is the husband I have always wanted. He is encouraging me to share the teachings with more and more people. Three of my sisters who have poor marriages are just now beginning to study the book. I wish everyone would read and learn about F.W. If in this day of equal rights all women would accept these feminine principles, what a beautiful change would be made in our society."

## Our Marriage Wasn't That Bad

"When I first enrolled in the F.W. course, I wasn't prepared for all the changes that were about to take place in my life! To begin with, our marriage wasn't 'that bad,' so I felt there was little room for improvement. Besides, I had read *The Fascinating Girl* prior to our marriage and had really applied it in our courtship days and the early days of our marriage.

"This class showed me how far I had slipped from being my husband's ideal woman in the past four years. I found out that the honeymoon didn't end just because 'it always does,' but that I had brought it to an end by trying to help my husband run his life. I was constantly offering well-meaning advice regarding education, careers, and finances. And he was constantly ignoring that advice or fighting it, which brought up a huge wall of reserve between us.

"Although we loved each other, we neither one were enjoying the other's company that much! And the funny part is that I honestly thought it was all his fault and that if he'd follow my suggestions we'd be happier. I might mention here that I rated our marriage as 'happy to very happy.' The 'extremely happy' definition seemed such a fairy tale I couldn't believe anyone could have that!

"When I suddenly began admiring my husband again and accepting him as he was, without offering my two cents' worth, he was skeptical. He said, 'Oh, that'll wear off in two weeks or so.' I really don't think he accepted anything I said for about a month, because it was so 'out of character' for me.

"The turning point of our marriage came when I made a book for our two-year-old son about 'My Daddy.' I used a lot of photographs of the two of them together and of my husband doing manly things. I glued them on construction paper pages, added captions making reference to how hard Daddy works, his *strong muscles,* and how smart he is! Then I covered each page with clear contact paper. When my husband saw the book he actually became misty eyed. He said, 'This is really beautiful—you are so creative . . . I think every child should have something like this to help them realize what daddies are for . . . ' I said, 'Well, we realize, and I really appreciate all you do for us.'

"From then on he's been a different man. He finally realized that the admiration was coming from my heart. Since that time we have truly had an extremely happy marriage. He's been working out of town lately and only comes home on weekends. In years prior to this I have spent similar weekends pouting and complaining about how little I saw him. This year the weekends are like honeymoons. He's anxious to come home and we spend the whole time together and are really communicating."

"He is much more physically affectionate and often tells me how happy he is. He brings me little gifts and surprises and I have absolutely no complaints.

"One of the nicest things he has done for me recently is to plan a vacation for us. He has always known that I love to travel by car and have wanted to take a trip to Missouri (where we met). Each year when I've asked him, he has said, 'You know I don't ever like to travel. If we go anywhere we'll fly . . . but there's nowhere I want to go.' This year I didn't even mention a vacation. One day out of the blue he said, 'Why don't we go to Missouri this May?' I nearly flipped. Slipping into my 'old self,' I began to help him plan. I said, 'We could probably fly and it would cost about the same.' He said, 'No, I want to drive. We've never been on a real vacation by car.' How's that for success?"

## Life Was Boring

"My husband and I had been married eleven years and I thought we were happy. I was alone much of the time with four children but he had his own business and I thought that was the way it had to be. The only time we had together was Sunday, and that always turned out boring and miserable, and I knew my husband was even more bored but I didn't know what to do. Then it got so bad that he even worked on Sunday.

"Then suddenly there was another woman. He went on with his affair, sometimes living at home, sometimes not. When this had been going on about two years I found F.W. I tried living it but it was almost impossible since I saw him so little and we talked even less.

"After I had the book six months I decided that I must file for divorce as I didn't believe it was helping the children to stay together—they knew too much. When I told him, he said he didn't believe me but said he would move out as soon as possible. It wasn't but a month until he started asking what he had to do to come back to us and then I poured on the F.W. thick and heavy. I told him that if he would give up the other woman, I wanted another chance to prove myself to him. We started dating and he was with us practically all the time. About three months later I dropped the divorce and he moved back home.

"He keeps saying over and over that he never thought he could be this happy with me. He said that when he asked to come back, he was prepared to give the other woman up but that he thought he would have to accept the boring miserable life. He says that I am just as innocent and sweet as I ever was but that there has been so much more added to me. Incidentally, I gave this book to my mother and she can't believe the change it has made in their marriage, which is forty-six years old. Also, the 'other woman' in my case is now breaking up another home and I have just recently given the wife my F.W. book and I certainly pray she will get the opportunity that I got to apply the principles."

# 15

## *Inner Happiness*

Inner happiness is a *happiness of spirit, serenity, tranquility,* and *peace of soul*. Agnes had this quality of spirit, a *placid* and *sweet expression,* a *tranquility* about her, a *quiet, good, calm, spirit*.

Inner happiness can carry you through the turmoil of life with a calm stability. Your life will not necessarily be free of problems and disappointments, but you will have the power to face these problems with a spiritual calm. Inner happiness is pretty important to a man. I know of at least two men in the throes of troubled marriages who would not consider a reconciliation unless their wives learned to be happy within.

When a man senses his wife is unhappy, if he is a kindly man he will be concerned and sympathetic. He will try to help her and cheer her up. But, this is *not* something men appreciate in women. It is looked on as a deficiency. They expect women to be happy within, so they can *shed joy around, and cast light upon dark days*.

What causes unhappiness? It arises from a failure within the individual—weakness of character, sin, failure to fulfill responsibility, or self-centeredness. We are *unhappy* when we are doing something wrong, failing to do something right, or in some way breaking the eternal laws of life. We become *happy* by *overcoming our weaknesses, performing our duties, losing our self-centeredness, and putting ourselves in harmony with eternal laws*. We will discuss these routes to happiness but first, let's define the difference between happiness and pleasure:

## Happiness Versus Pleasure

The word pleasure comes from the word *please*. Pleasure is derived from things which please the senses—the eyes, nose, ears, mouth, and sensual feelings. There are both good and bad pleasures:

Good pleasures are derived from wholesome things such as sunshine, rain, flowers, nourishing food, the laughter of little children, beautiful music, fine art, wholesome recreation, and the finer things of life. We receive good pleasure from attractive clothing, beautiful homes, gardens, furniture, and conveniences of modern equipment such as vacuum cleaners and washing machines. They enrich life, but bring pleasure rather than happiness. This is proven by people who have all the pleasures of earth but are *unhappy*.

Bad pleasures are derived from sin and bring harm rather than good—immoral sex, bad literature, sexy movies, improper food, alcohol, smoking, gambling, and riotous living. They are destructive to body and spirit and should be avoided completely. Other sources of bad pleasures are extravagance, too many worldly goods, and pleasures that waste time.

Happiness is quite different from pleasure. While pleasure comes from things which please the senses, happiness may arise from unpleasant experiences. The mother who desires the joys of a family first knows the pain of childbirth, then the tiresome labor to care for her children. The father knows the weariness, pain, and toil to secure comforts for his loved ones.

Dedication to high goals brings struggle and opposition. But with it comes a newfound joy, not only the joy of achievement but the joy of a newfound strength, a strength gained in conflict and experience. Sometimes happiness comes as a result of knowing misery, sorrow, pain, and suffering. Pleasure may be derived from sin, while happiness arises from the struggle to overcome sin. No person who lives a mere innocent life, devoid of unpleasant experiences, can be happy.

Although happiness can arise from unpleasant experience, even misery and pain, the feeling of happiness itself is the opposite of misery. Happiness is a deep feeling of spirit, a combination of peace, joy, and serenity. Even this cannot adequately describe it. It has always been difficult to describe the feeling of happiness.

The Apostle Paul, when he attempted to explain the eternal happiness in store for the faithful, said, *"Eye hath not seen nor ear heard, neither entered into the heart of man the things which God hath prepared for them that love him."* (I Cor. 2:9)

And so it is with earthly happiness. We cannot comprehend its magnificence without personal experience. But when experienced, it is unmistakable. How can we acquire inner happiness? What conscious effort can we make to achieve it?

## How to Gain Inner Happiness

We sometimes hear the statement, *"People are about as happy as they make up their minds to be."* Although there is some merit to this positive outlook, the statement is not entirely correct. A wicked person cannot be happy by merely determining to be. In fact, no one can gain inner happiness by suddenly deciding to be happy, such as when you decide to smile. Inner happiness is a feeling which must be earned.

Henry Drummond said, *"No one can get joy by merely asking for it. It is one of the ripest fruits of the Christian life, and like all other fruits, must be grown."* And Robert Ingersoll said, *"Happiness is the bud, the blossom, and the fruit of good and noble actions. It is not the gift of God. It must be earned."*

Inner happiness is acquired by following eternal laws. There are spiritual laws governing happiness, just as there are laws governing the universe. When people are *happy*, it is because they follow the laws upon which happiness is based; and when they are *unhappy*, it is because they have broken these laws. Inner happiness can be reached by everyone who obeys its laws. To gain true happiness, do the following:

## 1. Fulfill Domestic Role

If you are to be happy, the most basic area where you must succeed is in *the home,* serving as the understanding wife, devoted mother, and homemaker. Success in this area brings you in harmony with eternal laws which inevitably results in happiness. You may not fully realize that your *bluebird of happiness* lies within your own four walls. Of course, it takes a *wholehearted effort* to earn happiness from homemaking. You have to *go the second mile,* doing more than required. If you merely do enough to get by, you can't expect any great rewards.

If you were to fail in the home, you would inevitably reap *unhappiness*. When you break eternal laws, you must suffer the consequences. For a woman, a failure in the home is a failure in life. Even though you fail in only one area, such as homemaking, you are somewhat of a failure. You must succeed in all three duties—wife, mother, and homemaker—to gain the reward.

## 2. Develop Character

Happiness comes from righteous living and the development of a noble character. You can observe this by noticing that people who are truly *happy* are honest, unselfish, kind, responsible, and have high moral standards. On the other hand, *unhappy* people are invariably selfish, lazy, irresponsible, and lacking in self-discipline. And, people who are *miserable* tend to be immoral, dishonest, greedy, cruel, or in other ways dark in character. Sinfulness leads to depression, nervousness, and mental illness.

It is encouraging to find that modern psychiatry is turning to religion to cure the ills of the spirit. Dr. J. A. Hadfield, one of England's foremost psychiatrists, has said, *"I am convinced that the Christian religion is one of the most potent influences for producing that harmony, peace of mind, and confidence of soul needed to bring health to a large portion of nervous patients."* And the Bible promises, *"He who hath clean hands and a pure heart; who hath not lifted up his soul unto vanity, nor sworn deceitfully, he shall receive the blessings of the Lord."*

The struggle to overcome weakness or sin is not an easy one. Sin is addicting, and therefore a type of bondage. As we make progress in overcoming sin, there is always a tendency to slip back into old habits. Overcoming sin brings inner happiness, not only because of overcoming the habit itself, but because of the strength gained in conflict, a strength of spirit which is a newfound joy. Specific weaknesses we need to overcome and basic strengths we need to achieve in the development of a noble character are taught in the next chapter.

## 3. Give Service

The way to be happy is to be *involved in something,* something worthwhile. Benevolent service outside the home can greatly enrich your life. Your first responsibility is to your family, but you have an obligation to serve beyond your own sphere, for the betterment of society. If you limit your devotion to your own small family unit, focusing on *your* children and *your* household, your life will become narrow and your happiness limited.

Dr. Max Levine, psychiatrist of New York, has said, *"I speak not as a clergyman, but as a psychiatrist. There cannot be emotional health in the absence of high moral standards and a sense of social responsibility."* When you share the burdens of society to help make the world a better place, you gain a compensating inner happiness.

## 4. Do Creative Work

Did you know that working with your hands, creating things of beauty and worth, builds inner happiness? Don't think you lack this power within you. Boris Bali, former Dean of Fine Arts, Temple University, said, *"I am convinced that every human being possesses a creative urge to make beautiful things, that this urge can be brought out and put to work with proper encouragement, and that suppression of it results in maladjustment."* A routine therapy used in mental hospitals has been to give the patients creative things to do with their hands.

You can be creative in things you do at home, such as cooking, sewing, decorating, and gardening. It is not creative to merely copy someone else's idea from a pattern, recipe, or picture—another person's creation. Creative opportunities are found in the fields of art, sculpture, music, writing, designing, problem-solving, and almost every endeavor. You are creative when you have an original idea or produce something from your imagination, something that is good or beautiful.

And when you create something of *real worth or supreme beauty,* such as rare treasures of art, music, or literature, it goes beyond inner happiness to deep soul satisfaction. When we consider the great joy in the modest creative efforts of man, think how God must have felt when He created the earth and, viewing the workmanship of His hands, said, "It is good."

## 5. Accept Yourself

To be happy, accept yourself and allow for human errors and weaknesses. Don't let your mistakes get you down. In the process of becoming an angel, you are a human being, prone to errors in judgment. You may do silly things such as burn food, spend money foolishly, break an expensive object, lose something, or miss an appointment. You can become quite upset with yourself. Even little things disturb you and rob you of happiness. It's not fair to be hard on yourself. If you forgive others, do the same with yourself.

The businessman allows in advance for business failures. Do the same in your routine. Tell yourself that each year, each week, and even each day, you will make your share of mistakes or unwise decisions. When you go shopping remember, you may not choose wisely with every item. You learn by experience, and this means you will make mistakes. Accepting yourself, however, does not mean contentment—you are satisfied with yourself as you are and make no effort to improve. This attitude blocks progress.

## 6. Appreciate Simple Pleasures

To be happy, appreciate the simple joys of life such as rain, sunlight, and fresh, crisp curtains. It is not so much simple pleasures themselves that bring happiness as your ability to appreciate them. The following is a comparison between a woman who finds happiness in the simple joys of life and one who must have much more to be happy:

The appreciative woman enjoys drinking water from a tin cup, while another must have china dishes. One woman enjoys sitting on a box in her backyard, letting the warm sun shine down on her shoulders, while another must have patio furniture. An appreciative woman enjoys the song of a bird, the rustling of leaves, or the stillness of a great forest. Another must have grand opera. One enjoys a simple wardrobe of cottons, while another lives for the day she can buy her clothes on Fifth Avenue. One feels joy in pushing her baby carriage in the park, while another must have the bright lights and gay places. One enjoys the simplest cottage, while another must have a modern home with a view. One woman delights in the smell of fresh rain while another must have French perfume. The appreciative woman who learns to enjoy common pleasures around her always has a source of joy near at hand.

## 7. Seek Knowledge and Wisdom

Knowledge unlocks the door to happiness, and wisdom opens it. Knowledge comes first, and then the application of knowledge, which is wisdom. The search for wisdom should be the most important pursuit of our lives, and the attainment of it our most priceless possession. This thought is expressed in the Holy Scriptures, Proverbs 3:11–18:

*"Happy is the man that findeth wisdom and the man that getteth understanding. For the merchandise of it is better than the merchandise of silver, and the gain thereof than fine gold. She is more precious than rubies and all the things thou canst desire are not to be compared to her. Length of days is in her right hand; and in her left hand riches and honor. Her ways are the ways of pleasantness, and all her paths are peace. She is the tree of life to them that lay hold on her; and happy is everyone that retaineth her."*

If knowledge can bring happiness, then lack of knowledge can bring unhappiness. This thought is expressed by Dr. Abraham Maslow, psychologist: *"Knowledge, insight, truth, reality and facts are most powerful curative medicines. . . . If knowledge can cure, then lack of knowledge can sicken. . . . We must take seriously the fact that blindness can be sickness-producing and that knowing can be curative. The old saying, 'what you don't know won't hurt you' turns out to be false. Just the contrary is true. It is what you don't know that will hurt you. What you don't know has power over you; knowing brings it under your control."* A good example is in marriage. Those who are unhappy in marriage lack knowledge and wisdom. When they gain knowledge and apply it they find happiness.

## Is Love of Husband Necessary?

If you feel unloved, you may be inclined to think, "If my husband really loved me, then I would be happy." A man's love *is* essential to a woman's happiness in a complete sense, but not to the *inner happiness* I refer to. In fact, you must first find inner happiness before your husband can really love you. Men all over the country are turning from their wives to someone else because their wives are unhappy.

If you find inner happiness, and your husband doesn't love you, there is something missing. It is not *complete happiness*. A good example is Agnes Wickfield. Although there was a tranquility about her and a good calm spirit, she was not completely happy during most of the story. David Copperfield frequently noticed an unhappy expression in her beautiful face, not knowing it was due to unrequited love. An ingredient to happiness was missing, but it did not detract from her tranquility of spirit.

## How Do Others and Circumstances Affect Happiness?

Other people—your husband, children, relatives, and friends—can contribute greatly to your happiness, as do favorable circumstances. However, they are not absolutely necessary. If you don't have the advantage of these things, if other people have let you down or if circumstances are difficult, don't let this discourage you. You can be happy by living right principles. If you find happiness without the advantage of other people and circumstances, it proves you are a finer, more courageous, and stronger person.

## How to Find Inner Happiness

1. Fulfill domestic role.
2. Develop character.
3. Give service.
4. Do Creative Work.
5. Accept yourself.
6. Enjoy simple pleasures.
7. Gain knowledge and wisdom.

## Assignment

Make an evaluation of yourself to determine if you are happy within. If not, in which area of your life are you lacking? Review that part to see how to gain greater inner happiness.

Inner Happiness is a quality of spirit which must be earned by a victory over our weaknesses and an upward reach for the perfection of our character. It is like swimming upstream. It is found in the great efforts and achievements of life and in faithful devotion to duty.

# 16

## *A Worthy Character*

A man wants a woman of fine character, one he can place on a pedestal and hold in high regard. He expects her to be not only good, but better than himself. He hopes that she will be kinder, more patient, forgiving, unselfish, and hold more valiantly to principle. If *he* is thoughtless, critical or weak, he can overlook these human frailties in himself. But he expects a woman, the more angelic creature of the human race, to be above such things.

At times a man will shake a woman's pedestal by suggesting she do something wrong. He may do this deliberately to see if she is as worthy as she appears to be. In other words, he tests her. What a disappointment if she lowers her standards and falls to his level, and what a joy if she remains unshaken. Remaining on the pedestal is further proof that she belongs there.

When a man perceives *fine character* in a woman, it has a profound effect on his feelings for her. A perfect example is from the classic novel *The Little Minister* by Sir James Barrie. Babbie was a beautiful gypsy girl with enchanting ways, but Gavin, the little minister, considered her wild and even wicked. It wasn't until he became aware of her loving concern for a little old lady that he first loved her, as described in the following incident:

### Babbie

The Reverend Gavin Dishart and Dr. McQueen had arrived at Nanny Webster's cottage to take her to the poorhouse. Nanny was so pained over the disgrace of her poverty and being torn from her home that she had reached the point of suffering. Just as the two men had patiently and gently persuaded Nanny to leave, Babbie opened the door. *"This is no place for you,"* Gavin was saying fiercely when Nanny, too distraught to think, fell crying at the gypsy's feet.

*"They are taking me to the poorhouse,"* she sobbed. *"Dinna let them take me, dinna let them."* The Egyptian's arms clasped her, and the Egyptian kissed a sallow cheek ... No one had caressed Nanny for many years, but do you think she was too poor and old to care for these young arms around her neck? There are those who say that women cannot love each other, but it is not true. Woman is not undeveloped man, but something better, and Gavin and the doctor knew it as they saw Nanny clinging to her protector. When the gypsy turned with flashing eyes to the two men she might have been a mother protecting her child.

*"How dare you!"* she cried, stamping her foot; and they quaked like malefactors ... She turned to Nanny. *"You poor dear,"* she said tenderly, *"I won't let them take you away."* She looked triumphantly at both minister and doctor, as one who had foiled them in their cruel designs. *"Go,"* she said, pointing grandly to the door.

Then to the Egyptian, Gavin said firmly, *"You mean well, but you are doing this poor woman a cruelty in holding out hopes to her that cannot be realized. Sympathy is not meal and bedclothes, and these are what she needs."*

*"And you who live in luxury,"* retorted the girl, *"would send her to the poorhouse for them. I thought better of you."* The two men made a meager defense of their position, picked up Nanny's bags, and urged her to the door. *"We are waiting for you, Nanny."* *"Ay, I'm coming,"* said Nanny, leaving the Egyptian. *"I'll have to be going, lassie. Dinna grieve for me."*

*"No, you are not going. It is these men who are going,"* said Babbie. *"Go, sirs, and leave us."* *"And you will provide for Nanny?"* asked the doctor, contemptuously. *"Yes,"* said Babbie. *"And where is the money coming from?"* asked the doctor. *"That is my affair, and Nanny's. Begone, both of you. She shall never want again. See how the very mention of your going brings back life to her face."*

Babbie's charity for Nanny turned Gavin's feelings for her from contempt to love. He now saw a different woman, one he trusted. Never before had he seen anything but a vagrant girl, wild, and carefree. Now she was a woman with a heart and soul, her hand stretched out to the poor. Gavin considered himself a charitable person, but Babbie's charity surpassed his own. We will hear more of Babbie's fine qualities in a later chapter.

## Katherine

In *Captains and the Kings,* the author describes the effect of angelic character on a man's emotions. During the Civil War two trains stopped as they pulled aside each other. Joseph Armaugh was a powerful, yet unemotional man who seemed unaware of women, yet when the troop train passed and stopped by his window he peered out to see something which caught his attention and tugged at his masculine heart:

*A young woman in cap and apron straightened up from a youth she was attending and there were tears on her cheeks . . . She seemed to be exhausted beyond endurance. She stood up in a drooping attitude, a bloody bandage in her hand, her head lifted, her eyes holding the expression, far and distant, of one who had looked on too much pain . . . But her tiredness, her drooping posture, her manifest depletion of young vitality and her coarse apron and cap could not hide the slender loveliness of her body and the beauty of her face. . . .*

*Joseph sat up straighter and looked deeply into the girl's face. She would not submit to exhaustion. She would go on after a moment. A soldier spoke to her, a man out of sight and Joseph saw her bend her slight body. Her face was full of pity, it trembled with mercy and quickened concern. Then the troop train moved on to the depot . . . .*

*He pushed open the window. He saw the diminishing lights of the other train as it neared the depot and suddenly he wanted to jump from his own train and race after the other. So hot, so demanding, so turbulent were his feelings, so hungry, and emphatic that he lost his reason, his cold aplomb and disciplined self-control. Even in his turmoil he could dazedly ask himself what had struck him like this and with wonder, and to marvel at his emotions.*

*It had not been the girl's beauty alone which had blud-*

*geoned him, for he had seen prettier and younger and certainly more blooming . . . he had seen gayer—this girl was not gay in the least. He had seen prettier and more girlish, but they were nothing to this young woman who had such a gentle pride, such selfless compassion, such determined desire to serve and console.*

*"I have lost my mind," he thought, and forced himself to lie still. "What is she to me, a woman I'll never see again." Then at that thought he was bereft, torn with grief, savaged by longing and to his immediate horror, by desire.*

Before a man can have such deep and tender feelings, a woman must have a character which inspires those feelings. Your first impression may be, *"This subject isn't essential for me. I've been trained all my life in the virtues. I'm already honest, kind, and benevolent. You see, I have a fine character."* The virtues mentioned are essential but character includes much more. Dora was kind, honest, and benevolent, but David never completely loved her. There are many virtues, the following essential:

## 1. Self-Control

You need self-control to manage your life successfully, to keep commitments, manage time and money, control thoughts and words, subdue appetites, school feelings, overcome temptations, and reach goals.

The greatest person in history, with the most difficult goal, first prepared himself by self-mastery. Jesus Christ did not begin His ministry until He went into the wilderness and fasted forty days and nights. During this time He overcame the temptations of Satan and thus gained the self-mastery needed for His mission in life.

When you determine to improve your life or pursue a worthy goal, opposition appears in the form of self-doubt, discouragement, and the temptation to quit. You need self-control to overcome the opposition and move forward towards your goals. Here are the keys to gaining self-control:

1. *Self-worth:* To overcome self-doubt which keeps you from your goals, learn to appreciate yourself. If you knew who you are, and your inestimable worth in the sight of God, you

would expect more of yourself, be more confident, more in control. Develop a *good self-image* to gain an indestructible feeling of worth.

2. *Fasting and Prayer:* This means to abstain from all food and beverage for a period of time. A twenty-four hour fast is long enough if practiced regularly. There are two purposes of the fast—to develop self-control and to gain spiritual strength needed to reach the goal. When physical needs of the body are withheld, the spirit is more in tune with God. Accompany the fasting with prayer, asking God for spiritual strength to reach your goal.

3. *Train the Will:* Another way to gain self-control is to train the will. For example: Every day do one or more of the following:

  a.) *Do something unpleasant*—take a cold shower, exercise, or eat health food you don't like.
  b.) *Do something difficult*—do a hard job, stick to your diet, or work on a difficult goal, forego, coffee, candy, or smoking.
  c.) *Demand quotas of yourself*—get up at four thirty, get a specific job done at a given time, etc.

4. *Be Determined:* In addition to the suggestions given, you need *determination*. Keep your goal in mind and be determined to stick to it. Don't let others sidetrack you, discourage you, or waste your time. Be determined to do *whatever is necessary,* no matter how difficult, and to do it *when it needs doing*. You will reach your goals and gain self-control in the process.

## 2. Unselfishness

*Unselfishness* is a willingness to give up one's own comfort or advantage for the benefit of someone else. There must be an element of sacrifice in a truly unselfish act. This means giving up a pleasure, comfort, advantage, or material thing of value, or going to some trouble or inconvenience for the benefit of someone else.

There are acts which are imagined unselfish which in reality are not, such as giving away something you don't want or need, or doing something which is little trouble or expense. These may be acts of kindness, but are not unselfish. A good deed is unselfish only if it requires sacrifice. For example, you give away something you like or need but which someone else needs more, or you go to some trouble or inconvenience to help someone in need.

Unselfishness is different from charity in this way: Charity is a feeling of love and concern for others which moves us to act in time of their need. Unselfishness is not necessarily prompted by love. It can be a virtue one has come to accept as part of a moral code, a principle one believes in. Unselfishness is the first step in developing charity, in that it helps us lose our self-centeredness and focus on others.

## 3. Charity

Charity is the highest, noblest, strongest kind of love and concern we have for one another. It goes beyond the barriers of race, religion, and culture. It can be compared to the pure love of our Heavenly Father for each of us. Charity is the main goal of the true Christian and all who seek God honestly. Charity prompts us to give service to those in need. *Service*, however, is not always prompted by a feeling of charity. It can be given out of a sense of duty. In this case it is not considered charity. The Apostle Paul explained this in Corinthians 13: *"And though I bestow all my goods to feed the poor . . . and have not charity it profiteth me nothing."*

The virtuous woman described in Proverbs 31 was charitable. After carefully attending to the needs of her household— *arising while it was yet night, giving meat to her household, working willingly with her hands, bringing her food from afar, seeing that her children had double garments to keep out the cold, and herself coverings of tapestry—she stretched out her hand to the poor, "yea, she reacheth forth her hands to the needy."*

Your first obligation is in the home, building a happy marriage and family life. Beyond this your duty extends to the world, to the critical needs of others. We all share responsibility for the urgent problems of society. The fortunate and the morally strong should assist the less fortunate and the weak. Nothing will so enrich a woman's life and make her a better person and a better mother than her loving concern for others beyond her family circle. Three keys to charity are:

1. *Compassion:* Learn to value human life. Each person

is a child of God, of supreme worth. When you see your fellow men oppressed, discouraged, or suffering, care for them with a loving concern for their welfare. Such a compassionate feeling will move you to action in their behalf. This is charity.

2. *Perceiving Their Need:* Find out what people *really* need. There is no merit in giving goods or service when not needed, and fail to fill critical needs. Likewise, perceive *when* help is needed. Don't fail them in their hour of need.

3. *Sacrifice:* When someone in need is in a crisis, it may require your personal sacrifice. Often an urgent need for help cannot wait. It must be done at the moment. It may require you stop in the middle of your work and rearrange your schedule. But remember, service is *almost never convenient.*

Or, you may have to give up comforts, goods, money, or go to extra trouble for the person in need. We often hear the statement, *"Oh, I hope this isn't any trouble for you,"* or *"I hope this doesn't inconvenience you too much."* In truth, we should be willing to go to extra trouble or inconvenience for people in need. A willingness to sacrifice time, money, or comfort, for someone in need is necessary for true charity.

This is not to suggest you grossly neglect your family, but there may be temporary neglect. Other members of your household may have to make sacrifices too, as they support you in stretching forth your hand to the needy. Let them sacrifice. In so doing they learn charity. By involving them in the sacrifice you teach them *the gospel of love.*

In the story *Little Women,* by Louisa May Alcott, is an example of family charity: On Christmas morning the family prepared a delicious breakfast with their favorite food, popovers. Just as they were ready to serve, the mother returned from a visit to the poor. There was sickness in the poor family and an urgent need of food. The mother asked her daughters to help her gather up the breakfast, put it in a basket, and take it to the poor family. The disappointed girls reluctantly complied. By making their own portion of the sacrifice, they learned the true meaning of charity.

### Mrs. Carter

One day my little girl complained about my giving considerable time to a worthy cause. She said, *"Why can't you be like Mrs. Carter? She pays attention to her children all the time.''* This hurt me for a moment, and I had to stop and give careful thought to what I was doing. Then I thought of Mrs. Carter. She was truly a devoted mother. She gave her children the best birthday parties in the neighborhood and the most lavish Christmases. They took lessons of all kinds, so she was always driving them places or picking them up. Whenever there was a community project where children were involved, hers participated. Her devotion was unquestioned. I too wished I could be more devoted, like Mrs. Carter. But I felt the service I was rendering was even more important.

So I talked to my little girl and explained to her the meaning of charity. I told her about three mothers: Mother A loved her children, but got a little bored tending them all the time. She felt she deserved to get away part of the time, so she went shopping for long hours, golfing, and out of town. Sometimes the children got a little lonely and felt neglected, but they felt she really loved them.

Mother B loved her children very much. She spent most of her time with them. They had the best birthday parties in town and the best Christmases. They had lessons of all kinds and participated in projects. She took them places, played with them, took them on long walks, or went bicycling. (I was describing Mrs. Carter.)

Mother C, I explained, loved her children, but she loved other children, too, and other people, and wanted to help them with their problems. She took good care of her children, spent a lot of time with them and did all of the important things for them. But, she shared some of her time with others, helping them. Then, I asked my daughter which mother was living the most Christian life. She immediately understood the meaning of charity and has supported me in benevolent causes since, sometimes at considerable sacrifice.

The real enemy to charity is self-centeredness, an over-concern for our own. We focus on *our* children, *our* house, *our* husband and *our* problems. Surrounding us are people in desperate circumstances. They may need a helping hand, money, a word of wisdom, or encouragement. I received a letter from a mother who reflected back on earlier hard years:

*"Both of our children in their infant years were sickly and ran temperatures. Our little daughter had an eye defect*

*and almost died from a high fever and severe convulsions. After this I was scared to leave the children. My husband and I needed desperately to get away for a short time, but neither my mother nor my husband's mother wanted the responsibility for their welfare. We couldn't afford a nurse nor would I leave them with a young babysitter."* Very few are willing to follow the admonition of the Apostle Paul: "Bear ye one another's burdens."

## 4. Humility

Humility is freedom from pride or arrogance. A humble person is aware of his virtues, talents, and advantages but realizes his weaknesses, mistakes, and limitations. He is neither haughty nor self-effacing. He has a correct opinion of himself.

When you are humble you don't think of yourself as better, smarter, or more fortunate than another person. You may be better in some ways, but not as good in other ways. Although you may have abilities, talents, and accomplishments for which you can be honestly proud, you are not all you could be or should be. There is always room for improvement.

The Savior set a perfect example of humility. Although He was the chosen Son of God, without sin, and overcame all things, He lived among the common people and dined with sinners. Although His disciples worshipped Him, He did not rise above them in an attitude of superiority. In humility He bowed before them, washed their feet, and wiped them with the towel that was girded about Him. By this act He impressed upon them, in a dramatic way, the requirement that men remain humble.

Humility can be further understood by reviewing its opposite—arrogance, or pride. Arrogance is an ungrounded feeling of superiority and an inability to see one's own weaknesses or limitations. This fault can be commonly viewed in the following areas of life:

1. *Worldly Goods:* Those who have a lot of money and possessions find it hard to keep from being proud. Women who dress in fine clothes, drive expensive automobiles, and live in luxurious homes tend to feel superior to women with less. Some take pleasure in parading their fine possessions

before the less fortunate. They seem to derive a fiendish delight from making another person feel inferior, while increasing their own feeling of self-importance. Glorying in the corruptible things of the earth is an arrogance that indicates serious moral and spiritual weakness.

2. *Knowledge:* Another source of unwholesome pride is knowledge, which comes from higher education, learned skills, abilities, and achievements, or native ability, gifts, or talents. A realization of these gifts or achievements is not wrong, but a feeling of superiority because of them can be wrong and indicates lack of humility.

People who are intelligent and well educated are seldom proud and haughty. They tend to be humble. They realize that although they have knowledge, there is a vast sea of knowledge yet undiscovered. They stand between the past and the future. They recognize the greatness of those who have gone before, and the contributions that will be made in the future. Knowledge will come forth to dwarf the present accomplishments. They live between a realization of their own contributions and an awareness of their limitations. Others know far more about certain subjects than they. Their knowledge, great as it is, is limited to specific fields.

3. *Righteousness:* Women tend to be arrogant of their righteousness. For example, you may be making an honest effort to live a pure, wholesome life, hold to high standards and overcome your weaknesses. When you compare yourself to another person who doesn't appear to be making an effort, according to your terms, you are tempted to feel superior. To feel humble in this situation is difficult.

To overcome this tendency, tell yourself you are not the judge of another person's worth, or your own. Other people may appear week and irresponsible, but may yet live worthwhile lives. They may have hidden qualities that have not surfaced or been brought to the test. Consider their background. They may not have been inspired by good parents or had proper training. If given opportunities equal to your own, they may be as good as or better then you.

God has strongly condemned pride. We read in Proverbs 6:16–19: *"These six things doth the Lord hate; yea seven are an abomination to him; A proud look, a lying tongue, and hands that shed innocent blood, an heart that deviseth wicked imaginations, feet that be swift in running to mischief, a false witness that speaketh lies, and he that soweth discord among brethren.''* It is significant that pride is described as an abomination to God along with lying, wicked imaginations, and even murder.

Did you know that humility can cure criticism? When you are humble, ever aware of your own human frailties and imperfections, you are less inclined to criticize another. When you are tempted to criticize people, remind yourself that although some of their faults may be glaring ones, they may be superior to you in other ways. We are all more equal than we think. True humility brings with it patience, forgiveness, acceptance, and appreciation. With these qualities it is impossible to feel critical.

True humility is one of the most essential elements of a worthy character. All truly great people have been humble, regardless of their position or gifts. They have seen themselves in a true light—have recognized their greatness, yet acknowledged their weakness and limitations. No one is so great or good that he has no need of humility.

## 5. Responsibility

Responsibility means to assume work, *with a feeling of accountability for that work*. For example, if you were to work as a secretary, you would be given specific jobs to do and would be expected to take *responsibility* for these jobs. This means you must *see that the work is done*. You would also be expected to do a *good job,* and to see that it's done *on time*. Either a person has this sense of responsibility or he doesn't. It's a virtue of character, a part of a person's moral code.

Apply this to the ideal woman working in the home. She assumes the responsibility of running the household—cooking, shopping, cleaning, laundry, and tending the children. She may enjoy domestic work, as many women do. But what if she doesn't? Is she justified in neglecting it, or leaving it to someone else so she can do something she enjoys more? No, whether she enjoys her work or not is not a consideration. She assumes it with *a keen sense of responsibility*, realizing that it must be done and the job rightfully belongs to her. No matter how unpleasant or tiring, she rolls up her sleeves and gets to work, without complaint.

Who is more responsible for the welfare of the child than the mother? If you hire a baby-sitter or place a child in a day care center, they provide daily care but they don't take the responsibility to train the child, teach him refinements, mold his character, or instill a faith in God. This is the mother's responsibility.

And who is more responsible to create a clean, orderly home than the wife? She may call on her children or servants to assist her but she must see that it's done. Anything less indicates a weakness of character. To turn her back on her work is a *serious dereliction of duty*. The only exception is when a woman is physically or mentally incapable. In this case other arrangements must be made.

This keen sense of responsibility should extend beyond the home to the community, school, or church. Once you accept a job in an organization, *accept the responsibility to fulfill it*.

## 6. Diligence

> Whatsoever thy hand findeth to do,
> do it with thy might. (Eccl. 9:10)

Diligence means to *persevere,* or to do something with *careful attention*. It means to do a good job. The opposite is to be *lazy, careless, negligent, or indifferent*.

There is quite a difference in the quality of women's work. Some women are good at everything they do. If you ask them to bring a casserole to the church bazaar, you can be sure it will be a good one. Whether they are sewing a quilt, working in the nursery, or teaching a Sunday School lesson, you can count on them to do a good job. They run their homes the same way, because they have the quality of character called *diligence*.

At the other end of the pole are the women who are lazy and negligent. They are poor at everything they do. They can't sew a straight seam or bake a good loaf of bread. Their homes are run the same way. Take hold of a doorknob and it's sticky;

the laundry is stacked sky high; pots and pans are left in the sink; you can never find anything when you need it.

Between these two extremes are women who do fairly well. They make an honest effort with the important things and no one seems to complain. But beware of mediocrity. There is a tendency in everyone to do just enough to get by. Lean forward in the direction of diligence. It has everything to do with success and enjoyment of life.

## 7. Patience

Patience means to endure trials or pains *without complaint*, to bear stress and strain with *calm endurance*. When provoked or suffering, you *control yourself*. If something is out of reach you *forbear, you wait with calmness, without discontent, undisturbed by obstacles, delays or failures*. There are four ways we need patience:

1. *Patience With People:* There is no better place to learn patience with people than in the home, dealing with our own family. Little children do such things as put gum in their hair, spill food, muddy their shoes, and quarrel with each other. Teenagers have messy rooms, monopolize the phone, and don't eat right. Your husband may be late for dinner or fail to do his yard work. To develop patience with your family, accept problems as part of daily living, and *allow for them*. Instead of overreacting to a problem, *minimize* it. For example, a little girl spilled fingernail polish on her bedspread and ran to her mother in tears. Instead of the mother becoming upset, she said, patiently, "Well, honey, we've lived through worse things than this."

2. *Patience With Duties:* We also learn patience with our work at home, cooking three meals a day, washing that never ends, housecleaning that keeps repeating itself. The home is a wonderful school for developing patience for when you perform these tasks over and over you develop patience. Women show a lack of patience when they neglect their work, do it carelessly, complain, or turn from it altogether to seek relief in the career world.

3. *Patience With Desires:* It takes patience to reach certain goals or desires. Perhaps you want a better home, more furniture, new clothes, or a family vacation. These things may

not be obtainable at the moment, or not until some time in the future. To save, plan, and sacrifice for a long-range goal takes considerable patience. How wise are those who *have the patience to wait.*

Or, you may want *time of your own,* time to pursue talents or other personal interests. If you are rearing a family you may feel this time will never come. You want it *now.* If you insist on having everything now—wife, mother, homemaking, and outside interests—you overcrowd your time and deny yourself the enjoyment of raising a family. *How unwise.* The time will come when your little ones will be gone and you will have time on your hands. As Shakespeare said, *"How poor are they who have not patience to wait."*

And when you do have time, it takes great patience to reach high goals—develop musical skills, do creative writing, or create works of art. I remember watching a lady making a beautiful hooked rug. I asked her how long she expected it would take to complete it. *"Oh, about a year,"* she said. I innocently remarked, *"I don't have the patience to begin something I can't finish in a day or so."* A year or so later I conceived the idea of writing this book. What a lesson I had to learn in patience, in the endless hours and even years it took for its completion.

Learn patience in reflecting on the creations of mankind, the great cathedrals, sculpture, painting, music, literature, encyclopedias, and even the dictionary. Works of the past have left us a rich heritage. Today we have great bridges, intricate freeway systems, modern technology, and advancements in science to stagger the mind. All of these were produced by endless patience.

Learn patience by watching nature in her methods of reaching her objectives. In a limestone cave, you see the beautiful patterns built by drops of water falling from the ceiling over the centuries. How long does it take to grow an oak tree, or a giant redwood, or to carve the gorge of the Colorado?

4. *The Brighter Day:* Periods of your life may be filled with disappointment, discouragement, or even sorrow. Be assured that you are not alone. Cloudy days are everyone's experience. Have the patience to *let this time pass* and hope for a brighter day.

## 8. Moral Courage

Moral courage is *the courage to do what is right, at the risk of unpleasant or even painful consequences,* such as criticism, humiliation, loss of friends, loss of money, loss of position, or even bodily harm. It is one thing to set standards for ourselves and quite another to have the moral courage to hold fast to these standards. The following are common ways we need moral courage:

1. *Moral Standards and Goals:* Holding to our standards and goals often requires moral courage. An example is a young man who resolves not to drink, smoke, tamper with drugs, or attend X-rated movies. When he feels the pressure of friends to lower his standards and do as they do, and fears that if he doesn't he will lose status with the group, it takes considerable moral courage to say no. A young woman may determine to be sexually moral, but may lack the courage to say no to save her relationship. Mature adults are not as inclined to feel peer pressure, but not immune to it.

One of the finest examples of moral courage is Joseph, who was sold into Egypt, as recorded in the Bible. Torn from his father's house when he was seventeen, he was sold by his brothers into Egyptian slavery. Through diligence and faithfulness he worked himself up to be head of Potipher's house. Then, as his master's wife made sexual advances towards him, at the risk of offending her he had the moral courage to resist. As a result he was cast into prison.

It often takes moral courage to carry out a worthy goal. An example may be educating your children at home. You may be convinced of the worthiness of your project, but not everyone shares your views. You may find considerable opposition from the school system, or other parents who don't want to go to the trouble themselves. If you care what people think, you may find it takes moral courage to proceed toward your objective.

It may require moral courage to reach goals you set as a homemaker. You may resolve to be better organized or spend more time with your children. Then, someone urges you to do something else or calls you on the phone and wastes your time, sidetracking you from your goals. You may lack the moral courage to say *no* or to terminate phone calls for fear of offending them. What they think means more to you than your goals.

If someone is monopolizing your time on the phone, say, *"I'm sorry to interrupt but I have to go now. There is something I must do."* If someone urges you to do something you consider unimportant, say something like this: *"I'm involved in some other things right now,"* or *"There is something else I must do."*

2. *Defending Your Convictions, Beliefs:* It may take moral courage to defend your beliefs, especially if they are controversial or unpopular. This could be your religion, political views, educational ideas, racial issues, or anything which may invite unpleasant or painful consequences. We all know of the early Christians who held to their beliefs in the face of severe persecution and even death. Mankind has fought and died to defend principles they believe in.

3. *Defend the Abused:* Suppose an innocent person has been the topic of malicious gossip, his character has been defamed, or he is a victim of injustice. It is always easier to stay at arm's length. Why should you become involved in another person's affairs? You may invite sticky problems or risk your own reputation. If you fear consequences it may take considerable moral courage to defend the abused.

I am not suggesting you needlessly meddle in someone else's affairs, but when your voice could correct an injustice, have the moral courage to speak out. There are many fine examples in classical literature. In *Les Miserables,* by Victor Hugo, the most dramatic part of the story occurred when Jean Valjean had the moral courage to reveal his identity as an escaped convict, to save an innocent man who was about to be sent to the gallows.

4. *Admitting Your Wrongs:* Another time for moral courage is when you have committed a moral wrong. Sometimes consequences are serious—humiliation, disgrace, punishment, fines, or even imprisonment. This was the theme of the classic but true story *The Scarlet Letter*, by Nathaniel Hawthorne. The Reverend Arthur Dinsdale did not have the moral courage to confess his sin with Hester Prynne, and thus caused his own moral and physical degeneration. If you have committed a moral transgression, although it may mean painful consequences, have the moral courage to admit your wrong and clear

yourself before God and man. These are only a few of the ways we need moral courage. Always remember that moral courage is needed when there is *a need to do something right,* and an accompanying *fear of consequences*.

## 9. Honesty

Essential to a moral and successful life is honesty. Most of us have been trained in the basics of honesty in that we wouldn't think of stealing, cheating, or telling bold-faced lies. These standards, however, don't necessarily make us an honest person, for we may be dishonest in the more subtle forms.

Subtle forms of dishonesty are to lie about a child's age, return items to a store under false pretenses, buy items wholesale by deceptive means, illegally copy videos and cassette tapes, fail to leave identification for a damaged car, make excuses which are not entirely true, exaggerate the truth, fail to return money or goods which have been given by mistake, take pay for jobs not completed, accept a reward not earned, give false reasons for mistakes or bad behavior. We are dishonest when we *attempt to deceive anyone or misrepresent ourselves,* even if only by the tone of our voice or the raising of an eyebrow.

Subtle forms of dishonesty usually have something to do with money, inconvenience, or the fear of humiliation. To overcome dishonest tendencies *improve your values*. Tell yourself that honesty can be costly but *it's worth it*. Be willing to pay the price for it, in the way of money, inconvenience, or humiliation. Be determined to live an honest life, no matter what the cost. *Do what is right and let the consequences follow*. Whatever the consequences, honesty is rewarded a thousand-fold, for strength of character gained, and its contribution to a successful life.

## 10. Chastity

Chastity means to be sexually pure, to not have sexual relations with anyone but the person to whom you are legally married, and to not have any impure thoughts or actions. To be *unchaste* means to commit fornication, adultery, homosexuality, or any sexual act which is impure. Fornication is *un-*

*married* persons having sexual relations; adultery is *married* persons having sexual relations with someone other than their own wives or husbands; homosexuality is persons of the same sex having sexual attraction, feelings, or practices.

Sexual immorality is an old problem which dates back to the beginning of time. Prophets throughout the ages have cried out against it, terming it an *abomination,* and warning people of dangers involved. This practice continues in present society but with new dangers: Participants are pleading for society to accept their sins as *acceptable life-styles.*

There are some in this generation that claim there is no harm in sexual immorality if intimacies are practiced by two consenting adults. They blame society for the feeling of guilt imposed upon them and urge society to accept their sinful practices to ease the pain of an outraged conscience. They ignore the harm that comes to themselves and society:

## Harm in Sexual Immorality

1. *Sin in the Eyes of God:* "*Thou shalt not commit adultery*" was written on tablets of stone for the Children of Israel. This instruction was reinforced in scripture many times. Sexual immorality was considered a serious sin, punishable by death in some periods. In God's eyes it is just as serious today.

2. *Distraction:* Sexual sin is a distraction to a man in his work, and to a woman in her devotion to her family. As the interest and energies are focused on immorality, the duties of life are neglected. This can lead to failures in many areas of life.

3. *Damaged Relationships:* Attachments formed in promiscuous sex can lead to damaged relationships and broken homes. In sexual parties of several married couples, whole neighborhoods have been disrupted, resulting in broken homes and families. The damage has been awesome.

4. *Emotional Illness:* We live under spiritual laws which emanate from God. When we commit an immoral act, we come into conflict with spiritual laws, resulting in a feeling of guilt, and emotional distress. Again I quote Dr. Max Levine, the psychiatrist referred to in the last chapter: "There cannot be emotional health in the absence of high moral standards."

When immorality is committed over a period of time, the

conscience becomes callous, reducing the feeling of guilt. The numbing of the conscience destroys the finer, more noble elements of the spirit. As the conscience is eased, it fails to function as a warning, leaving the individual free to indulge in other sins, one sin provoking another.

5. *Losing the Spirit of God:* Those who commit immoral acts alienate themselves from God and therefore lose the Spirit of God. Being cut off from communication with our Heavenly Father is a frightening loss. The Spirit of God is greatly needed to guide us to a successful life, to help us make wise decisions, lay sound plans, and use good judgment. When we lose the Spirit, we are left to grope along life's path alone. This can bring failure in all areas of living.

6. *Eternal Punishment:* We read in 1 Cor. 6:9, *"Know ye not that the unrighteous shall not inherit the kingdom of God? Be not deceived; neither fornicators, nor idolaters, nor adulterers, nor effeminate, nor abusers of themselves with mankind."* The initial day of judgment at the Second Coming of our Lord Jesus Christ, as recorded in Mal. 3:5, *"will be a swift witness...against the adulterers and they shall be burned as stubble."* Why God has placed such severe punishment on this particular sin is not entirely clear, but in His noble purposes He follows undeviating principle.

7. *Downfall of Nations:* Again I quote from my husband's book, *Man of Steel and Velvet:* *"The greatest threat of any country lies in immorality, and especially in sexual immorality. Like the columns of the temple of Gaza which Samson pulled down, causing the entire temple to collapse, so will immorality lead to the weakening and eventual destruction of an entire civilization. Sexual immorality was the principle cause of the disintegration of the Roman Empire, Greece, Persia, Babylonia, Sodom and Gomorrah, and others. It is the greatest threat in America today as well as many other countries, and supersedes all other problems. It does, in fact, create most of them. If for no other reason than love of country and love of life should we avoid immorality and run from it as the greatest enemy of mankind. It will tear from us all that is near and dear."*

Related are the sins of pornographic literature, sensual music, movies, and stage plays. These, too, bring discord to the spirit. Those who expose themselves to erotic influences transgress spiritual laws and bring discord to themselves. If beautiful literature, music, and art can affect mankind favorably and enhance the spirit, then bad literature, music, and art can affect the spirit in a damaging way.

This concludes our review of character traits. There are other virtues of character. These are only the most essential. To further the study of character become aware of the common weaknesses of mankind to which we are all subject, human frailties that deter our progress and keep us from peace, happiness, and success.

## Human Frailties

My purpose here is to review only a certain category of human frailties, the weaknesses of the faithful. By faithful I mean good people who go to church, pay their tithes, are honest, fair, and basically moral. They are not adulterers. They are faithful in marriage and love their children. Yet, among such faithful are serious flaws which cause problems and deter them from success in many areas of life. The most common weaknesses are the following:

1. Laziness
2. Selfishness
3. Lack of self-discipline
4. Criticalness
5. Lack of dependability
6. Greed
7. Arrogance

These are human frailties to which we are all prone. If you think about it you will see how they cause problems and keep us from reaching success in important areas of daily living.

## How to Acquire a Worthy Character

You acquire a worthy character the way you acquire anything worthwhile, by *diligent effort*. However, with character it is difficult to reach success without daily prayer. The goal is too high and the forces of evil too strong to gain success without the guidance of the Holy Spirit. You can become a good pianist, tennis player, or public speaker by persistence alone but the perfection of a noble character is not within reach without the promptings of the Holy Spirit.

When you bring the Holy Spirit into your life you receive accompanying virtues, without a conscious effort on your part. The Apostle Paul promised, *"the fruit of the spirit is love, joy, peace, long suffering, gentleness, goodness, faith, meekness, and temperance."* This is why people who are converted to the Lord change so suddenly, having *no more disposition to do evil*.

### Is Good Character Beyond Your Reach?

Don't think that fine character is beyond your reach. Your character is not fixed or unchangeable. It was made to grow. We never know what is in our character. It is always more or less an unexplored mine. We are familiar with only a few surface details which trick us into imagining we know ourselves; but let a great crisis come, let us be thrown upon our own resources, let a dear one meet with disaster, or let a great responsibility be thrust upon us, and there can arise from the unexplored depths qualities of character which neither we ourselves nor others ever suspected.

*"But,"* you may insist, *"I am just an ordinary human being with serious faults. I can't aspire to be **the living form of a benediction**. I can never hope, with my ordinary character, to arouse such reverence and adoration as Deruchette or Amelia."* Are you so far from such reverence as you think? You may not have done anything in the past deserving of particular reverence, but how do you know what you can do in the future?

Look at the millions of ordinary women who have become the world's extraordinary mothers; or wives who have proved to be the inspiration of their husband's success and greatness. They were once ordinary young women whom no one particularly recognized as noble in character. They only *became* great mothers and wives. Each of us has within us the seeds of fine character if we believe in ourselves and work to that end.

### *Princess Maria*

In the classic novel *War and Peace* is an example of a supremely virtuous woman. Princess Maria lived with her aged father who was so harsh that Maria had to cross herself and pray each morning before she greeted him. Each day he tried to teach her geometry lessons. *She was so terrified of him that fear prevented her from understanding his explanations. She couldn't see or hear anything and was only conscious of her father's stern, withered face close to her, and her one thought was to get away as quickly as she could to work out the problem in peace in her room.*

*The old man would lose all patience, noisily push back his chair . . . then draw it forward again, making efforts to control himself and not fly into a rage but he almost always broke into a fury, storming and sometimes flinging down the exercise book. The princess made a wrong answer. "What an idiot the girl is," roared the prince. . . . Princess Maria returned to her room with the sad, scared expression that rarely left her face and made her plain, sickly face still less attractive . . . In another place he made the remark when he knew she was listening, "If only some fool would marry her."*

As the father grew older he became more difficult, but Maria endured with a quiet, spiritual resignation, not blaming him and loving him still. Later, when she thought he was near death, she sat by a window, trying to imagine how it would feel to be free from his oppression, then reproached herself mournfully for daring to think such wicked thoughts.

Maria had large luminous eyes but a rather plain face and a heavy walk. Because of her sad, sickly face men were not attracted to her. She thought she would never marry but her life took a different turn.

During the war when they were forced to flee, the servants refused to go or cooperate with her efforts. She found herself in a difficult and dangerous situation. She appealed to a nearby regiment of soldiers for help. When the commander, Nikolai Rostov, heard of her plight he came to her rescue. Princess Maria was sitting helpless and distraught in the large sitting room when Nikolai was shown in.

*When she saw his Russian face and recognized by his*

*manner and the first words he uttered that he was a man of
her own walk of life, she looked up at him with deep, starry
eyes and began speaking in a voice that faltered and trembled
with emotion. Nikolai found something romantic in the meeting. A defenseless girl alone, abandoned to the mercy of the
coarse, rebellious peasants. "And what strange destiny has
brought me here," he thought as he watched her and listened
to her story. "And what sweetness and nobility there is in her
features and expression." There were tears in Nikolai's eyes.
Princess Maria noticed it and looked grateful to him with the
luminous eyes that made one forget the plainness of her face.
And later on ...*

*She held out her delicate hand to him and for the first
time deep womanly tones vibrated. In his presence, sensing
his appreciation of her, she was transformed. Mademoiselle
Bourienne, who was in the drawing room, stared at Princess
Maria in bewildered surprise. Herself an accomplished coquette, she could not have maneuvered better on meeting a
man whom she wanted to attract. Had Princess Maria been
capable of reflection at that moment she would have been even
more astonished than Mademoiselle Bourienne at the change
that had taken place in herself.*

*For the first time all the pure, spiritual travail of which
she had lived till then came out into the open. All her inner
searchings of spirit, her sufferings, her striving after goodness,
her resignation, her love and self-sacrifice—all this shone forth
in those radiant eyes, in her sweet smile, in every feature of
her tender face. Nikolai saw all of this as clearly as though
he had known her whole life. He felt that the being before him
was utterly different from and better than anyone he had met
before, and above all, better than himself. Nikolai was struck
by her particular moral beauty ... In Princess Maria that very
sorrowfulness which revealed the depth of a whole spiritual
world foreign to him was an irresistible attraction.*

After they were married Maria kept a diary *in which she
recorded everything in the children's lives ... indicative of
their characters. The entries consisted mainly of the most tri-
fling of details but they did not seem so to the mother, or the
father now reading this journal for the first time. Nikolai put
down the book and looked at his wife. The radiant eyes gazed
at him questioningly: Would he approve or disapprove of the*

*diary? There could be no doubt, not only of his approval but also of his admiration for his wife.*

*"Perhaps it need not be done so pedantically," Nikolai thought, "perhaps it need not be done at all." But this constant, tireless spiritual application, the sole aim of which was the children's moral welfare, enchanted him. If Nikolai could have analyzed his feelings he would have found that his proud, tender, assured love for his wife rested on this very feeling of awe at her spirituality, at the lofty moral world almost beyond his reach, in which she had her being.*

*He was proud that she was so wise, and he fully recognized his own insignificance beside her in the spiritual world, and rejoiced all the more that a soul like that not only belonged to him but was part of his very self. "I quite approve, quite approve, my dearest," he said with an expressive look.*

*Maria's spirit was always striving towards the infinite, the eternal and the absolute, and could therefore never be at peace. An austere expression, born of hidden, lofty suffering of spirit, burdened by the flesh, appeared on her face. Nikolai gazed at her. "My God, what would become of us if she were to die, which is what I dread when she looks like that," he thought, and placing himself before the icon he began to say his evening prayers.*

## Traits of Character

1. Self-control
2. Unselfishness
3. Charity
4. Humility
5. Responsibility
6. Diligence
7. Patience
8. Moral Courage
9. Honesty
10. Chastity

## Assignment

Make a self-analysis of your character. List your strong points and your weak points.

# 17

## *The Domestic Goddess*

What is a Domestic Goddess? First, she is a good home-maker. She keeps a clean, orderly home, has well-behaved children, cooks delicious meals, and is successful in her overall career in the home. Second, the term relates to the woman herself and her orientation towards her work. She accepts her work as a sacred trust. Hers is a career of worldwide importance and infinite purpose. Because she glorifies her work, because she loves and serves her family as a goddess, they respect her as one. She is the queen of her household, bringing a sort of glory to her role as a homemaker.

Examples of the Domestic Goddess are found in our studies of Agnes, Amelia, and Deruchette. Agnes was as *"staid and discreet a housekeeper as the old house could have."* Amelia was a *"kind, smiling, tender, little domestic goddess whom men are inclined to worship."* And Deruchette's occupation was *"only to live her daily life."* Hugo compared her to a little bird that *"flits from branch to branch, or rather from room to room."*

### *Qualities of the Domestic Goddess*

The Domestic Goddess serves faithfully as the understanding wife, the devoted mother, and the successful homemaker. She is skilled in the feminine arts of cooking, sewing, cleaning, organizing, managing a household, caring for children, handling money wisely, and interior decorating. Not only does she do these jobs, *she does them well,* going beyond the call of duty, doing more than required.

She is *a good manager of time and values.* She is not

necessarily the most *perfect* housekeeper in town or the *best* cook or even the *most devoted* mother. But, she does succeed in her *overall responsibility* in the home, dividing her time and devotion between husband, children, and homemaking, putting the emphasis where it counts the most—*at the moment*. Of course, she may be the best housekeeper in town or the best cook. It all depends on her situation. But she is not a Domestic Goddess if she spends most of her time cleaning, while neglecting her family, or hours playing with her children, while neglecting her housework. She balances her time to meet the needs.

The Domestic Goddess adds *feminine touches* to her homemaking—gingham curtains, a basket of fruit, soft pillows, a cozy rug at the door, flowers, a row of plates above a cross beam, cheerful wallpaper—to give a homey feeling to the house. She adds feminine touches to her meals—cheerful tablecloths, pretty dishes, and delicious aromas. Men long remember the smell of their mothers' cooking—homemade bread baking, onions frying, cinnamon rolls, beef stew.

She also adds a *warmth of spirit* to her household. She scatters sunshine. It is she who makes a house a home, filling it with understanding, love, and happiness. She is the central figure in the home, its heart, its tree of life. Deruchette, you will remember, radiated warmth. *Her presence lights the home; her approach is like a cheerful warmth; she passes by and we are content; she stays awhile and we are happy*. Deruchette *shed joy around . . . cast light upon dark days*. Without Deruchette, the house would have been an empty shell. This warm presence is what every man needs when he returns from work, and what every child needs when he returns from school. The home should be their refuge, their source of comfort, understanding, and love.

The Domestic Goddess *honors her position in the home*. She looks upon her career in the home as the most important career in the world. Creating a happy marriage and family life and raising honorable children are the greatest contributions she can make to the well being of society. Even though she does nothing more than live her daily life, if she does it well it is of immeasurable value. No success compares to the success in the home; no failure a worse failure.

She is also *happy in her homemaking role*. She is not

bored. She is not looking to the world of men for fulfillment. Her glory is *the esteem of her husband, the happiness of her children, and her overall success in the home*. She may serve humanity in additional ways outside the home but she is not dependent upon it for fulfillment. In summary we can say that the Domestic Goddess has the following qualities:

### The Domestic Goddess

1. Does her jobs well, beyond the call of duty.
2. Is a good manager of time and values.
3. Adds feminine touches to her homemaking.
4. Adds warmth to her household.
5. Honors her role in the home.
6. Is happy in her role, fulfilled.

### How to Find Happiness in Homemaking

An essential quality of the Domestic Goddess is her ability to find joy and satisfaction in her work. This satisfaction comes as a result of her *attitude* about her work, her *control* of her life, and her *diligence* in performing her work, as here expressed:

1. *Accept Drudgery:* If not all of your work seems pleasant, face it honestly. Accept your work in the home as part pleasant and part unpleasant. Some jobs are just not joy producers, at least not for you. Look at it this way: Every occupation has its boring, monotonous tasks. Think of the farmer, doctor, salesman, secretary, or teacher. A certain amount of their work is drudgery. You may not find joy in changing babies, cleaning toilets, and scrubbing floors, but you *can* find *happiness in the overall accomplishment*.

Many of our duties *are* a source of real enjoyment. Caring for children, cooking delicious meals, and cleaning the house can be pleasant experiences. Some women delight in scrubbing floors, cleaning windows, washing, ironing, and organizing closets. Actually little of our work is unpleasant, but when it seems so to you, face it honestly, realizing that the world's work consists of a certain amount of drudgery.

2. *Don't Become Crowded for Time:* If you want to enjoy homemaking, don't become involved in too many activities

outside the home. The most time-consuming are outside employment, assisting your husband in his business, or doing masculine jobs around the house, such as yard work, painting, handling money, or bookkeeping.

Also, limit your time for clubs, service organizations, self-improvement programs, education classes, or lessons. Although these programs may be a fine thing if you have time for them, don't let them rob you of time to enjoy homemaking.

Activities within the home may crowd you for time, such as talking on the phone, browsing through magazines, watching T.V., extensive sewing, or canning. These time robbers can cause you to be in a last minute rush for the important things. When such is the case, it's difficult to enjoy your work. When anything crowds you for time, so you hurry through your jobs to get them over with, it's difficult to enjoy them.

Observe a little girl playing house. She doesn't hurry to get her work done. She puts her doll in a crib, folds the little blankets, tucks them in carefully, and when she is finished, takes them off and does it all over again. She does the same with a little tea set, setting and unsetting the table, over and over again. She enjoys her work because she is unaware of time. I doubt if she would enjoy it if she were to watch a clock. I believe our natural instinct is to enjoy domestic work, as little girls do, and being crowded for time robs us of enjoyment.

If you are thinking, "I don't have time to play house as little girls do," ask yourself, "What am I doing that is more important than *doing domestic work and enjoying it?*" Perhaps you are giving important service. That may have to come first for a time. Measure each activity for its value, always regarding home duties and your enjoyment of them of major importance.

3. *Go the Second Mile*: To find joy in your work, *do it well*. This doctrine was taught hundreds of years ago by Jesus when He said, *"If anyone compel thee to go one mile, go with him twain."* Going the second mile, or beyond the call of duty, lifts the burden from work and makes it seem easy and enjoyable. Perhaps this is what Jesus meant when he said, *"My yoke is easy and my burden light."*

Many women fail to find happiness in homemaking because they go only the first mile. They give only the bare stint of requirement—just enough to get by. They feed and clothe

the family and keep the house reasonably clean, but not an ounce more. Their meals are all quick and easy, and then they're off to an outside diversion. Women who give just enough to get by never enjoy homemaking. You have to go the second mile to enjoy anything. This is what Jesus taught when he said, *"He who loseth his life for my sake, shall surely find it."*

## Fundamentals of Good Homemaking

The difference between a good homemaker and a poor one is a matter of following correct principles. Here are the fundamentals which lead to a clean, uncluttered, well-organized household:

1. *Concentrate:* The management of a household requires concentration. You can't daydream, ponder problems, and at the same time work with efficiency. Work such as ironing, cleaning windows, and doing dishes can be done while daydreaming but most work requires thought as well as hands, especially organizing and meal preparation. Put other things out of your mind and concentrate on the jobs at hand. What is considered lack of homemaking ability is usually mental laziness.

2. *Simplify:* You cannot become a good housekeeper if you have too many things, such as too much furniture, too many dishes, unnecessary clothes, old papers and magazines, too many toys, objects, ornaments, or heirlooms. They are of value only if they are useful or add beauty to the home. When they make housekeeping difficult they should be removed. For greatest efficiency, have only enough goods to serve the family. Anything more clutters the household and burdens the homemaker.

If you have a cluttered household and want to turn it into an organized one, the first step is to *get rid of things you don't need*. Begin by setting aside a day to *whittle life down to the bone*. Get a lot of corrugated boxes. Label them: *Throw Away, Give Away, Put Away, Store Away,* and *Can't Decide*. Go through your cupboards, drawers, and closets, quickly. Keep only those things *you know* are essential and discard the rest in the boxes. Also consider all objects sitting on open shelves, tables or hanging on walls. When you have covered your entire household do the following:

- First, get rid of *Throw Away* boxes.
- Put *Store Away* boxes in the attic, basement, closet.
- Put *Give Away* boxes in the trunk of your car.
- Put away the things in the *Put Away* boxes. If there are too many, stack the boxes in a corner and go through them in the next few days.
- Put the *Can't Decide* boxes in your garage, attic, or basement and sort through them when convenient. After you have sorted through them, if there are items you still can't decide what to do with, leave them in the box for about six months. At the end of this time if you have not needed them, you will know they are not essential and can give them away.

In simplifying a household, everything should be *either useful* or *beautiful*. Have only enough useful and beautiful goods to serve your needs. In other words, an egg beater is useful and drinking glasses are useful, but you don't need two egg beaters or forty glasses. Better to have too few than too many. As for beautiful ornaments or pictures, limit them to those which enhance the beauty of your home. Too many art objects look cluttered and ugly. As for family heirlooms, art treasures, and things of sentimental value, store them if you can but if they burden life rather than enrich it, they may not be worth saving.

3. *Organize Things:* To be well organized, *have a place for everything*. In the kitchen every dish, bowl, glass, or pan should have a place of its own. The same with the shoe polish, scissors, stationery, string, newspapers, or magazines. Organize bedroom closets with enough rods, shelves, baskets, and hooks. Provide drawers, or just a box under the bed. When everything has a place of its own, do the following: Always put things back in their exact place and teach all family members to do the same. When things in your house are this well organized you can get up in the night without turning on a light and find what you need.

Very useful is a large, walk-in storage closet lined with

shelves. This could be added to the basement, attic, garage, or as a small wing on your house. Into this put anything not currently needed such as off-season clothes, old shoes, extra fabric, thread, old patterns, Christmas decorations, heirlooms and pictures.

4. *Organize Work and Commitments:* First, list work and commitments you do *routinely*—meals, laundry, make beds, tidy the house, vacuum, grocery shop, take child to piano lesson, mend, shop, weekly clean. Then arrange them on a *schedule* so you have a specific time to do everything. Next, list things you do *occasionally,* such as appointments, phone calls, social events, special cleaning, shopping, sewing, outings. To be well organized in getting your work done and keeping your commitments, use a *calendar notebook.* For information about a planning notebook produced by *Fascinating Womanhood,* refer to the appendix.

5. *Organize Priorities:* Work out *wise* priorities. Put first things first. To arrange priorities, list your six most important duties, then arrange them in order of importance. Consult your husband and children for their opinions. For example:

### Priority List

> My Appearance
> Regular Meals on Time
> House tidy
> Washing and ironing
> Imperative Shopping
> Auxiliary things:

An infant in the family requires top priority. Small children must also be high on the list. Auxiliary jobs are such things as doctors' appointments, school events, scouts, transporting children to music lessons, etc. When small children require priority, you may have to forgo some things on your auxiliary list and have your husband do the imperative shopping. If you don't get anything done beyond your priority list, you will be doing the most important things.

Next, create a secondary list—clean the house, wash windows, sweep garage, sew, shop, train children, time for self and others. Also make a third list for occasional jobs—special cleaning, organizing closets and drawers, seasonal shopping, home decorating.

To keep priorities, avoid time wasters such as talking on the phone for long periods, sewing to excess, spending hours of time reading, watching T.V., or browsing through shops. You may justify time spent on these things because you enjoy them. Such may be the case, but when you determine to be a Domestic Goddess you must be willing to make such sacrifices.

6. *Work:* Although you concentrate, simplify, organize, and have priorities well in mind, you will not reach success unless you are willing to work. Good homemaking requires *diligent effort* as does any worthy achievement. The only way to run a household is to put on your apron, roll up your sleeves, and go to work. But it's fun to cook, clean, and organize— the most wholesome, rewarding work in the world.

7. *Make Him Comfortable:* With all of your diligence in homemaking, allow your husband to be comfortable. Remember, *his home is his castle*. Let him hang his coat on a chair, lie on his bed without concern for the spread, stack his papers on his desk, put his glasses on the dresser, and his shoes by the bed. This doesn't mean you invite him to be slovenly to the point of imposing on you, but let him be relaxed and comfortable in his own home. This too is part of being a Domestic Goddess.

For example, a man was married to a fussy, perfectionist housekeeper. She followed him around picking up after him, straightening the pillows. smoothing the rugs, picking lint from the carpet, and removing his clutter. Finally he tired of this foolishness, divorced her, and married a woman who was the opposite. She was a good housekeeper, but allowed him to relax and be comfortable. In comparing the two women, he said, "The change in wives was like taking off a pair of tight shoes and putting on a pair of soft, comfortable, slippers." Children should not be given the same *relaxing* privileges as their father. They should bend to your training and instructions.

## Motherhood

The Domestic Goddess finds joy in bearing children. This is a natural instinct in the truly feminine woman. You don't have to teach her, it is *inborn*. She is like Rachel and Hannah in the Bible who, when they discovered they were barren, cried to the Lord for children. Theirs was an inner yearning to fill the measure of their creation.

The feminine woman has a natural instinct to *care for* her little ones. Like the mother robin, she is consumed in feeding her offspring and guarding the nest. Moved by an instinctive concern for their physical welfare, she sees that they are properly fed, bathed, and free of danger. She would never allow them to go hungry, cold, or unprotected, if within her power to prevent it. She takes pride in their appearance by keeping them clean, well groomed, and attractively dressed. She is gentle, loving, and understanding. She teaches them how to be happy, and gives them praise and encouragement—providing bread for their souls as well as their bodies.

How does a man view all of this? Men respect women who delight in bearing children. The man himself may complain about the responsibility, and even oppose the birth of more children, but he doesn't admire women who complain. How unfeminine it sounds when a woman complains sorrowfully, *"Oh, I'm pregnant again."* Men admire women who want children and devote themselves to their care, no matter what the sacrifice.

## Meal Preparation

Meals are highly important to most husbands and children. Imagine how they feel when they come home after a busy day, hungry and tired, but know they can count on a good meal as a regular part of family life. As they open the door they smell bread baking, onions frying, or a delicious pot of soup brewing on the stove. This sets a wonderful atmosphere in the home. Elaborate meals aren't necessary. What is important is that meals be *on time, nutritious, and taste good.*

Of all domestic tasks other than the care of little children, the most urgent is feeding the family. Other things can wait. Meals are in daily demand. To succeed, *allow enough time.* It takes time to cook a good meal. Don't skimp by preparing something in a last-minute rush. Instead of setting a time to *serve the meal*, set a time to *begin preparation.* Also important is an attractive table setting with a tablecloth if possible.

Many women fail in meal preparation. They go for the quick, easy, meals with an emphasis on speed. Their goal is to get in and out of the kitchen in as short a time as possible, using the fewest dishes and making the least mess. They rely on frozen dinners, cold cuts, packaged mixes, canned foods, macaroni, and other quick and easy foods. Even worse, some families don't have regular meals together—just snacking.

One reason women go for the quick and easy meals is because they don't want to get the kitchen dirty. But what is a kitchen for? It's not for looking at admiringly, but for working in diligently. The Domestic Goddess may have pots and pans strewn around the kitchen, steam on the windows, dishes in the sink, and flour on her face, but the results—a good home-cooked meal, the center of family life.

## The Housedress

Many women of today don't understand the meaning of the term *housedress*, so I will explain: A housedress is a cute cotton dress, made comfortable enough to work in, usually worn with an apron. Wear it to function in your career as a domestic goddess. It is more or less your uniform or identification mark. When you wear a feminine, domestic-looking housedress and apron, there will be no doubt in the minds of your family about who you are—the queen of the household.

## Housekeeping, a Matter of Character

You may never have thought of it before, but keeping the house clean, preparing meals, and managing the household is a matter of character. The woman who fails in these areas shows a weakness of character, in the following ways:

1. *Self-centeredness:* Poor homemaking is usually traced to self-centeredness, wherein the wife thinks too much of her own comforts and pleasures, and spends her time talking on the phone, browsing through magazines, loafing, visiting, or gadding about the community, rather than on things that would make her family comfortable and happy.

2. *Lack of Organization:* God, who is our pattern of perfection, sets before us the work of His creations—a masterpiece

of organization and system, from the human body to the planets in the heavens. He has said, *"I am a God of order, not confusion."* Failure to follow this eternal example indicates lack of character.

3. *Lack of Knowledge:* Poor homemaking may be due to a lack of knowledge. This is understandable in the newly married woman, but when she makes no effort to learn, it indicates a lack of caring, and therefore a lack of character. This can be compared to a man who is not making an adequate living, but makes no effort to gain knowledge to improve his earning capacity. If knowledge is not available, turn to God for help. As we are taught in the Bible, *"If any of ye lack wisdom, let him ask of God, Who giveth to all men liberally."* (James 1:6)

4. *Lack of a Sense of Responsibility:* One of the major reasons for poor homemaking is a lack of a sense of responsibility, or a failure to assume work that belongs to us. As explained in the chapter on character, a keen sense of responsibility is a virtue. When it is lacking there is a deficiency of character.

5. *Laziness:* This is also a flaw in character, a lack of diligence. In addition, the woman who will not care for her family because she is lazy demonstrates a lack of love for them, a lack of concern for their comfort, a lack of character.

### Don't Let Life Become Narrow

There is a tendency for women who focus their time and attention on homemaking to become narrow in interests and viewpoint and therefore stunted in personality. Friends, strangers, and even their own husbands may find them a little dull or even boring. Avoid being narrow by extending your interests beyond your home and family. Keep your eyes open and learn to listen. You'll learn a lot from people. Keep up with current events to learn what is going on in the community and the world. Read as widely as you can. Develop an interest in people.

### Beyond Your Role as the Domestic Goddess

If you are an efficient homemaker you will have time for things beyond your role in the home, time to pursue other interests, develop talents, and give service. This can enrich your life and make you a better person, a better wife, a better mother. It will broaden your horizons and keep you from being narrow. Although family life should always be your first concern, you can be a part of the world beyond. Don't, however, become involved in things which are too time consuming, demanding, or inflexible, or which distract you from your priority in the home. The greatest hazard is employment or a career. Here are true experiences to prove the rewards in store for a Domestic Goddess:

## *I Was So Sure Our Marriage Was Over*

"I never thought any book could save a marriage, but after eight weeks of *Fascinating Womanhood* I'm convinced it has. I was so sure our marriage was over. We just couldn't get along—so many fights that left us both miserable for days, not knowing from one day to the next when the next blowup would be. We talked about divorce a few times but for the children's sake we decided to stay together. We were both very unhappy.

"I decided to go to work to see if that was what I needed. For awhile it seemed to make things a little better but after about nine months I could see we were growing even further apart. And I just didn't care about the house or the children anymore. I couldn't look at myself in the mirror because I didn't like what I saw. Deep down inside I was searching for something. I wasn't even sure what it was I wanted. Was it to be free? I was so sick of the hassles of marriage, children, housework, etc. Things were looking pretty bad all around. I'm really surprised when I think of it that my husband didn't leave. I suppose he felt the same way I did in all respects.

"I decided to quit work and try to straighten things out as much as possible. Little did I know that what I was searching for was right at my fingertips all the time. I had a bad attitude about everything and it must have shown, because a friend said she was going to go to classes called *Fascinating Womanhood* to learn how to be fascinating. She asked me to come along.

"I listened to our teacher that first night and all through the class all I could think was, 'What a fool I have been for so many years, sixteen, as a matter of fact!' I have kicked myself over and over for being so self-righteous, thinking that all of our problems were because of things my husband had done to me. I decided that if I was to live F.W. I would put my whole heart into it.

"Well, to my surprise I found out what a wonderful thing it is to be a fascinating woman. During the first three weeks I could see a change in myself, and in my husband. So many good things have happened. I keep saying to myself, 'It's really working. I can't believe it!' We have been able to face our problems much more easily. Things just don't seem so bad anymore.

"One thing I have noticed is that I'm enjoying life and the things around me. I'm happy to be a wife, mother, house-keeper, and all that goes with it. My attitude has changed completely and so has my husband's. Now, whenever we have a problem that makes us feel down and out, I just go to my husband, wrap my arms around him and tell him that I love him and that everything is going to be all right, and you wouldn't believe how he just seems to relax. I'm sure it means a lot to him just to know that I care enough about him to try to be a fascinating woman.

"I could go on for a week telling of all the successes I have had. There is one thing for sure. Anyone who thinks that there are more important things than a happy marriage and the peace and contentment of a happy home needs to read *Fascinating Womanhood*. Thank you so much, dear Lord, for bringing *Fascinating Womanhood* into my life."

## He Wanted to Come Home to a Woman

"I was so happy on my wedding day. Somehow my hus-band was stronger, braver, and more chivalrous than I ever dared hope for. Yet things rapidly went wrong. So much so that after only one year of marriage we were planning to live entirely separate lives. He would have one room of our house to live in alone, and I would have the rest of the house for myself and our son. The only reason we didn't separate com-pletely was because he said he couldn't afford to run two houses.

"I also remember him saying sadly one evening, 'I want

to come home to a woman.' This hurt, but I didn't really understand what he meant. Then, I remember thinking, 'From the bottom of my heart I wish I knew how to be a wife.' I really had no idea what I should do.

"Shortly after this I found F.W. in a local bookstore. Amazingly I actually had enough money in my purse to buy it, although we were very poor at the time. I can hardly describe how I felt when I first read it. I can only say it 'spoke to my heart.' I did not need any convincing of the truth of the teachings. During the year of applying the teachings the following incidents come to mind:

"Applying the seemingly small principle of *joy in bearing children:* I was pregnant at the time with our third child, and enjoying it deeply. I was sitting down one evening with no shoes on, and here I must add that my feet are the largest size in ladies footwear. I have bunions and hammer toes and, in short, my feet are not my best feature. My husband suddenly got up from his chair, sank to his knees, and while still on his knees walked across the room, and kissed my feet! Evidently that moment of my contented serenity in my condition moved him deeply. The fact that my feet are not beautiful made it even more meaningful.

"Another incident that stands out: Our house was in poor decorative condition and in need of repair. This used to upset me. One day, using the principle of childlikeness, I said simply, 'Can I have some money to make the house nice?' He smiled and said, 'OK, will two hundred dollars be all right?' I said, contriving with childlikeness, 'Oh, no! two hundred dollars is not enough. I need two thousand dollars.' (We were lacking basic kitchen amenities and other costly items. I also knew he had made an unusually large profit in his business.) To my amazement he said, 'OK, when do you want it?' Shortly after this he insisted on buying me a car, so I could have some freedom. This made me feel loved and understood.

"Another remarkable incident was when his work caused him to live away from home for sixteen months. He was compelled to take this job, and I must say I was rather worried as to how it would affect our marriage. This time the principles of *making sure he feels needed and he felt my full support in doing what he felt was necessary* came to my rescue. When I put into words how much I needed him, I realized how profoundly true it was. How would I manage without his *strong arm to lean on?* He assured me that he would telephone and come home regularly. When the time came he was more than true to his word.

"My dear husband, in his concern for us, telephoned us every day he was away (except one day that I was supposed to call him) to check that we were all right. He did this every day at the same time, so we wouldn't be kept anxiously waiting for his call. This was a great comfort to me in his absence and I could ask his advice whenever I needed it. In addition, he came home every weekend. He calculated that he drove approximately 24,000 miles to come home during that time. For a man who dislikes long-distance driving, this is truly remarkable. With the help of F.W. I have become the *real woman he longed to come home to.*

"However, even after twelve years F.W. is a real challenge to me. I still have trouble with overweight, due to sugar dependency. I also have a battle with anger that I grew up in a dirty, ugly home, although Mum was earning a good salary. I interpreted the awful food and dirt as lack of love, and became rebellious as a teenager. I turned to drugs and sex and was, in fact, pregnant on my wedding day. But with F.W. I not only found married happiness beyond my dreams, the journey to become *fascinating* led me to Christianity. Thank you is a very small word for such a big gift."

## Qualities of the Domestic Goddess

1. Does her job well.
2. Is a good manager of time and values.
3. Adds feminine touches to her homemaking.
4. Adds warmth to her household.
5. Honors her position in the home.
6. Is happy in her role.

## How to Find Happiness in Homemaking

1. Accept drudgery.
2. Don't become crowded for time.
3. Go the second mile.

## *Assignment*

1. List in order of importance your six most essential responsibilities. Check with husband and children, for their ideas.
2. List your strong points in domestic skills.
3. List your weak points. Improve these areas.
4. Read from the Bible: Proverbs 31:10–31

# Part II
# THE HUMAN QUALITIES

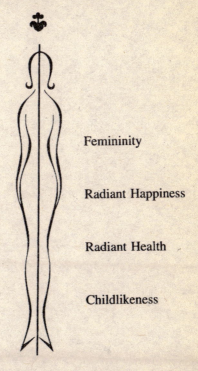

Femininity

Radiant Happiness

Radiant Health

Childlikeness

The human side of a woman fascinates, amuses, captivates, and enchants a man. It arouses a desire to protect and shelter.

To become an ideal woman from a man's point of view it is essential that you have not only the angelic qualities just covered but the human. The following chapters are devoted to a study of the human qualities and how to acquire them.

# Introduction to Femininity

## What Is Femininity?

Femininity is a gentle, tender quality found in a woman's *appearance, manner,* and *nature.* A feminine woman gives the impression of *softness,* and *delicateness.* She has a spirit of *sweet submission,* and a *dependency* upon men for their care and protection. Nothing about her appears masculine—no male aggressiveness, competence, efficiency, fearlessness, strength, or *the ability to kill her own snakes.*

Femininity has great appeal to men, for it is such a contrast to their own strong and firm masculinity. This contrast, when brought to a man's attention, causes him to feel more masculine, and this realization of his masculine strength and ability is one of the most enjoyable sensations he can experience.

Femininity awakens a man's tender, romantic feelings. When femininity disappears, his romantic feelings disappear. He may continue to respect and appreciate a woman who has lost her femininity, but will not feel the same.

The feminine woman is naturally oriented towards her womanhood. She is proud to be a woman and happy to fill her destiny as a wife and mother, anxious to make a happy home for her loved ones. Her career is a career in the home. Her occupation is to live her daily life. Her glory is the esteem of her husband and the happiness of her children.

Think of femininity in two categories—*outer* femininity and *inner* femininity. Outer femininity has to do with her *appearance* and *manner,* whereas inner femininity has to do with her *feminine nature,* and her *orientation towards her feminine role.*

Femininity is acquired by *accentuating the differences* between yourself and men, not the similarities. This is applied to the *feminine appearance, manner, nature,* and *the feminine role.* In Part 2 we study *the feminine role versus the working wife,* and how working outside the home affects femininity.

# 18

## *The Feminine Appearance*

A noticeable characteristic of the feminine woman is that she *gives careful attention to her appearance*. She doesn't neglect her hair, face, figure, or clothes. She looks as pretty as she can at all times. This is instinctive in her nature. An *ideal* woman, however, doesn't focus unduly on her looks. She doesn't spend endless hours on her appearance, and in so doing neglect important duty. She devotes herself to those things which need her time and attention, but manages to find time to look attractive.

A wonderful example of a woman who manages the affairs of her household, while at the same time taking care of her appearance, is the virtuous woman described in Proverbs 31: She arises before daybreak to take care of the needs of her household; works *willingly* with her hands; gathers wool and flax and spins it into yarn; plants a vineyard; stretches out her hands to the poor and the needy; makes warm clothes for her children; and makes fine linen and sells it.

In addition, she manages to find time for herself. *"She maketh herself coverings of tapestry; her clothing is silk and purple."* Please note the fabrics. Tapestry is an intricate, beautiful design woven into the fabric. Silk is the most feminine of all fabrics. The color purple is significant, suggesting she cares about her appearance, and goes to some trouble to look her best.

### How to Acquire a Feminine Appearance

To acquire a feminine appearance, *accentuate the differences between yourself and men*. Wear only those materials

248

and styles which are the least suggestive of men's and which make the greatest contrast to their apparel. Men never wear anything fluffy, lacy, or gauzy. Use such materials, therefore, whenever you can. Men seldom pay much attention to the latest style, so keep up your interest in current fashions. In developing a feminine appearance, observe the following rules:

1. *Fabric Weave:* Avoid such fabrics as tweeds, herringbones, hard finish woolens, denims, glen plaids, pin stripes, or any fabrics commonly used by men. They can be used, however, if distinguished by an ultrafeminine *style, color,* or *trim.* Otherwise they give no help in making him realize how womanly you are! They cannot strive to bring out any contrast between your nature and his.

Do wear soft or crisp cottons, soft or fine woolens, linens, silks, or anything silky, soft, or womanly. The extremes of feminine fabrics are chiffon, lace, velvet, satin, angora, and organdie. Try to include some of these in your wardrobe. Wear them when trying to appear the most feminine.

2. *Fabric Color:* Colors which are feminine are pastels, soft colors, clear colors, rich colors, and even black. Avoid drab colors used by men, such as browns, grays, and khaki. They may be used, however, if of a soft fabric, feminine style, or trim.

3. *Fabric Design:* In selecting a print, take care that it is a *good design.* Avoid anything which is loud, gaudy, or lacking in good taste. The print should not dominate the woman. The design of the fabric should suggest softness, modesty, womanliness.

4. *Style:* Avoid tailored styles or any suggestion of masculinity such as pants, mannish jackets and coats, buttoned cuffs, and top stitching. These styles can be used, however, if made of a feminine material or color. Extreme feminine styles are full skirts, ruffles, puffed sleeves, gathers, and drapes. Use them when in style and appropriate. Even a plain dress is feminine, since it is not part of a man's wardrobe.

5. *Pants*: Should women wear pants? Pants are *not the most feminine of dress.* You *can* wear them, however, if of a feminine material and style, and a color becoming to you. Soften the masculine effect by wearing a feminine top, ac-

cessories, and hair style. If you have a chunky figure be sure the pants are not too tight. Better if they are a little loose. Unless you are very young, avoid denims and fabrics used by men.

6. *Trim:* Trim can give a feminine effect to an otherwise plain dress—lace, ribbon, colorful tie, embroidery, beads, braid.

7. *Accessories:* Avoid purses which resemble men's briefcases and shoes of masculine style. Wear soft scarves, flowers, and jewelry.

8. *Grooming and Makeup:* For generations women used rags to curl their hair, pinched their cheeks for color, applied eye makeup, and used fragrances. The bath was their routine, as was clean, squeaky hair and laundered clothes. Women who came over on the Mayflower may not have had enough water to drink, but they sneaked enough to wash their white collars and caps. Traditionally women have claimed the right to their sacred toilette.

Women today are essentially the same. Much time, effort, and money is spent on looking pretty. Hairstyles are important. Women bathe as never before. They primp, glance in the mirror from time to time to fix their hair or touch up their makeup. Their tools are combs, brushes, curlers, hair pins, dryers, perms, and a wide variety of makeup.

Careful attention to makeup and hairstyles is feminine, accentuates your natural endowments, and makes you more fascinating. Your husband may or may not notice it, or may fail to comment, but if you *neglect* your appearance he *will* notice it. He wants you to look pretty. Does he want you to look pretty to all men? Yes, unless a man is terribly jealous or overly possessive he wants his wife to look pretty to everyone.

9. *Modesty:* Still another part of the feminine appearance is modesty. In spite of the worldly emphasis on low-cut, scanty clothes, decent men don't respect women who expose too much of their bodies to the public. Not only should the *body* be modestly covered, but the *underwear*. Men dislike visible slips, bra straps, or exposed underwear. Higher types of civilization have traditionally been modest. It seems to go with intelligence and refinement.

## What the Feminine Appearance Does:

When you dress in feminine clothes and are well groomed, it increases your feeling of self-esteem. You feel better about yourself. You are encouraged to act more feminine in the way you walk, move your hands, sit, and conduct yourself. The outer appearance encourages the feminine manner.

A feminine appearance brings out a favorable response in a man. As you acquire a more feminine appearance, he will notice you more, find you more appealing and respect you more, as suggested in the following success stories:

### He Didn't Recognize Me

"*Fascinating Womanhood* is so foreign to my nature that it was difficult to apply. I'm loud, obnoxious, and dominating. I was about as feminine as a man. But I don't want to be anymore. My husband and I separated. I see why now. Then I didn't. The children were the ones who suffered most. I have a teenager who was absolutely crushed by it. My husband left for a harlot, left his job, everything for her. I couldn't understand it.

"Then a friend gave me F.W. to read. I let my hair grow, let my nails grow, lost twenty pounds and bought dresses. I'd always been heavy with short, slicked, black-brown hair. I went from a fourteen to a perfect nine. I bleached my hair like it was when I was young and got a new feminine hairstyle.

"When my husband came to visit he didn't even recognize me. The children and I applied *Fascinating Womanhood*. The funny part is that everything I said was the truth. I hadn't realized what I had. He really is a marvelous man. I just never told him that before.

"The harlot—he gave her up in a week. He has never needed her since. We are very happy and so are the children. F.W. has saved so many lives. I also think my husband's life is much improved, and I have really benefited.

"I quit work so we could have more time together. I don't know any knowledge that can change a person's life so much, can cause so much happiness for so many. I want to thank the author. I owe her so much."

## I Bought Feminine Dresses

"I'm not very good at expressing myself but I must tell you how *Fascinating Womanhood* has changed my life. My husband and I married very young. I wanted so badly to be a good wife, the kind you read about in love stories. I wanted to be fascinating, and loving, and soft. Only I came from a family where my mother hated housework, cooking, kids— everything womanly. I had no one to copy or to show me how to be who I longed to be. I didn't fit in my mother's world or in the women's lib world. I looked at marriage with both wishfulness and fear.

"I wanted marriage but I wanted a special kind of marriage, one where outsiders could just feel the love surrounding my family. I didn't want the kind of marriage I found with all my neighbors and friends, with the wife telling the man what to do, always yelling and screaming, demanding her way. I wanted more than just a man and a woman living under the same roof. Only I felt that maybe the only people who live like this are the ones in children's bedtime stories.

"Then I met my husband. He was young, but he had good basic qualities and soon he had my heart. I thought with this boy I could have the kind of marriage I dreamed of. Anxious to be a wife, homemaker, and mother we started a family right away. I got pregnant within a few months, just in time to see my dreams all falling apart.

"My husband spent most of his time with the boys. When he was home he was always drinking, yelling, and slapping me around. He never asked me to do anything, he ordered. I feared him and almost hated him, but I came from a family who believed: 'You made your bed, you lie in it.' I had nowhere to go and a baby due any day. I felt helpless, trapped, and a complete failure as a woman. Where had things gone wrong?

"When my baby was born my husband started to change and I could see part of that person I once loved return. He was a fabulous father, but things didn't change between us. He still slapped me around, wouldn't come home every night till ten or later from being out with the guys, and would pick fights when he was home. This went on for four and one-half years. I hated being married, I hated being a mother, and I hated men. I wanted a divorce. My dream of marriage was just that, a dream. I tried so hard to be a good wife; how had I failed?

"One day I was reading the paper and saw an article about *Fascinating Womanhood*. They described marriage just like my dream! Maybe, just maybe, I could fit with them. Maybe they could help me find who I am. I had hit bottom. How I hoped this was the answer to my prayers. I was so hopeful I rushed down to a bookstore to buy a copy of F.W. weeks before the classes began. Once I started to read I knew this was the answer to my prayers! And I decided to start right then to live this way.

"All this time I had blamed my husband for our bad marriage. How wrong I was! Bit by bit I started to change, not him, *myself!* I bought some new feminine dresses in soft colors with full skirts, let my nails grow, put a permanent in my hair. So much for the outside. Now I had to change the inside. I started looking at just my husband's good points. He was a good father, generous with his money, a hard worker, and a good leader. I could go on and on, and I did, to *him*.

"When I got up in the morning I tried to look at the good things that would happen that day, such as the pretty wild-flowers growing, or the beautiful sunset. I thought of little things I could do to make my husband happy such as cooking what he liked or writing love notes to him, telling him about the things he's done or said that made me happy. When he wanted to talk, I made a point of forgetting *all* else to listen to him, even if it meant turning off the dinner, or stopping folding the clothes. I did these and much more, trying to show him in all ways, at all times, that I accept him as he is, a man, and leader.

"I have been living *Fascinating Womanhood* for a year and a half now and you would never believe we are the same couple. He takes me out to lunch, fishing, and almost every-where he goes. Lots of times we just go for drives or window shopping. And where before he never bought me presents, even on my birthday or Christmas, now I get presents just because he loves me. He now enjoys buying me clothes and things for the house. Would you believe we are even thinking about having another baby, an absolute no-no just eighteen months ago! Thanks to *Fascinating Womanhood* I don't dream of a beautiful warm, friendly, and loving marriage. I'm living it.''

### To Acquire a Feminine Appearance:

*Accentuate the differences between you and men in:*

1. Fabric Weave
2. Fabric Color
3. Fabric Design
4. Style
5. Pants
6. Trim
7. Accessories
8. Grooming/Makeup
9. Modesty

### Assignment

Make or buy a feminine housedress and apron. Add feminine touches (ribbon or pearls). Groom your hair in a feminine style and if you wear makeup, apply it with skill. Watch your husband's reaction. Record his favorable reaction in your love booklet.

*To achieve a feminine appearance, the important thing to remember is the over-all impression you make. It is not necessary to wear ruffles and lace, but do work for a striking contrast to masculinity.*

# 19

## *The Feminine Manner*

The *feminine manner* is the motions of a woman's body, the way she walks, talks, uses her hands, the sound of her voice, her facial expressions, and her laugh. The feminine manner is attractive to a man because it is such a contrast to his masculine strength and firmness. David Copperfield was fascinated by Dora's enchanting manner—the way she patted the horses, spanked her little dog, or held the flowers against her chin. *"She had the most delightful little voice, the gayest little laugh, the pleasantest and most fascinating little ways."*

The feminine *appearance* is highly important, as emphasized in the last chapter, but if you do not add a feminine *manner*, the effect can be disappointing, even amusing. For example, if a woman is dressed in a soft, frilly dress, but moves about with a stiff, brusk manner, her manner doesn't seem to fit the dress. We have all seen women who wear the most feminine dresses, but who wear them as if they were on the wrong person. They do not carry themselves in a way to harmonize with their clothes. They are *professors in chiffon, bears in lace,* or *wooden posts in organdie.*

### Margaret and Gerard

In the classic novel *The Cloister and the Hearth*, by Charles Reade, is an illustration of the feminine manner and its enchanting effect on a young man: Margaret and her father had stopped by the wayside when a stranger, Gerard, stopped to help them with their difficulties. As they were about to proceed on their way:

"*Gerard could not tie his ribbon again as Catherine, his mother, had tied it. Margaret, after slyly eyeing his efforts for some time, offered to help him; for at her age girls love to be coy and tender, saucy and gentle, by turns . . . then a fair head with its stately crown of auburn curls, glossy and glowing through silver, bowed sweetly towards him; and while it ravished his eye, two white supple hands played delicately upon the stubborn ribbon and molded it with soft, airy touches.*

"*Then a heavenly thrill ran through the innocent young man and vague glimpses of a new world of feeling and sentiment opened to him. And these new exquisite sensations Margaret unwittingly prolonged; it is not natural to her sex to hurry ought that pertains to the sacred toilet.*

"*Nay, when the taper fingers had at last subjugated the ends of the knot, her mind was not quite easy till, by a maneuver peculiar to the female hand, she had made her palm convex and so applied it with a gentle pressure to the center of the knot—a sweet little coaxing hand kiss, as much as to say, 'now be a good knot and stay so!'*

"'*There, that was how it was!*' *said Margaret, and drew back to take one last survey of her work, then looking up for a simple approval of her skill, received full in her eyes a longing gaze of such adoration as made her lower them quickly and color all over.*"

Acquire a feminine manner by *accentuating the differences* between yourself and men, not the *similarities*. Since the masculine manner is strong, firm, and heavy, yours should be gentle, delicate, and light. Apply this in the way you walk, talk, use your hands, and carry yourself.

## 1. The Hands

Avoid stiff, brusque movements. Don't wave your hands in the air or use them firmly in expressing yourself. Never pound on the table to put over a point. Never grasp the sides of a lectern or pulpit. Never slap anyone on the back. Learn how to shake hands with men. Never shake a man's hand with strength and vigor, regardless of how happy you are to see him. The handshake should be gentle but firm.

## 2. The Walk

Avoid a heavy gait or long strides, such as the way men walk. Don't copy the fashion model walk. It is arrogant and unfeminine. Walk in a light, graceful, natural, manner, with legs somewhat straight. To induce a *light* walk, imagine you weigh ninety-five pounds. Have someone tape a video of you walking. It will give you a visual view of how you need to improve.

## 3. The Voice

If you are learning to walk and use your hands correctly, you tend to modulate your voice to harmonize with your manner. If you find your voice is spoiling the impression you are trying to create, make an effort to change it.

Don't talk too loud. And don't let your voice suggest mannish efficiency or coarse boldness. No man likes a coarse, loud, or vulgar tone in a woman any more than a woman likes an effeminate tone in a man. And no man likes a mumbling, dull, monotonous, or singsong voice, because it indicates the character behind the voice is equally dull and uninteresting.

Your voice should be clear and variable. If you have difficulty with your voice, record it on a tape player. If your voice sounds dry or raspy, you may sleep with your mouth open. This can dry out your vocal cords. If you can't overcome this habit, hang a wet towel in your room at night. A raspy voice can also be caused by eating junk food. Smoking *ruins* the voice.

To improve your voice, practice speaking or reading aloud to yourself in the privacy of your room. If your lips, cheeks, or tongue are tight, practice with marbles in your mouth. When you read to yourself, do so with expression— enthusiasm, delight, eagerness, wonder, love, pity, and every sentiment or emotion. Raise or lower your voice as needed for expression. In the humorous parts put laughter in your voice; in sad parts put sorrow. Old fairy tales are excellent for practice as they cover good and evil, joy and sorrow. A half hour once a day should be effective, if kept up for three or four weeks.

There are good books on the market that give instruction on improving the talking voice.

## 4. The Laugh

Avoid any tendency to the masculine laugh such as a deep or loud tone. Don't open your mouth wide, throw your head back, slap your hands on your thighs, roar, cackle, snort, or anything coarse or vulgar. If these extremes are avoided, the laugh will probably be at least acceptable.

## 5. Cooing and Purring

When a very feminine woman feels close to the man she adores, she sometimes coos and purrs. Deruchette *made all kinds of gentle noises, murmurings of unspeakable delight to certain ears*. After Dora married David Copperfield, she talked *baby talk* to him. Probably every woman who has been a feminine coquette has impulsively spoken this way to the man she loves.

When women feel the tendency to coo or purr, they tend to suppress it, thinking it silly. It comes forth more naturally when we are around babies. Have you noticed when women talk to their babies or tiny children they tend to make gentle noises? This is called baby talk. It can be fascinating to a man, even when bestowed on an infant.

## 6. Bewitching Languor

Languor is a calm, quiet air similar to that of a cat relaxing before a fireplace. It's a touch of velvet. Deruchette had at times an air of *bewitching languor*. The opposite of languor is nervous and high-strung behavior, such as biting fingernails, jingling keys, twisting a handkerchief, or fingering the hair. To be feminine, work to overcome these habits.

## 7. Facial Expressions

Avoid frowns, hardness in the eyes, tight lips, and a drooping mouth. Feminine expressions are gentle, tender, sweet, with a soft look in the eyes.

Facial expression has its roots in character. If you have a gentle character, it's natural and easy to have a gentle expression. On the other hand, if you have a harsh, critical, impatient, character you'll have difficulty keeping these unwholesome traits from creeping into your face.

If this is a problem, work on your character. Make sure you have a sound philosophy of life based on moral values. Learn to accept people, be patient with them, and forgive them. The key to this change of heart lies in humility, for through this virtue we learn to accept, forgive, and not judge.

While you are working on character, try to *control* your facial expressions. This helps to train your character within to be more gentle. The face acts as a teacher to the character, reminding it to be patient and forgiving. You can't keep this practice up for long, however, if you continue to hold grudges and have ill will towards people.

## 8. Feminine Conversation

Take care that your conversation is feminine: First, *don't talk too much*. Almost all women talk too much! Make sure your conversation is *not centered on yourself*—your children, your husband, your house, your problems, and your successes. Such a conversation is boring. Don't dominate the conversation. Every time someone brings up a new topic, don't turn the conversation back to things you are interested in. Don't focus on menial matters which are of no consequence to you or anyone else.

Don't let your conversation become crude, vulgar, harsh, overbearing, or critical. Be certain your remarks reflect gentleness, kindness, and love. If a discussion centers around an unfortunate person, show forth sympathy and concern. Don't make an unkind remark such as, *"Well, he deserves it"* or *"He had it coming to him."* Take every opportunity to defend people, to be long suffering, and understanding.

Avoid talking about people you dislike as you may be tempted to make an unkind remark. Remake your attitude toward them before you bring them into the conversation. Avoid subjects which may lead to heated arguments. Avoid negative statements. All of your conversation should reflect tenderness, patience, forgiveness, understanding, tolerance, and love.

In your conversations with children, don't wait for an emergency to show tenderness. When your little boy passes by, pat him on the head and make a kind remark. Take your little girl in your arms and say, "I always wanted a little girl just like you." Or, put your arm around your older son and say, "I'm proud of you." Give them a steady diet of tenderness. It will bring them closer to you and improve your feminine manner.

## 9. Refinement

One of the marks of a feminine woman is refinement, which implies *good social breeding*. This means to be tactful, courteous, diplomatic, considerate, sensitive to the feelings of others, and the picture of propriety, good taste, and graciousness. A refined person is careful to not offend anyone, is never rude, impolite, inconsiderate, crude, coarse, or vulgar.

To be refined: Never interrupt anyone, bring up a subject which would embarrass someone, monopolize the conversation, or focus it on yourself. Never point a finger of scorn at anyone. Never speak your mind to someone in a blunt, brutally frank way, even though you may technically be in the right. If you can see that you are on a subject which is making someone uneasy, have the courtesy to quickly change the subject.

Never use vulgar language, profane, swear, or tell vulgar jokes. Never pick your nose, scratch yourself, or blow your nose in public. Never rub your husband's back in public, stroke his hair, or fondle him. Such actions in public are *very* unrefined. Don't bring up topics of conversation which are inappropriate or unrefined. Although these coarse habits are not becoming in a man, they are more repulsive in a woman.

Cultivate refined taste in the way you dress, style your hair, and apply makeup. Use good taste in designing the interior of your house, the selection of your furniture, and dishes. Cultivate refined taste for art and for music. Never ignore social invitations. They should be promptly accepted or declined with graciousness. by phone or letter.

Another mark of refinement: Be courteous to everyone you meet, regardless of age, situation, financial or social standing. Every person is a human being, entitled to respect. The higher your respect of human beings generally, the higher your tendency to refinement. Any tendency to arrogance shows a lack of consideration expected of a refined person. Nothing is more quickly calculated to make you appear coarse and unrefined than to ignore or shun another individual.

To demonstrate your consideration for people, never do anything to hurt their feelings. Never, for example, show indifference for their opinions or downgrade things they say or do, especially things they consider important. Be considerate of the feelings, opinions, accomplishments, ideas, traditions, religious customs, or way of life of others.

If, for example, you happen to meet a little old lady who has spent a lifetime devoted to a worship of traditions, don't show disrespect for her feelings by trampling on those traditions. Or if you have dinner with some honest soul who takes pride in her cooking, don't refuse a second helping or give any indication that you are any less than delighted with her meal.

If you are in the home of an exceptionally refined person, don't show a disregard for her way of life by boisterous conduct or heated arguments. On the other hand, if the hostess is fun-loving and set on everyone relaxing and having a good time, show consideration for her thinking by being lighthearted yourself. The greatest mark of refinement you can show is a genuine delight in the company you keep with a respect and consideration for their way of living.

Also, learn to respect another person's enthusiasm. For example, if a gentleman tells you of an adventurous journey he is about to take, and as he unfolds his plans gets into a state of excitement, don't throw cold water on his enthusiasm by acting bored. Even worse, don't make a negative remark which would destroy his enthusiasm altogether, such as reminding him how expensive or foolhardy it might be. Instead, share his enthusiasm. Or, if he is merely enthusiastic about a piece of cake he is eating, don't dampen his enthusiasm by a negative remark such as, *"I can't stand that kind."*

Still another lack of refinement is *cheekiness,* an old-fashioned word which means to be nervy or impose on people. Cheekiness is an attitude of *expecting favors,* with a lack of consideration for the imposition it might be on the other person. Young people are guilty of this practice by asking for things to eat while in the homes of their friends, or by asking to borrow clothing, perfume, cars, or even money. There are emergencies when asking favors is justified but borrowing is ordinarily considered nervy and unrefined.

## The Tiger's Whisker

A woman's tender, feminine manner can tame the most difficult man, as the following old Korean tale illustrates:

Yun Ok came to the house of a wise sage for counsel. Her problem was this: *"It is my husband, wise one,"* she said. *"He is very dear to me. For the past three years be has been away fighting in the wars. Now that he has returned, he hardly speaks to me or to anyone else. If I speak he doesn't seem to hear. When he talks at all it is roughly. If I serve him food not to his liking he pushes it aside and angrily leaves the room. Sometimes when he should be working in the rice field I see him sitting idly on top of the hill looking towards the sea! I want a potion,"* she said, *"so he will be loving and gentle as he used to be."* The wise sage told her to bring him a whisker from a living tiger, from which he was to make the magic potion.

At night when her husband was asleep Yun Ok crept from her house with a bowl of rice and meat sauce in her hand. She went to a place on the mountainside where a tiger was known to live. Standing far from the tiger's cave she held out the bowl of food, calling the tiger to come and eat, but the tiger did not come. Each night she returned doing the same thing and each time she came a few steps closer to the tiger. Although the tiger did not come to eat he did become accustomed to seeing her.

One night she approached within a stone's throw of the cave. This time the tiger came a few steps toward her and stopped. The two of them stood looking at one another in the moonlight. It happened again the following night, and this time they were so close she could talk to him in a soft, soothing voice. The next night, after looking carefully into her eyes, the tiger ate the food she held out for him. After that, when Yun Ok came in the night she found the tiger waiting for her on the trail.

Nearly six months passed since the night of her first visit.

At last one night, after caressing the animal's head she said, *"Oh, generous animal, I must have one of your whiskers. Do not be angry with me."* And she snipped off one of his whiskers.

Yun Ok ran down the trail with the tiger's whisker tightly clutched in her hand. When she brought it to the wise sage, he examined it then tossed it into the fire. *"Yun Ok,"* said the sage, *"Is a man more vicious than a tiger? Is he less responsive to kindness and understanding? If your gentleness and patience can win the confidence of a wild and bloodthirsty animal, it can do the same with your husband."*

## You Need Not Be Beautiful to Be Feminine

You need not be beautiful to have all of the charms of femininity. There are thousands of rather plain women with irregular features and faulty builds who succeed in being attractive to men because they are models of femininity. On the other hand, there are thousands of other women who have beautiful faces and features but who, because of woodenness, or masculinity of manner, never impress men as being especially attractive. When a woman is tender, soft, fun-loving, lovable, and also innocent and pure, who stops to inquire if she has beauty in the classical sense? Regardless of her feature or form, to most men she seems a paragon of femininity. To them she is beautiful!

Even when a woman is so homely that the fact cannot be overlooked, men are often attracted nevertheless. While they may not find her beautiful, they may consider her pert, cute, charming, dainty, lovable, saucy, and everything else that is highly fascinating. Very often such a woman has the most enchanting personality of all and succeeds in captivating the most sensible men, the more virile characters for whom beauty without femininity has no attraction; and frequently such a woman can make a merely beautiful woman seem insignificant beside her.

You must not, therefore, let the absence of beauty discourage you; nor must you let the possession of beauty, if you have it, lull you into a false security. The presence or the absence of beauty is of minor consequence in the attainment of true femininity. As always, evidence of the truthfulness of these teachings is the testimonies of women who have accepted and lived them, such as the following:

### I Was Tall and Unfeminine Looking

"Before I found out about F.W. I was extremely unhappy. I had doubts about whether or not I even wanted to get married, because there are so many marriages that fail. I didn't know if I could make a marriage that would not only survive, but be happy in the process.

"I had been raised to be very aggressive, independent, and competent, and added to that was the fact that I am very tall and unfeminine looking. *Fascinating Womanhood* helped me to realize my mistaken frame of mind and become a fascinating woman.

"My husband has become more of a man through my application of the principles and he says I have made him so happy he just doesn't know what to do sometimes. I feel anything that can change a person like I was into a soft, feminine, woman needs to be taught to every woman, especially Women's Libbers! They don't know what they're missing."

### A Whole New World Opened Up

"I was married at age eighteen and at the time thought I was mature and a wonderful wife. It was nice to be so young and so sure of myself. But, as the years went on I began to get faint inklings that maybe I had a few things to learn. We had a happy life together in spite of my inability to handle squabbles and heartaches.

"In the spring of last year I was introduced to *Fascinating Womanhood,* and a whole new world seemed to open to me. I happily practiced its principles and went out of my way to make my husband happy, and found myself happier than I had ever been and the goal of Celestial Love becoming more and more a reality.

"One day I really backslid! I was watching T.V. while the children ran and yelled and my husband tried to talk to me. I forgot all about being fascinating and yelled for everyone to 'shut up.' That did it! My husband jumped up and stomped out of the house. Realizing what I had done I went after him, but he made it known that I wasn't welcome when we drove off.

"I apologized and put everything I had learned to work on him. Within a half hour I accomplished what used to take days, and we spent a lovely evening together, riding in the desert, talking and loving each other.

"I will always be grateful to F.W. for that evening, because it was the last we ever had together. My husband was critically injured the next day. As I sat by his bedside hoping and praying, I was so thankful we didn't part on a sour note. I used this time to again put F.W. to work, and told him how important he was to me, how brave and masculine he was and how much I loved him. He lived thirty days. Now I am a widow with very tender memories and thankfulness for the few very, very special months we had and the joy we knew thanks to *Fascinating Womanhood*."

## Feminine Wiles and Ways

"I was raised on a farm and worked like a boy, gardening, doing chores, etc. I never had any frilly feminine things as a girl, and never thought such things necessary. Perfume, nail polish, eye makeup, frilly lingerie were for fancy town women who never did anything useful, or helped their men.

"I married my husband with the idea of making him into something acceptable. I thought he should appreciate my efforts. He had been dominated a great deal by his father and so took a lot of my bossiness without comment. Between his Dad and me he's never really had a chance to be himself. I felt responsible for what he did and he let me.

"I worried about money and church. He blithely spent whatever he liked, writing out checks, going into debt. His family was not religious, mine was. I tried to get him to go to church, and he did, but embarrassed me by acting bored, etc. He continued a few bad habits he'd promised to break before we were married. In spite of this we had a pretty good marriage. We were in love and thought our problems were normal ones. But our quarrels grew more frequent and violent.

Money was the main bone of contention, along with his refusal to give me things I thought rightfully due me.

"Worry over money was making me old before my time. He refused to try to get a really good job after getting fired from an excellent one. I tried to budget on what little was left after his weekly 'pocket expense and check writing.' I bravely chased and bribed creditors. I even left my three little kids and went to work.

"But while I worked he spent enough on dog food, ice cream, cola, treats for buddies, car repairs, gas, etc., that our rent checks bounced and we ended nearly three hundred dollars in the hole. The way things were going, separation was inevitable. I had plans to leave him as soon as the kids were in school.

"About this time he became active in scouts, at my insistence. Soon we had scouts 'coming out our ears.' He spent so much time with them we hardly saw him. He broke promises of carnivals with me and the kids to go hiking with the scouts.

"I was taking a chorister class once a week, and the night of my first class my husband was planning to stay home and paint the floor on my back porch for me. When I got home I found he'd called three of the scouts to do it so they could get their 'floor painting' merit badge. Not only was the floor painted, but the walls were spattered. It looked awful and I was furious!

"The very next night a friend told me about Fascinating Womanhood. I know we would have separated by now without it. My husband is a changed man now. I've never been so blissfully happy. Freedom, acceptance, praise, feminine wiles and ways and love, these are my secrets. It's really fun to be a feminine woman. I'm hardly unfulfilled.

"My husband has an extremely good job now and he loves it and is making as much in one week as he used to in two. His love and consideration for me has doubled. It is apparent in all he does. He acts romantic as a school kid. He brings me presents, helps me with the dishes (occasionally) and our love life is wonderful. I couldn't ask for more."

## *Outdoor Parties*

Women tend to relax their feminine manner at outdoor parties and games. This is partly due to their clothes. Pants and casual clothes encourage unrestrained actions. Women slap men on the back, whistle, yell, speak loudly, laugh noisily, gulp their food down, sit with legs apart, or one leg resting on another as men do, roar at jokes, and throw their head back when they drink. Be on guard at such parties to retain your feminine manner.

## *Don'ts for the Feminine Manner*

1. Don't use your hands in a stiff, brusque, efficient, firm, or strong manner.
2. Don't walk with a heavy gait or long strides.
3. Avoid the following qualities in the voice: loudness, firmness, efficiency, boldness, dullness, mumbling, monotonous, singsong.
4. Don't laugh loudly or in a vulgar manner.
5. Don't use facial expressions that suggest anger, coldness, bitterness, resentment, disgust, or stubbornness.
6. Don't indulge in conversation that is harsh, bitter, critical, impatient, crude, vulgar, or unrefined.
7. Don't pick your nose, scratch yourself, or blow your nose in public. (Wiping your nose is OK)
8. Don't stroke your husband's back in public, caress his hair, or fondle him.
9. Don't slap anyone on the back.
10. Don't talk loud, whistle, or yell.
11. Don't roar at jokes.
12. Don't gulp food or eat noisily.
13. Don't drink by throwing your head back.
14. Don't sit with legs apart, or one leg across the other.

## *How to Acquire a Feminine Manner*

1. Hands
2. Walk
3. Voice
4. Laugh

5. Cooing and Purring
6. Bewitching Languor
7. Facial Expressions
8. Conversation
9. Refinement

## *Assignment*

Analyze your feminine manner. Take your weakest point and work on it for at least a week. A month is better.

# 20

## *The Feminine Nature*

In the feminine nature there's a kind of *weakness, softness,* and *delicateness.* The feminine woman is inclined to be *trustful, adaptable,* and *fearful, with tender emotions for the innocent* and *the suffering.* In addition, she has a spirit of *sweet submission, and a dependency upon men* for their care and protection. There is no male aggressiveness, competence, or fearlessness, no male air of command, no masculine strength or ability.

This feminine nature sharply defines the difference between men and women, enhancing their attraction for one another. We should be grateful for this difference, and try in every way to preserve it. For generations various cultures of people have recognized and appreciated the difference. Hence comes the expression *"Vive la différence!"* or in English, "Long live the difference!"

The feminine nature awakens a man's chivalry for a woman, his impulse to protect her and provide for her. Don't think that chivalry is an imposition on a man. *One of the most pleasant sensations a real man can experience is his consciousness of the power to give his manly power and protection. Rob him of this sensation of superior strength and ability and you rob him of his manliness. A man delights in protecting and sheltering a feminine, dependent woman. The bigger, manlier, and more sensible a man is, the more he seems to be attracted to this quality.*

## How Men Feel in the Presence of Capable, Independent Women

What happens when the average red-blooded man comes in contact with an obviously able, intellectual, and competent woman, manifestly independent of any help a mere man can give, and capable of meeting him or defeating him on his own ground? He simply doesn't feel like a man any longer. In the presence of such strength and ability in a mere woman he feels like a futile, ineffectual imitation of a man. It is one of the most uncomfortable and humiliating sensations a man can experience, so that the woman who arouses it becomes repugnant to him.

*A man cannot derive any joy or satisfaction from protecting and providing for a woman who can obviously do very well without him. He only delights in protecting and sheltering a woman who needs his manly care, or at least appears to need it.*

## How Men Feel in the Presence of Feminine, Dependent Women

When a man is in the presence of a tender, gentle, trustful, dependent woman he immediately feels a sublime expansion of his power to protect and shelter this frail and delicate creature. In the presence of such weakness, he feels stronger, more competent, bigger, manlier than ever. This feeling of strength and power is one of the most enjoyable he can experience. The apparent need of the woman for care and protection, instead of arousing contempt for her lack of ability, appeals to the very noblest feelings within him.

### Amelia

An excellent illustration of the *feminine nature* is found in Amelia in *Vanity Fair: "Those who formed the small circle of Amelia's acquaintances were quite angry with the enthusiasm with which the other sex regarded her. For almost all men who came near her loved her; though no doubt they would be at a loss to tell you why. She was not brilliant, nor witty, nor wise over-much, nor extraordinarily handsome. But wher-*

*ever she went, she touched and charmed everyone of the male
sex, as invariably as she awakened the scorn and incredulity
of her own sisterhood. I think it was her 'weakness' which was
her principle charm; a kind of 'sweet submission' and 'softness'
which seemed to appeal to each man she met for his sympathy
and protection.''*

## Mrs. Woodrow Wilson

Writing to his wife Ellen, President Wilson said: *"What
a source of steadying and of strength it is to me in such
seasons of too intimate self-questioning to have one fixed
point of confidence and certainty—that even, unbroken, excellent perfection of my little wife, with her poise, her easy
capacity in action, her unfailing courage, her quick efficient
thought—and the charm that goes with it all, the sweetness,
the feminine grace—none of the usual penalties of efficiency—
no hardness, no incisive sharpness, no air of command, or
of unyielding opinion. Most women who are efficient are such
terrors.''*

## The Capable, Independent Woman Men Admire

Occasionally we notice a capable, efficient, masculine
type of woman who is very much admired by men. She may
be exceedingly skilled in management, or have ingenious ideas
about how to make the business or industrial world tick. Don't
let a man's admiration for such a woman confuse you. His
admiration for her doesn't mean he finds her attractive. He
undoubtedly admires her as he would another man, for her fine
ability.

There are many women, in all walks of life, who possess
great personal magnetism, whom all, including the men, admire as great and powerful characters, but who can never
change a man's admiration into love. One such woman, a
famous Sunday School teacher, illustrates this situation.

Her magnetic personality and noble character drew
hundreds of young people to join her class. Thousands of men
and women of all ages attended whenever she gave a public
lecture. In spite of this almost universal respect and admiration,
the average man would never think of seeking her private

company. It would never cross his mind to indulge in an intimate conversation with her, or to make her his *little girl,* to cherish and protect throughout a lifetime.

Everyone knows of such women, healthy, charming, enjoyable, whom men admire greatly but whom they don't seem to be fascinated by. The reason for this is that they lack an air of frail dependency upon men. They are too capable and independent to stir a man's sentiments. The air of being able to *kill their own snakes* is just what destroys the charm of so many business and professional women. And it is the absence of this air that permits many a *brainless doll* to capture an able and intelligent man, whom one would expect to choose a more sensible companion.

The kind of woman a man wants is first an angelic being whom he can adore as better than himself, and second a helpless creature whom he would like to gather up in his arms and cherish and protect forever. The admirable women just mentioned fill the first requirement but not the second. Though it is absolutely necessary to fill the first, you can't afford to do as these women do, and neglect the second.

What if you happen to be a big, strong, independent woman, or have a powerful personality, or in some other way overpower men? How can you possibly appear to be tender, trustful, delicate, and dependent? In the first place, size has nothing to do with the feminine nature. No matter what your size or your capabilities, you can appear fragile to a man if you follow certain rules. It is not important that you actually be little and delicate, but that you seem so to the man.

## When the Large Woman Attracts the Little Man

Occasionally we see a rather small short man, married to a large woman. It is interesting to observe that she does not seem large to him because she has given him the impression of smallness. Such a man is even apt to call her *his little girl*. She has managed, in spite of her size, to give him the impression of delicacy. By letting him know that she can't get along without him, that she is utterly dependent upon him, she has been able to disguise her rather large, overpowering figure.

## *Characteristics of the Feminine Nature*

1. *Weakness:* The feminine nature is *weak, soft,* and *delicate,* compared to the man's strong and firm nature. This does not imply weakness in a negative way, such as weakness of character, or lack of moral courage.

2. *Submissiveness:* The feminine nature is *submissive, trustful,* and *adaptable,* all yielding qualities which make her a good follower. This makes it more natural for her to surrender to her husband's leadership.

3. *Dependence:* Feminine dependency can be defined as *a woman's need for masculine care and protection.* She needs a strong arm to lean on, a breadwinner to depend on, and a protector to feel safe with. Why? Because she is weaker and more delicate, and because her whole purpose in life is home-oriented. All of her energies are directed towards the home, making a nest for her little ones and a castle for her king. If she is to succeed in her domestic career, she must devote her time and energy in that direction. Therefore, she must have a man to provide the living, do the strenuous work, and protect her and her children from harm.

4. *Tenderness:* Feminine women are inclined to have tender feelings for the helpless, the innocent, and the suffering. They are easily awakened to pity or sympathy. Amelia, in *Vanity Fair,* is a typical example of tender emotions for, *"She cried over a dead canary, or a mouse that the cat had seized upon, or the end of a novel, were it ever so stupid."*

The trouble is that most women feel ashamed of their tender feelings and try to withhold them. How many times have you read a book or watched a movie with a tragic ending, and deliberately tried to hold back the tears? *Never try to stifle a tender emotion in the presence of a man.* This betrayal of tenderness of heart is fascinating to men.

5. *Fearfulness:* Feminine women have a natural fear of dangers, whereas men are inclined to be unafraid of dangers, especially if they are in control of the danger. Men will, in fact, sometimes take women into danger, just to see how fearful women are and how unafraid they are. For example, a man loved to take his sailboat into dangerous waters and keel it over on its side. His wife was terrified, but in spite of this fact,

he did it again and again. She asked me, *"Why does he do this when he knows I am so afraid?"* I answered, *"He does it because you are so afraid, and he is so unafraid."*

Women are also afraid of *unreal dangers*, such as lightning, thunder, strange noises, spiders, mice, and even dark shadows, much to the amusement of men. Men love this trait in women, for in the presence of such weakness, the man feels stronger. If she shrinks from a spider, or hops on a chair at the sight of a mouse, how manly he feels that he can laugh at such tremblings and calm her fears. It does a man more good to save a woman from a mouse than a tiger, since he feels more power over the mouse.

Feminine women tend to be fearful in the presence of heavy traffic. When such a woman approaches an intersection she doesn't charge forth with all confidence. Instead, she hesitates at the curb for a moment, clings to the man's arm a little tighter, waiting for him to lead the way. Rather than be offended, the man appreciates her fearfulness and his ability to give protection.

## How to Awaken Your Dependent, Feminine Nature

Some of the following points may appear as a repeat of subjects covered earlier. Earlier chapters, however, focused on *the man,* and his need to function, feel needed, and excel you in the masculine things. Now the emphasis is *you,* and what you must do to develop your femininity.

1. *Acquire a Feminine Attitude:* Dispense with any air of masculine strength, ability, competence, or fearlessness, and acquire an attitude of frail dependency. Let him know that his help is needed and appreciated and that you could not get along in this world without him. Be adaptable to his life and his circumstances. Get rid of an attitude of bossiness, control, or command, and acquire a spirit of sweet submission.

2. *Eliminate the Masculine Work:* You can never be a truly feminine woman unless you eliminate the masculine work. To do this, first decide what work you want to eliminate. Do you want to quit your job? Do you want to be relieved of paying the bills, keeping the books, or have him take over the yard work, painting, fixing, repairing, and other fix-it jobs around the house?

Once you decide what masculine work you want to eliminate, explain your intentions to your husband. Ask him to take over the masculine jobs. Discuss each one with him so he will clearly understand. Tell him you *need him* to do these things so you can devote yourself to your feminine role in the home. Also tell him you feel unfeminine doing them, and would like to be relieved so you can become a truly feminine women.

If he accepts, *let go completely*. Don't worry about the outcome. If he fails to follow through on a job don't complain or pressure him to get things done. The concern is his now. He may never take hold until you let go. If his negligence provokes you, try to understand his world. What may seem important to you may seem insignificant to him compared to demands of his work away from home. If you hammer a point on small home repairs you display a narrow, self-centered, unsympathetic attitude.

If he refuses to accept the masculine work in the home, don't make an issue of it. Do what *must be done* yourself and let the rest go. Continue to live *Fascinating Womanhood* and his attitude will change. A little later you can approach him again.

3. *If Stuck With A Masculine Job:* As you try to unload the masculine work, there will be times you'll be stuck with a masculine job. If so, do it *in a feminine manner*. You need not perform masculine tasks with manly efficiency. If you must fix the furnace, repair the leaking roof, or handle the finances, do so *in a feminine manner*. Your husband will soon realize you need masculine assistance. If you can work as well as he can, he'll never come to your rescue. You may be stuck with the job permanently.

4. *Be Submissive:* The word *submissive* means to yield to a higher authority, or to leave matters to the discretion or judgment of others. The opposite: To be stubborn, unyielding, rebellious, or disobedient. To develop your feminine nature, yield to your husband's rule with a *spirit of sweet submission*. This is one of the most charming qualities in *Fascinating Womanhood*, measuring greatly in the success of marriage.

When in discussions with your husband or any man, avoid *unyielding opinions* which lead to heated arguments, as this is unfeminine and offensive to men. A man wants a woman to express her viewpoint and defend it to a degree, but is offended when she takes such a firm stand on an issue that he cannot convince her with even the soundest logic. This is stubbornness, the opposite of submissiveness. It's better to surrender your point of view to a man than win an argument. It's more feminine. I am *not* suggesting you be submissive in your *moral convictions*. They should be defended firmly.

5. *Don't Subdue Fearfulness:* Don't subdue your natural tendency to be afraid of dangers. In the face of danger, need his masculine protection, or at least appear to need it.

6. *Don't Subdue Tender Emotions:* As has been explained, don't subdue your tender emotions for the innocent and the suffering. Don't try to hold back your tears. Let yourself go. Such tender sympathy is attractive in a woman.

7. *Don't Try to Excel Him:* To preserve your femininity, don't compete with men in anything which requires masculine ability. For example, don't try to outdo them in sports, lifting weights, running, or repairing equipment. Don't compete with men for advancement on a job, higher pay, or greater honors. Don't compete with them for scholastic honors in men's subjects. It may be all right to win over a man in English or social studies, but you're in trouble if you compete with a man in math, chemistry, or science. Don't appear to know more than a man does in world events, the space program, science, or industry. Don't try to excel men in anything which has to do with masculine fields of endeavor.

8. *Invite His Care and Protection:* Let him open doors for you, pull up your chair, or help you on with your coat. If he doesn't offer, perhaps you did it yourself too quickly. Next time you need to put on your coat, hand it to him, then turn your back to make it easy for him. Ask him to lift in the groceries or open tight jar lids. Confine your requests to things women need men for, and not things women can just as well do for themselves. And always, always, thank him.

9. *Live Your Feminine Role:* The best way to develop femininity is the home, as you function as the wife, mother, and homemaker. This is the most ideal workshop for acquiring all of the gentle traits of femininity.

## The Sweet Promise

Although men are fascinated by frailty in women, there's a balancing quality they appreciate. A man needs the assurance that, with all of your helpless dependency on him to take care of you, protect, and wait on you, that somewhere hidden within is *your ability to meet an emergency*. He needs to know that in times of urgent need, you would have the womanly courage, strength, endurance, and ability to solve difficult problems, that you would not, in this case, be helpless. This is known as the *sweet promise*. It should be somewhere within your character, and he must perceive it is there.

Many women show forth this promise when put to the test. Take for example a young widow left with several small children to support. She sets out single-handed to battle against all odds. She slaves and struggles, dares and suffers in her effort to provide for her children. When defeat stares her in the face, she doesn't whimper. Taking her lot as a matter of course, she grits her teeth and braves the struggle again.

No matter what pain she suffers from overwork, she has a smile of comfort for her little ones; no matter how weary, she forgets her own weariness at the slightest hint of danger to her children. Look to the widows of this earth and you'll find many compare to the angels of heaven. This sweet promise arises from a noble character which includes love, faith, endurance, and determination.

## What the Feminine Nature Awakens in a Man

As a woman becomes more feminine a man begins to offer his care and protection. And as he more fully devotes himself to her care his *love and tenderness* grows. This is true of any individual who shelters and cares for another. We tend to love whom we serve. On the other hand when we neglect someone we are responsible for, we may cease to love them.

A mother, for example, who grossly neglects her child may cease to love him. This is why some mothers run away from their children. Likewise, when a man neglects his wife he may cease to love her. Therefore, it is extremely important that you develop your feminine nature, so he will *want* to take care of you, do things for you, protect you, devote himself to you, and in so doing love you more.

You care for your husband in a similar way. You prepare him nourishing meals, wash his clothes, and watch over him to see that he doesn't neglect his health. You give him comfort, understanding, and sympathy. You also protect him in your own way. You try to prevent others from taking unfair advantage of his generous nature, try to keep his foolhardy courage from endangering his safety, and try to make certain his manly indifference to detail doesn't lead him into trouble. Your devotion increases your love and tenderness for him.

Remember, a man does not offer his care and protection unless a woman appears to need it. Therefore, to win his devoted care and magnify his love for you, *develop your feminine nature*. The rewards of such femininity is evident in thousands of testimonials, such as the following:

### The Reason He Loved Me

"While sitting with my husband he picked up my F.W. book and glanced through it. He noticed the quality of tenderness and said that it was the main reason he loved me. Can you imagine my inner glow and delight and satisfaction to hear those kind words, especially since he had never ever put them into words before and told me why he loved me. And then he said he had observed this same tenderness in our two-and-a-half-year-old daughter."

### We Were Poles Apart

"In no way was I dependent on my husband. I was a college graduate and my husband high school only. I have a quick mind. His is slower, more methodical. We were highly successful in our chosen careers. When we married both of us were used to being completely independent. On top of this, when my parents realized I had to beg my husband for every penny I got, they made me *financially* independent. Since there was nothing dependent about me, this part of F.W. was rough for me.

"My husband made big money but spent most of it on himself. He always said he wanted it all spent when he died, and proved this by canceling his life insurance the day he was told he had cancer. His attitude in the home was, *'If Liz does it right, it's her duty; if she does it wrong, she catches heck.'* It was not a happy marriage for either of us. Yet we were stable and neither sought divorce.

"His work was exciting and carried us all over the world. Both of us created good lives for ourselves, outside of each other. We lived in the same house, slept in the same bed, our sex life was good, but we were poles apart—no common interests, no sharing. He rarely confided in me, nor permitted me to confide in him. When I tried to share he would cut me down with 'I'm not interested.'

"Then I took the *Fascinating Womanhood* course. I took it *seriously*. I gave it a real try! I did everything F.W. suggested, whether I agreed with the principle or not. Sometimes I felt like a fool trying. I especially worked on becoming dependent and trusting, even though I feared trusting my husband.

"Let me tell you what actually happened: This husband who one year before was harsh, critical, overbearing, and a tightwad, turned into a tender, thoughtful, loving man. Not perfect, but it was a miracle. This man who wanted nothing left for his wife, should he die, has now paid off the mortgage on our home and set up a handsome pension for me. He brings me coffee in bed. There's a delightful companionship and sharing between us. I believe the real miracle began when I started being dependent."

## A Voice From Beijing

"I'm a Chinese woman in my late twenties. Occasionally I saw your book *Fascinating Womanhood* in a bookstore and picked it up. After reading the introduction at the back very briefly, I was immediately drawn and bought it without any hesitation, though such purchase shocked my friends because it cost me a half my monthly salary.

"After reading the whole book I could not help but wishing my English better, so as to tell you how a Chinese lady feels, in spite of different culture, education, moral, etc. All I could say right now is, thank you very much, dear Ms. Andelin, you have brought a wonderful world to all the women of this land who have been searching desperately for love, tender, and happiness, which they are perfectly deserved of. You have brought a peace and harmony to those disturbed and fragile hearts and souls and brought self-confidence to them too. I wish I could see you sometime and talk to you in person.

"Before I read your book, I was just one of those women who thought man would appreciate our capability, unyieldingness, toughness, suggestions to them of dos and don'ts. Especially they would admire our bright career and love us because we are no brainless doll and equal to them or even better, superior to them in job.

"I used to be fond of three smart boys and I assumed they were fond of me too, as I was no plain and normal girl and have got a bright career future. Yet all of them declined me with bad excuses. I was extremely sad, hurt, and lost. Still I did not know the real reasons. As a female, I was so ready to be loved, yet nobody loved me whom I loved too. Up to yesterday I had been dreadfully seeking and longing for the heart-melting love and fulfillment of repeated dreams without actually knowing how to find.

"But today I'm very glad to tell you now you have taught me the techniques, and I'm ready to go ahead equipped with both Angelic's and Dora's qualities. Of course I understand that such self-reforming is no easy. But I am quite convinced that with your book as my Bible I'll succeed and be loved by my beloved, as I still think I'm quite special and deserved the best love in this world.

"In addition, I would request your consent to my translation of your books into Chinese language because China has got the largest population and around half of them are females. We Chinese women also have the right, if we wish, to pursue our happiness and success, which is dependent upon our male's happiness and success, and we need to know how to do so. I want to translate your books so that much more kind and sweet hearts will be calmed down and relieved."

## Characteristics of the Feminine Nature

1. Weakness, softness
2. Submissiveness
3. Dependence

4. Tenderness
5. Fearfulnesss
6. Sweet Promise

## *Assignment*

1. Analyze your feminine nature. List your feminine traits. List those you lack.
2. Ask your husband to do something for you, something which takes masculine strength or ability.
3. If stuck with a masculine job, do it in a feminine manner.

# 21

## *The Feminine Role vs. The Working Wife*

*The moon, when it moves from its sphere of night into day, loses its luster, its charm, its very poetry.*

The most important way to enhance your femininity is in the home, serving as the wife, mother, and homemaker. Here you have a field in which to grow as a woman. As you love and care for your children, cheerfully devote yourself to the ordinary chores of the household, and serve as the understanding wife, you acquire gentle, feminine, traits. Yet, in spite of this ideal feminine workshop, women are moving away from the home into the working world. Let's take a look:

The Department of Labor reports that 54.3% of *married women with spouses living at home* are now employed outside the home—39.4% working full-time and 14.9% working part-time (1988 data). Of those with children under the age of eighteen, 29.3% are employed outside the home—20.4% working full-time and 8.9% working part-time. Of those with children under the age of six, 12.4% are employed outside the home—8.2% working full-time and 4.2% working part-time. These figures do not include women working in home industries or a family business, helping on the farm, or baby-sitting children of other mothers.

This report is of mothers with a husband present in the home, and does not include the single, widowed, or divorced. If this group were included, figures would be much higher.

### When Women Are Justified in Working

If you are widowed, divorced, single, or your husband is disabled, you may be justified in working. It depends on your need for money. *If you are married and your husband is physically able,* you are justified in the following situations:

1. *Compelling Emergencies:* You are justified in working when a financial emergency gives you no alternative. In this case, *when you work because you have to,* the family more easily accepts the situation. They may even consider your working a noble sacrifice. In a situation such as this, if the family works through the crisis together little harm results.

2. *Furthering the Husband's Education or Training:* If your husband is attending college or training for a career you may be justified in working, especially if he has no other alternative to secure an education. Since his training will prepare him to provide a more adequate living, and since your situation is only temporary, you may be justified in helping him reach his goal. This depends on the number of children, their age, and their care while you work.

Beware of this danger, however: If you help your husband through school there's a temptation to continue after he graduates. He'll need to get established. You'll need many things after going without for so long. Is there any harm in your working a little longer? Perhaps not, but after the necessities you add a few comforts, then luxuries. Soon you become accustomed to the extra income, then dependent upon it. This is one of the ways mothers become trapped into a lifetime of working.

3. *The Older Woman:* If your children are married and you have time on your hands, you may want to work to occupy your time. Useful employment may seem better than idling away your time on things of no importance. In this case, you may be justified in working but consider the following:

If you are married you still have a household to run and a husband to care for. Your married children may need you. If you are tied to employment you may not be available when needed. Your influence is important in the lives of your grandchildren. You may also be needed in the community, giving benevolent service. Your devotion to your household, family, and charity *enhances feminine charm,* whereas employment outside the home does little or nothing for it.

## When Women Are Not Justified in Working

1. *To Ease the Pinch:* You may not have enough money to cover expenses. There are too many things you need and can't afford. You grow tired of never having enough money, so you seek employment, perhaps with your husband's approval. The problem with getting a job is that it's not worth the price you pay. Your presence in the home is worth far more. Instead of going to work, *cut expenses:* Move to a less expensive home, sell one car, dispense with music lessons, buy clothes at secondhand shops, and in other ways be thrifty.

2. *For Luxuries:* You may work for additional comforts, luxuries, and conveniences—the latest household equipment, new furniture, draperies, carpet, a better house, or better clothes. Your husband may encourage you to work to satisfy his taste for luxuries—a boat, swimming pool, or cabin in the mountains. Or you may want greater advantages for your children—music lessons, college, or better clothes. Justified as these desires may seem, the sacrifice is too great. It's better to *trim the luxuries*.

3. *When You Are Bored at Home:* You may be bored with the menial tasks of housekeeping and tending children. You seek relief in the exciting world of work. Your husband may support the idea, to keep you happy. And it may end your boredom, and make you happy, temporarily. The problem is that you are buying happiness at the expense of your family. You are putting your desires ahead of their needs. This is never justified.

4. *To Do Something Important:* You may feel that what you are doing from day to day in the home is relatively unimportant, and that men have the more important jobs. Noble contribution to mankind, you may reason, are made in the fields of science, industry, government, or the arts.

Women who think this have a false notion. They exaggerate the importance of the man's work, and underestimate the importance of the woman's work in the home. Noble as the contributions of men are, they do not surpass a well-brought-up family. A doctor spends his time *saving lives*. You, on the other hand, in the simple routine of your home, are *saving souls*. Learn to see the distant scene, how your patient devotion to family produces men and women of worth, the greatest contribution to any society.

5. *To Ease the Load for the Man:* When you see your husband under pressure and strain, concerned about meeting expenses for a growing family, you may feel it your duty to help him by getting a job. Benevolent as this seems it is not justified or necessary: *God blessed the man with strength, endurance, and the emotional makeup for his work. Rather than share his burdens, strengthen him for them. Give him appreciation. This builds his confidence and helps him succeed in his work. Ease his burdens at home by reducing demands on his time and money, and by providing a peaceful home life where he can be renewed.*

## Careers

If you have talent as an artist, writer, designer, actress, singer, scientist, or in the technical fields, should you pursue a career? Think twice before you take this step. Your foremost duty is to your marriage and family. Here you must succeed. A career may sidetrack you from your family. Not only will your career demand your time, but your interest, and sometimes your soul. If your husband and family must be second place, you are making an unwise choice. The price you pay is too high. Listen to those who have had experience:

## Taylor Caldwell:

The late Taylor Caldwell, one of the most widely read authors in the English language, made the following statement to the press: *"There is no solid satisfaction in any career for a woman like myself. There is no home, no true freedom, no hope, no joy, no expectation for tomorrow, no contentment. I would rather cook a meal for a man and bring him his slippers and feel myself in the protection of his arms than have all the citations and awards I have received worldwide, including the Ribbon of Legion of Honor and my property and my bank accounts. They mean nothing to me and I am only one among the millions of sad women like myself."*

### Beverly Sills

Beverly Sills, the well-known opera star and impresario, recently addressed graduating students of Barnard College in New York City. She stated: *"Women are told today they can have it all—career, marriage, children. You need a total commitment to make it work. Take a close look at your child. He doesn't want you to be bright, talented, chic, or smart—any of those things. He just wants you to love him. He will be the one who pays the price for your wanting to have it all. Think carefully about having that baby. Not to have it would be a great loss. To have it too late greatly increases the health hazards for you and the child. To have it without a commitment to it would be a great tragedy."*

### A Career Woman Writes

"I am in my early thirties, single, a corporate officer, and executive. I serve on three boards of directors, one a national organization. With all my customer contacts, employee supervision, and peer contact, my total influence doesn't constitute a drop in the bucket to what a wife and mother contributes to society. She directly affects the mental outlook of her husband and children. She has the power to make her home *heaven* or *hell*. That's what I call *woman power*."

### My Own Career

Several years ago I received a letter from a lady in Huntsville, Alabama which reads: *"Mrs. Andelin, you are fooling yourself. You tell women to stay home and run their households and not have a career but you are the most professional of all women. In fact, you are a business woman par excellence. Hence, your fulfillment. All marriages of my acquaintance where wives are professionals are stable marriages. Husbands of stay-at-home wives are blatantly unfaithful with secretaries with whom they have something in common. They say their house-frau wives bore them to death. Many women follow your recipe and it doesn't work anymore in the twentieth century."* Here is my answer:

"For twenty years I was a full-time homemaker. I was

the typical *stay-at-home* wife and mother, with only a few small interests outside the home. I loved to clean, cook, bake bread, and try to look pretty. I looked forward with great anticipation to the birth of a baby. My husband often refers to the beautiful bassinet I prepared for our third child, with hand-quilted pink satin lining, quilted heart inside the hood, ruffles, bows, and sheer skirt. He said it was such a visual demonstration of the welcome I was preparing for the little one.

"Although I had a full schedule of homemaking duties, I spent time with the children. I read them stories, taught them crafts, and kept a watch over their playing. On summer afternoons I washed their faces, combed their hair, put my baby in a carriage, and took them for a walk in the park. There was no prouder mother anywhere.

"We lived in a cold climate so I was sometimes isolated at home for two weeks at a time. But I read a lot—marvelous books that helped shape my philosophy of life. I began to be a better person, a more interesting one. The world seemed broad to me. Life was exciting and I couldn't understand why anyone could be bored. When I was tired of reading, I painted pictures for my children's rooms, or decorated my house. On summer mornings I went outside in the sunshine, sat on a box, and watched my children play or helped them dig in the dirt. I was enjoying life and felt important.

"Then, we moved to California and lived in the country. We had eight children by now, all living at home. Shortly after my eighth child was born I looked out the living room window and said to myself, *'This is the happiest day of my life.'* I had everything worthwhile—eight adorable children, a husband who loved me, and good friends. I worked hard but it didn't matter. We had financial problems but this was life. In the evening my husband and I went for walks down a country lane. He confided his dreams, problems, and his feelings for me. His world was my world. I didn't think of anything else. I lived for him and the children.

"In the business world he had plenty of chances to notice secretaries if he had wanted to. But I never worried. He spent his spare time at home and when away, hurried home a day or so early. A woman knows when she is secure in her husband's love and I felt secure. When I was away for a week he put my shoes by the back door so he could look at them every time he went outside. He wrote to me, 'You are the joy of my life.' But, I wasn't a dull frau wife. I was an interesting person.

"Then I began teaching *Fascinating Womanhood*, sharing my secrets of married happiness with women in need. My classes were successful and grew rapidly. This gave me the impetus to write my book. It became widely known and I became more involved. But I didn't look on it as a career. To me it was a mission, a service.

"*Fascinating Womanhood* became more widely known. A career woman would have envied my position of importance and acclaim, would have wondered why I didn't glory in it. I became more involved, not knowing how to reverse the situation, responding to demands with a spirit of sacrifice. I confined office work to home and traveled only occasionally, but I was definitely *over my head* in this work.

"Call me what you like, business executive, career woman, or working wife, but I never looked at it this way. To me it has been a mission of charity. It was a unique work which had to be done by a woman. Many lives have changed for the better. The personal sacrifice has been well worth it. But I always put my marriage and family first. This is no doubt why they survived."

Several years ago I received a letter from a lady who challenged my ideas about women and careers. Here is her story:

## Back to Work I Go

"*During the fifteen years I worked outside the home I felt guilty and dreamed of the time I could be a full-time homemaker like my mother was. When my husband finally earned enough money I quit. At first I was elated. It was exciting doing all the things I had never had time to do before, but soon I ran out of things to do and found I was not really interested in them after all. My years of working double roles had forced me to be organized and efficient. I got my work out of the way quickly, my house sparkling clean and cooked gourmet meals but there were empty afternoons. There was never a need to rush, plenty of time tomorrow for what I didn't do today. I quit wearing makeup and sat around in an old robe. Why should I be all dressed up and nowhere to go?*

*"I took classes in macramé but dropped out because of boredom. The women's small talk of recipes and their cute kids seemed unimportant compared to balance sheets and sales motivation discussions of my former job. I felt puzzled over my feelings. I had crying spells, became resentful, depressed, and sarcastic. My husband responded with a growing distance. My young son didn't seem to care if I was home or not. He liked hamburgers better than my gourmet meals.*

*"Things worsened until my husband and son suggested I get a job again. They wanted me, above all, to be happy. Working seemed the right route for me, regardless of what my mother did. I got a part-time job and everything straightened out. I am happy now and so is my family."*

My comments are these: If a woman has only one child and he is eight years of age or older, there is no reason she can't get a part-time job if she wants to. But it isn't the only solution or the best one. If she were creative she could have made more of her marriage and life in the home, and given service to the community.

She accused her homemaker friends of *small talk* about recipes and their cute kids. This is somewhat true, but what makes her think *balance sheets and sales motivation discussions* are more interesting, or even more important? And not all homemakers engage in small talk. A Hollywood talk show director told me the following: *"In my ten-year experience talking to thousands of women in my radio audience, I find the housewife more interesting and more widely read than the career woman. I assume this must be because she has more time to read."*

## Should Daughters Be Trained for Careers?

You may think your daughters should prepare to make a living in the event of widowhood, divorce, or other compelling emergencies. Consider the seriousness of this step from the following viewpoints:

1. *Makes Her Independent:* If one of the features of femininity is *dependency,* it doesn't seem wise to direct her to a

career which makes her *independent*. By so doing she loses her need for manly care, one of the charms which attracts a man to a woman. She is also in danger of acquiring masculine efficiency, a fault of so many professional women.

There are, of course, some professional women who manage to stay feminine, either through a nature so strongly feminine that it cannot be subdued, or by conscious effort. But it seems a mistake to encourage a girl in the direction of a career, when disadvantages arise which she must work to overcome.

2. *Encourages Her to Work:* Training for careers encourages women to continue working after marriage. The intensive training seems wasted if put on the shelf. They are tempted to use their knowledge, whether they need to work or not.

3. *Training Becomes Out of Date:* Qualifications for a job change from year to year. The woman who is qualified at one time may be out of date a few years later. When she marries and has children she drops out of the work force. When she returns she must take further training to qualify for her work. Was the earlier training worth it? Could her time in college have been better spent on other subjects?

4. *Easy Escape from Marriage:* The independence which results from the ability to make money can be a dangerous thing for a woman, serving as an escape. When difficulties arise in marriage the woman who is independent has less incentive to make the adjustment. Since she can support herself, divorce seems an easy way out.

5. *Deprives Her of a Liberal Education:* It doesn't seem logical for a woman to train for a career in the event of widowhood or a rare emergency, if by so doing she bypasses a rich cultural education which would make her a better wife and mother. A man may as well train for motherhood and homemaking if this logic is sound.

The best education for a young woman is a broad, liberal, education. It better prepares her to understand her children, and help them with their education and their life ahead. It helps her equally as a wife. She's more interesting, more open to new ideas. She has a better understanding of the world and is therefore a better citizen.

The woman with a liberal education is actually better prepared to meet an emergency than the woman who has been trained for a career. Her broad education is more inclined to develop creativeness, intelligence, sound reasoning, and wisdom. When faced with an emergency she has more ingenuity to solve problems. If she must work, she can find her way into the working world and qualify for a job better than the woman who trained for a career ten years earlier and now finds it out of date.

## Harm in Women Working

1. *Harm to the Man:* When you work, you rob your husband of his right to meet ordinary challenges, and to grow by these challenges. And, as you become capable, efficient, and independent, he feels less needed, and therefore less masculine. This weakens him. As you lift, *he sets the bucket down*.

2. *Harm to the Woman:* When you work by choice, you tend to lose some of your womanliness. *The moon, when it moves from its sphere of night into day, loses its luster, its charm, its very poetry. And so it is with a woman, when she attempts to play a part not intended for her, gone is the luster, the charm, the poetry that says, "She is a phantom of delight."*

When you work you tend to take on masculine traits, to be aggressive, bold, capable, efficient, and independent, resulting in a loss of feminine charm. How much charm you lose depends on the type of work. Less masculine jobs are secretarial, clerical, nursing, school teaching, and child care. But any type of work which earns money encourages *independence*, an enemy to feminine charm. Again, I quote from my husband's book, *Man of Steel and Velvet:*

*"When a woman divides herself between two worlds it's difficult for her to succeed in either. In her world alone she has challenge enough to achieve the domestic excellence she desires. Here she is the understanding wife, the devoted mother and homemaker, and gains great satisfaction from a job well done. This takes great effort. To divide her time and interests between two worlds makes success in either difficult.*

*"Even if she rejects her home sphere and turns her heart and soul to the working world, she will have difficulty. In many jobs she will have a natural disadvantage. She will not meet man's excellence in his world, but will always be secondary*

*to him. So she wanders between two worlds, having rejected her own where she could have been superior and chosen another where she will never be anything but a second-rate man.*

"When a woman works because it is her husband's idea, an even greater harm comes. His suggestion that she work casts doubts in her mind as to his adequacy as a man. If he must lean on her, she will question his ability to solve his problems and face responsibility that is his. This brings insecurity.

"Still another harm to consider is the woman's relationship to her employer, especially if he is a man. She's accustomed to looking up to her husband as the director of her activities. When she finds herself taking orders from another man, it is an unnatural situation. She owes him obedience as her employer, and in countless hours of close contact she may find herself physically attracted to him. Seeing him at his best and perhaps as a more dynamic and effective leader than her husband, she makes comparisons unfavorable to her husband, whose faults and failings she knows all too well."

3. *Harm to the Children:* "When a mother works due to a compelling emergency, children adjust to this situation. They're able to understand when a genuine emergency exists. They may suffer neglect but don't feel lack of love or concern.

When a mother works by choice, great harm can come to the child. When he realizes she prefers to work instead of taking care of him, that she places her interests or luxuries ahead of his basic needs, this raises doubt about her love.

"The children of working mothers usually suffer considerable neglect. Not in all cases but in most. The woman who works must dedicate herself to her job in order to succeed and justify her pay. During the working hours her job's a priority. At times it will be demanding. Her children are less demanding. They're naturally the ones who suffer."

Working mothers often make this statement: "*It is not the quantity of time you spend with your children that counts, but the quality.*" When they come home they try to make up for their absence by spending *quality* time with their children. Most of this is just talk. A working mother is too busy in the evening to do anything extraordinary with her children. But, even if she does give her child quality time here is something else to consider:

The mother's *presence* in the home during the day means everything to the child's feeling of well-being, even though she is busy with homemaking tasks. It isn't always possible or even necessary for a busy mother to take time away from her work to play with her children. And too much attention can harm the child and make him demanding. But her presence in the home provides security for the child and helps him develop normally.

When a child comes home from school he may not pay much attention to his mother or be overly aware that she is home, but her presence is felt and the child is benefited. If the mother is away from home for long hours, the child may not complain, but will miss her presence. Even an infant senses the lack of his mother's presence. If the mother is missing for an extended time, the infant can become seriously retarded in growth and development. Early medical studies have proven this to be true.

4. *Harm to Society:* To quote again from *Man of Steel and Velvet:* *"The trend for the mother to be out of the home is a pattern of living which has extended for many years in America, since the emergency of World War II took millions of women into the factories. It has been during this time that we have developed some of our most threatening social problems—marriage problems, divorce, violence in the streets, drug abuse, and rebellion against social customs and moral standards. Many of these problems can be traced to homes of working mothers."*

Dr. David V. Haws, chairman of psychiatry, General Hospital in Phoenix has said, *"Mother must be returned to the home. The standard of living is a fictitious thing. It is a woman's primordial function to stay home and raise children. She should not join the hunt with men. A man, too, feels less of a man when his wife works. If you don't leave a family of decent kids behind, you have left nothing. Basic to the solution of adolescent problems of any generation is an intact home."*

The working wife has also upset the *economy* of our country so that now she feels *locked into working.* In 1975 I made a prediction on national TV. It was a time when women were crying for the choice to work outside the home. I addressed such women with this statement: *"If you don't stop crying for the choice to work, you will so upset the economy of this country that the time will come when you will not have a choice—you will have to work."* That time has come. Employers have now lowered pay to fit a two-income family. In many cases a mother feels she must work. She seems to have no choice. She feels locked in.

## Solutions:

If you are a working wife who feels locked in, the situation is not irreversible. First, learn the womanly art of thrift so you can live on your husband's income. If necessary, sell your home and move to one less expensive, in a less prestigious neighborhood. If you have two cars, sell one. Cut out vacations and spend time at the park or go to the mountains. Meals can be made simpler and less expensive without losing nutritive value. Be content with fewer clothes, content to wear them over and over. Shop for children's clothes at used clothing stores.

The next step is to quit work. Do all you can to provide a peaceful home life, build your husband's self-confidence, and live all of F.W. These things motivate your husband toward success, toward a more adequate income.

The courage required to take this step, and the faith you demonstrate in doing that which is morally right, bring unexpected blessings from God. Benefits come that you have no way to anticipate. Solutions appear that make life better than before. You cannot lose by doing what is right.

When you quit it brings immediate peace in the household. Mother is home when the children come home from school. She is rested, composed, not in a hurry. The house is tidy and homey. All is well. This will bring more lasting memories than fine material comforts.

## The Feminist Movement

Women in the feminist movement are inclined to feel that women's work in the home is inferior to men's work. When doing their domestic chores they feel like second-class citizens, *not like goddesses.* They think the only important, exciting work is in the world of men. Therefore, they seek fulfillment in careers outside the home. I quote from their own words:

*"While my husband has the freedom and opportunity to be out in the working world experiencing new people, new ideas, and perhaps the creative joy of seeing the world change for the better by the fruits of his own efforts, I am at home in the isolated household with no one to talk to but little children and friends in the same situation as myself."* And from another woman:

*"I am assuming a role that frustrates the development of my own capabilities and prohibits me from being a companion who can truly understand my husband's experience and feeling through direct experience of my own."* And another: *"In too many cases women are a shadow to their husbands and a servant to their children."*

Women of high intelligence and education complain that homemaking requires only moderate mentality. Because of their superior gifts, they feel their calling is outside the home in making a contribution to society such as did Madam Curie, or in the fields of science, industry, technology, or government. Thus, they can help make the world a better place.

I agree, it takes little intelligence to merely feed and clothe a family and do the minimum requirements. It does, however, require our very best in mental ability to make a success in the home, such as a Domestic Goddess would achieve. She must be alert, comprehending, and in tune with her husband's needs. She must meet the mental challenge of making a secure home for her children in a world of uncertainty. And she must have the mental astuteness to guide her children through difficult years. When she finally sees them become useful citizens, she experiences *the creative joy of seeing the world change for the better*.

But the mind isn't all that is required to succeed in the home. What about the heart? Aren't love and kindness equally important? Don't they do as much or more for society? The world isn't short of brainpower. It's short of love, kindness, and spiritual values. The workshop for such teaching is the home and the mother the master teacher.

Feminists fail to realize that *someone must do the woman's work. Someone must tend the children.* Isn't the mother and wife the logical one? Is brain-power being wasted in the home? No, our career in the home requires the best within us. This thought is advanced by a great lady, Leah D. Widstoe, from whom I quote:

*"The training of the human soul for advancement and joy here and in the hereafter calls for the greatest powers of mind and heart. Psychologists and students generally admit that the first years of life are crucial in determining what shall be the future of the child physically, mentally, and spiritually; that grave responsibility belongs by right of sex to the women who bear and nurture the whole human race. Theirs is the right to bear and rear to maturity as well as to influence for good or ill the precious souls of men."*

To be a successful mother is greater than to be a successful opera singer, writer, or artist. One is eternal greatness and the other a short-term honor. One day my young son said to me, "Mother, boys are more important than girls, aren't they, for they can become presidents and generals and famous people." I replied, "But it is mothers who make presidents and generals and famous people. *The hand that rocks the cradle is the hand that rules the world.*"

Every woman can make a worthy contribution to society through her children, but not every man can through his work. Some jobs are unimportant or even destructive. If women feel they must serve their country, the best way is in the home, making a success of family life. Calvin Coolidge, former U.S. president said, *"Look well to the hearthstone. Therein lies all hope for America."*

The work in the home is a different kind of glory than career women enjoy. A great mother lives in obscurity, and the perfect wife is even less known. Her reward is a quiet, unacclaimed honor. *Her glory is the esteem of her husband, the happiness of her children, and her overall success in the home.* She enjoys rich fulfillment and Celestial Love, as in the following experiences:

### There Can Be Happiness Here on Earth

"The teachings of F.W. opened my eyes to so many things. The uniqueness of the book is that I don't have to worry about forgetting everything in a week or so, like so many other books, because it changes one's whole outlook and attitude, so most other things you mention come naturally.

"I've always felt guilty about wasting my brains to be only *a housewife*. F.W. lifted a huge burden from me. I've always thought I'd committed a great sin for not using my God-given talents for some fabulous career, never realizing how fabulous and important a wife and mother really are! Right here, under my own roof, lies such a responsibility and lifelong career. I'm so happy and relived to know I've always been where God wanted me! I can finally stop waiting for some *golden opportunity* because I already have it right here at home. I've neglected my husband in every way for so long.

"Now I don't treat him like I'm wasting my time or that he's dragging me down. Ever since I read your book he's shocked with happiness. I almost wish he wasn't so nice to me this soon. I've blown ten years of his life and have so much to make up for. My poor children have suffered plenty too. I've been cruel and selfish, you name it. I've been misled for so long and am eagerly running down the road to recovery. Thank you, and thank God for opening my eyes. Praise the Lord! There can be happiness here on earth. I never knew it in all my life—only misery."

## I Was a Woman's Lib

"I've been studying *Fascinating Womanhood* and applying its principles over the last year and a half. I was so blind before. I needed instruction in all areas. My marriage is more loving and fulfilling because of it. What a blessing it is.

"I'm twenty-seven years old and brought up on the idea of the Women's Liberation Movement. All that was offered me through school, through the media, and by example was the limited choice of a full-time career. As editor of my high school newspaper I wrote pro Women's Lib articles and worked for the E.R.A. We had to prove we were just as good as the men and needed to be treated the same. This ugly competitive drive continued through college. The spirit of feminism stole my femininity.

"Four and a half years ago Jesus stepped into my life. He touched my hardened heart and started changing my mind. I longed for that gentle and quiet spirit that the Bible tells us is precious in the sight of God. Then a neighbor friend loaned me her copy of *Fascinating Womanhood*. I was thrilled to see God's principles spelled out. Eternal laws for the modern woman; a map to marriage bliss; how to fulfill my role as a fascinating woman, as a wife and helpmeet, as a mother, as a woman God intended. Yes, I echo those many success stories. *Fascinating Womanhood* has helped me gain back my stolen femininity.''

## A Single Career Girl Speaks

''All the glamour the women's movement has given to the working world isn't there that much. Our nation's working world, especially at the executive level, is negative-oriented rather than positive or creative-oriented. This is due in part to high inflation, excessive government control, excessive litigation which has driven insurance rates sky-high, just to name a few. The women's movement has also given rise to the concept that a career outside the home will make a woman more organized and efficient. This isn't exactly correct either.

''Like the homemaker, executives have *some unpleasant tasks*. Two of my unfavorite tasks are 1) bidding eighty-page government contracts, and 2) handling very delicate customer complaints which have been improperly handled at a lower level. If every woman could give as much *time and thought* to their children and husbands as I give to answering and handling problem customers alone, this would indeed transform the world. Right answers and solutions to a problem take much thoughtful consideration and even prayer. The customer is not always right.

''Working mothers receive dozens of phone calls from their children, but are not there with them when they may need the mother most. A recent experience sums it up best: A dear relative of mine died suddenly. A neighbor girl said this dear lady was closer to her than her own mother. While her own mother worked, this lady was always available to help her with her problems. When the girl married and had children of her own, she kept in close contact with her. When I meet my Prince Charming I intend to change careers and be a full-time wife and mother, and do *really important work*.''

## I Quit My Job to Stay Home

"After nine years of marriage I felt I had a good marriage, exactly what was expected for a young successful couple. My husband and I had good jobs, two children, a house, a car, and the necessary ingredients for happiness. But we were not happy.

"The one main event I can pinpoint as a reason for our problems was when I received a promotion into upper management. I felt I owed my company more of my time; therefore, my job became my number one priority and my husband and family were pushed down the priority ladder. As the arguments between my husband and me increased, so did the tension level in our home. As we tried to talk things out my husband kept saying I had changed. I agreed that I had changed, but only into the *ideal career woman and working mother*.

"After coming home from a ten-day vacation with my husband things were no better between us. The mailman arrived with a flyer advertising *Fascinating Womanhood*. My mother had highly recommended it so I bought the book and read it. Up to now I thought I liked my job. After reading Fascinating Womanhood and mulling it over, I realized I really did not like my job. My boss pressured me in areas that were compromising my values and family life. After a lot of thought I asked my husband if I could quit my job to stay home and take care of him and the children. He said *yes!*

"From that day forward my marriage has been wonderful, marvelous, unbelievable! The tension has left our home, since I'm not trying to be a liberated woman and make my husband do my domestic jobs. I'm not trying to put out fifty percent and wait for my husband's fifty percent to make my marriage successful. As the tension left, my husband and I talked without arguing. I found out that my job threatened him as a provider, because I could have supported the children on my salary and he felt I did not need him anymore. Now that we were talking, boy did Pandora's Box open up. I followed F.W. to the letter on how to handle Pandora's Box and I have kept on following the teachings.

"Thanks to F.W. my life is going in the right direction. My husband is happy, the children are happy, and I am more content than ever before. I take pride in being a Domestic Goddess and look forward to following the teachings of F.W. to become my husband's ideal woman.''

## Assignment:

1. If you work outside the home, ask yourself why you work.

2. If you work because of economic need but would like to quit, determine which ways you can reduce expenses. Discuss the idea with your husband. Explain the disadvantages of working and advantages of staying home.

# Summary on Femininity

As we come to the end of the chapters on femininity, you should have gained new insights. Femininity, as you can see, is more than ruffles and lace. Although a feminine appearance is important, it is of little use without the feminine manner, and neither are of any merit without the feminine nature—softness, gentleness, weakness, a spirit of sweet submission and a dependency on men for their care and protection. There must be no trace of masculine strength, aggressiveness, or competence.

You have learned of your feminine role in the home, in caring for the needs of your family. Here you have a field in which to grow as a woman. As you devote yourself to your family you acquire the traits of patience, gentleness, tenderness, and love—all feminine traits.

To be the most feminine, make your career a career in the home. Learn the feminine arts and skills—how to cook, clean, and care for children. Learn how to make a house a home. Let your husband make the living, and you make life worth living.

Of course you have a choice of what your life will be, and society should respect your choice. When you make a choice, however, you bear the consequences. If you move out of the feminine sphere into the working world, remember: *The moon, when it moves from its sphere of night into day loses its luster, its charm, its very poetry.*

Of all the qualities a woman may possess, femininity outweighs them all as far as men are concerned. Without femininity you may have a magnetic personality or a noble character but in men's eyes you will not be a woman. A man isn't interested in a great and noble character. He wants a gentle, tender, feminine woman.

# 22

## *Radiant Happiness*

What is radiant happiness? How does it differ from inner happiness, taught earlier? Inner happiness must be *earned* by building the character, whereas radiant happiness is a *voluntary* quality such as when you suddenly decide to smile. It is cheerfulness, laughter, singing, joyfulness, smiles, bright eyes, sparkle, vivacity, enthusiasm, optimism, a sense of humor, a sunny disposition and, like Deruchette, the power to lift the spirits of others.

Radiant happiness is one of the real charms men find fascinating in women, counting far more than beauty of face and form. Beautiful women should not make the mistake of *resting on their laurels,* hoping their pretty faces alone will make them attractive to men. Without a smile and sparkling eyes they have little appeal. Men admire pretty girls as they do beautiful pictures and scenes from nature, but they search for radiant, smiling women to be their life's companions.

Women who lack beauty of face and form due to irregular features often turn out to be the real charmers. This is because they have worked diligently to make up for their defects by acquiring the qualities that really count with men. Amelia, you will remember, was chubby and stout, with a short nose and round cheeks, but succeeded in winning the love of all men who came near her. Her defects were obscured by her smiling lips, eyes, and heart. Deruchette had freckles and a large mouth. Her beauty was her dangerous smile and vivacity.

Women have always tried to be attractive to men. Their emphasis, however, has been on clothes, hairstyles, and makeup. This outer shell is important, but more important is their smiling face and sunny disposition. If, for example, a woman is a picture of beauty in clothes, hairstyle, and makeup, but wears a sour expression, she will not be attractive to men. If, on the other hand, she wears the most ordinary clothes and hairstyle with little or no makeup but has a sunny smile, men will be fascinated.

### Deruchette, Amelia, and Dora

The most fascinating trait of Deruchette was her ability to radiate happiness to others, to *shed joy around,* and *cast light upon dark days.* Her smile had the *power* to lift the spirits of others; her presence radiated joy and light to her entire household; her approach was like a cheerful warmth. As the author says, *"She passes by and we are content; she stays awhile and we are happy."*

Amelia was *kind, fresh, smiling,* with a *smiling heart.* Dora had a *gay little laugh and a delightful little voice.* President Woodrow Wilson said of his wife, Ellen, *"She was so radiant, so happy!"* Men don't enjoy women who are glum, depressed, or even overly serious. They seek out women who are vibrant, alive, and happy!

### Dolly Madison

One of the longest reigning and most vivacious of all first ladies of the White House was Dolly Madison. During the eight years her husband presided she won the hearts of her countrymen and was known as the most popular person in the U.S., and the most loved. In Parisian turban, topped with a plume, her neck and arms strung with pearls, she was the perfect hostess—bubbly and natural, tactful and gracious. Her zest for life never ran out. Without becoming ill, one day at age eighty-two she simply passed from a nap to death. *"She sparkled,"* reported a friend, *"up to the very verge of the grave."*

### Ninon de Lenclos

Ninon de Lenclos of the seventeenth-century court of France was another woman of special charm and radiance. Some of the greatest men of the century loved her, and she is said to have won the hearts of three generations of men in a single family, for she lived and retained her beauty and charm into her eighties. The most interesting women of France were her devoted friends. The most wonderful thing about her, everyone said, was her eager delight in everything around her. In her own words she said, *"You never hear me say, 'this is good' or 'this is bad,' but a thousand times a day I say, 'I enjoy, I enjoy.'"*

## Natasha

Natasha, the heroine of *War and Peace*, had spark and verve, pluck and audacity with a bit of mischief. At times she had a roguish expression. She was happy and radiant. Prince Andrei was first attracted to her love of life. As he was trying to sleep by an open window he heard her voice from a window above saying to her cousin, *"Oh, how can you sleep. Just look how lovely it is! Oh, how glorious! There never, never was such an exquisite night! Look, what a moon! Oh, how lovely! Do come here. There, you see, I feel like squatting down on my heels, putting my arms around my knees like this, tight as tight can be, and flying away like this . . .*

*"All was silent but Prince Andrei knew she was still sitting there. . . . 'What is she so glad about? What is she thinking of? Why is she so happy?' . . . Her charm mounted to his head like wine. . . . Prince Andrei enjoyed meeting someone not of the conventional society stamp. And such was Natasha with her wonder, her delight, her shyness, and even her mistakes in speaking French. He admired the radiance of her eyes and her smile which had to do with her own inner happiness and not with what they were saying."*

The author does not describe Natasha as being especially beautiful. She is considered charming, enchanting, and by some even pretty. At one point the author even elaborates on her defects by saying, *"Natasha's large mouth widened, making her look quite ugly."* So, as in other examples of charming women, their appeal is not so much in the shape of their face as their angelic and human qualities.

*"In Natasha, Prince Andrei was conscious of a strange world, completely remote from him and brimful of joys he had not known. . . . He looked at her while she sang and something*

*new and blissful stirred his soul. . . . His soul was so full of joyful sensations that it seemed to him as if he had just emerged from a stuffy room into God's fresh air. . . . It did not enter his head that he was in love with her. . . . He was not thinking of her but only picturing her to himself, and in consequence all life appeared in a new light. And for the first time for a very long time he began making plans for the future. His feeling for her helped him believe in the possibility of happiness.*

*" 'Yesterday I was in torment, agony,' said Prince Andrei, 'But I would not exchange that agony for anything else in the world. . . . I have never lived until now. Only now am I alive, but I cannot live without her.' Prince Andrei seemed and really was an utterly different, new man . . . What had become of his ennui, his contempt for life, his disillusionment? . . . He marveled at the feeling which had taken possession of him, as something strange and apart, independent of himself. . . . 'The whole world is split in two halves for me: She is in one half and there is all joy, hope and light: The other is where she is not and there everything is gloom and darkness.' "* And such is the tremendous feeling a man can have for a woman.

### A Sense of Humor

When I say a woman should have a sense of humor, I am not referring to telling silly jokes or playing pranks. This can detract from feminine charm. I am referring to seeing the amusing side of ordinary situations. This is not only attractive in a woman, but can serve a useful purpose. It can be a means of handling rough moments, can even turn tears to laughter. I came from a family who handled mishaps in this way, so I learned it early in life, and therefore will give you some personal examples:

Shortly after I met my husband he drove me to our college campus. As he helped me out of his car I caught my coat on something and tore a hole in it. I can't explain why, unless it was my upbringing, but it struck me as funny and I started giggling. My husband, coming from a more serious family, was truly amazed at this reaction. I'm not sure he knew quite what to think, but he had the impression I would be comfortable to live around and we started dating about this time.

After we were married I had another mishap. I was carrying a bowl of spaghetti across the kitchen floor, slipped on a rug, and splattered spaghetti all over myself and the kitchen. Now I could have sat on the floor and cried, but instead I saw the ridiculous humor of it all and began laughing. My husband still has fond memories of this occasion. It was during World War II, when there wasn't much to laugh about.

Next time you have a mishap, try to see the humor. For example, suppose you run out of gas on the freeway, lock yourself out of your house in your nightgown, lose a ten-dollar bill, accidentally put your plane ticket in the trash can, bring home someone else's coat in place of your own, or any other ridiculous human error. You can do like most people do—grumble, complain, and make yourself feel miserable. But will fretting do any good to solve the problem? You may as well see the humor in it. In fact, keeping your spirits up helps you think through your problem and find a solution.

## How to Acquire Radiant Happiness

1. *Work for Inner Happiness:* You can more naturally and consistently radiate happiness to others if you are happy within. Work on this continually.

2. *Make a Conscious Effort:* After you have applied your makeup, stand before the mirror and practice smiling. Try to look radiant. The radiance, however, must be of the lips, eyes, and the entire countenance, not a stiff wooden smile. Leave the room with a happy face. Your family will reflect this same expression and your day will begin well. Next, add a cheerful attitude. Try not to be skeptical or dubious about life. Certainly some things we must look upon with doubt but our attitude should be optimistic, hopeful, with an emphasis on the brighter side of life. We can't have a smile which lifts the spirits of others unless we maintain a bright outlook.

3. *Radiate Happiness to All:* The best way to form the habit of being radiant is to have a smile for everyone, not just your family and friends. The world delights in sunny people; there are more than enough serious ones. Bring sunshine to the sad, depressed, and disconsolate. Shed joy to the frowning and disagreeable. They need it most of all. Give whether they

deserve it or not. God *"sendeth rain on the just and on the unjust."* Or, as an old Oriental proverb says, *"The lotus blossom gives fragrance to all in the room."*

4. *Smile Through Adversity:* It seems to be a natural part of life to have periods of discouragement. Smiling at such times may seem unnatural but, as with all Christian and moral teachings *we are expected to do the supernatural thing.* A mark of true character, especially womanly character, is to smile through adversity, as expressed in the following lines by Ella Wheeler Wilcox:

> *It is easy enough to be pleasant*
> *When life flows by like a song.*
> *But the one worthwhile is the one who can smile*
> *When everything goes dead wrong.*
> *For the test of the heart is trouble*
> *And it always comes with the years.*
> *And the smile that is worth the praises of earth*
> *Is the smile that shines through tears.*

5. *Health:* You can more easily smile and look radiant if you feel well. If you don't, if your body is sickly, depleted, weak, or tired, it is difficult to look radiant. Health is the topic of the next chapter, an important part of radiance and the whole of *Fascinating Womanhood.*

## When Not to Smile

There are times it is best not to smile or to radiate happiness. For example, when you are in the presence of someone who is extremely sorrowful, your happy attitude may suggest a lack of sympathy. In this case it is best to be serious to show an understanding for what the other person is suffering. Try to perceive situations in which gravity and sympathy seem more appropriate. If you are not sure, notice their reaction to your smile. If they seem offended by your happiness you can be sure it is not in harmony with their low spirits, and they wish you would stop. Mourning is even a virtue sometimes, when appropriate.

## The Real Charm

*"There is in this world no function more important than that of being charming—to shed joy around, to cast light upon dark days, to be the golden thread of our destiny, and the very spirit of grace and harmony. Is not this to render a service?"*

## Assignment:

Practice smiling before the mirror. Include the lips, the eyes, and the whole countenance.

# 23

## *Radiant Health*

The foundation of beauty is fresh, radiant health, not only for the health itself, but for the fresh and joyful spirit it lends to the appearance, actions, and attitude. How attractive are sparkling eyes, lustrous hair, a clear voice, buoyancy of manner, and the animation which good health brings to the face, and the vivacity it communicates to the thoughts. We cannot attach too much importance to this qualification.

What is good health? Are we healthy if we never get sick, never have to visit a doctor or spend time in a sick bed? Are we healthy if we feel reasonably well most of the time? Not necessarily. The sparkling countenance described above is not derived from just average good health. A fresh, radiant appearance arises from *health in rich abundance*.

What is the secret of this abundant health? Like happiness, health is based on laws. We attain good health by understanding these laws and applying them. The following are the fundamental laws of good health:

### 1. Eat Properly

A super wholesome diet is the following: About fifty percent or more of the diet should be comprised of fresh fruits and vegetables, altered as little as possible, much of it raw and freshly prepared. When possible, buy or grow organic, unsprayed, fruits and vegetables. About twenty-five percent or more of the diet should be comprised of whole grains (wheat, oats, corn, rye, millet, barley, buckwheat). About ten percent or more should be comprised of legumes (peas, lentils, lima beans), seeds, and nuts. The remaining ten to fifteen percent can consist of lean meat, low- fat dairy products, and oils, used mainly to flavor other foods.

When you cook, use no fats or cooking water. Use tightly covered pans at temperatures below the boiling point of water. Allow considerable additional cooking time. Don't overcook. If you haven't been feeling well, this diet will make a remarkable difference within a few days. If you're already in good health, you'll notice more abundant health than you thought possible. If you don't wish to follow it to such an extreme, use it as a guideline to improve your diet.

### Foods to Avoid:

1. *Processed Foods:* Avoid all processed or refined foods such as white flour, white sugar, white rice, or foods which contain them such as macaroni, crackers, cold cereal, cookies, cakes, pies, doughnuts, pizza, spaghetti, candy, gum, or ice cream. Beware of foods which come in boxes, bottles, cans, or packages. Avoid canned or frozen food. Avoid cold cuts of meat, ham, bacon, sausage, or wieners. Why avoid these processed foods? For two reasons:

First, when foods are processed vital elements are removed or destroyed—vitamins, minerals, enzymes, and natural fiber. Freezing and cooking, for example, destroy enzymes. Milling grain into refined flour removes the bran, and therefore vitamins and fiber. Refining sugar removes every trace of mineral and vitamin content so there is nothing left but a product that cannot be classified as a food. In an effort to make up for these losses, processors add vitamins and minerals, but they don't compare to those they removed, and they can't add enzymes since they are too perishable.

Second, processed foods contain additives—preservatives, emulsifiers, colorings, and flavorings. Additives are harmful to the body and cause a variety of ailments. Food coloring, for example, can cause hypersensitivity in children. If foods are labeled *natural,* don't be fooled. Food processors use this term with an intent to deceive. Carefully read all labels to avoid being *poisoned.*

2. *Salt:* Use only small quantities.

3. *Poison Sprays*: Avoid fruits and vegetables which have been sprayed with pesticides while growing, or treated with chemicals after being picked to preserve freshness.

4. *Chemical Fertilizers:* Avoid buying fresh foods grown in chemically fertilized soil. Such chemicals are destroying our topsoil, encouraging plagues of insects, and producing fruits and vegetables which are high in yield but deficient in essential vitamins, mineral, enzymes, and trace minerals.

## 2. Get Enough Sleep

To be assured of getting enough sleep, set a specific time to go to bed. If you find it hard to get to bed on time, is it because you have too much to do? If so, ask yourself if the things you must do are more important than sleep, or your health. This may require a review of priorities.

For sleep to be the most restful, avoid eating after six P.M., go to bed before ten P.M., and sleep on a good, firm, mattress. The hours of sleep before midnight are more restful than those after. Why this is I don't think anyone knows but experience has proven this to be true.

## 3. Exercise Regularly

Exercise is as important as the food we eat in producing good health and preserving life. You may feel you get enough exercise by walking about the house, bending, and reaching. The problem is these motions don't invigorate the heart or bloodstream, nor bring into play all of the muscles.

Exercise should do two things: First, it should be vigorous enough and sustained enough to *raise the heartbeat* and maintain it for thirty to forty minutes. This stimulates the cardiovascular system, strengthens the heart, and brings oxygen into the bloodstream. When such exercise is maintained regularly for six months or longer it lowers the pulse, or blood pressure, thus improving and insuring health. Second, exercise should involve as *many muscles* as possible, to both *strengthen them* and *limber them*.

Some good forms of exercise are gymnastics, aerobics, calisthenics, bicycling, weight lifting, swimming, very brisk walking, and running. To include all of the muscles, however, some must be combined. What are the rewards of exercise? When you exercise vigorously and regularly, you require *less sleep*, feel *less hungry*, are in *better health*, and *feel better*.

## 4. Drink Plenty of Pure Water

Calculate the amount of water to drink in a day by your weight. Drink half as many liquid ounces of water as your total weight in pounds. For example, if you weigh 128 pounds, you should drink 64 ounces of water per day, which is exactly two quarts. Make certain the water is pure. Most public water systems are not fit for drinking. Many contain pesticides and other impurities which have seeped from the surface into the underground water systems. If you haven't done so, have your water tested. If inadequate, buy a water purifier or bottled water.

Be sure you drink *enough* water. Don't deprive your body of one of its most important elements for health. If you don't drink enough water, your body is forced to use its water over and over again. Your whole system suffers unless refreshed frequently with a new supply of water.

## 5. Get Plenty of Fresh Air

A good air supply consists of three things: First, the air should be *fresh*, so it has an ample oxygen content. Second, it should have a sufficient *moisture* content. Third, *breathe deeply* so you take sufficient oxygen into your lungs. Oxygen is our most important food. What good food is to the stomach, oxygen is to the blood. To be assured of enough oxygen, see that fresh air circulates in your rooms; keep your posture erect so your breathing is deep rather than shallow; increase your oxygen intake by vigorous exercise.

The moisture content of the air is very important to health, especially in preventing illness of the respiratory system such as colds, sore throat, and bronchitis. Most modern heating systems dry the air, so that even in a moist climate the air in the house is dry. To solve this problem, have a moisturizer installed in your furnace, use a humidifier, or hang wet towels in rooms which are occupied. At night, if the weather permits, turn off the furnace and open the windows.

## 6. Relax, at Work or Play

Relaxation promotes health and charm whereas tension deters it. While doing work which makes you tense, how can you make yourself relax? By mind control. The mind controls the body, making it tense or relaxed. When you merely tell your body to relax, you immediately feel a relief of tension. Additional things which help you relax are exercise and a good mental attitude.

## 7. Have a Healthy Mental Attitude

Wholesome attitudes arise from virtues such as faith, hope, optimism, love, kindness, cheerfulness, sympathy, forgiveness, and enthusiasm. These pleasant attitudes harmonize with body functions and invigorate the system, promoting good health. In contrast, unwholesome attitudes arise from defects of character such as worry, fear, anxiety, pessimism, hate, resentments, impatience, envy, or anger. Any negative mental attitude has a detrimental effect on the health. Its destructive influence is carried through the nervous system to the entire body. People have been known to die of extreme fear or rage.

## 8. Control Weight

There are two main reasons to control your weight. The first is *your health*. Excess weight is detrimental to health. It is harmful to body functions, can interfere with proper breathing and walking, and is the cause of a number of diseases such as diabetes and heart trouble. You can greatly improve your health and vitality and extend your life by getting down to normal size.

The second reason to lose weight is *your appearance*. If you have a chunky figure you cannot appear dainty, feminine, or girlish, even with the help of soft, flowing, feminine clothes. No matter what you do to disguise it, you cannot hide excess weight. When you get down to normal size, you will look many times more attractive in your clothes. You will appear younger and more feminine, and will acquire a new vitality to your face and features. Just from the standpoint of appearance it is well worth it to lose excess weight.

## Guidelines for Losing Weight:

1. *Diet:* Follow a good, nutritious diet such as the diabetic diet, Weight Watchers diet, or the one suggested in this chapter. You must have plenty of fresh fruits and vegetables and the most nourishing food possible. This helps to satisfy your appetite and preserve your health.

2. *Off Limits:* Eliminate sweets and fats from your diet— pie, cake, ice cream, candy, gum, soft drinks, cookies, pastries, puddings, syrup, and jam. In a month or two your desire for sweets lessens or entirely leaves. This step not only reduces weight but improves health, preserves teeth, and lengthens life.

3. *Time Limits:* Avoid eating after six P.M. Foods you eat in the evening when you are more relaxed, are more easily assimilated. Never eat late at night for the same reason. You may want to consider eating only two meals a day. This could be breakfast at ten A.M. and dinner at four P.M.

4. *Support Group:* You may want to consider joining a weight loss program. They offer diet suggestions, encouragement, incentives, and group support.

5. *Radical Diets:* Avoid radical diets and diet pills as they are harmful to the health.

Are you discouraged with the idea of losing weight? Do you look upon it as a lifetime struggle, not worth the continual effort? To be slim, must you *starve yourself for the rest of your life?* No. Take courage with this thought: When you finally reach your normal weight, and better still, a few pounds below, it is not the struggle it once was. Your appetite becomes more normal, or at least more controllable with only reasonable effort. You reach a point where it is not a major problem any longer.

After you reach your normal weight, make it a habit to weigh yourself *once a day or at least twice a week*. If you gain even one pound during this time, go on a diet the next day to lose that one pound. With reasonable effort you can keep your slim figure for the rest of your life.

## 9. Correct Internal Disorders

If you eat properly and follow the principles of health just covered, many internal ailments will be corrected. When the body is properly nourished and exercised, it works to correct itself. After considerable time on a strict health program if you still have internal problems such as disorders of the blood, glands, or internal organs, or chronic infections, seek competent treatment. Most of these ailments can be eliminated by proper attention.

### A Healthy Appearance

A clean, fresh, healthy, appearance is attractive to a man. How is such an appearance achieved? The following are guidelines:

1. *Health:* The main way to achieve a healthy appearance is by genuine good health. Good health adds color to the cheeks, clearness to the eyes, sheen to the hair, a glow to the skin, and vitality to the face and feature.

2. *Cleanliness and Grooming:* This is also important. Take care that your teeth, hair, nails, feet, and entire body are clean and well cared for.

3. *Clothing:* Clothing also contributes to a fresh, healthy look, such as fresh starched collars, flowers, polished shoes, and clean, well-pressed clothes. Certain fabrics appear fresh—fabrics with fresh colors, clean stripes, polka dots, or just a fresh look.

4. *Makeup:* This is also important in achieving a clean, fresh, healthy look, especially eye makeup, rouge, and lipstick. Men are not opposed to artificial beauty if it makes a woman appear more fresh and radiant.

### If Health Is Beyond Your Reach

If you, because of permanent damage to your body, cannot attain this ideal of abundant health, try to maintain *a healthy mental attitude*. When you do, you appear more healthy than you actually are. Elizabeth Barrett Browning was an invalid, yet one of the truly charming women in history. Her husband, Robert Browning, adored her. Her physical weakness, although a disadvantage, did not destroy her feminine charm. This was due to an abundance of other womanly qualities which overcame the physical deficiency. Radiant health is only one quality of The Ideal Woman. If you have a healthy mental attitude, you can still be a fascinating woman.

## Fundamentals of Good Health

1. Eat Properly
2. Get Enough Sleep
3. Exercise Regularly
4. Drink Plenty of Pure Water
5. Get Plenty of Fresh Air
6. Relax, at Work or Play
7. Have a Healthy Mental Attitude
8. Control Weight
9. Correct Internal Disorders

## Assignment

Evaluate your health in comparison with the ideals taught in this lesson. If you have weak points, outline a program of self-improvement.

# *Introduction to Childlikeness*

*Except ye be converted and become as little children*
*ye shall not enter the kingdom of heaven. Mat.18:3*

What is meant by the Biblical statement, *except ye become as little children?* Doesn't it imply they have traits we should copy? Children tend to be trustful, teachable, believing, and forgiving.

We should copy the manner in which children express emotions, especially the emotion of anger. When a child is offended he doesn't respond with an ugly, cutting remark, nor does he conceal his feelings. His emotions surface quickly and dramatically! He is honest and outspoken. Instead of holding a grudge, he tends to be forgiving.

Childlikeness teaches you how to handle difficult and common problems in marriage. You learn how to express yourself when you are angry, and how to react when he is angry with you, or when he is stern, harsh, or cross. With a childlike response you can, in a small moment, turn the night to day. You learn the right way to ask for things, and he responds by *wanting* to do things for you.

Up to now I have suggested you do a lot of giving— accept your husband's weaknesses, appreciate him, admire him, make him number one, honor his leadership, and be an ideal wife. Childlikeness is a balance to this. Now the concern is with you, your needs and feelings, your moments of pain. You learn to handle these moments in a way to preserve your self-dignity, to keep from feeling like a doormat. In so doing you command his respect, his tenderness, and his love. This adds a new dimension to your relationship, a new ingredient to your love. It takes the thorns out of marriage and makes it fun.

Childlikeness is one of the most charming traits taught in

*Fascinating Womanhood*. It is the spice and spark of the subject and keeps the angelic side from becoming cloysome. Men love this trait in women. It amuses and fascinates them because it is a contrast to their masculine strength.

# 24

## *Childlike Anger*

Are you ever upset or angry with your husband? If so, why? Think for a moment. Isn't it because he has *mistreated* you in some way? I am referring to times he has been *harshly critical, unkind or unfair, or has insulted you, neglected* or *ignored you.* He has *hurt your feelings, disappointed you,* or in some way *upset you.*

When he does these things how do you handle it? Do you fly off the handle with a nasty temper? Do you shrink back as if wounded? Do you retreat into your shell? Or, do you hold your tongue, but smolder inside? The trouble with these reactions is they create resentments, cool feelings, and provoke arguments. And they make you look ugly and feel terrible. Since none of these methods work, consider a childlike response:

### Childlike Anger

Childlike anger is the cute, pert, saucy anger of a little child. There is no better school for learning childlike anger than watching the antics of little children, especially little girls who have been spoiled by too much loving. They are so trusting and innocent, and yet so piquant and outspoken, they are often teased into anger. They are too innocent to feel hate, jealousy, resentment, and the uglier emotions.

When such a child is teased, she doesn't respond with some hideous sarcasm. Instead, she stamps her foot and shakes her curls and pouts. She gets adorably angry at herself because her efforts to respond are impotent. Finally, she switches off and threatens never to speak to you again, then glances back at you over her shoulder to see if you thought she really meant it, only to stomp her foot in impatience when she sees you're not the least bit fooled.

A scene such as this invariably makes us smile with amusement. We feel an irresistible longing to pick up such a child and hug it. We would do anything rather than permit such an adorable little thing to suffer danger or want; to protect and care for such a delightfully human little creature would be nothing less than a delight.

This is much the same feeling a woman inspires in a man when she expresses anger in a childlike way. Her ridiculous exaggeration of manner makes him suddenly want to laugh; makes him feel, in contrast, stronger, more sensible, and more of a man. This is why women who are little spitfires—independent and saucy—are often sought after by men. This anger, however, must be the sauciness of a child, and not the intractable stubbornness of a woman well able to *kill her own snakes*.

## Dora's Anger

An example of childlike anger is found in the story of David Copperfield. In this particular situation, David criticized Dora because she didn't manage the hired help well; because of this, one of them had stolen Dora's gold watch. David put the blame on Dora. *"I began to be afraid,"* said David, *"that the fault is not entirely on one side, but that these people turn out ill because we don't turn out very well ourselves."*

*"Oh, what an accusation!"* exclaimed Dora, opening her eyes wide, *"to say that you ever saw me take gold watches. Oh! Oh! you cruel fellow, to compare your affectionate wife to a transported page!* [hired boy]. *Why didn't you tell me your opinion of me before we were married? Why didn't you say, you hard-hearted thing, that you were convinced that I was worse than a transported page. Oh, what a dreadful opinion to have of me! Oh, my goodness!"*

Please note that Dora used *strong adjectives* to describe David's treatment of her such as *cruel* and *hard-hearted*. She also *exaggerated* his treatment of her by saying he had implied she was a thief. Such means of expressing anger are childlike.

## How to Express Childlike Anger

1. *Character:* To express anger with the innocence of a child there must be an absence of bitterness, resentment, hate, sarcasm, or the ugly emotions. If you have a harsh, critical, disposition you'll not be able to express childlike anger until you overcome these serious weaknesses of character.

2. *Manner:* Learn childlike mannerisms by studying the antics of little girls: Stomp your foot, lift your chin high, square your shoulders, pout, put both hands on your hips, open your eyes wide, mumble under your breath, or turn and walk briskly away, then pause and look back over your shoulder. Or, beat your fists on your husband's chest. You may have to be an actress to succeed, if only a ham actress. But, remember, you'll be launching an acting career which will save you pain, tension, frustration, a damaged relationship, and perhaps even a marriage. Is any acting career of greater importance? No, so turn on the drama. It is guaranteed to ease tension and bring humor into your life instead of pain.

3. *Use Adjectives:* Acquire a list of adjectives which *compliment his masculinity,* such as *big, tough, brute, stubborn, obstinate,* or *hairy beast.* Other appropriate adjectives are *unyielding, determined, difficult, hard-hearted, inflexible, unruly, stiff-necked, indomitable,* and *invincible.* Be certain your words compliment his masculinity. Never use words which belittle masculinity such as *little, imp, pip-squeak, insignificant, weak, simpleminded,* or *dumb.*

4. *Exaggerate:* Exaggerate his treatment of you by saying, for example: *"How can a great big man like you pick on a poor little helpless girl like me!"* Or, *"So this is the way you treat a poor little defenseless woman."* Or, *"Oh, what a dreadful thing to do!"* Or, be charmingly defensive by saying, *"I'm just a poor, erring, wayward little human being."* Or, *"Everyone has at least one little fault. Nobody's perfect!"*

Or, make exaggerated childlike threats by saying, *"I'll never speak to you again."* Or, *"I won't do anything for you anymore."* Or, *"I'll tell your mother on you."* Or, if he insults you in public say, *"Wait until I get you home alone."* Or, *"I'll get even with you."* Be sure your expressions represent a trustful, feminine woman of high character, not a vulgar, overbearing, or suspicious one.

Why do children tend to exaggerate? Because they feel little and helpless in the presence of adults or even other children. Unconsciously, in moments of frustration, they try to make up for their smallness by exaggerations. Therefore, when a woman uses this same method, she gives the man the impression she is little, helpless, and therefore childlike.

5. *Tears:* If you feel the impulse for tears it can be childlike. Be certain it reflects the innocence of a child and not the emotional turmoil of a deeply disturbed woman. There is nothing which so frustrates a man as a hysterical woman.

### When You Have a Right to Be Angry

You have a right to be angry when you have been in any way mistreated—treated unfairly, insulted, criticized, imposed on, neglected, ignored, or teased.

You *don't* have a right to be angry when your husband has failed in his world of responsibility, when he has made a stupid mistake in his work or lost his job, or neglected to cut the lawn, balance the budget, or wash the car. He has a right to be himself, even if it means to be weak and lazy, to neglect his duty, or even to fail. This is his department.

Also, *don't* express anger when you feel the emotions of hate, bitterness, resentments, or any of the ugly emotions. Instead, pour out your angry feelings to a trusted friend or parent, or engage in hard physical work. Work on your character, especially the qualities of humility, acceptance, and forgiveness. Only when ugly emotions have been overcome can anger be expressed in a childlike way.

Express childlike anger *at the moment of offense*, not sometime later when you've had time to decide what to say. This means you'll have to think quickly or plan some reactions ahead of time. If you don't respond *at the moment*, consider it your failure. You may as well forgive and forget. Review the situation and be prepared with a response next time. Don't blame your husband. It is you who have failed. So, even though you may not always respond with childlike anger, just knowing you should have done, and could have done, softens your feelings.

Also don't use childlike anger as a means of reforming his treatment of you, thinking he will stop insulting and neglecting you. He may, but on the other hand, he may continue to mistreat you. If he does, continue to respond with childlike anger. The only purpose of childlike anger is to *vent troubled feelings, ease painful moments, preserve self-dignity,* and *be fascinating.*

Express anger in times of *medium offenses.* In other words, it's best to overlook trifles, lest we appear picky. Major offenses may be so disturbing they are difficult to approach with childlikeness (not impossible). But, do apply childlike anger in times of *medium offenses.*

## Major Offenses

There are serious ways men mistreat women—infidelity, physical abuse, gross neglect, nonsupport, and lack of respect for human rights and liberty. If your husband mistreats you in any of these serious ways, live the entire philosophy of *Fascinating Womanhood* for a period of time to soften his heart and bring about a reformation in his behavior. You may be the one who has brought out his ugly side by lack of acceptance, admiration, and sympathetic understanding, and a failure to place him number one. Give him a chance to respond to the new you. If he is physically or mentally dangerous, remove yourself and your children from the household.

## A Word to Those Who Resist Childlike Anger

Some women think the idea of childlike anger ridiculous. They wonder, ''How can a grown up woman like me take the part of a little girl who stomps her foot, shakes her curls, and pouts? How can I look adorable when I am angry?'' Why not try it? It may seem absurd to you, but why not let your husband decide? Of course, if you don't play your part well, if you laugh and act ridiculous you'll make a fool of yourself. You don't *have* to stomp your foot and shake your curls. You can just use adjectives, exaggerations, and amusing statements.

Other women claim they don't need childlike anger, that everything is going along fine for them. This may be true, in some cases, but as long as we have men who are thoughtless and critical, and sensitive women who become upset, angry, or resentful towards their husbands, we need childlike anger or an effective alternative.

If you can't express anger in a childlike way, do find an acceptable means of expressing it so you won't form resentments toward your husband and thus harm your marriage relationship. In fact, you owe it to your husband as well as yourself to express anger. You do him no favor to smother your angry feelings and hold resentments. Eliminating these problems is the main purpose of childlike anger. It builds better marriages.

## How to Overcome Anger

As long as you are angry, as long as you experience the troubled feeling within, seek effective means of dealing with this problem. In the mean time, overcome the tendency to anger in the following ways:

1. *Spiritual Growth:* Learn to be forgiving, understanding, and patient. Allow for the mistakes and human frailties of others. This leads to spiritual growth. In this way you overcome the tendency to anger. You no longer experience the turmoil and distressing feelings which accompany anger. However, on the path to perfection you are still a human being, prone to anger. Deal with this human fault by expressing childlike anger.

2. *Self-esteem:* When you have a good self-image you are less likely to be offended and therefore less prone to anger. With self-esteem comes an invulnerability of spirit which keeps you from being hurt, a *"sticks and stones will break my bones but words will never hurt me"* attitude. When you are invulnerable to criticism or abuse you feel, *"I know you neglect me, criticize me, or treat me unfairly, but I know you love me too much to do this intentionally."* In this way you are marvelously freed from the damaging effects of offenses. The following are childlike success stories:

### Saucy

"When I tried a saucy response to my husband's thoughtlessness, he said, 'That was so cute, let's do it again.'"

## A Pout

"I had my doubts about applying childlikeness, for I didn't think I could do it. Then one time when I was offended I just stuck out my lower lip, just slightly and my husband said, 'You look so cute when you do that,' and we both forgot what we were upset about."

## I Stomped My Foot

"Before breakfast one morning I was cooking pancakes. My husband was in a cross, ugly mood and finally snapped something ridiculous at me. I stamped my little foot (size nine) and exclaimed, 'You cross old bear! You great big bully, talking that way to me.' I tossed my head and turned back to the stove. 'I think I'll just burn your pancakes,' I added, glancing back over my shoulder with a mischievous look, to see if he was watching. He was grinning from ear to ear and the black, ugly mood was gone. It took me four months to try childlikeness because it seemed so silly. For months I practiced in front of a mirror, using the right adjectives!"

## Pillow Fight

"We had just experienced one of those terrible weekends where every flick of an eyelash is misinterpreted and the tension so thick you could cut it with a knife. So my husband could have the peace and quiet he wanted I took our five-year-old to the park and kept her until dinnertime, then quickly rushed her to bed.

"Very soon afterward I dejectedly, resentfully, and rather tearfully crawled into bed with my *Fascinating Womanhood* book. What should I read but the part about sauciness. I didn't have any idea how to be saucy and I didn't have any curls to toss. Try to imagine me sitting up in bed, talking to myself as to what I would say and practicing sauciness. I became so involved that I completely forgot about my resentment and began to laugh at myself.

"When my husband came to bed I popped up with a pout on my face and said saucily, 'I hope you have enjoyed your ole peace and quiet because I have been utterly miserable.' He was so amused that he picked up a pillow and threw it at me and I threw it back and we had a good laugh. He said he realized he had been unfair and he would take our child to the park the next weekend and I could have the peace and quiet. Without *Fascinating Womanhood* I'm afraid this story would have had a different ending. Through sauciness there was a happy ending.''

### From a Little Girl

''I am ten years old and going into the sixth grade. My mom has the book *Fascinating Womanhood*. One day about two months ago she told me to take *Fascinating Womanhood* to my teacher and let her read it. But it was too late. Her husband had died about six years ago. But it still didn't hurt for her to read it. She didn't have time to read it in class because she was too busy getting mad at some boys who had been playing hooky the day before.

''I told her she could take it home with her to read and she did. The next morning she came to school with a real pretty dress on. She said, 'That's a fantastic book. If more people would read it and do what it says there wouldn't be any more divorces. Can I borrow it again?' 'It's OK with me,' I replied. Now, whenever she gets mad she uses sauciness and has a soft voice. Thanks to *Fascinating Womanhood* for everything.''

### My Hairy Beast

''My marriage was like so many, an armed truce. We had vowed 'for better or for worse' and it had been mostly 'worse.' My husband never wore his ring, and spent little time with me or our two children. He made it very clear that he didn't need me at all. His father had often yelled at and beaten his mother, so my husband went the opposite direction. He seldom spoke and never touched me.

''In the fall, just half a year after buying a new home, he was transferred 2,200 miles away. The children and I stayed behind to sell the house. He went on to get a new house. I was to live in what *he* picked. I was not considered at all.

''One lonely day I was pouring my heart out to a friend, telling her what I had decided to do. I can't count the times she said, 'That's not what you should do!' or 'That is not the way to handle it!' I got mad at her, but undaunted she persisted with F.W. and more F.W. I called her a *Fascinating Womanhood* fanatic!

"My husband flew home on weekends. I planned all week. It is a good thing he left on Sunday evening for my self-control lasted about two days. Over those two days I pretended that things were as I wanted them to be and I acted the part. When I met him at the airport I went early, parked the car, and went to the gate. (Usually I met him out front.) I dressed my most feminine. I built myself up to a breathless pitch. When I saw him coming I ran to meet him and flung my arms around him, telling him I was glad to see him and that I had missed him. Everyone in the area was looking. One would have thought he was returning from a year as prisoner of war. He had always shunned any emotional display, even in private, calling it disgusting. Now he didn't say anything but he was touched. In the car I sat close and kept my mouth shut, my hand lightly touching him, and with my eyes I drank him in. He was overwhelmed.

"That was the beginning. Three weekends later he suggested I leave the children with my mother and join him for a week to select a house from several he had seen. On that trip I expressed admiration for the beauty of the area, searched for the good, and delightfully enjoyed. I was the epitome of understanding. The high point of the trip came one evening after we had decided to build. We were staying at the home of a bachelor friend of his.

"I was doing the dinner dishes while my husband was showing the bachelor, who was very desirous of marriage, our plans. My husband began saying over and over things like, 'So you want to get married. Boy, you don't know when you're well off . . . look at the headaches a wife can bring.' At first I took it as a joke, but soon it wasn't funny anymore.

"As I scrubbed one plate I thought, 'If I hear him say that once more I'll really tell him.' Then I thought, 'What have I read in F.W. about anger?' I gave it a try. I turned around, stomped my foot, and said, 'You big hairy beast! I'm never going to like you again, ever!' and walked out of the room, turning as I went to glance over my shoulder with a tiny smile. I don't think he saw it. He was grinning from ear to ear. 'Did you hear what she called me?' he asked our host. 'Did you hear?'

"I found myself in the bedroom thinking, 'Great, but what now?' My husband had never in eight years of marriage apologized for being inconsiderate. Yet not minutes later he entered the bedroom, sat down beside me, and said, 'I am sorry and I didn't mean to hurt your feelings. Will you forgive me?' I'd have forgiven him anything at that moment.

"A couple of months later I received my first birthday card from my husband. It was special, not only because he remembered it, and even got the date right, but because he had selected a tiny card showing a cute little hairy beast, suitcase in hand. It said *Happy Birthday, Lovingly, your Hairy Beast*. He had actually looked for a special card.

"It is now five years later. They have been the best five years of my life. There are many things I could tell, but one highlight stands out above the rest. Our third child was born in January. It was an emergency C section. My wonderful husband, who truly can't stand sickness or pain, was with me every minute he could be. The day I left the hospital the nurses told me they, all of them, voted my husband the most loving, tender, romantic husband they had ever met. And he is!

"Our marriage isn't perfect. There are still things which cause me pain. I have a long way to go, but I know that when I am perfect he will be perfect too. My prayer is every woman can know and accept *Fascinating Womanhood*."

### How to Express Childlike Anger:

1. Develop character to eliminate the ugly emotions of hate, bitterness, sarcasm, or resentments.
2. Use childlike mannerisms.
3. Acquire a list of adjectives which compliment masculinity.
4. Exaggerate his treatment of you.

### Assignment

1. Make a list of adjectives which compliment masculinity.
2. Create exaggerated expressions for moments of childlike anger.

# 25

## *A Childlike Response*

*When a Man Is Angry, Cross, Irritable, or Stern*

There are two sources of anger in a marriage. One is when you are angry with your husband. The other is when he is angry with you. Always keep these two situations separate and don't confuse them. *When you are angry with your husband,* respond as suggested in the last chapter. *When he is angry with you,* respond in a different way:

### The Gentle Way

Women have thought of all sorts of things to say when a man is angry or cross. In *Mary Poppins*, when George Banks was cross, his wife said gently to him, *"The trouble with you, George, is that you are out of sorts."* An early Christian hymn suggests, *"You can speak a gentle word, to the heart with anger stirred."* The gentle response tends to soften anger, and is feminine and angelic.

### The Childlike Way

Another way to respond when a man is angry, cross, or stern is with childlikeness. Basically the method is this: 1) Exaggerate by words or manner. 2) Distract his attention. 3) Change the subject. 4) Be submissive, in a childlike way. 5) Be teasingly playful. For example:

1. *My Prince:* One of my nephews is inclined to be stern and sometimes cross. His little girl has learned to tame him and have everything going her way. For example, when he is overly stern or cross with her, she puts her hands on his cheeks, looks into his face and says, *"My prince, my handsome*

*prince.''* This adorable childlike response disarms him. He absolutely melts.

2. *Flowers:* When my uncle is cross with his wife she changes the subject by saying, *"Have you seen the flowers on the church grounds lately?"* She always says the same thing, which makes it so ridiculous it amuses him and he forgets why he was cross.

3. *Babbie:* One of the best examples of a childlike response to a man's anger is in *The Little Minister* by Sir James Barrie: This is a very long quote, but it is so full of childlikeness, it is a method of teaching it:

### Babbie

Babbie had tricked the little minister into helping her escape through a line of solders by pretending to be his wife: Gavin was furious. *"It was beautiful,"* she exclaimed, clapping her hands merrily. *"It was iniquitous,"* he answered, *"and I, a minister."* After listening to his scolding, *Babbie's* face changed and she became as a child. *"I am very sorry,"* she said, as if he had caught her stealing jam. The hood had fallen back, and she looked pleadingly at him. She had the appearance of one who was entirely in his hands. . . .

*"I do not understand you,"* Gavin said weakly. *"Only a few hours ago you were a gypsy girl in a fantastic dress . . . Now you fling a cloak over your shoulders and become a fine lady. Who are you?"* Babbie answered mischievously, *"Perhaps it is the cloak that has bewitched me."* She slipped out of it. *"Ay,"* she said, as if surprised, *"it was just the cloak that did it, for now I'm a poor ignorant little lassie again. My goodness, but clothes do make a difference to a woman."* This was sheer levity, so the dignified minister walked away, but he was charmed.

Gavin looked with horror on Babbie's wild gypsy ways. When he met her at the old mill to receive the money for Nanny, he intended to reprimand her. Before she arrived he was practicing aloud what he intended to say to her: *"How dared you bewitch me? In your presence I flung away the precious hours of the Sabbath; I even forgot the Sabbath . . . I am an unworthy preacher of the Word . . . Nevertheless . . . I call upon you, before we part, never to meet again, to repent*

*of your— . . .''* and then he heard Babbie singing from a fir
tree.

*"Where are you?"* Gavin cried in bewilderment. *"I am
watching you from my window so high,"* answered the Egyptian; and then the minister, looking up, saw her peering at
him from a fir. *"How did you get up there?"* he asked in
amazement. *"On my broomstick,"* Babbie replied and sang
on. *"What are you doing up there?"* Gavin said, wrathfully.
*"This is my home,"* she answered. *"I told you I lived in a
tree."* *"Come down at once,"* ordered Gavin, to which the
singer responded by continuing her Scottish ballad.

The next instant a snowball hit his hat. *"That is for being
so cross,"* she explained . . . *"Why are you so nasty today,
and oh, do you know you were speaking to yourself?"* *"You
are mistaken,"* said Gavin, severely. *"I was speaking to you,
or rather I was saying to myself what—"* *"What you decided
to say to me?"* said the delighted gypsy.

*"Do you prepare your talk like sermons? I hope you have
prepared something nice for me. If it is very nice, I may give
you this bunch of holly."* *"I don't know that you will think it
nice,"* the minister answered slowly, *"but my duty—"* *"If it
is about duty,"* entreated Babbie, *"don't say it. Don't, and I
will give you the berries."* She took the berries from her dress,
smiling triumphantly the while like one who had discovered a
cure for duty; and instead of pointing the finger of wrath at
her, Gavin stood expectant.

*"But no,"* he said, remembering who he was and pushing
the gift aside, *"I will not be bribed. I must tell you—"* *"Now,"*
said the Egyptian sadly, *"I see you are angry with me. Is it
because I said I lived in a tree? Do forgive me for that dreadful
lie."* She had gone down on her knees before he could stop
her, and was gazing imploringly at him, with her hands
clasped. *"You are mocking me again,"* said Gavin, *"but I
am not angry with you. Only you must understand—"*

*"She jumped up and put her fingers to her ears. *"You
see I can hear nothing,"* she said. *"Listen while I tell you—"*
Gavin continued. *"I don't hear a word. Why do you scold me
when I have kept my promise? If I dared to take my fingers
from my ears I would give you the money for Nanny. And,
Mr. Dishart, I must be gone in five minutes."*

*"In five minutes,"* echoed Gavin, with such a dismal face

*that Babbie heard the words with her eyes and dropped her
hands. "Why are you in such haste?" he asked, taking the
five pounds mechanically, and forgetting all that he had meant
to say. "Because they require me at home," she answered,
with a sly look at her fir.*

*"Would you like to hear all about me?" she asked. "Do
you really think me a gypsy?" Then, in the middle of the
conversation she had him stand back to back to see which was
the taller. "Let us measure," she said sweetly, putting her
back to his. "You are not stretching your neck, are you?"
This was not the best thing to say to Gavin, for he was sensitive
about his height, but it was childlike. When she could see he
was offended, she was ashamed of herself and quickly changed
the subject.*

*Then, just as she was to go she said, "I know why you
are looking so troubled. You think I am to ask you the color
of my eyes and you have forgotten again." He would have
answered but she checked him. "Make no pretence," she said
severely; "I know you think they are blue." She came close
to him until her face almost touched his. "Look hard at them,"
she said solemnly, "and after this you may remember that they
are black, black, black." At each repetition of the word she
shook her head in his face. She was adorable. He was enchanted. He would have put his arms around her but she ran
away."*

Note that Babbie did not respond to Gavin's anger by
acting hurt or sullen, or by trying to correct him, or fight back.
Instead she playfully distracted his attention away from his
anger. She sang the Scottish ballad, told him she lived in a
tree, offered to give him the holly berries, and asked him the
color of her eyes. Or, on bended knees with hands clasped,
she put herself at his mercy and asked forgiveness. She put
her fingers in her ears so she couldn't hear him. All of these
things were childlike.

And Gavin, who was watched by his congregation from
the time he arose in the morning until he went to bed at night,
and who did all he could to resist his feelings for her, found
her so enchanting, so essential to his happiness, that he risked
his ministry for her, a ministry he had sacrificed many years
to obtain. Babbie was not perfect. She made a few mistakes.
But she was a superb example of character and childlikeness.

# 26

## *More Childlike Ways*

### *How to Ask for Things*

Are there things you've wanted for a long time but still don't have? Think for a moment. It may be something as simple as an extra shelf in the pantry, new dishes, or a silk dress. You may want to visit a friend in a distant state, take violin lessons, or join a talent club. I'm not referring to selfish whims, but things you deserve and he can afford, perhaps with a little personal sacrifice on his part. You may have tried asking for these things but he doesn't take you seriously. Or, he says he'll do it and then never gets around to it, or makes excuses. Or, he turns you down flat. If so, you are probably asking in the wrong way. The following are the usual ways of asking, the ways that usually fail:

### *The Usual Way of Asking*

1. *Hints:* When you hint for something you want, does your husband respond? Or, does he usually ignore it or forget it? If he does, do you tend to interpret it as lack of love? You may even say to yourself, *"If he really cared about me he would remember to do these things for me."* Is his neglect due to lack of love? Not usually. More often it is because he is too preoccupied with his own problems. Or, he may count your hints as womanly whims. Whatever the reason for his neglect, this method usually fails.

2. *Suggestions:* You might say, *"Why don't we go to the lake this summer, or wouldn't it be nice to build a bookcase in the family room."* Such suggestions are fine if you are not

334

sure what you want and are seeking his opinion. If you know what you want this method doesn't do anything to encourage a positive answer, unless he is already in the frame of mind for it. This approach is more likely to invite an opposing view.

3. *Convince Him:* You may think of all the reasons you are justified in asking for something. Then you take the matter to your husband and try to convince him, backing it up with your reasons. This method sometimes works, but it more often invites opposition. He may think of reasons you are *not justified* in having it. In addition, you appear as a *decision-making equal*, prompting him to say "no," *just to show his authority*. He may be in favor of granting your request but says *no* automatically, not realizing he took a negative stand to preserve his position as the leader.

4. *Demand:* You become so frustrated trying to get what you want and deserve you resort to demanding it. When your husbands feels pressure from you he may give in, but not with good feeling. Or he may flatly refuse. This may lead to an argument in which, if he wins, you are the one with bad feelings. This creates contention. Demanding your rights will not make him *want to do* things for you.

If you've had a difficult time getting what you want or need you may give up entirely. You may rather go without than face the ordeal of trying to get him to do things for you. The problem is, if you give up asking and go without things which mean so much, you tend to form resentments toward him. It strikes you as unfair for him to ignore simple requests when you have done a great deal for him.

Don't give up. Important to any man-woman relationship is filling each other's needs and desires. If he is to love you he must do things for you. Instead of giving up learn to ask in the right way so he will want to do things for you. Here is the method suggested:

## The Childlike Way to Ask

Again, we copy this art from little children. How do they get what they want? They just *ask for it,* in a trusting manner. They don't justify, explain, or try to convince you. When a little girl wants something, she approaches her parents trustingly, respecting their right to say yes or no. She will say,

*"May I please?"* or *"Will you please?"* or, *"It would mean so much to me."* All kindhearted parents are inclined to say *yes* to such a childlike request.

When you ask him for something in a trusting, childlike way you show respect for his leadership. When he senses your respect for his position, your dependency on him for all you have, he is prompted to do his utmost to fill your request. He may even jump at the chance to do things for you. *Men have often broken their necks to cater to the whims of femininity.* I am not suggesting you ask for whims, but I advise you to ask for things you need, want, and deserve, things which are important to your well-being. Your husband will love you more and you will feel more kindly toward him for heeding your requests.

## What Not to Ask For

There are a few things you should not ask for. Don't ask for things which are selfish or which he can't afford. Don't ask for something which would require he neglect an important duty. Don't ask for things which would be against his judgment or principles. Don't ask for anything which would place a heavy burden on him, or a worry. As a rule, don't ask for love, tenderness, or affection. They are of value only when given voluntarily. They should be *awakened*. There may be men who respond to this but most men don't like this much aggression in a woman.

## When Not to Ask

Don't ask for things when you have not been doing your part as a wife. If you have been neglectful of your homemaking, his meals, your appearance, or your sex life, it's best to not ask him for anything special until you make improvements.

## The Self-Sacrificing Wife

Do you go without things you need because you think it's noble to sacrifice? For years you may have wanted something but every time the thought crosses your mind you subdue the impulse to ask so there'll be more money for your husband and children. It sounds noble, but unfortunately it isn't good for a marriage.

During an emergency he appreciates your willingness to set aside personal needs to solve problems, but when there's no urgent reason he won't appreciate your sacrifice. You are his queen, deserving of the best he can offer. He doesn't want you to place his comforts and those of the children ahead of your important needs.

Another point is this: When you are overly self-sacrificing you rob your husband of the opportunity to serve you, and therefore to love you more. We love those we serve. You owe it to your husband and your marriage relationship to see that he does things for you. But *you must ask*. A man is not a mind reader.

### Expecting Things

This is another method of asking, and although it is not childlike, it is effective for some purposes. An illustration is in the life of Abraham Lincoln. Abraham's parents, Tom and Nancy Lincoln, and their children lived for years in a little log cabin with a dirt floor. Tom was negligent and rather lazy, so he never got around to building a wooden floor, and Nancy didn't know how to get him to do it.

Then Nancy died and Tom married Sarah. She was a very fine person, but different from Nancy. When Tom brought her home to the log cabin she brought with her several wagonloads of fine furniture and home furnishings. She took one look at the dirt floor and said, *"Oh, my goodness, Tom, I couldn't think of bringing all of my nice things in here on this dirt floor. I will just leave them in the wagons and you can build me a wooden floor tomorrow."*

Tom Lincoln did build her a wooden floor the very next day. Wasn't it sad to think poor Nancy lived all those years on a dirt floor because she didn't know how to motivate a man to action? Notice Sarah was pleasant, but *definite,* and placed *a time limit* on the task. With the furniture sitting outside, her request was urgent. When you have a similar situation of urgency, your husband may respond to this method.

## Childlike Joy

In studying the joy of little children, note it takes very little to make them happy. They delight in catching a ray of sunshine, splashing in a tub of water, walking in the rain, stepping in mud puddles, picking up rocks, patting a puppy dog, or eating an ice cream cone.

A woman who can get excited over the common joys of life is bewitching to a man. A few rare women genuinely feel the joy of a summer day, a sunset, the first flowers of spring, or a full moon. They delight in going down to the bay to watch the ships come in as the ocean waves break against the pier and they feel the sea air.

Referring again to the joy of little children, when they are rewarded a pleasant surprise or promised a forthcoming good time, what happens? Their eyes sparkle with excitement or they clap their hands and jump up and down. They tend to exaggerate by saying, *"This is the prettiest or the best in the whole world."* As parents, when we see this pleasant response we are prompted to repeat our favors.

When a man buys a woman a gift or does something special for her he appreciates a joyful response. Women who get excited over every little thing a man does for them are usually pampered and spoiled. On the other hand, women who respond with a bland *thank you,* or *oh, how nice,* or *how thoughtful of you,* do nothing to encourage a man's generosity. Even worse, some women receive favors from a man as though he *owed it to them*.

Childlike joy is not appropriate for every occasion. When a man gives a woman something of unusual value or does something for her which required considerable sacrifice, even childlike joy may not be sufficient. A deeply expressed appreciation, warm affection, or even tears of joy may be more significant.

## Problems in Gift Giving

1. *Negligence:* If your husband ignores or forgets your birthday and this troubles you, do the following: First, ask yourself if you are to blame. When he gave you something in the past, did you fail to show appreciation? Did you make a

negative remark or take it back? If so, this explains his lack of interest in giving you anything.

If you are not to blame, try to be understanding. Men are known to be negligent about gift giving. They never quite know what a woman wants and tend to dislike the compulsion of giving. Some men prefer to buy something when they feel like it rather than when tradition dictates. Don't therefore, be too concerned about this negligence, or interpret it as a lack of love.

If you can't overlook his negligence, next time your birthday comes around make gift giving easier for him. You might say, *"There is something I have really been wanting."* Make certain it is something easy to find and he can afford. Or say, *"I know you never quite know what to get me for my birthday. Would you like me to go with you to pick it out?"*

If this makes you feel better, do it. The problem is, it takes the joy out of giving and receiving. When it's your idea it tends to lose its value. It's better to live the whole of F.W. and thus prompt him to give spontaneously.

2. *When You Don't Like the Gift:* Never make the mistake of showing disappointment or criticizing the gift. On the other hand, don't be insincere and act as though you like a gift when you don't. Appreciate, not the gift, but the *giver*, or *the act of giving*. Show appreciation for his thoughtfulness. The gift is of little consequence compared to the generosity of the giver.

If it's the wrong color, try it on and ask him how you look in it. If it passes his judgment, keep it and wear it. If it's the wrong size it's OK to exchange it. Otherwise don't make the mistake of returning it, exchanging it, or putting it away and not using it. Whatever the gift, use it at least for awhile.

3. *When He Can't Afford It:* If your husband has a habit of buying you things he can't afford, don't make an unkind remark about how he should have known better. Instead, give him suggestions of inexpensive things you appreciate. Tell him you appreciate expensive gifts but appreciate other things as much.

## Childlike Trust

Childlike trust is a confidence such as children have in their parents, that their parents have their best interests at heart and will always take care of them. You show this same trust for a man when you trust in his ability to take care of you, to safely lead you, guide you, protect you, and provide for you, and that he has the capabilities of doing so. You show lack of trust when you doubt his ability to take care of you.

You should not, for example, tell him what to do or how to do it. Nothing so irritates a man as when his wife gives him directions or instructions in something he is supposed to know more about than she does. I remember being in the company of a man and his wife who were showing us the city in which they lived. She was at his elbow telling him every turn to make. When a man is driving, never make the mistake of telling him where to turn, unless he asks. It's better to let him make a mistake and have to backtrack, than to doubt his common judgment. This is especially irritating in something as simple as finding his way around in life.

You show lack of trust when you doubt his ability to solve his problems such as finding his way out of financial difficulty or reaching a challenging goal. Don't give him too many suggestions about how to succeed. It's better to turn your back on the problem, with a childlike trust that one way or another he will be victorious. However, don't give him the impression you think it will be easy, but do help him feel he has the power to win.

When you trust him, don't expect perfection. Not everything he does will turn out well. You trust, not so much the outcome of events, as *the intent of his heart*. Try to believe he means well, acts on his best judgment, and intends to take care of you. He is likely doing a better job than you could.

You may wonder, how can you trust a man who has made foolish mistakes? This may seem difficult but remember, we all make mistakes and learn by them. Mistakes of the past sharpen judgment for the future. But even a man who has learned good judgment is not free of mistakes. It's a continual part of life for all of us. But, move ahead with a childlike trust, willing to risk time, comforts, and security to achieve worthy goals. This is how the greatest objectives in life have been reached.

What will trust do? When you put your trust in a man, you impel him to measure up to your expectations of him.

There is nothing which so inspires a man to action as when someone puts their trust in him.

## Outspokenness

Another way of being childlike is to be outspoken. This is not to imply you have an *unbridled tongue*, or speak too frankly, with little concern for the feelings of others, a common fault with adults. But, be direct in conversation, not evasive. Don't beat around the bush, make excuses, or fail to come to the point.

A little girl who has been reared by kind and loving parents of whom she is not afraid, tends to be honest and outspoken. For example, if you ask a little girl if she would like to visit a lady down the street and the child doesn't want to go, she doesn't hunt for excuses or ask to put it off until another time. She simply says, *"I don't want to."* This is childlike.

Or if you ask her why she didn't pick up her toys as she was told, instead of making a tedious explanation she simply says, *"I forgot."* This is childlike. However, when a child is a little afraid of his parents, he tends to lie, or put the blame on someone else. But a child who is unafraid tends to be outspoken. This is the response a man appreciates in a woman.

If you are shopping with your husband for such things as furniture, clothes, or even a house, and he suggests you buy something you don't like, it isn't necessary to go into a long explanation to justify your objections. Be honest and outspoken and say, *"Honey, I just don't think I want this one."* This comment not only settles matters but is appreciated and less likely to insult his tastes than an elaboration of your objections. Of course, it's important to please your husband, especially in home decor, but not at your expense. It is important to please both of you.

I knew a lady who had this charm of outspokenness. On the occasion I remember, her husband and several other men had just announced plans to sail down the Colorado River on a raft. The lady, thinking the trip extravagant, especially since she had been going without things she needed, said in a child-like voice, *"But what about me! I need some new cotton dresses and some high-heeled shoes."*

Her husband looked up in surprised wonder and amusement. How much better this was than if she had complained, accused him of selfishness, or even worse, said nothing and held a grudge. But please note: In some instances you should encourage your husband's plans, with eagerness and excitement. This would depend on your situation. In this case the trip was beyond their means, and her outspoken words brought him back to reality and kept him from making a mistake.

## Changefulness

You are more interesting when you are changeful—not the same all the time. Charles Reade states in *The Cloister and the Hearth*: "*Girls love to be coy and tender, gentle and saucy by turns.*" This adds variety to your personality, and makes you more mysterious and therefore more interesting, especially to a man. If you are unpredictable so he can't count on your mood or reaction in a situation, you are more fascinating.

Deruchette was changeful—sweet, good, childlike, birdlike, innocent, vivacious, graceful, giddy, with a dash of melancholy, the teasing playfulness of a child, an air of bewitching languor, and certain mischief in the eye.

Little children are changeful in *emotions*. Notice that, when hurt or disappointed, they run to their mothers with tears streaming down their cute little faces. When comforted with a kiss or pleasant surprise they instantly burst into a smile, with tears still wet on their cheeks. Little children hold no grudges, which is one reason their emotions are free to fluctuate.

Also observe children when they listen to bedtime stories. Their emotions fluctuate with every turn of events. When the story shows uncertainty they display anxiety. When things take a turn for the worse, their anxiety increases. When great danger appears they work themselves into quite a state of emotion. When things work out better, they express delight.

## Youthful Manner

Women with a youthful manner have a zest for living, a spring in their step, a lightheartedness of spirit, an alert interest in life, and enthusiasm for the future. This is the spirit of youth.

It can, however, be retained into old age. I recently had a conversation with a lady who said, *"You know, I am seventy-four years old but I still feel young and kind of cute."* This youthfulness of manner is part of being fascinating, and makes you forever attractive.

To be youthful in manner, eliminate any tendency to matronliness, especially in your walk. Older women tend to slant forward, drop their chin, round their shoulders, walk with legs apart and wobble the upper part of their body. This is the walk of age. To appear youthful do the opposite. Also avoid a forlorn look in the face which stems from a foreboding about the future or being bored with life, as these are symptoms of age.

### Youthful Appearance

To achieve a youthful appearance, *avoid matronly styles,* or styles, worn by older women. Also avoid styles which are *out-of-date*—dresses, hairstyles, shoes, and makeup that were in vogue ten or more years ago. There's a tendency for women to hang on to styles that were popular when they were young. To look youthful, avoid doing this.

To avoid a matronly appearance, refuse to let yourself get overweight, even ten pounds over. There's nothing which will more quickly destroy the appearance of youth as a chunky figure. It's almost impossible to appear youthful in either manner or appearance if you are overweight.

To accentuate youthfulness in dress, visit young girls' shops. You may not end up buying your clothes there but you'll get the picture of what's in fashion. There's a tendency for young women to go for *mod,* or *fad* styles. Avoid these completely, lest you look ridiculous. But young women do keep up with the latest style. In fact, being style-conscious is typical of youth. Let their styles influence you, just a little.

If you want to create some youthful styles of your own, especially housedresses, visit a little girls' shop. There you will see buttons and bows, checks, plaids, pleats, stripes, jumpers, daisies, and even satin, lace, and velvet. All of their clothes are pretty.

Also be conscious of hairstyles. Avoid styles you wore ten years ago which are now out-of-date. You need not go to extremes but do lean toward current or youthful hairstyles.

Little girls wear ribbons, bows, barrettes, and flowers in their hair. They wear cute little hats.

If you think it ridiculous for a grown woman to wear youthful styles, wear them in your own home and let your husband be the judge. He may not want you to wear them in public, but will probably like them at home or for informal occasions.

## I Wore a Childlike Hat

I received a letter from a lady who had not paid much attention to childlikeness until she had the following experience:

*"This is a little thing but my husband was recalling a hat I wore eight years ago when I went fishing with him. He said it was like a hat I had on when I was a very little girl. I had no idea he noticed either one. Through F.W. I can understand that he liked it because it was girlish."*

## Childishness

*Childlikeness* should not be confused with *childishness*, which is a negative quality. To be childish is to copy the faults of children, whereas to be childlike is to copy their virtues. Childish traits in children are self-centeredness, lack of responsibility for their actions, and expecting too much of others. Those who retain childish traits in adult life fret when they don't get their way, blame others for their unfortunate circumstances, fail to acknowledge their mistakes and failures, and make unreasonable demands of their associates.

When we were young we expected much from our parents and thought they could do almost anything. To project this unrealistic thought into adult life is to expect too much from our associates and is therefore childish. Childishness in a grown woman is very *unattractive*.

## Conclusions

There are a few women who resist the idea of acting childlike, who consider it an insult to their good sense for anyone to expect them to act the part of a little girl. They insist on believing that really sensible men, the kind they admire, would be repulsed instead of attracted to such a childlike creature. The only way to prove to yourself if childlikeness is charming to men is to try it in your own life to test your husband's reaction.

Even when women agree a childlike woman is the most attractive, many mistakenly assume that for themselves the acting of such a part is impossible. Be assured that every woman can become childlike, for we all have this trait in our nature. It's part of being a woman. Remember, it was not long ago you were a little girl, when these traits were natural to you. You can recapture this manner and charm and make it part of your personality.

When a woman matures there's a marked tendency for her to lose this childlike trait, especially when she gets married. She somehow feels that now she must grow up, without realizing that men never want women to grow up completely. Truly fascinating women always remain somewhat little girls, regardless of age.

### Childlike Ways:

1. Childlike Anger (When you are angry)
2. Childlike Response (When he is angry or cross)
3. Asking for Things
4. Childlike Joy
5. Childlike Trust
6. Outspokenness
7. Changefulness
8. Youthful Manner
9. Youthful Appearance

### Assignment:

1. Think of something you really want, and ask your husband for it in a childlike way.
2. Make a youthful housedress.

# Fascinating Womanhood *Applied to Sex*

The most important thing to do to attain an enjoyable sex life is to build the marriage relationship. As you apply the principles of *Fascinating Womanhood,* most sex problems are resolved and sex life improves along with the marriage relationship.

Information here is for the following purpose: First, to establish the morality of sex, according to the moral requirements of God. Second, to suggest how to apply the principles of *Fascinating Womanhood* to attain an enjoyable sex life. Third, to review common sex problems and how to resolve them.

### The Morality of Sex

As a first principle, *sex is reserved for those who are married*. This is well established in God's laws, in both the Old and New Testaments. Violation brings painful consequences, whether you understand the law or not. To be assured of a happy marriage and a successful life ahead, adhere to this principle: *Never have sexual relations with anyone other than your legally wed husband*.

Instill this principle in the minds and hearts of your children. Teach them to be chaste, that they may come to the alter of marriage clean before God. Uphold virginity as the most precious of virtues. Help them understand that violation brings serious consequences, whereas strict adherence brings inner strength and blessings.

As a second principle, keep your sexual life with your husband pure. A marriage license is not a license to do wrong.

Don't engage in a sexual practice which is impure. The Holy Spirit will prompt you. Listen to the still small voice within which tells you right from wrong.

Don't expose your mind to anything which encourages impure sex thoughts, such as sexy stage performances, movies, TV, magazines, or any type of pornographic material. Don't listen to rock music or any music which encourages unwholesome feelings. Give your children these same instructions. Don't allow your husband or anyone else to bring unwholesome material into your home. If they do, burn it. You have as much right to do this as to rid your house of an infestation of cockroaches.

## How to Achieve an Enjoyable Sex Life

What is an enjoyable sex life? In simple terms, it is when both husband and wife enjoy sexual experience to the utmost, and with a frequency desirable for both. To achieve this, keep this fact in mind: Women are inclined to be less highly sexed than men. Therefore, achieving a good sex life may mean doing some things to turn yourself on.

## Frequency of Sex

How many times a week should you have sexual relations? Statistics indicate that most couples have sex from one to five times per week. However, it is not uncommon to be happy on either side of these averages. The concern here, however, is not the frequency per se, but arriving at a frequency which is desirable for both.

You need not feel you owe it to your husband to give sex whenever he expects it, and never refuse. I doubt if there is any merit in this. There may even be harm. Women who do, I have noticed, are not the ones who are idolized by their husbands. They are more often taken for granted, neglected, and sometimes even treated with contempt. In fact, they are about the most poorly treated wives I have known.

No man appreciates sex which can be had so readily. It is simply too cheap. Although you owe your husband a generous amount of sex, he doesn't own your body. To give him sex every time he asks is to spoil him, just as you spoil a child if you give him cookies every time he asks. Children respect us more if we don't give them every little thing their hearts desire. Husbands do the same. When we feel it is right, we give to our children willingly. When it is not for their good or our own, we withhold. We can apply this same principle to a man's sex needs.

Don't give your husband sex if he has seriously mistreated you. This is not to suggest you withhold sex as a punishment, but because of an inborn womanly dignity that shrinks from a man's advances when he has trampled on her. Regard your intimate life as too precious to surrender when you have been shown disrespect. To yield is to cheapen sex, whereas to withhold places a higher value on it.

Never give your husband sex if he tries to insist. When a woman gives in to her husband's demands against her own feelings it can make her feel resentful. His sex drives appear more important to him than her feelings. This removes love and consideration from sex so that sex become repulsive. Her husband appears to gratify his passions at her expense. This causes her to regard sex as a degrading experience.

Her husband also experiences bad feelings. He feels ashamed for his loss of control and lack of consideration for her feelings. He may hold her responsible for yielding. Her refusal would have preserved his self-respect, which is more important to a man than a release of his passions. Even worse is the disrespect he feels for her. Although it seems unfair, a man doesn't respect a woman he takes unfair advantage of. An illustration is the account of Amnon and Tamar in 2 Samuel, 13.

### How to Say No

In saying *no* to your husband, the most important thing to remember is his sensitive masculine pride. Dr. David R. Mace, former director of the American Association of Marriage Counselors, once said, "To make a sexual advance and be refused is deeply humiliating to a husband. Of course, there are times when a woman may say no, but it needs to be done with great tact, or the man's pride can be sorely wounded."

In the first place, you should never actually say no. It is

softer to say, some other time, or later, or indicate by your actions that you are not interested at the moment. Never make him feel ashamed for asking or imply he is like a beast with uncontrollable passions. Never make statements such as, "I've about had it up to here with sex," or "Don't you ever think of anything but sex," or "Why don't you get interested in something else."

In refusing your husband sex, be understanding of his feelings. You are attractive to him. He is easily aroused by your body. But, be firm in saying no. Don't keep him dangling. Don't allow him to remain in an unsettled state of mind, wondering if you will respond or not. Take the initiative to settle matters. Make up your mind quickly and stick to your decision with firmness.

If he interrupts you in the middle of the day, you may want to stop what you're doing and show consideration for his feeling, but this is not your obligation. If you feel imposed on, don't do it. Tell him it's not on the agenda at the moment.

## Turn Yourself On

To receive the utmost from sex, do some things to turn yourself on. This is important, not only for your own enjoyment but your husband's as well. His enjoyment of sex lies not only in your participation but in your full enjoyment. A man's self-esteem is deeply rooted in his ability to awaken his wife and bring her satisfaction. If he fails to do so he can feel inadequate as a man. Turn yourself on by doing the following:

1. *Eliminate Resentments:* A resentful attitude toward your husband can injure your sexual feelings for him, or even cause them to disappear. In Dr. Marie Robinson's book, *The Power of Sexual Surrender,* she deals with the problem of resentments and sexual arousal, making it clear that resentments must be removed if sexual desire is to be increased. Following are two methods of removing resentments:

First, apply the principles of *Fascinating Womanhood*. Accept your husband at face value, allow for his human weaknesses, be forgiving, and appreciate his better side. Be understanding of his world of worry and concern. Allow for his bad behavior or his negligence. When he is thoughtless or unfair, respond with childlikeness. If you don't respond with childlikeness, realize that you could have done. Even this reduces a resentful attitude.

After you have taken these measures to reduce your resentments toward him, if you still feel deep wounds which affect your attitude, your husband may need to take a good look at himself. At this point, it may not be within your power to remake your feelings towards him. Your husband may have to do something about it. If he has emotionally abused you, or been seriously unjust, he cannot expect you to respond to him sexually until he heals the wounds he inflicted. It is difficult for a woman to respond to a man sexually unless she feels kindly towards him and knows he truly loves her.

In *Education for Marriage,* by James A. Peterson, this thought is supported. *"The need for psychological security is of extraordinary importance to a woman. If she cannot feel that her husband truly loves her and would stand by her in any circumstance, she finds it difficult to give herself sexually to him. Where all of these conditions are met, the atmosphere is conducive to good sexual development."*

If your husband has seriously trampled on you so that your sexual response has been injured, speak to him honestly. Tell him that his actions have injured your sexual feelings for him, beyond your control. This may be a painful realization for him but if he can be made to see his mistakes and admit them, and you can forgive him fully, some adverse conditions can be swept clean.

2. *A Wholesome Attitude Toward Sex:* In the past many women held to an old Victorian attitude about sex. They acknowledged that men enjoyed sex but regarded it for themselves as an act of duty. Some Victorian women considered sex carnal and even dirty. A resulting pregnancy was a hush-hush subject, in an effort to conceal the sensual act in which conception took place. Women made their baby clothes in secret and retired from public view when their pregnancy became evident. In general, women looked upon sex with shame and embarrassment.

Today the Victorian attitude has been cast out and stress is now on the naturalness, wholesomeness, and enjoyment of sex for both partners. Great strides have been made. However, new unwholesome attitudes are being formed:

Many children in good families are growing up with a perverted attitude about sex. Parents, in an effort to withstand rampant immorality, teach their children to keep themselves clean. This gives children the impression that sex must be unclean. There is not a clear differentiation between the wrongness of sex before marriage and the rightness of it after marriage. Without intention, the thought is placed in their minds that there is something evil about sex. Sex is linked with dirty words written in public rest rooms, trashy books, magazines, and X-rated movies.

After marriage children find it difficult to change attitudes and regard sex as wholesome. The solution lies in more specific education in the home, to stress the immorality of sex before marriage and the purity of sex after marriage. Too often we assume children know these things.

Essential to a woman's sexual arousal is a proper attitude towards sex. Unless she regards sex as a natural, wholesome, and an enjoyable experience for both her husband and herself, her desire will he limited. A good attitude can be created, in most cases, by proper instruction. If this does not remake a wrong attitude there may be deeply rooted problems that need psychiatric attention.

3. *Don't Be Too Busy or Preoccupied With Other Things:* If you are sexually under par, take a good look at your life. Are you under stress and strain with demands made of your time? Do you work with time limits, appointments, or having to get work done by a specific time? If so, trim life down and focus on the important things. Certainly sex life is one of them, particularly from a man's point of view. Give sex life the priority it deserves. This will increase your sexual desires.

4. *Awaken the Senses:* Sexual feeling is derived from the senses. Therefore, sexual feelings can be awakened by stimulating the senses. The most fundamental way to awaken the senses is to promote good health. Nourishing the body with healthful food, exercise, fresh air, and sound sleep helps to preserve and increase the sense of feeling. Destructive to the senses are tea, coffee, tobacco, alcohol, drugs, and bad food.

The beauties of nature also awaken the senses—grassy meadows, hills, trees, flowers, beautiful skies, rivers, lakes, and streams. There is something about nature's waters that awakens romantic, sensual feelings. A woman can turn on by watching a waterfall or the churning of the ocean. Fragrances of nature are also awakening—fresh cut grass, flowers, and fresh rain. Strange as it may seem, tasty food can awaken the senses. A night out at a good restaurant has its benefits. Food with a sharp taste such as pickles, cheese, sharp salad dressings, or foods with a zing can help in its own way. It may not do everything, but it does its part.

5. *Husband's Affection:* Still another means of awakening sexual desire is the husband's tender affection. When he speaks kindly, expresses his love and devotion, gently touches her hair, neck, and arms, she is more responsive. You can awaken this tender affection in your husband by living the principles of *Fascinating Womanhood*.

6. *Herbs:* Certain herbs are known to arouse the sex passions. Common vegetables suggested are celery, lettuce, and onions. Herbs recommended are Asiatic ginseng, carline thistle, English walnut, fenugreek, jasmine, lovage, saffron, savory, saw palmetto, and water eryngo. Use herbs with extreme care, following directions carefully. My own experience in the use of these herbs is limited, but they could be something to investigate.

### The Sex Act

We have now covered the means of sexually turning on so you want sex and look forward to it. Let him know you want it. As already stated, this is important because his enjoyment of sex lies not only in your participation, but in your full enjoyment of it. Be a warm, responsive sex partner. When you are, you invite the flowers rather than the weeds.

The techniques of sex have not been covered here. This is because when a man and woman have a wholesome attitude about sex, when they truly love each other, and are sexually awakened, they don't need instructions about how to have sex with each other. It comes about naturally.

### The Oversexed Man

A common problem in men is overactive sex glands. The problem I refer to here is the man who is so highly sexed that his wife, willing though she may be, cannot keep up with him. For solutions, consider the following:

1. *Allow for His Erotic Nature:* First realize that men are more quickly aroused than women. A sexy picture or story can quickly arouse a man's passions. This problem is exaggerated in today's world where men are exposed to sexual stimulation at every turn. They can't pass a row of magazines without viewing sexually arousing pictures or suggestions. A woman can view these things with only a slight arousal, but they can erupt a man's sexual feelings.

Try to understand that men were born with strong sex drives implanted by Deity to encourage the birth of children. These drives must be strong to overcome the natural reluctance of men to assume the continuing burden of family responsibility. A man's sex drive can be quite overpowering, even to him, and he is sensitive to his control, or lack of control. But with only a few exceptions, a man is not a beast or antagonist seeking gratification at the woman's expense. Have a sympathy for his sex needs and try to turn yourself on. If his sex passions seem out of hand, take measures to calm them.

2. *Avoid Sensual Stimuli:* If you are trying to calm your husband's sex passions, don't make the problem worse by undressing in front of him, giving him a passionate kiss, talking about sex, or giving him a sexy glance. He should avoid sensuous movies, pictures, and books. Eliminate any pornographic or sensuous material in your home.

3. *Fill His Emotional Needs:* Sometimes a man turns to sex as an outlet, a relief from tension, frustration, or worry. If problems in the outside world are severe, a man may require more sex than usual. To reduce his sexual desire, fill his emotional needs: Appreciate him, admire him, and do everything you can to build his self-esteem and help him feel good about himself. This will reduce his need for sex as an outlet.

4. *Hard Work and Exercise:* One of the best things to normalize overactive sex glands is hard work and vigorous physical exercise. It diverts the interest away from sex, and promotes physical and mental relaxation and sound sleep. There is probably nothing better as a therapy.

5. *Medicinal Herbs:* If your husband has overactive sex glands, you may want to investigate medicinal herbs as a means of reducing his sex passions. For information seek the name

of an herbalist from your local health store, or refer to an herb book. Herbs listed to correct this condition are belladonna, black willow, coriander, mouse-ear, skullcap, star grass, and wild marjoram. Use herbs with great discretion, however, following directions carefully. Some medicinal herbs are very potent and can be dangerous to the health. Medicinal herbs are different from herbal teas. Herbal teas are not considered dangerous and can be used more freely.

## Impotency in Men

If your husband suffers a lack of sexual desire, the most important thing to do is *be understanding*. He can be sensitive about this problem because his sexuality is one of the ways he proves his masculinity to himself. Masculine pride is at stake here more than in anything he does. If he finds himself to be impotent, he can suffer great anguish, a feeling he is no longer a man. Your understanding is vital to his happiness and to eventually overcoming the problem. The causes of impotence are usually not physical, but emotional. Ranking high among the causes are the following problems:

1. *Bruised Ego:* When a man is humiliated, when his masculine pride is brutally cut down, his sexual feelings can be injured. How this takes place is interesting. In Dr. Edrita Fried's book, *The Ego in Love and Sexuality,* referred to previously, she explains why injured pride can affect sexual feelings:

*"When we are physically injured—for instance, when we are deprived of food over a long period, or when we are exposed to unbearable temperatures—we eventually become apathetic. When we are emotionally injured over and over— for instance, when we are exposed to repeated derision or contempt—eventually apathy sets in like a drug, to dull the sting of pain. The man who is humiliated on his job protects himself from the pain by hardening himself against it. He learns not to care. He stops feeling, so that it won't hurt."*

But unfortunately, and again we quote Dr. Fried, *"We pay dearly for the self-induced numbness, for while it relieves our pain, it also reduces our ability to respond to pleasant stimulation."* The man who has learned to protect himself from the pain of humiliation no longer feels the hurt, but neither does he respond to his wife's love. His sexual feelings diminish and he can even become impotent.

To help a man overcome sexual impotence, respect his masculinity. Admire his masculine body, his masculine skills, abilities, and achievements; don't wound his masculine pride; heal the wounds others inflict. By admiring his manliness, you build his self- image and awaken his sexual feelings.

2. *Drive for a Career:* If your husband is wrapped up in his career, it could diminish his sexual desire. This is especially true if he has set a high mark for himself with time limits and pressures such as in higher education, or advancement to a top position. Or he may be intensely interested in his career, or excited about it.

With his dedication to his career he is apt to neglect you or fail to give you the affection you need. When he goes to bed he may turn over and go to sleep. You may attribute this to a failure in yourself, such as a loss of appeal, when in reality it is merely his drive for a career. This problem requires your understanding and patience. You may have to accept this situation until he has finally reached the mark he has set for himself.

3. *Wife Lacks Femininity:* Remember, it is femininity to which masculinity responds. When a woman loses her feminine charm, to a great extent she loses her ability to arouse a man sexually. For example, when a woman loses her gentle, tender qualities and takes on the masculine traits of aggressiveness, boldness, drive, masculine efficiency, and independence, she can turn a man off sexually. On the other hand, when she returns to her gentle, tender, frail, and dependent nature, she can awaken his sexual feelings, affection, and love.

4. *Wife Is Too Aggressive in Sex:* On occasion, a man may like his wife to be aggressive in sex. Her advances can be reassuring to him that she likes and wants sex. This can boost his ego. But a woman can be too aggressive, to the point of turning him off. If he is already sexually under par, her advances can make bad matters worse.

For example, take a man who is driving for a career so that he has lost some of his sexual desire. His wife may be greatly concerned, thinking she may have lost her appeal. She may dress in a frilly nightie, spray herself with perfume, give him a sexy look, and squeeze his hand. Ordinarily, a man may love this advance toward sex but when he has lost the desire himself, it can strike him as too aggressive. It is simply the wrong psychology.

If you have been turning him off by your advances, apply reverse psychology. When you have a sexual desire, don't let your feelings show. Even a look in the eye can be a giveaway. Instead of dressing up in frilly nightwear, stay up late and read a book. Or, when you go to bed, wear an unsexy nightgown, turn over, and go to sleep. Act disinterested in sex and interested in other things. If he squeezes your hand or pats you on the shoulder, pretend you didn't notice it. Be busy. Don't be cold, just be interested in other things. This should straighten things out. But don't carry this too far. When he indicates a serious interest in sex, respond.

Remember, the man is the pursuer, the woman the pursued, even after marriage. Always keep this straight. The only time to vary this is when you're certain he wants you to be aggressive. Be sensitive to his reaction. He'll let you know when he likes it. Sometimes the sole cause of a man's sexual decline is an overly aggressive wife. A reverse psychology may be the only action needed to eliminate the problem.

The solutions outlined here aid men and women in solving sex problems and producing a more enjoyable sex life. Sex is not everything in marriage so we must not exaggerate its importance, but since it's an integrated part of the marriage relationship, problems should be faced honestly and solutions sought earnestly.

Contrary to popular belief, a good sex life is not the tie that binds a marriage securely together. Marriage counselors find many couples have a good sex life right up to the time of divorce. A mistress finds it difficult to feel secure in her relationship, not solely because she lacks a marriage license, but because important elements are missing in her relationship.

The tie that binds a man and woman securely together is a mating of spirit with spirit. This is built on a moral foundation by God's standards and requires commitment, trust, understanding, and unselfish devotion. The entire purpose of *Fascinating Womanhood* is to build such a relationship. When achieved, good sexual relations usually follow, as in the following testimonial:

## *We Had No Relations for Three Years*

"I am so thankful for F.W. I just read one chapter at a time and couldn't wait to apply the assignment when my husband came home. After just three nights I found myself lying in bed just thanking God over and over again. Psalm 1:1 became very real to me. I was delighting in the law of the Lord and became so aware of His grace to me.

"My marriage had been a mess. I was all of the women mentioned in F.W. I did everything wrong, trying to fight for my right to be loved. How sorry I was when F.W. showed me the truth. And how anxious I was to change it all and make it good. Almost immediately my love for my husband returned and with it a desire for him again. (We'd had no relations for three years.) How anxious I am to find and develop my femininity which I had never really had.

"I see a movement in our churches for men and women to work together and compromise to solve their marital problems. I hope to introduce F.W. to our church. How we can mess up God's law so totally is amazing. F.W. makes it so clear."

# Summary

Within these pages I have presented a way of living, one which leads to a happy marriage. To reach the goal, much is expected of you. Marriage is no longer a fifty-fifty proposition, but a willingness to give ninety percent. In giving wholeheartedly you receive rich compensation. *When you cast your bread upon the waters, it comes back buttered.*

When you live these concepts devotedly, your husband will be tender and romantic. You will be not only loved, but *cherished, honored,* and *adored.* This happy marriage will be the heart of a happy home. *Fascinating Womanhood* makes women happier, husbands happier, and children happier. One lady said, "Even my dog is happier."

You may be reluctant to yield decision-making control to your husband. You may have worked hard to gain control, or at least joint control, and fear surrender means you'll give up too much. This is an unnecessary concern. When you walk away from the masculine role, if you give up anything it is headaches, heartaches, frustration, disappointments, hard work, and discouragement. If you give up freedom, you gain more than you lose. When you are truly fascinating he will do anything in his power to make you happy.

You are in a precarious position as the wife. *You can build or destroy him.* You destroy him by needling him to change, stealing his leadership, wounding his pride, and ignoring his important needs. You build him by appreciating him, admiring him, understanding him, healing his wounds, and helping him function as the guide, protector, and provider.

The most basic principle taught in *Fascinating Womanhood* is this: If you want to awaken a man's love and tenderness, you must 1) *Be a person worthy of that love*, a woman of both angelic and human qualities. 2) *Make him feel like a man*. To do this, admire his manly qualities, make him feel adequate and needed in his role as a man, fill your role as a woman, be feminine and childlike—traits which make him feel manly in contrast.

Don't become discouraged if you occasionally backslide. This is normal. It usually takes about a year to form new habits. Keep going and you'll create a new way of living and find you're in a new world. Once you have a glimpse into the new world of *Fascinating Womanhood* you'll never be content with the old one. You may stand astride for awhile between the two worlds, unable to reach the higher goals but discontent with the unhappy days of the past. But, eventually you'll advance to the *banquet of life,* never again to *eat the crumbs.*

Once your husband has experienced you as a fascinating woman, he'll not be content with *the old you* again. Having tasted the sweet, he'll dislike the bitter more than ever. Determine in the beginning that once you start on the road to *Fascinating Womanhood,* there's *no turning back.*

The greatest help you'll find in living this idealistic way of life is to *turn to God for strength.* Let me explain it in this way: Your greatest enemy to success is the weakness of human nature, or the tendency of human beings to give way to the weaknesses of the flesh. You may have every intention and desire to live these teachings, but human nature enters in by way of selfishness, laziness, lack of self-discipline, criticism, and pride, to deter you from your goals. Some women all but despair over their own weakness to live these teachings.

When you turn to God and are *born of the spirit,* you'll find a new strength to sustain you in daily living. You'll overcome the weaknesses of human nature much better. If you are not affiliated with a religion which inspires a faith in God and love of fellowmen, let this be your first step in living the teachings of *Fascinating Womanhood.* If you put your trust in God and ask for His strength, success is assured.

Another thought is this: People everywhere suffer from a poor opinion of themselves, more commonly called a *poor self-image.* Good books and teachings suggest ways to improve your self-image. Fundamental to improving your self-image, however, is to become a better person.

Through *Fascinating Womanhood* you have a wonderful workshop for becoming a better person. As you advance toward the Ideal Woman you advance toward becoming a better person. As you perform your duties, grow in character, build your husband, become more womanly, and *cast light upon dark days,* you build your self-image.

A tremendous encouragement in living *Fascinating Womanhood* is reviewing the phenomenal success stories of other women, such as those cited throughout this book. Many thousands more have been written. Here are additional ones to review:

## The Power of the Spirit

"My husband and I were married very young—he was seventeen and I was nineteen. We were married out of necessity and struggled to make our marriage work from the very beginning. Five years and two children later, our marriage was in serious trouble. I acquired F.W. somewhere and read it. I was excited about it and tried to follow the ideals taught but gave up too soon. I returned to the work force, gave up the F.W. ideals and 'did my own thing.' Shortly after my husband and I divorced.

"During the next couple of years I searched for happiness by trying whatever current trend the world was offering but only became more unhappy. In the meantime my ex-husband had become a Christian and prayed for me. After some time had passed, I too became a Christian and again picked up F.W. to learn how to become a godly woman. My husband and I were remarried to each other three years after our divorce.

"That was over thirteen years ago and I am happy to report that we have a good marriage. I am a slow learner and very stubborn at times so it hasn't been easy for me to learn to be a fascinating woman. I believe that the only reason I am making any progress is because I have the *power of the Holy Spirit* working these things out in my life. God has given us back *the years that the locust took* and we now have a wonderful restored family. We have adopted more children and work very hard at trying to teach these same values to them. Now I am doing the very thing that is more satisfying than anything the world can offer—being a devoted wife and mother! Thank you again for your excellent teachings.

## Write Your Own Romance

"My marriage was a very rough road from the beginning—nothing like I dreamed it would be. Before we were married my husband adored me and did anything and everything for me. He was so romantic and affectionate. After getting married he was not the same man and I suppose I was not the same woman. We didn't know each other, although we lived across the street from each other as children.

"My husband and I were from two totally opposite families: His family used very little discipline. His dad was never around, worked offshore, and when home hung out in bars. His mom let his dad walk all over her and do whatever he wanted. He never gave her respect or affection. My family was strongly disciplined. My dad adored my mom like a queen, didn't drink, and never went out with the guys. And my mom was a very demanding and ungrateful wife.

"We went into marriage not realizing how different we were. My husband didn't know how to respect and adore a woman. He didn't feel it was necessary and felt I should accept being treated like a doormat. After all, that was how his mom was treated. I thought if I demanded and bossed him around he would change and I would get respect and adoration that way. My mother was demanding and she was respected and adored by my father.

"The more demanding and bossy I was, the less I saw of him. He never came home from work on time, stayed out drinking with his friends, and avoided me. I didn't drink, never went out with friends, and sat at home alone crying and wondering what was wrong. Not once did my husband ever ask me to go anywhere. I was the doormat at home, a convenience, to cook, clean house, pay the bills, wash clothes, and use in the bedroom. I felt more like his mother and maid than his wife. He would say things like *'I miss my freedom. This choke chain you have around my neck is choking me. My time off is my own, not yours. I do what I want to do.'*

"I became the most depressed person in the world. I would sit home alone, hurting, suffering, not having anyone to talk to. So many times I wanted to just leave, to make it easier for us both, but I was never a quitter. I'm a strong and determined person so I stayed, looking for a better way. I had the full responsibility of working and keeping up the house. I don't mind housework but felt it unfair to go out to work.

"After three years of this hell I got pregnant. Now I really felt trapped. But even having a son didn't change my husband. He didn't share in this joyous event. Now I had not only a full-time job and care of the house, but a baby. He never lifted a finger to help and when I asked he would say, 'My dad didn't so I'm not.' Only by the grace of God did I make it through that period.

"A very dear friend at work introduced me to F.W. I scanned through the book, not having time to study it's principles. I loved what I read and found myself hungry for this wisdom. I had never heard any of the information before. I was desperate to find something to hold on to my marriage because we now had a son to consider.

"The first thing I did was to quit my job. I wanted more than anything to be home with my child, taking care of him and the house. The next thing I did was to find God and gave my life to Him. I knew that I could not change on my own. I noticed in F.W. that you often spoke of God, and being on the road of hell I was on I needed a miracle in my life. Giving my life to Him was the best thing I have ever done. Only then was I able to study and apply the F.W. principles. As I grew spiritually, I realized I didn't have to change myself. Jesus was doing it for me. It seemed as though He was working on me through F.W., telling me *'this is the way to be the woman you were meant to be.'*

"Now came the test of faith to apply the principles I was studying. It was difficult to say verbally the things I was reading so I used cards and letters. Coming from where we were for eight years it was really hard to practice these principles but I sought my strength from my Lord.

"The first thing I did was to mail a card to his job, telling him I accepted him as he was and I was glad he didn't allow me to push him around. That seemed to break the ice and he was really touched by my sending him a card. Next I sent him a card once a week, admiring him. He was smiling now and came home on time more often. I got braver, verbally admiring him, and he ate it up.

"One night I wrote down ten things I admired about him and asked him to do the same. To my amazement he did and the things he wrote filled me with joy because he had never said any of these things to me before. He even began giving me cards expressing his feelings for me. This was a great accomplishment for him, considering his Great Wall of China from his childhood hurts and pains. I didn't know anything about a reserve until I read about it in F.W. This helped me be sympathetic because of his childhood.

"Things were better than they had ever been but something was still wrong. I still wasn't totally number one in his life. There was a problem I couldn't put my finger on. But I kept praying and practicing the principles with diligence.

"Then suddenly God opened my eyes to the part in F.W. about the alcoholic husband and problems that went along with it. I came to realize that he was an alcoholic. His drink was number one. Now, my eyes were opened and I had the truth to stand on so I understood what was wrong.

"As I kept on living F.W. with diligence and the grace of God, he slowly began to confide things he never had before. He woke me up at one-thirty one morning to tell me he needed help, that he had a problem. I took the action necessary and he sought help.

"Since that time he has given his life to our Lord and Savior and has truly become a beautiful person. Because I am the woman I am today he has been able to be totally honest with me about the past and all the mistakes he has made. He has even admitted to other women he's picked up in bars. This wasn't easy to accept but I know that he sees in me what a woman is supposed to be. He often tells me he could never easily replace me. He would never have said or thought that if I had not changed.

"Today he tells me that because of the changes in me, he wants to change but doesn't know how. He looks at me and wants to be like me and what I am about. Today my marriage is beautiful. It's more than I've ever dreamed of and I realize that we have what very few couples have in this world and to make it even better, God is the center of our family.

"My story is not an overnight success. It took three years of diligence, prayers, and hard work, but the rewards are worth far more than the effort. I would like to say to every woman suffering and hurting in her marriage, don't give up, keep on praying, and using the principles in F.W. because if my marriage has survived, miracles do happen!

"Mere words cannot express how important I think F.W. is to the world. As I look around at women today I often feel so sad because so many of them place material things and careers ahead of their families, not to mention how unfeminine and forward they are. If women would read and practice *Fascinating Womanhood* they wouldn't have to read romance novels and lust over soap operas. They would have what they're looking for and could write their own romance stories.

"I'd like to express my deepest appreciation and tell you how grateful I am for this information. Rightfully, I must give all the glory to God but I know God used you to write this book. I know God has worked in me through F.W. and you've saved two souls in my household.

"Thank you for teaching me what a real woman is all about. I strongly believe that we should strive to be all that we were meant to be in the eyes of God. After all that I've been through in my marriage I am positive that I'm a wife who cannot easily be replaced. Each and every night I get on my knees and pray to become a fascinating woman, and I know God answers prayers."

### How I Won My Husband Back from a Harlot

"*Fascinating Womanhood* was, literally, an answer to prayer. I remember when the book arrived at my house. I had been praying that the Lord would show me what I could do to improve myself, wherever I was wrong in my crumbled marriage. One day I decided to call an old college roommate, whom I hadn't seen in years. She came over for a visit. When she asked me how my husband felt about the fourth baby I was expecting, I hedged—I knew he was furious about it. I finally broke down and told her he had sued for divorce twice, separation once, and that he had gone to one psychiatrist and a marriage counselor and I had gone to the counselor, a hypnotist, our minister, every friend we had, and my obstetrician, and nobody could say any more than either to pray about it or to get a divorce. And I had tried so hard.

"Every complaint he had I had done something about.

The house was super clean, the children kept quiet and out of the way when he came around. If he said he didn't like something, I jumped and corrected it. I tried hard not to act pregnant, because I knew how disgusted he was with my situation. I had, in turn, mailed him lovely good-bye letters, called him every name I knew, threatened divorce or never to let him have one, not answered the phone, had only the children talk with him, or run to answer the phone myself on the first ring with the sexiest voice I could muster. All the tricks women think of to handle a man, using his weaknesses, I had tried. They brought temporary relief but no change.

"The next night my college friend drove forty miles to bring me *The Fascinating Girl.* I read a little in a few chapters and was so excited I had butterflies. The next morning I dumped the children in the car and drove twenty miles to the nearest bookstore to buy both *The Fascinating Girl* and *Fascinating Womanhood,* seriously damaging the family food budget. When I started reading *Fascinating Womanhood,* I kept it with me all over the house—in the kitchen, bathroom, bedroom— and read it as a man nearly dead of thirst would drink water. My face felt hot and burning when I read about not comparing your man to other men, being happy within yourself, even when he is not, accepting his faults and not trying to change him, looking to his better side, losing your temper in a childlike way, not allowing yourself to be stepped on, accepting him at face value, and what criticizing a man can do to him. You can see that I did not understand men at all.

"About a month after I had read *Fascinating Womanhood* for the twenty-fifth time came what I had been hoping for— my husband told me I had changed. He didn't know how but he sure liked it. About four months after that, he spilled out to me that in his utter misery in our situation he had picked up a harlot and had been living with her for three and a half years. She was ugly, uneducated, sick, divorced three times at the age of twenty-four, near alcoholic, and wouldn't hold down a job. She had given her only son to her parents to raise. But she was fascinating. My husband was like a god in her eyes. His enemies were hers, his friends were hers. She made him feel important, accepted, and understood.

"When my husband confessed his affair to me, I temporarily forgot all about *Fascinating Womanhood* and completely lost control of my temper. I broke a glass door and a couple of glass-covered pictures, ended up getting beaten, and my husband leaving the house, going to a motel, taking about two bottles of aspirin, and calling his mistress for comfort. Even after he came home and calmed down, he went on secretly seeing her for a couple of weeks. But I kept that image before my eyes of taming the terrible tiger with kindness and patience, and eventually the rewards were what I had been praying for during the eight years of our marriage. When I began to learn the difficult lessons of how to be fascinating, apparently the bottom fell out of his relationship with the harlot—in fact, these were my husband's own words.

"I don't mean to say that these changes were easy to make. My husband had become addicted to this woman, and I had to be understanding and loving and mop his brow when he lay in bed and shook because he hadn't talked to her for three days. When he would lapse into moods or end up referring to her in his conversations, I had to find inner strength and happiness to carry me over it and sometimes I would truly give way to despair. During this period when my husband was trying to rid himself of his addiction, he brought home a Gideon Bible and started reading it. I was so thrilled. About seven weeks after his confession to me, we were baptized together into our church. In about two months after that my husband became what our church has been praying for, in charge of our 'tape ministry' and got it into a functioning and prospering position.

"My husband's Bible reading continued at a phenomenal pace, and he kept growing and growing in Christianity until now, one year later, and he is still growing and studying. He has an understanding of God that I am sure very few men have—it's like living with a prophet, a man like Paul or David in the Bible. He has completely built his own business and in five years has prospered to the point where he told me he has 200,000 dollars in the bank. But he, like Tolstoy, doesn't want to let the world separate him from God, so he won't use the money on material needs. He doesn't know yet what the Lord would have him do with the money and he talks of adopting some children. Thank you, Mrs. Andelin, and even more, I thank God for sending your message to me and to my family."

## Heartbreak With a Happy Ending

"My husband and I were married when I was eighteen years old and he was nineteen. We went through school together and went together for six months after graduation before becoming engaged. After a one-and-a-half year engagement we were married, and eight days later he was sent overseas by the air force. I lived with his parents for the next five months while saving up enough money so that I could join him. His folks were closer to me than my own. He was their only son, and they accepted me lovingly into their home as their only daughter. I thought I knew everything there was to know about my husband when I finally joined him.

"Well, I was wrong, and completely oblivious to the really important things a wife should know about her husband and, most important, herself. I ignorantly stumbled through seven years of marriage. The last four of those years were pure hell for me emotionally, for when our first child was three months old, my husband finally confessed (after a million times I'd accused him of not loving me) that maybe I was right, because he didn't think he did love me anymore. Now it was at last out in the open and we didn't know what to do about it. We are both very conscientious people with extremely high moral standards, and we decided to seek professional help to determine if there was enough left of our marriage to salvage.

"Our minister suggested Family Service Association, and so for two years after that we went weekly to our marriage counselor. We had another baby seventeen months after the first, and shortly thereafter I was critically burned in an auto accident, which I know was the answer to my prayers. Dumb? Yes, but I was desperate, emotionally falling apart at the seams. Since counseling obviously was not providing the answers to our problems (my problems, really), I prayed to God every day to help me find a way out, or to take me out of my misery by taking my life, or by making something horrible happen to me, so my husband would be jolted into realization and know one way or the other whether he loved me or not. The constant pressure of not knowing was too much for me to go on bearing.

"Well, it worked, or at least I thought it did for a while. As I lay in the hospital in intensive care, I heard my husband say 'I love you' for the first time in three years. It was wonderful at first and I suffered greatly for that; and that 'I love you' was all that kept me going the whole two months I was in the hospital, for I was sure that when I got home, everything would be wonderful and happy again in spite of my ugly scarred face and hands.

"Again I was wrong. Things were worse than ever, and the next two years I spent praying for the good Lord to show mercy on the wretched human being who was really at the end of her rope. I tried so hard and changed my ways just like the counselor said, but nothing helped. The problem definitely was not solved and I had no emotional control left. I was a complete wreck in every sense of the word.

"Last July, my husband was speaking cruelly and disrespectfully to me in front of our children and I thought that was the very last straw, so I helped him pack his bags and asked him to leave. He did, somewhat to my surprise, and he was ready for it. Merciful peace reigned at last, and I truly felt this was God's answer to my prayers.

"Again I was wrong. For two months we were the happiest separated couple the world has ever known. The children made great strides in that short time. The baby, now two years old, completely potty trained herself, and the two boys were happier than they'd ever been. Then my sister Sally brought me the book *Fascinating Womanhood,* and I immediately began the most intensive study program I ever partook of in my life. I read slowly, thoroughly, and then I thought and thought and then I'd apply one chapter at a time. An explosive revolution was going on inside me and I was so happy at last to have God's answers to all my problems, but at the same time I hated myself with a passion I never knew existed. 'How could I have been so dumb—so blind—so stupid!!!'

"My husband was everything good I'd ever wanted in life, and I hated myself for never having understood him as a man. By the time I finished the book I looked in the mirror and saw myself as I really was—how my husband saw me. I despised what I saw. Oh, how ignorant and self-righteous I was. I cried for two days after I read about the Russian author of *War and Peace,* Tolstoy, and how his wife made herself so offensive that he couldn't stand the sight of her. I was sure it was too late to ever repair the damage I had caused my husband. He had a wall of reserve that made the Great Wall of China look microscopic!

"Thank goodness our God is a truly merciful God, for I followed step by step the principles of *Fascinating Womanhood* and my husband responded miraculously. I will always be in debt to *Fascinating Womanhood,* Helen Andelin, and God for showing this wretched creature how to make others happy and how to be happy—for just that reason and none other.

This is how it happened: I called my husband and asked him to stop by one evening on his way to work. I wanted to tell him of my newfound knowledge and tell him all the things the 'ice breaker' said to say as a start. He came, and I stammered for awhile until I finally told him that in my loneliness I had been doing a lot of reading and that I was at long last able to see how wrong I had been all the years (seven) of our marriage.

"I told him that I couldn't expect him to forgive me for making his life into a hell on earth, but I wanted to apologize just the same and that I was truly and deeply sorry for the misery I had caused him. I told him I could now see that the failure was my fault and mine alone and he was the best husband a woman ever had. I told him I admired his strength of character and that he never once gave in to my nagging criticism and never allowed me to make him putty in my hands. He had to know this for his future happiness, for I never wanted him to think our marriage failed through any fault of his. He could rest assured that someday he would find someone who could be the kind of wife he deserved and know that he couldn't ever cause any problems because he was the best guy in the world and I hated myself for not seeing it in time.

"All of the while I was telling him these things he just sat there looking alternately into space, not seeing anything and then in blank disbelief at me, and then into space again. When I'd finished, I had tears running down my face and the whole house was so quiet. He didn't move his blank stare and I just sat nearby, waiting, waiting, waiting. That two or three minutes seemed an eternity. His first words were, 'I'm dumbfounded. I don't know what to say.' I told him I didn't want or expect him to say anything but I simply wanted him to know how I felt. He left for work still somewhat dazed with disbelief.

"I did not leave the house for three days, waiting for a call or something, and finally he called to ask if he could come over for his weekly visit with the kids and I said, sure. That night I admired him before the children for his long legs, broad shoulders, manly physique, and neat good looks, and he just ate it all up. He'd grin from ear to ear and chuckle and tell the children not to believe everything their mom told them. After we put the kids to bed, he asked me to a dinner dance a month away and I was once again happy, happy, happy. This meant that there might still be some hope for me to reinstate myself with him, and again I thanked God for being so merciful to such an unworthy human being. Weekly visits came and went and always the children consumed his full attention, but occasionally he would compliment me on the improvements I'd made in my appearance, homemaking, etc. But never a hint about moving back home to us, so in one of my loneliest moments I asked him over to watch TV with me, and he came.

"After bedding down the kids, we talked a bit and I told him that I wanted him to know that I truly loved him and saw the error of my ways, that I felt I understood him as a man and that I thought I could make him happy if he could forgive me enough to move home. I told him I certainly didn't expect him to, but that I'd love to have the chance to make him happy and to please think about it. 'I just want you to know that I want you more than anything in this world and that if by some miracle you should want to come home, we love you and would be the happiest family to have you back.' He said it was too soon to decide and that he was sorry I hadn't changed sooner. That's the way it went, and the next two months went by with not one single word or ray of hope from him that he even ever thought of returning.

"It had been seven years since we said 'I do' and five months since our separation when he came up to the house with some papers for me to sign. He had just bought a car and needed my signature as it was to be in our names. I floated around the house for days and days (seven to be exact), clinging to that first ray of hope that he might be considering giving me another 'last chance' to make good our marriage. I was so happy, but never pressed him about it.

"One week later his refrigerator broke down at his apartment and he brought down all of his food to store in ours until his could be fixed. In a joking way, as he was trying to figure out how to work picking up his food each day and plan his meals, I suggested he could move home with us and not worry about all that. He stopped and smiled (to my amazement) and I just waited for his response. When it finally came, I was up on 'cloud nine' because he said, 'Well, I guess I could at that.' I wrapped myself around him and bawled my eyes out with joy and the only words I could utter were, 'You mean it? You mean you would really give me another chance?'

"After several moments when I'd calmed down a bit, he sat me down in a chair and said that before he could move home he had to know how I would be in regard to his newfound and dearly loved freedom. He said that while on his own he realized that his freedom to be himself and to indulge in his hobbies (woodworking, electronics, etc.) and not to have to adhere to set schedules was his most precious possession he'd discovered while on his own and that he couldn't give that up for anyone or anything. I told him I understood and I guess he knew I did (at last), and as he walked out the door to get his things, he turned and held out his hand. In his hand was a brand-new set of keys for his new car, and he said, 'Here, I guess you'll need these now,' and he left, but only so that he could return again and this time for good. That was three weeks before Christmas and we had the happiest Christmas any family ever had. Since that glorious day, almost six months have passed and not one week goes by that he does not comment in a bewildered way that he just can't believe how much I've changed. (He'd remind me of how I would have reacted before.)

"*Fascinating Womanhood* has been the salvation of my soul, my marriage, and my family, and I will strive the rest of my days to live up to its teachings. I never did one thing— not one thing—right before, and I have got a lot to learn yet before my old habits and thinking patterns have been wiped out of existence and replaced by the more mature and proper *Fascinating Womanhood* way. Not one *Fascinating Womanhood* applied principle has failed me and I know it's the right way to be even though every day is a challenge; I know it is, because my husband can't believe I have changed so much. I thank God in heaven and you on earth for giving me this 'last chance' to make my family happy. Thank you, thank you, thank you.''

### How I Pitied Myself!

"As my plane took off from Miami I looked out the window with tears in my eyes, asking God to please help me. I felt so tired, angry, frustrated, lonely, empty. It was not the first time I was seeking relief from thirty years of living with a self-centered, uncaring, indifferent, clone of a man, who also was a chauvinistic, bitter, spiteful, jealous, old _____. I have accused him of faking a heart attack eight years ago just so he could retire and try to manipulate me.

"I didn't care that he'd have to close up the condo by himself and drive back to New York alone. The only happiness I felt was knowing I'd be alone and peaceful for a few weeks away from this pathetic excuse of a husband. 'Where are you going; why did you buy that; you don't need it; why do you do so much laundry; why don't you clean the house?' and me retorting with 'Mind your business, leave me alone, drop dead, go back to work, or shut up.' Even though I had left him before like this, it seemed different this time. I really felt somehow this was different. My future was questionable.

"In my possession at this time was a book called *Fascinating Womanhood*. My daughter had sent it to me a month before. I promised her I'd read it but I knew it wouldn't help. I've read many books before—how to please men, how to be sexy, how to cater to them. Who needs it now. My life is over. I'm in my fifties and I'm tired. I even read *Wendy's Dilemma*. It made me more dissatisfied with my life and our marriage worsened, because he didn't change one bit. So I shelved the idea of another book and just laid my head back and started thinking about my life. How wasted, how disappointing, how lonely, not at all the way I'd dreamed it would be when I was young and hopeful. How I pitied myself. Life sure had played a dirty trick on me.

"When I was young I was beautiful, tough, capable, arrogant, independent—on the surface. Yet the inner me has always felt vulnerable, insecure, sensitive and so dependent, but I've been careful never to reveal this side of me, except to the wrong people. I expected marriage to be as in the movies. If Betty Grable or Joan Crawford walked out on a man or slapped his face, naturally the next day he'd bring flowers, run after her, knock her door down. She could say or do anything and he'd still crawl. I believed all a woman had to do was be attractive and she'd have men at her feet and live happily ever after.

"I was widowed with a one-year-old when I met Bill. After one month I proposed to him and he said OK. I was so lonely for love. My first husband, Michael, died of cancer within one year of our marriage. He was so caring, I needed a replacement to take care of me. Bill was different, though. From the start he was corporate-minded. Climbing the ladder of success was first in his life. Never home. No phone calls. Many disappointments. I started making demands, yelling, complaining, withholding, unknowingly doing my Joan Crawford imitation, but this leading man wasn't following the script.

"The more I shouted and screamed the more he'd stay away at work. Why weren't things going the way it was supposed to? How confusing. I didn't understand. I needed his love, companionship, help, a hug. I couldn't get through to him. Most of the time he'd just go out and slam the door, leaving behind a hysterical, screaming, wife and by now three children to suffer all the repercussions of our battles. How I hated him for his lack of understanding. I'd tell people, 'If you ever see him cry at my funeral, throw him out.'

"During all of this chaos I found a religion. Looking back I see now how self-righteous I became. He also joined but his faith was a more honest veneer. Mine was more hypocritical. The few times we ate together as a family I'd ask him to say prayer and he'd pray mechanically. Sometimes he'd refuse to pray for spite. I'd attack him for his obvious blatant un-Christian act, reminding him he's the head of the house and should set a good example. I'd prod him to come to Bible lectures. He'd spitefully fall asleep. He always knew what button to push—picnics, weddings, covered-dish socials—he'd wait till the last minute to inform us he'd changed his mind. I'd blow up and take the kids myself. I'd take the children to religious meetings once a week and let him not forget it.

"He caused me to run everything—house, religion, bills, repairs, lawn, paint, children, just about everything. I'd complain about this but I certainly was not uncomfortable in this leading role. I'd parrot the words, 'If a woman wants something done she has to do it herself.' Sometimes after hanging up the phone feeling rejected, I'd send the poor children scattering. My nerves couldn't stand any more, especially since he told me he was once again not coming home for dinner. And I cooked special!

"Time and life were disappearing, the children were older, and I was starting to sip wine at night before dinner, and he was approaching the top of the ladder. Yes, I kept my secret rendezvous with my bottle of Chianti and the children kept suffering. Any pleas, criticism, arguments, sent him either to lie down, to watch TV, take a nap, tell me 'please, I have enough of my own problems,' or out the door. How I hated him for not understanding. I'd stop drinking, then I'd start again, sometimes a year would lapse before I'd start again. It's been a fight but I think I've got a handle on it now.

"Soon the children were grown. Thank God they have turned out well. Perhaps they did understand after all. But I grew older still living quite independently and alone most of the time. I successfully went into real estate for awhile which caused me to be more tolerant of Bill's schedule. I continued my religious meetings but there was still the emptiness, the not feeling loved. Something was so wrong, even though there was a movie once in awhile, the dinners, etc. I still didn't feel complete.

"Suddenly things changed drastically. This man who for the sake of pride, power, and success, for years sacrificed his wife, children, religion, and friends, ended up in the hospital with a near-fatal heart attack. I thanked God he survived and I immediately devoted myself to him, though I hadn't really been with him for twenty years. I waited on him hand and foot and loved every minute of it. I was making up for all the years of not having him at home and he loved it. But after six months I was resenting his directing and ordering me from his recliner chair. I started feeling used, drained, waiting on him hand and foot. The doctor told him to walk and exercise and he'd eventually return to almost normal health. All this while I couldn't understand. I was doing everything in my power to please him, make him happy, yet I felt empty, unloved, dissatisfied with his response to my devotion. What was wrong?

"As my resentments grew I started saying things like, 'Don't you think it's about time you remembered to take your own medicine?' 'Why don't you get up and get it yourself?' His hostility toward me surfaced and we were back in the front lines again. He'd be home now twenty-four hours a day, telling me how to shop, cook, make a bed, close drapes, wash clothes, when to shop, etc. Now, after twenty years of leaving me to do it all by myself, I need a caretaker? Again, I'd tell him to mind his own business, drop dead, butt out, etc.

"But I'd still play the Christian and go to my Bible meeting, sing praises to God and pray, putting on my martyr's cloak, really believing in my heart (self-righteous heart) what sacrifices I was making being married to such a man. He would come to the meetings once in a while for his needed nap. During all this we bought a condo in Florida to escape from New York during the cold weather. We bought a smaller new house in N.Y. state and I'd work like a man side by side with him— lawn, finishing work, driveways, shrubs, wallpaper, etc. I worked my buns off with him. He had the nerve to not appreciate all the hard work I did, but to complain that I didn't cook dinner.

"When I'd tell him how selfish and ungrateful he was, and I'm only trying to lighten his load because of his heart condition, he'd say, 'Go in the house and do your own work. Go cook my dinner.' I hated him so. What an ingrate. After all, I was sure he'd fall apart without my help. After all, who would show him his mistakes? Who would advise him and show him how the patio or garage should be done? Who would be there to show him how to paint, wallpaper, mow the lawn? He needed me. Hadn't I been doing this for the past twenty years? But of course this would lead to arguing and screaming at each other. I started holding out sexually too.

"The same was happening after we bought our condo in Florida. But things got worse there because I'd see all the men down there catering to their wives and I'd fume. These men washed floors, cleaned windows, did laundry, and even shopped for their wives. Bill would have no part of this. These men would tease me and Bill when they'd see me washing my own windows. How I hated being taken advantage of—this chauvinistic pig.

"The last straw of this saga was, after a long estrangement

between my firstborn Michael and me, he finally wanted to talk to me on the phone. (Bill never intervened or encouraged a reconciliation during all the time Michael wouldn't talk to me.) Now Bill made no bones about his open hostility against our reconciliation. I couldn't believe it. How could he. He's done some lousy things in his life but this—I realized right then that he enjoyed and probably promoted our estrangement. How sick. How hateful! I hated him more than ever now. That's when I packed my bags and got on the plane to New York. Oh yes, I've left him before many times. But this time I knew it was different. My thoughts of the future were hazy and confused and any chances for happiness at my age was questionable. I only knew I didn't want to look at him again.

"I got off the plane and went home thanking God I was alone, able to set down and think in peace—no interruptions, no quarreling. My daughter again encouraged me to read F.W. After a few days of isolation I thought to myself, what have I got to lose.

"Well, the first two pages opened my eyes. *My fault??* This statement made me curious to see how the author would prove her point. I read on—*My age doesn't matter?? Law to follow? I'll have power in my hands? I can learn how to cause a man to want to do things for me? I'll lose none of my dignity? I'll have rewards and surprises???* I felt skeptical yet curious. How would this writer justify all these promises?

"I lay around for two week reading, underlining, rereading, meditating. I felt I was being slapped over and over again, was defensive, angry, crying in discouragement, then hopefully happy, encouraged. I hated the author, then loved her. F.W. was a rude awakening for me. I cried many times as I read and reread it. I was beginning to believe that this writer was making sense. Everything I resented and hated in my husband was brought on by his *fight to hold on to his masculinity*. What a fool I've been, all these years wasted. Why didn't I find F.W. sooner?

"I contemplated what I would do as an icebreaker. I'll wait until he drives home to N.Y. It will give me more time to keep my independence. No, stupid! Call him now. The book promises happiness in our *dependence*. Oh God, what should I do. I'm so peaceful without him. But who wants empty peace. Call him! No, I'll have to be in subjection, then he'll really be hell to live with. No, the author says my life will be enjoyable and filled with rewards and surprises. Oh God, help me. I believe in it—and I don't. Why do I hesitate. Everything F.W. says is in the Bible.

"I decided to go for it. I was so nervous. How I wanted all the wonderful things F.W. promised, if I followed the rules. But, what if I failed? I was afraid to give up that domineering, independent person. I needed my tough skin. I needed to hold *some* reins. Stop hesitating. Do it now! Now! I dialed Florida. He answered. Oh God, how frightened I was. There was some small talk at first, then—I went blank. I said, 'Wait a minute.' I ran for the book, found the icebreaker. Then fumbled through the words. How sorry for the past, happy he never gave in to me. I waited for a response—silence—'Did you hear me, Bill?' 'Yes, I heard you, but have you been drinking?' I said, 'No, Bill, it's Sunday morning. I'm on my way to Bible meeting. But I mean every word I've said. I'll be a much better wife from now on, I promise.'

"He said he was happy and peaceful there and was seriously thinking of staying there and letting me live in the house. He couldn't take any more. Thanks to F.W. I didn't reply, 'What about my peace.' I just told him I didn't blame him for feeling this way and I deserve everything he's saying to me, like 'We've tried before and it always ends the same.' I had tears in my eyes and begged his forgiveness. 'Let me return to Florida and give me another chance, please! This time it will be different. I'll call you after meeting.'

"That afternoon I called back and he was actually waiting by the phone. I repeated more of the icebreaker to him. He seemed confused, dumbfounded. He said, 'Where are you getting all this stuff?' I told him I've been reading books, along with the Bible and meditating. I pleaded. 'Bill, when I left before I'd always fantasized that when we reconciled you would be a changed man, and you'd be all the things I decided you should be. But it's different this time. I've been the wrong one. I've been the fool. I don't want you to change. I love you the way you are. It's been me all along. I'm so ashamed of myself. I'm so sorry. Please let me return to Florida and I'll drive home with you. Please trust me and give me another chance. It's only seventy-nine dollars now on Eastern. It will be the best seventy-nine dollars you'll spend, I promise. And if it doesn't work you can send me home again.'

"He cautiously said I could come back but added, 'You know I'm going to want to hold you and touch you and feel you close to me. I need to feel a woman in my arms.' (I had spitefully withheld sex from him for five years, like a good Christian.) I said, 'Yes, Bill, I know and I need to feel your manly arms around me too. I've missed it so.' He said, 'I don't know where you're getting all this stuff but I'll give it a try. If it doesn't work I'll stay here and you fly back.' I said, 'Bill, I promise you won't be sorry.'

"I was so scared, praying all the time on the plane. Please, God, don't let me fail. After thirty years, how can I change! We were clumsy and polite to each other, making small talk in the car, on the way to the condo. After dinner with his family next door (no candlelight as I fantasized) I came down with such a headache. I fell asleep in my rocking chair. I woke with a start. I can't believe this, I thought. What a way to start the new me. But the next morning, thanking him for his understanding and patient heart, I made it up to him.

"He spent the next few weeks observing me with delight and confusion, being cautious as a serpent. I played my part well but to my surprise I wasn't putting on an act. Right from the start things worked out as F.W. promised. I too was confused and delighted. Obeying him was easy, not a drudge, and the more I saw things working out well the more I delighted in practicing F.W. I started feeling a happy, dignified woman, not a sex object, not a slave, not being taken advantage of, not being yelled at. I felt good, good about him, good about me. I felt, for the first time, peace with God Jehovah.

"My Bill is not a demonstrative person and never will be. But he doesn't have to be. He shows his love and appreciation by the things he happily allows me to do. He is so agreeable now. When I help him do everything in a feminine way now, not man to man, I love it. He loves it. He laughs delightedly when I can't pick up something heavy, comes running over to take over. He is a beautiful person, with qualities I would never have discovered had it not been for F.W. A day never goes by that I don't talk about how smart, or manly, or aggressive, etc. he is, being cautious to mean what I say. To my surprise he now stops at any garage sale, store, or shop I ask for, if he's not pressed for time, without yelling and degrading me.

"He came to our religious convention this week because he wanted to, without my prodding and pushing him. The other evening he said to me, 'How would you like to go to Steak and Stein,' a restaurant in town. I said I'd love to. To my delighted surprise he added as an afterthought, 'Yes, just you and me together.' The other morning as I was fixing breakfast he actually made the bed and put my things away. I kissed him and thanked him.

"I still slip back now and then and he graciously accepts my apologies. I have become a contented Domestic Goddess, and Bill is so pleased and happy. He also smiles with embarrassment when I remind him how strong and competent he is at everything he tries to do. It's the truth. How could I have been so stupid, so blind in not recognizing it in the past. I'm so grateful to F.W. for opening my eyes to the sensitive makeup of my husband's nature. I don't know where I'd be now or what miserable circumstance we'd both be in now if it weren't for you. Even at our ages we found happiness together. How can I ever repay you! Thank you sincerely.

"P.S. I think that if people are retired and around each other constantly, bickering and arguing, they should separate for a few days or a week and let this vital information digest and sink in. I don't know if I would have been as successful if we were together at the time of my reading F.W., mixing it with confrontations, arguments, demands, snide remarks, and fighting.''

# Bibliography

THE PRICELESS GIFT, by Eleanor Wilson McAdoo. Copyright 1962 by Eleanor Wilson McAdoo. McGraw-Hill Book Co., New York, N.Y.

THE EGO IN LOVE AND SEXUALITY, by Dr. Edrita Fried. Copyright 1960. Grune & Stratton, Inc., New York, N.Y.

THE POWER OF SEXUAL SURRENDER, by Dr. Marie N. Robinson. Copyright 1959 by Marie N. Robinson. Doubleday & Co., Inc., New York, N. Y.

MARRIAGE FOR MODERNS, by Henry A. Bowman. Copyright 1960. McGraw-Hill Book Co., New York, N.Y.

WOMEN AND SOMETIMES MEN, by Florida Scott-Maxwell. Copyright 1957 by Florida Scott-Maxwell. Alfred A. Knopf, Inc., New York, N.Y.

THREE WISE MEN OF THE EAST, by Elizabeth Bisland. Copyright by University of North Carolina Press.

THE LAND OF POETRY, BOOK 2, published 1930. James Nisbet & Co. Ltd., Welwyn, Herts., England.

EDUCATION FOR MARRIAGE, by James A. Peterson, copyright © 1964. Scribner and Sons, New York, N.Y.

MODERN BRIDE, Summer 1973, "How Men Feel About Sex," by Dr. David R. Mace, Copyright © 1973, by Ziff-Davis Publishing Co., New York, N.Y.

# Appendix

**Fascinating Womanhood *Classes***

Throughout this book many of the testimonials refer to *Fascinating Womanhood* classes. These classes have been taught in churches, educational programs, rented halls, and private homes. They have been taught by authorized teachers, ministers' wives, or leaders of study groups. The teachers have been helpful in clarifying the concepts, strengthening the message, and offering encouragement in living the teachings. In addition, the classes have served as support groups. As women have associated with other women in the class, they have felt support in launching a new way of life and sticking to it.

Many women who have never attended a class, however, have been very successful in living these teachings. By only reading the book, they have understood and applied the teachings with phenomenal success. These principles are clearly stated in the text and there are no secrets or special techniques needed to achieve the results promised. So, it isn't necessary to attend a class to have success in living *Fascinating Womanhood*. Once you have these concepts in mind and visions of rewards in store, you can make these changes on your own.

For up-to-date information about the *Fascinating Womanhood* program visit our web site:

**Marriage, The Fascinating Way**
www.andelin-2000.com

# Index

### Scripture

### Success Stories